Cisco Networking Academy Program: First-Year Companion Guide, Revised Printing

Vito Amato, Series Editor
Wayne Lewis, Contributor

CISCO SYSTEMS

CISCO PRESS

Cisco Press
201 West 103rd Street
Indianapolis, IN 46290

Cisco Networking Academy Program: First-Year Companion Guide, Revised Printing

Vito Amato, Series Editor

International Standard Book Number: 1-58713-003-3

Library of Congress Catalog Card Number: 00-100255

02   01   00   4

Interpretation of the printing code: The rightmost double-digit number is the year of the book's printing; the rightmost single-digit, the number of the book's printing. For example, the printing code 00-1 shows that the first printing of the book occurred in 2000.

Printed in the United States of America

Trademark Acknowledgments

All terms mentioned in this book that are known to be trademarks or service marks have been appropriately capitalized. Cisco Press cannot attest to the accuracy of this information. Use of a term in this book should not be regarded as affecting the validity of any trademark or service mark.

Warning and Disclaimer

This book is designed to provide information about Cisco Networking Academy Program studies. Every effort has been made to make this book as complete and as accurate as possible, but no warranty or fitness is implied.

The information is provided on an as-is basis. The authors, Cisco Press, and Cisco Systems, Inc., shall have neither liability nor responsibility to any person or entity with respect to any loss or damages arising from the information contained in this book or from the use of the discs or programs that may accompany it.

Feedback Information

At Cisco Press, our goal is to create in-depth technical books of the highest quality and value. Each book is crafted with care and precision, undergoing rigorous development that involves the unique expertise of members from the professional technical community.

Readers' feedback is a natural continuation of this process. If you have any comments regarding how we could improve the quality of this book, or otherwise alter it to better suit your needs, you can contact us at ciscopress@mcp.com. Please make sure to include the book title and ISBN in your message.

We greatly appreciate your assistance.

Publisher	*John Wait*
Executive Editor	*Dave Dusthimer*
Managing Editor	*Patrick Kanouse*
Development Editor	*Kitty Wilson Jarrett*
Technical Reviewers	*Denise Hoyt*
	Mark McGregor
	Wayne Jarvimaki
Senior Editor	*Jennifer Chisholm*
Indexers	*Kevin Fulcher*
	Tim Wright
Acquisitions Coordinator	*Amy Lewis*
Associate Editor	*Shannon Gross*
Manufacturing Coordinator	*Chris Moos*
Cover Designer	*Louisa Klucznik*
Production	*Argosy*
	Gina Rexrode
	Steve Gifford

About the Series Editor and Contributor

Vito Amato is a senior technical writer at Cisco Systems for World Wide Education. Previously, he was the Information Technology Director at the Arizona Department of Education. Vito earned his Ph.D. at Arizona State University, specializing in curriculum and instruction with an emphasis on educational media and computers. In addition, Vito is currently teaching distance education theory and practice at ASU. During the last three years, Vito has been involved in the planning, writing, and implementation of the Cisco Networking Academy program. Lastly, his research, writing, and teaching focus is the integration of information technology into the teaching/learning environment.

Wayne Lewis is the Cisco Academy Training Center Coordinator for Honolulu Community College. He provides training to Cisco Academy Instructors in Japan, Taiwan, Indonesia, Hong Kong, and the U.S. Wayne received a Ph.D. in math from the University of Hawaii in 1992. He is a Cisco Certified Network Professional (CCNP), Cisco Certified Design Associate (CCDA), Cisco Certified Design Professional (CCDP), Cisco Certified Academy Instructor (CCAI), and Microsoft Certified Professional (MCP). In his free time, Wayne enjoys surfing the North Shore of Oahu.

About the Technical Reviewers

This book's reviewers contributed their considerable practical, hands-on expertise to the entire development process for *Cisco Networking Academy Program: First-Year Companion Guide*, Revised Printing. As the book was being written, these folks reviewed all the material for technical content, organization, and flow. Their feedback was critical to ensuring that *Cisco Networking Academy Program: First-Year Companion Guide*, Revised Printing, fits our readers' need for the highest-quality technical information.

Denise Hoyt has been a teacher for 16 years. She received her bachelor's degree from California State University, Chico, and her master's degree in administration from the University of Redlands. She received her Cisco Networking Academy Program Instructor certification in the summer of 1998. In the fall of 1998, she became the Cisco Systems Academy Regional Coordinator for San Bernardino County. Denise also serves as the county's technology coordinator and teaches the Cisco Networking Academy Program Curriculum at Yucaipa High School in Yucaipa, California.

Mark McGregor, CCNA, is a Cisco Networking Academy Program Instructor at Los Medanos College and Antioch Adult School in Northern California. He holds a bachelor's degree in English from the University of California, Davis, and has taught in public schools for five years with a focus on at-risk youth and alternative education.

Wayne Jarvimaki, CCNA, CCAI, is an Instructor and Program Director at North Seattle CATC. He has been training Regional and CATC instructors since 1989. As a Networking Instructor, he was responsible for developing the Certificate/Degree option for Cisco Specialist at North Seattle Community College. Wayne also serves on the Cisco Networking Academy Curriculum Review Team.

Acknowledgments

This book would have not been possible without the vision and commitment of George Ward, Kevin Warner, Alex Belous, and David Alexander to the Cisco Networking Academy Program Program. Their support for the book has been tremendous. I would like to acknowledge their support not only in making the book a reality, but also in making the Cisco Networking Academy Program Program come alive. I also would like to acknowledge Jai Gosine and Dennis Frezzo for sharing their subject matter expertise, which allowed me to organize the content of this book. Most importantly, I would to thank my wife, Bonnie, and my kids, Tori, Michael, Matthew, and Laura, for their patience and support.

This book is a synthesis and integration of many Cisco educational publications. I would like to thank the education marketing development team at Cisco for their contribution. Finally, I would like to thank the team at Cisco Press, Dave Dusthimer, Amy Lewis, and Kitty Jarrett, for guiding me through the publication of this book.

Overview

Table of Contents

Preface

With the full implementation of the Cisco Networking Academy Program program over the past two years, Cisco has instituted an online learning systems approach that integrates the multimedia delivery of a networking curriculum with testing, performance-based skills assessment, evaluation, and reporting through a Web interface. The Cisco Networking Academy Program curriculum goes beyond traditional computer-based instruction by helping students develop practical networking knowledge and skills in a hands-on environment. In a lab setting that closely corresponds to a real networking environment, students work with the architecture and infrastructure pieces of networking technology. As a result, students learn the principles and practices of networking technology.

The Cisco Networking Academy Program provides in-depth and meaningful networking content, which is being used by regional and local academies to teach students around the world by utilizing the curriculum to integrate networking instruction into the classroom. The focus of the Cisco Networking Academy Program is the integration of a Web-based network curriculum into the learning environment. This element is addressed through intensive staff development for teachers and innovative classroom materials and approaches to instruction, which are provided by Cisco. The participating educators are provided with resources, the means of remote access to online support, and the knowledge base for the effective classroom integration of the Cisco Networking Academy Program curriculum into the classroom learning environment. As a result, the Cisco Networking Academy Program provides the means for dynamic exchange of information by providing a suite of services that redefine the way instructional resources are disseminated, resulting in a many-to-many interactive and collaborative network of teachers and students functioning to meet diverse educational needs.

What makes the Cisco Networking Academy Program curriculum exciting to educators and students is the fact that the courseware is interactive. Because of the growing use of interactive technologies, the curriculum is an exciting new way to convey instruction with new interactive technologies that allow instructors and trainers to mix a number of media, including audio, video, text, numerical data, and graphics. Consequently, students can select different media from the computer screen and custom design their instructional content to meet their instructional needs, and educators have the option of either designing their own environment for assessment or selecting from the applicable assessments.

Finally, by developing a curriculum that recognizes the changing classroom and workforce demographics, the globalization of the economy, changing workforce knowledge and skill requirements, and the role of technology in education, the Cisco Networking Academy Program program supports national educational goals for K–12 education. As support for the Cisco Networking Academy Program, Cisco Press has published this book, *Cisco Networking Academy Program: First-Year Companion Guide,* Revised Printing, as a companion guide for the curriculum used in the Cisco Networking Academy Program program.

Introduction

Cisco Networking Academy Program: First-Year Companion Guide, Revised Printing, is designed to act as a supplement to the student's classroom and laboratory experience with version 2.1 of the Cisco Networking Academy curriculum. Since the first version of this book was published in the spring of 1999, the online curriculum has gone through two revisions. This revised printing was developed to provide you with a companion text that includes all of the information added to the curriculum. Because the publication of a book is an expensive and time-consuming endeavor, we have added the material new to version 2.1 in five appendixes in the back of the book. We did not reorganize the entire book. Instead, we have included a detailed mapping guide in this introduction that will help students and teachers track the reading assignments from this book to the chapters in version 2.1 of the curriculum. We have also included tracking references for the *Cisco Networking Academy Program: Engineering Journal and Workbook*, Volume 1.

Semester 1 v2.1 is structured entirely around the OSI model, with a structured cabling project midway through the semester. With these changes in the mind, the book includes a "Computer Basics" appendix, which provides foundational material essential to the course. In addition, the "Electronics and Signals" and the "Signaling and Data Transmission" appendixes have been introduced to make the media and electronics section of the course more meaningful. The "Binary and Hexadecimal Conversion" appendix reflects the binary and hexadecimal math content in the curriculum, which is taught separately from IP addressing to allow students time to master the math before applying it. The book also includes a "Network Troubleshooting" appendix to support the curriculum.

Finally, this book aims not only to prepare you for your CCNA test and certification, but also to prepare you for the CompTIA Net + networking certification exam. The OSI model is absolutely essential for all networking students preparing for the CCNA exam. The sections on collisions and segmentation are also very important for the CCNA exam, along with Ethernet, which is important to understand the dominant LAN technology. The IP addressing chapters are perhaps the most conceptually difficult, yet are very important chapters, especially for the CCNA exam. Lastly, the skills in the structured cabling and electricity chapters are crucial if you are seeking network-cabling related employment.

This mapping guide will help you implement the Companion Guide and Engineering Journal/Workbook with version 2.1 of the curriculum.

Curriculum Mapping Guide

The online curriculum is the most dynamic part of the Networking Academy Program. We suggest that you begin your study of each chapter with the online material and then move to the print products. Use the mapping guide to ensure that you get the most from the various components of the program.

Online Curriculum		1st Year Companion Guide, Revised Printing		1st Year Engineering Journal/Workbook	
Ch.	Title	Ch.	Title	Ch.	Title
1	Basics of Computing	D	Computer Basics	1	Basics of Computing
2	The OSI Model	1	Networking and the OSI Reference Model	2	The OSI Model
3	Local Area Networks	1	Networking and the OSI Reference Model	3	LANs
		3	Networking Devices	17	LANs: Layers 1, 2, 3
		4	LANs and WANs		
4	Electronics and Signals	E	Electronics and Signals	4	Electronics and Signals
5	Media Connections and Collisions	2	The Physical and Data Link Layers	5	Layer 1: Networking Media
6	Layer 2 Concepts	2	The Physical and Data Link Layers	6	Layer 2: Data Link Layer
7	Layer 2 Technologies	4	LANs and WANs	7	Layer 2: Technologies
8	Design and Documentation	8	Structured Cabling and Electricity	8	Design and Documentation

Online Curriculum		1st Year Companion Guide, Revised Printing		1st Year Engineering Journal/Workbook	
Ch.	Title	Ch.	Title	Ch.	Title
9	Structured Cabling Project	8	Structured Cabling and Electricity	9	Structured Cabling
10	Layer 3: Routing and Addressing	5	IP Addressing	10	Layer 3: Routing and Addressing
		7	Topologies		
		11	The Network Layer and Routing		
		G	Binary and Hexadecimal Conversion		
11	Layer 3 Routing Protocols	6	ARP and RARP	11	Layer 3: Routing Protocols
12	Layer 4 Transport Layer	9	The Application, Presentation, Session, and Transport Layers	12	Layer 4: The Transport Layer
				18	Layers 4, 5, 6, and 7
		10	TCP/IP		
13	Layer 5 Session Layer	9	The Application, Presentation, Session, and Transport Layers	13	Layer 5: The Session Layer
				18	Layers 4, 5, 6, and 7

Online Curriculum		1st Year Companion Guide, Revised Printing		1st Year Engineering Journal/Workbook	
Ch.	Title	Ch.	Title	Ch.	Title
14	Layer 6: The Presentation Layer	9	The Application, Presentation, Session, and Transport Layers	14	Layer 6: The Presentation Layer
				18	Layers 4, 5, 6, and 7
15	Layer 7: The Application Layer	9	The Application, Presentation, Session, and Transport Layers	15	Layer 7: The Application Layer
				18	Layers 4, 5, 6, and 7
Semester Two					
1	Review	1	Networking and the OSI Reference Model	16	OSI Review
2	Routers	4	LANs and WANs	19	WANs
		13	Displaying Router Configuration Information	20	Routing
3	Using the Router	12	The Router User Interface and Modes	21	Using the Router
4	Router Componets	13	Displaying Router Configuration Information	22	Router Components

Online Curriculum		1st Year Companion Guide, Revised Printing		1st Year Engineering Journal/Workbook	
Ch.	Title	Ch.	Title	Ch.	Title
5	Router Startup and Setup	14	Router Startup and Setup Configuration	23	Router Startup and Setup
6	Router Configuration	15	Router Configuration	24	Router Configuration
7	IOS	16	Sources for Cisco IOS Software	25	IOS
8	Individual Router Config Practice				
9	TCP/IP	10	TCP/IP	26	TCP/IP
10	IP Addressing	17	Configuring Router Interfaces with IP Addresses	27	IP Addressing
11	Routing	11	The Network Layer and Routing	20	Routing
12	Routing Protocols	18	Router Configuration and Routing Protocols: RIP and IGRP	28	Routing Protocols

This Book's Features

Many of this book's features help facilitate a full understanding of the networking and routing covered in this book:

- *Chapter objectives*—At the beginning of each chapter is a list of objectives to be mastered by the end of the chapter. In addition, the list provides a reference to the concepts covered in the chapter, which can be used as an advanced organizer.

- *Figures, listings, and tables*—This book contains figures, listings, and tables that help explain theories, concepts, commands, and setup sequences; they reinforce concepts and help you visualize the content covered in the chapter. In addition, listings and tables provide such things as command summaries with descriptions, examples of screen outputs, and practical and theoretical information.

■ *Chapter summaries*—At the end of each chapter is a summary of the concepts covered in the chapter; it provides a synopsis of the chapter and serves as a study aid.

■ *Review questions*—After the summary of each chapter are 10 review questions that serve as an end-of-chapter assessment. In addition, the questions reinforce the concepts introduced in the chapter and help you test your understanding before you move on to new concepts.

Conventions Used in This Book

In this book, the following conventions are used:

■ Important or new terms are *italicized*.

■ All code examples appear in `monospace` type, and parts of code use the following conventions:

— Commands and keywords are in **bold** type.

— Arguments, which are placeholders for values the user inputs, appear in *italics*.

— Square brackets ([ ]) indicate optional keywords or arguments.

— Braces ({ }) indicate required choices.

— Vertical bars (|) are used to separate required choices.

This Book's Organization

This book is divided into 19 chapters, 8 appendixes, and a glossary.

Chapter 1, "Networking and the OSI Reference Model," discusses networking terms and concepts, local-area networks (LANs), and wide-area networks (WANs). In addition, it covers the seven-layer Open System Interconnection (OSI) reference model and the communication process between the model's lower layers.

Chapter 2, "The Physical and Data Link Layers," presents the network functions that occur at the physical and data link layers of the OSI reference model and the different types of networking media that are used at the physical layer. In addition, it discusses the fact that access to the networking media occurs at the data link layer of the OSI model and how data is able to locate its intended destination on a network.

Chapter 3, "Networking Devices," describes networking devices, which can be used to filter traffic across a network and reduce large collision domains, which are areas where packets are likely to interfere with each other.

Chapter 4, "LANs and WANs," presents LAN and WAN technologies, standards, and networking devices that operate at the physical, data link, and network layers of the OSI model.

Chapter 5, "IP Addressing," describes IP addresses and the three classes of networks in IP addressing schemes, as well as the IP addresses that have been set aside by InterNIC and cannot be assigned to any network. Finally, it discusses subnetworks and subnet masks and describes their IP addressing schemes.

Chapter 6, "ARP and RARP," discusses devices on LANs that use Address Resolution Protocol (ARP) before forwarding data to a destination and what happens when a device on one network does not know the MAC address of a device on another network.

Chapter 7, "Topologies," describes the topologies that are used to build networks.

Chapter 8, "Structured Cabling and Electricity," presents structured cabling and electrical specifications used in LANs and wiring and electrical techniques used in building networks.

Chapter 9, "The Application, Presentation, Session, and Transport Layers," discusses the four upper layers of the OSI reference model. It describes in detail the processes used at the transport layer to provide reliable delivery of data as well as to provide effective control of traffic flow.

Chapter 10, "TCP/IP," describes Transmission Control Protocol/Internet Protocol (TCP/IP) and its operation to ensure communication across any set of interconnected networks.

Chapter 11, "The Network Layer and Routing," describes the router's use and operations in performing the key internetworking functions of the OSI reference model network layer.

Chapter 12, "The Router User Interface and Modes," discusses the network administrator's role in operating a router to ensure efficient and effective delivery of data on a network with routers.

Chapter 13, "Displaying Router Configuration Information," describes the correct procedures and commands to access a router, examine and maintain its components, and test its network connectivity.

Chapter 14, "Router Startup and Setup Configuration," explains how to start a router when it is used the first time by using the correct commands and startup sequence to do an initial router configuration.

Chapter 15, "Router Configuration," explains how to use router modes and configuration methods to update a router's configuration file with current and prior versions of Cisco IOS software.

Chapter 16, "Sources for Cisco IOS Software," explains how to use a variety of Cisco IOS software source options, execute commands to load Cisco IOS software onto the router, maintain backup files, and upgrade Cisco IOS software.

Chapter 17, "Configuring Router Interfaces with IP Addresses," describes the process of configuring IP addresses.

Chapter 18, "Router Configuration and Routing Protocols: RIP and IGRP," describes the initial configuration of a router to enable the IP routing protocols RIP and IGRP.

Chapter 19, "Network Management," discusses the basic fundamentals of managing a network by using techniques such as documenting, auditing, monitoring, and evaluating.

Appendix A, "QuickTime Movie Reference," contains cross-referenced information about each of the QuickTime movies on the CD-ROM.

Appendix B, "Command Summary," describes and defines the commands related to configuring and using Cisco routers utilized in this book. It is alphabetically arranged so you can easily find information on a given command.

Appendix C, "Answers to Review Questions," provides the answers to the review questions you'll find at the end of each chapter.

Appendix D, "Computer Basics," provides backup reading for the new online Chapter 1.

Appendix E, "Electronics and Signals," covers the additional electricity and electronics information added to the online curriculum version 2.1.

Appendix F, "Signaling and Data Transmission," covers the new signaling information added to the online curriculum version 2.1.

Appendix G, "Binary and Hexadecimal Conversion" includes text and practice problems to increase your understanding of this critically important topic.

Appendix H, "Network Troubleshooting," covers the new information added to the online curriculum dealing with troubleshooting.

The Glossary defines the terms and abbreviations related to networking utilized in this book.

Objectives

After reading this chapter, you will be able to

- Define *networking*
- Define *protocol* and its importance in networking
- Define *LAN*
- Define *WAN*
- Describe the challenges and advantages of networking (software and hardware)
- Define and describe network standards
- Identify the functions of each of the seven layers of the OSI reference model
- Describe the process of encapsulation and communication between layers

Chapter 1

Networking and the OSI Reference Model

Introduction

In this chapter, you will learn about important networking terms and concepts. In addition, you will learn about two different types of networks:

Local-area networks (LANs), which make it possible for businesses using computer technology to efficiently share such things as files and printers

- Wide-area networks (WANs), which make it possible for businesses to communicate with each other even though they are geographically distant from each other

Finally, you will learn about the Open System Interconnection (OSI) reference model and the communication process between the lower layers of the OSI reference model.

Networking

Networking is the interconnection of workstations, peripherals (such as printers, hard drives, scanners, and CD-ROMs), and other devices. In networking, it is possible for different types of computers to communicate. It is not important what type of computer is used on a network. It may be a Macintosh, a PC, or a mainframe. In networking, what is important is that all the devices speak the same language, or *protocol*, which is a formal description of a set of rules and conventions that govern how devices on a network exchange information. For example, if a group of people are assigned to work as a team to complete a project, it does not matter if those people are French, German, Italian, American, Chinese, or Mexican. What is important is that they be able to communicate through a common language. In today's world, the team most likely would speak English. In computing, a protocol would function like English in this example because, like English, the protocol is a common language that can be understood by all devices on a network.

Why and How Did Networking Start?

Early computers were *standalone devices*. In other words, each computer operated on its own, independently from other computers. It soon became apparent that this was not an efficient or cost-effective way for businesses to operate. A solution was needed that would successfully address three problems:

- Duplication of equipment and resources
- Inability to communicate efficiently
- Lack of network management

Two solutions that addressed these three problems were LANs and WANs.

LANs

LANs connect workstations, peripherals, terminals, and other devices. LANs make it possible for businesses using computer technology to efficiently share such things as files and printers. As a result, a business can use a LAN to tie together its data, communication, computing, and file servers.

LANs are designed to

- Operate within a limited geographic area
- Allow many users to access high-bandwidth media
- Provide full-time connectivity to local services
- Connect physically adjacent devices

WANs

As businesses began to use computers more and more, however, it soon became apparent that even LANs were not sufficient. In a LAN system, each department or business was an electronic island.

Businesses needed a way to move information efficiently and quickly from one LAN to another. The solution was the creation of WANs. *WANs* interconnect LANs to provide access to computers or file servers in other locations. Because WANs connect networks that serve users across a large geographic area, they make it possible for businesses to communicate with each other even though they are geographically distant.

By networking or connecting computers, printers, and other devices on a WAN so they can communicate with each other, as shown in Figure 1-1, it is possible to share information and resources, as well as to access the Internet.

The Need for Standards

During the past two decades there has been a tremendous expansion of WANs. As organizations realized how much money they could save and how much productivity they could gain by using network technology, they began adding networks and expanding existing networks almost as rapidly as new network technologies and products were introduced. Consequently, many of the networks were built using different hardware and software implementations. As a result, many of the networks were incompatible and it became difficult for networks using different specifications to communicate with each other.

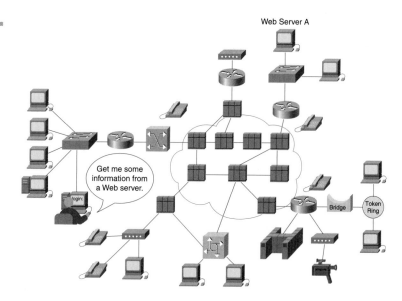

FIGURE 1-1
It is possible to share information by connecting computers and printers on a WAN.

To address the problem of networks being incompatible and unable to communicate with each other, the International Organization for Standardization (ISO) researched network schemes. The ISO recognized that there was a need to create a network model that would help vendors create interoperable network implementations; it released the OSI reference model in 1984. The OSI reference model quickly became the primary architectural model for intercomputer communications. Although other architectural models have been created, most network vendors relate their network products to the OSI reference model when they want to educate users about their products' compatibility and interoperability between the various types of network technologies that are produced around the world. Thus, the OSI reference model is the best tool available to people hoping to learn about network technology.

The OSI Reference Model

The OSI reference model is a descriptive network scheme; its standards ensure greater compatibility and interoperability between various types of network technologies. Further, the OSI reference model illustrates how information travels through networks. It is a conceptual framework specifying the network functions that occur at each layer. The OSI model describes how information or data makes its way from application programs (such as spreadsheets) through a network medium (such as wires) to another application program located on another computer on a network. As the information to be sent descends through the layers of a given system, it looks less and less like human language and more and more like the ones and zeros that a computer understands.

The OSI reference model divides the problem of moving information between computers over a network medium into seven smaller and more manageable problems. Each of the seven smaller problems was chosen because it is reasonably self-contained and, therefore, fairly easily solved without excessive reliance on external information. The separation of the seven smaller and more manageable problems into networking functions is called *layering*. As shown in Figure 1-2, each layer of the model solves each of the seven problem areas.

FIGURE 1-2
The seven layers of the OSI reference model.

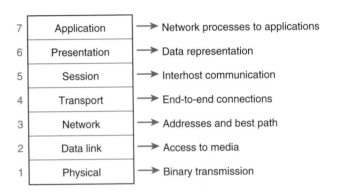

Because the lower layers—Layers 1 through 3—of the OSI reference model control the physical delivery of messages over the network, they often are referred to as the *media layers*. Because the upper layers—Layers 4 through 7—of the OSI reference model provide for the accurate delivery of data between computers on the network, they often are referred to as the *host layers* (see Figure 1-3). Most network devices implement all seven layers; however, to streamline operations, some network implementations incorporate functions of multiple layers at once.

The OSI reference model is not a network implementation. Instead, it specifies the functions of each layer. In this way, as shown in Figure 1-4, the OSI model is like a blueprint for building a car. After a car blueprint is complete, the car must still be built. Any number of automobile manufacturing companies can be contracted to do the actual work. If the blueprint is complete, then all the cars should be the same mechanically. Their appearance might differ in color or in the amount of chrome used as trim; however, they are all the same functionally.

FIGURE 1-3
On the network, the media layers control the physical delivery of messages, and the host layers provide the accurate delivery of data.

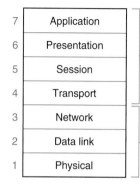

7	Application
6	Presentation
5	Session
4	Transport
3	Network
2	Data link
1	Physical

Host layers: Provide accurate data delivery between computers

Media layers: Control physical delivery of messages over the network

FIGURE 1-4
The OSI model is like a blueprint for the building of a car: It specifies the functions of each layer.

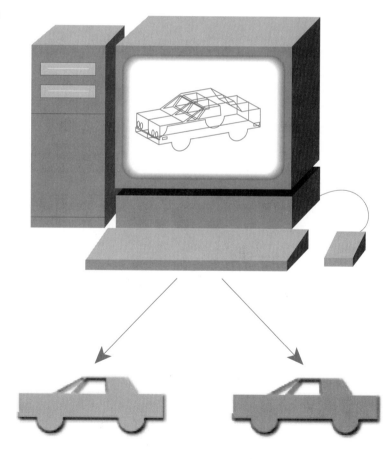

What accounts for the differences between implementations of the same car blueprint or protocol specification? In part, the differences are due to the inability of any specification to consider every possible implementation detail. Also, different manufacturers interpret the blueprint in slightly different ways. Consequently, inevitable implementation errors cause different implementations to occur in execution. This explains why one company's implementation of Protocol X does not always interoperate with another company's implementation of that protocol. Therefore, each layer of the OSI model serves a specific function, which is defined by the OSI and can be used by any network products vendor.

Why a Layered Network Model?

In the OSI model, seven numbered layers indicate distinct network functions. Dividing the network into these seven layers provides the following advantages:

- Divides the interrelated aspects of network operation into less complex elements
- Defines standard interfaces for plug-and-play compatibility and multi-vendor integration
- Enables engineers to specialize design and promote symmetry in the different internetwork modular functions so that they interoperate
- Prevents changes in one area from affecting other areas, so each area can evolve more quickly
- Divides the complexity of internetworking into discrete, more easily learned operation subsets

The Seven OSI Reference Model Layers

Now that the basic features of the OSI layered approach have been described, each individual OSI layer and its functions can be discussed. Each layer has a predetermined set of functions it must perform for communication to occur. The functions are described in the following sections.

Layer 7: The Application Layer

The application layer is the OSI layer closest to the user; it provides network services to user applications. It differs from the other layers in that it does not provide services to any other OSI layer, but rather to application processes outside the scope of the OSI model. Some examples of such application processes are spreadsheet programs, word processing programs, and banking terminal programs.

The application layer identifies and establishes the availability of intended communication partners, synchronizes cooperating applications, and establishes agreement on procedures for error recovery and control of data integrity. It also determines whether sufficient resources for the intended communication exist.

Layer 6: The Presentation Layer

The presentation layer ensures that information sent by the application layer of one system is readable by the application layer of another system. If necessary, the presentation layer translates between multiple data representation formats by using a common data representation format.

Layer 5: The Session Layer

As its name implies, the session layer establishes, manages, and terminates sessions between applications. Sessions consist of dialogs between two or more presentation entities.

The session layer provides its services to the presentation layer. Moreover, the session layer synchronizes dialog between presentation layer entities and manages their data exchange. In addition to basic regulation of conversations (sessions), the session layer offers provisions for dialog unit synchronization, class of service, and exception reporting of session-layer, presentation-layer, and application-layer problems.

Layer 4: The Transport Layer

The transport layer segments and reassembles data into a data stream. Whereas the application, presentation, and session layers are concerned with application issues, the lower four layers are concerned with data transport issues.

The transport layer attempts to provide a data transport service that shields the upper layers from transport implementation details. Specifically, issues such as how reliable transport over an internetwork is accomplished are the concern of the transport layer. In providing reliable service, the transport layer provides mechanisms for the establishment, maintenance, and orderly termination of virtual circuits, transport fault detection and recovery, and information flow control (to prevent one system from overrunning another with data).

Layer 3: The Network Layer

The network layer is a complex layer that provides connectivity and path selection between two end systems that may be located on geographically diverse networks. You'll learn more about Layer 3 in Chapter 3, "Networking Devices."

Layer 2: The Data Link Layer

The data link layer provides reliable transit of data across a physical link. In so doing, the data link layer is concerned with physical (as opposed to network, or logical) addressing, network topology, line discipline (how end systems use the network link), error notification, ordered delivery of frames, and flow control.

Layer 1: The Physical Layer

The physical layer defines the electrical, mechanical, procedural, and functional specifications for activating, maintaining, and deactivating the physical link between end systems. Such characteristics as voltage levels, timing of voltage changes, physical data rates, maximum transmission distances, physical connectors, and similar attributes are defined by physical-layer specifications.

Peer-to-Peer Communication

The OSI model's layering precludes direct communication between peer layers in different systems, as shown in Figure 1-5. To perform these tasks, it must communicate with its peer layer in the other system. Each layer's protocol exchanges information, called *protocol data units* (PDUs), between peer layers. A given layer can use a more specific name for its PDU.

FIGURE 1-5
In order to communicate with its peer layer in the other system, each layer uses its own layer protocol.

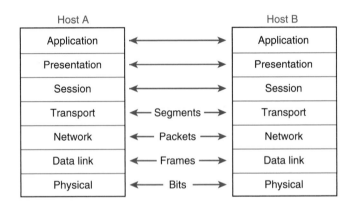

This peer-layer protocol communication is achieved by using the services of the layers below the communicating layer. The layer below any current layer provides its services to the current layer. Each lower-layer service takes upper-layer information as part of the lower-layer PDUs it exchanges with its layer peer.

For example, in TCP/IP, the transport layer of TCP communicates with the peer TCP function using segments, as shown in Figure 1-5. Thus, the TCP segments become part of the network-layer packets (also called *datagrams*) exchanged between IP peers. In turn, the IP packets must become part of the data link frames exchanged between directly connected devices. Ultimately, these frames must become bits as the data is finally transmitted by the physical-layer protocol using hardware.

Data Encapsulation

To understand how networks are structured and how they function, you should remember that all communications on a network originate at a source and are sent to a destination, as shown in Figure 1-6. The information that is sent on a network is referred to as *data* or *data packets*. If one computer (source) wants to send data to another computer (destination), the data must first be packaged in a process called *encapsulation*, which wraps data in a particular protocol header before network transit. This process can be compared to preparing a package to be sent—wrapping it, boxing it, putting source and destination addresses on it, putting stamps on the package, and dropping it in a mailbox.

FIGURE 1-6

Data packets on a network originate at a source and are sent to a destination.

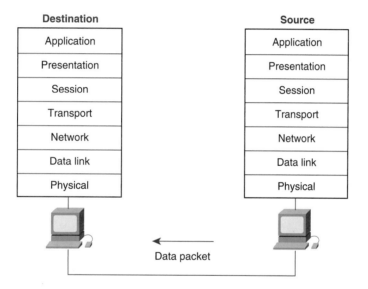

Each layer depends on the service function of the OSI layer below it. To provide this service, the lower layer uses encapsulation to put the PDU from the upper layer into its data field; then it can add whatever headers and trailers the layer will use to perform its function. Subsequently, as data moves down through the layers of the OSI model, headers and trailers are added.

For example, as shown in Figure 1-7, the network layer provides a service to the presentation layer, and the presentation layer presents data to the internetwork subsystem. The network layer has the task of moving that data through the internetwork. It accomplishes this task by encapsulating the data within a header. This header contains information required to complete the transfer, such as source and destination logical addresses.

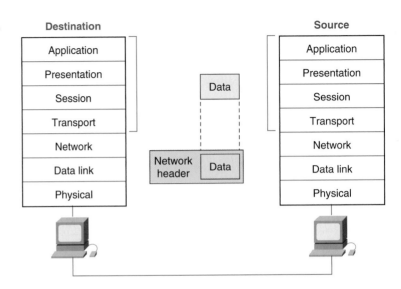

FIGURE 1-7
The network layer provides a service to the presentation layer by encapsulating the data within a header.

The data link layer in turn provides a service to the network layer, as shown in Figure 1-8. It encapsulates the network-layer information in a frame; the frame header contains information (for example, physical addresses) required to complete the data link functions.

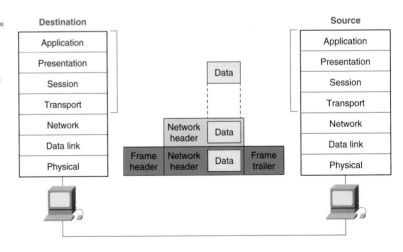

FIGURE 1-8
The data link layer provides a service to the network layer by encapsulating the network-layer information in a frame.

The physical layer also provides a service to the data link layer. As shown in Figure 1-9, the physical layer encodes the data link frame into a pattern of ones and zeros for transmission on the medium (usually a wire).

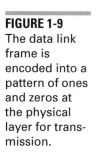

FIGURE 1-9
The data link frame is encoded into a pattern of ones and zeros at the physical layer for trans-mission.

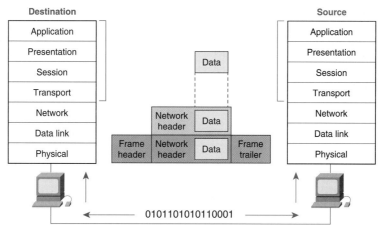

As networks perform services for users, the flow and packaging of the infor-mation changes. In the example of encapsulation shown in Figure 1-10, five conversion steps occur:

1. *Build the data*—As a user sends an e-mail message, the message's alphanumeric characters are converted to data that can traverse the internetwork.

2. *Package the data for end-to-end transport*—The data is packaged for internetwork transport. By using segments, the transport function ensures that the message hosts at both ends of the e-mail system can reliably communicate.

3. *Append network address in header*—The data is put into a packet or datagram that contains a network header with source and destination logical addresses. These addresses help network devices send the packets across the network along a chosen path.

4. *Append local address in data-link header*—Each network device must put the packet into a frame. The frame allows connection to the next directly connected network device on the link. Each device in the chosen network path requires framing to connect to the next device.

5. *Convert to bits for transmission*—The frame must be converted into a pattern of ones and zeros for transmission on the medium (usually a wire). A clocking function enables the devices to distinguish these bits as they traverse the medium. The medium on the physical internetwork can vary along the path used. For example, the e-mail message can originate on a LAN, cross a campus backbone, and go out a WAN link until it reaches its destination on another remote LAN.

FIGURE 1-10
Headers and trailers are added as data moves down through the layers of the OSI model.

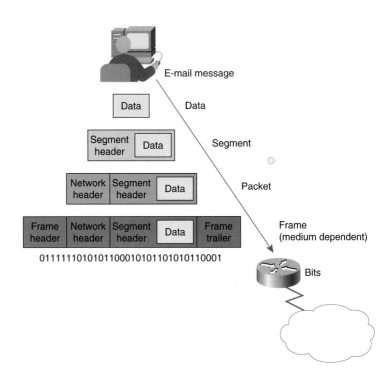

Summary

- *Networking* is the interconnection of workstations, peripherals (such as printers, hard drives, scanners, and CD-ROMs), and other devices.

- A *protocol* is a formal description of a set of rules and conventions that govern how devices on a network exchange information.

- The OSI reference model is a descriptive network scheme whose standards ensure greater compatibility and interoperability between various types of network technologies.

- The OSI reference model organizes network distinct functions into seven numbered layers:
  - *Layer 7*—The application layer
  - *Layer 6*—The presentation layer
  - *Layer 5*—The session layer
  - *Layer 4*—The transport layer
  - *Layer 3*—The network layer
  - *Layer 2*—The data link layer
  - *Layer 1*—The physical layer
- The OSI model's layering precludes direct communication between peer layers in different systems.
- *Encapsulation* is the process in which data is wrapped in a particular protocol header before network transit.

Review Questions

1. Which of the following is *not* a reason why the OSI model is a layered network model?

   A. A layered model increases complexity.

   B. A layered model standardizes interfaces.

   C. A layered model enables specialized development effort.

   D. A layered model prevents changes in one area from affecting other areas.

2. Which layer of the OSI model handles error notification, network topology, and flow control?

   A. The physical layer

   B. The data link layer

   C. The transport layer

   D. The network layer

3. Which layer of the OSI model establishes, maintains, and manages sessions between applications?

   A. The transport layer

   B. The session layer

   C. The presentation layer

   D. The application layer

4. Which best describes the function of the presentation layer?

   A. It provides data representation and code formatting.

   B. It handles error notification, network topology, and flow control.

   C. It provides network services to user applications.

   D. It provides electrical, mechanical, procedural, and functional means for activating and maintaining the link between systems.

5. Which layer of the OSI model provides network services to user applications?

    A. The transport layer

    B. The session layer

    C. The presentation layer

    D. The application layer

6. Which of the following correctly describes the five conversion steps of data encapsulation when one computer sends an e-mail message to another computer?

    A. Data, segments, packets, frames, bits

    B. Bits, frames, packets, segments, data

    C. Packets, segments, data, bits, frames

    D. Segments, packets, frames, bits, data

7. An e-mail message is sent from Host A to Host B on a LAN. To send this message, the data must be encapsulated. Which of the following best describes the first step of data encapsulation?

    A. Alphanumeric characters are converted into data.

    B. The message is segmented into easily transportable chunks.

    C. A network header is added to the message (source and destination addresses).

    D. The message is converted into binary format.

8. An e-mail message is sent from Host A to Host B on a LAN. Before you can send this message, the data must be encapsulated. Which of the following best describes what happens after a packet is constructed?

    A. The packet is transmitted along the medium.

    B. The packet is put into a frame.

    C. The packet is segmented into frames.

    D. The packet is converted to binary format.

9. An e-mail message is sent from Host A to Host B on a LAN. Before you can send this message, the data must be encapsulated. Which of the following best describes what happens after the e-mail message's alphanumeric characters are converted into data?

    A. The data is converted into binary format.

    B. The data has a network header added.

    C. The data is segmented into smaller chunks.

    D. The data is put into a frame.

10. Which best describes a datagram?

    A. A message sent to the source to confirm receipt of uncorrupted data

    B. A binary representation of routing information

    C. A data packet less than 100 bytes in size

    D. A network-layer packet

Objectives

After reading this chapter, you will be able to

- Describe Layer 1—the physical layer—of the OSI reference model
- Describe encoding
- Name, identify, and define four types of networking media
- Describe the criteria for judging appropriate-quality media
- Describe Layer 2—the data link layer—of the OSI reference model
- Define and describe the purpose of a MAC address
- Define and describe the purpose of a NIC

The Physical and Data Link Layers

Introduction

In Chapter 1, "Networking and the OSI Reference Model," you learned that LANs and WANs are different types of networks that businesses use to share computers, files, and devices. In addition, you learned that the OSI reference model has become the primary model for network communications. You learned that although other models have been created, most network vendors today relate their network products to the OSI reference model when they want to educate users about their products. You also learned that all data sent out on a network is from a source and is going to a destination.

In this chapter, you will learn about the network functions that occur at the physical and data link layers of the OSI model. You will learn about different types of networking media that are used at the physical layer, including shielded twisted-pair cable, unshielded twisted-pair cable, coaxial cable, and fiber-optic cable. In addition, you will learn that the type of connecting material used by a network can help determine such things as how much data can travel across the network and how fast. Finally, you will learn that access to the networking media occurs at the data link layer of the OSI reference model. In particular, you will learn about how data is able to locate its intended destination on a network.

The Physical Layer

In this chapter, the terms we use to describe how a network functions are linked to the OSI reference model. Similar to a house needing to have a foundation before it can be built, so too must a network have a foundation on which it can be built. In the OSI reference model, shown in Figure 2-1, this foundation is called the *physical layer*. The physical layer is the layer that defines the electrical, mechanical, procedural, and functional specifications for activating, maintaining, and deactivating the physical link between end systems.

The function of the physical layer is the transmission of data. Data, which can be information such as text, pictures, and sounds, is represented by the presence of either electrical pulses, referred to as *voltage*, on copper conducting wires or light pulses in optical fibers. This transmission process, referred to as *encoding*, typically is accomplished through the use of such things as cables and connectors, referred to as networking media.

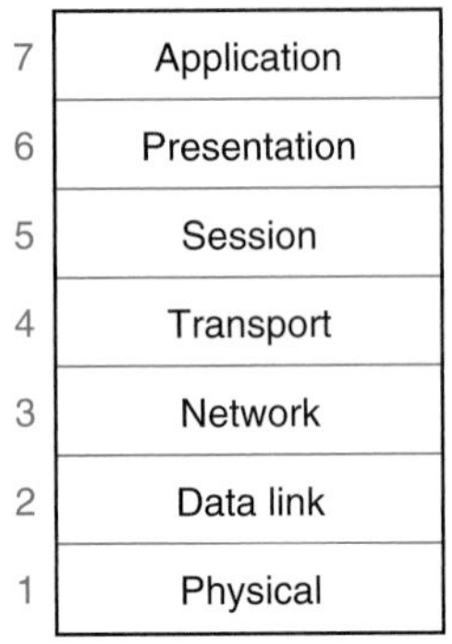

FIGURE 2-1
In the OSI model, the foundation layer is called the physical layer.

7	Application
6	Presentation
5	Session
4	Transport
3	Network
2	Data link
1	Physical

Networking Media

Networking media are the various physical environments through which transmission signals pass. For computers to communicate encoded information with each other, networking media must physically connect them to each other. The networking media used to connect computers vary. Several kinds of networking media can be used to connect computers (some of which are shown in Figure 2-2):

- Coaxial cable
- Unshielded twisted-pair cable
- Shielded twisted-pair cable
- Fiber-optic cable

Coaxial Cable

Coaxial cable, which is illustrated in Figure 2-3, consists of a hollow outer cylindrical conductor surrounding a single inner wire conductor. Coaxial cable consists of two conducting elements. One of these is located in the center of the cable and is copper. This center copper conductor is surrounded by a layer of flexible insulation. Over this insulating material is a shield composed of woven copper braid or metallic foil that acts as the second wire in the circuit. As its name implies, this outer braid acts as a shield for the inner conductor. Thus, it can help reduce the amount of interference. Outside this shield is the cable jacket.

FIGURE 2-2
Common networking media include coaxial, twisted-pair, and fiber-optic cable.

Coaxial

Unshielded twisted-pair

Fiber-optic

FIGURE 2-3
Coaxial cable is made up of a single inner wire conductor that is surrounded by a hollow outer cylindrical conductor.

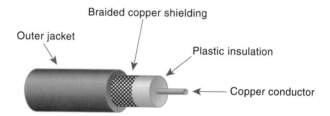

For LANs, coaxial cable offers several advantages. Coaxial cable can run unboosted for longer distances than either shielded or unshielded twisted-pair cable. This means that it can run for longer distances between network nodes without needing a repeater to reamplify the signal than can twisted-pair cable. Coaxial cable is less expensive than fiber-optic cable. Also, because it has been in use for a long time for all types of data communication, the technology is well-known.

Coaxial cable is available in different thicknesses. As a general rule, the thicker the cable, the more awkward it is to work with. This is an important point to remember, especially if cable must be pulled through existing conduits and troughs that are limited in size. Because it is stiff due to the shielding and because its jacket is a distinctive yellow color, this type of coaxial cable has frequently been referred to as *thicknet*. As is implied by its nickname, this type of coaxial cable can be too rigid to install easily in some situations. As a general rule, the more difficult networking media is to install, the more expensive it is to install.

Unshielded Twisted-Pair Cable

As shown in Figure 2-4, unshielded twisted-pair (UTP) cable is a four-pair wire medium used in a variety of networks. Each pair of wires is insulated from the other pairs.

FIGURE 2-4
A variety of networks use UTP, which is a four-pair wire medium.

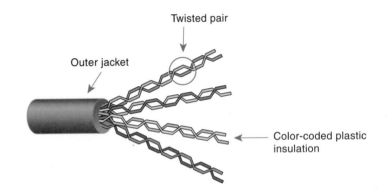

Outer jacket
Twisted pair
Color-coded plastic insulation

When used as a networking medium, UTP cable has four pairs of either 22- or 24-gauge copper wire. UTP has an external diameter of approximately 0.17 inch; its small size can be advantageous during installation. Because it can be used with most of the major networking architectures, UTP continues to grow in popularity.

UTP cable is easy to install and is less expensive than other types of networking media. In fact, UTP costs less per foot than any other type of LAN cabling. However, UTP's real advantage is its size. Because it has such a small external diameter, UTP won't fill up wiring ducts as rapidly as will other types of cable. This can be an extremely important factor to consider, particularly if you are installing a network in an older building. Moreover, UTP cable often is installed using a registered jack (RJ) connector (shown in Figure 2-5). RJ connectors are standard connectors originally used to connect telephone lines and are now used in connecting networks. Using RJ connectors, a good, solid connection is practically guaranteed; therefore, potential sources of network noise can be greatly reduced.

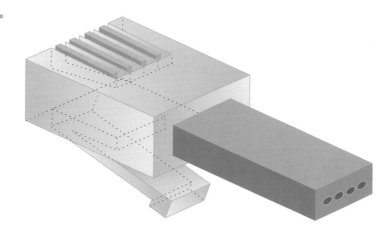

FIGURE 2-5
UTP uses RJ
connectors.

Generally speaking, UTP cable is more prone to electrical noise and interference than are other types of networking media. At one time, it could be said
that UTP was not as fast at transmitting data as other types of cable. However,
this is no longer true. In fact, UTP today is the fastest copper-based medium.
The distance between signal boosts is shorter for UTP than it is for coaxial.

Shielded Twisted-Pair Cable

Shielded twisted-pair (STP) cable combines the techniques of shielding and
twisting of wires. As specified for network installations, when properly
installed, STP cable provides great resistance to both electromagnetic interference and radio frequency interference without significantly increasing the
weight or size of the cable.

STP cable has all the advantages and disadvantages of UTP cable. In addition,
STP affords greater protection from all types of external interference than UTP
cable. Moreover, generally speaking, STP cable is more expensive than UTP
cable.

Unlike coaxial cable, in STP cable, the shield is not part of the data circuit.
Therefore, the cable must be grounded only at one end. Usually, installers
ground STP at either the wiring closet or the hub. This is not always easy to
do, particularly if installers attempt to use older wiring hubs that were not
designed to accommodate STP cable. In such cases, improperly grounded STP
can become a major source of problems because it allows the shield to act as
an antenna, absorbing electrical signals from other wires in the cable and from
sources of electrical noise outside the cable. Finally, STP cable cannot be run as
far unboosted as other networking media.

Fiber-Optic Cable

Fiber-optic cable, which is illustrated in Figure 2-6, is a networking medium capable of conducting modulated light transmissions. Fiber-optic cable is not susceptible to electromagnetic interference, and it is capable of higher data rates than UTP, STP, and coaxial cable. More specifically, fiber-optic cable does not carry electrical impulses as do other forms of networking media employing copper wire. Instead, on fiber-optic cable, signals that signify bits are changed into beams of light. Fiber-optic communication is rooted in inventions from the 19th century. But it was not until the 1960s, when solid-state laser light sources and high-quality impurity-free glass were introduced, that fiber-optical communication became practical. The widespread use of fiber-optic cable was pioneered by telephone companies, which saw its benefits for long-distance communication.

FIGURE 2-6
Fiber-optic cable is a networking medium capable of conducting modulated light transmissions.

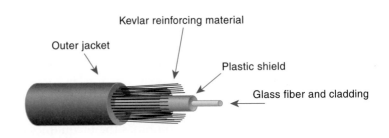

Fiber-optic cable used for networking is made up of two fibers encased in separate sheaths. If you were to view it in cross-section, you would see that each fiber is surrounded by layers of reflective cladding, a plastic coating called *Kevlar* (a protective material commonly used in bulletproof vests), and an outer jacket. The outer jacket provides protection for the entire cable and is usually made of plastic; the outer jacket conforms to appropriate fire and building codes. The purpose of Kevlar is to furnish additional cushioning and protection for the fragile hair-thin glass fibers. Where buried fiber-optic cables are required, a stainless steel wire is sometimes included for added cable strength.

The light-guiding parts of an optical fiber are called the *core* and the *cladding*. The core is usually very pure glass with a high index of refraction. When the core glass is surrounded by a cladding layer of glass or plastic with a low index of refraction, light can be trapped in the fiber core. This process is called *total internal reflection*; it allows the optical fiber to act like a light pipe, guiding light for tremendous distances—even around bends.

Not only is fiber-optic cable unaffected by electromagnetic interference, it is completely immune to radio frequency interference as well. Because of this freedom from internal and external noise, signals can go farther in fiber-optic cable than in other media types. Because it cannot carry electrical signals or power, fiber-optic cable is ideal for connecting buildings that might have different electrical grounds. Whereas long cable spans of copper cable between buildings could serve as an entry point for lightning strikes, fiber-optic cable used in the same type of situation would not. Moreover, like UTP cable, fiber-optic cable is small in diameter. In addition, fiber-optic cable is relatively flat, much like a lamp cord. Therefore, a single conduit can accommodate several fiber-optic cables. Thus, it is ideal in older buildings with limited space.

Fiber-optic cable is more expensive and more difficult to install than other types of networking media. Because fiber-optic connectors are optical interfaces, they must be polished perfectly flat and be free of scratches. Thus, installation can be difficult. Typically, even a trained installer requires several minutes to make each connection. This can quickly drive up the hourly cost of labor, and in large installations this cost can become prohibitive.

Selecting the Right Networking Media

Various criteria, such as rate of data transfer and cost, help determine which networking medium should be used. The type of connecting material used in a network determines such things as how much data can travel across the network and how quickly. Other factors, such as expense and where the cable will be used, are important as well.

To ensure optimal performance, it is important for the networking media to carry the signal from one device to another with as little degradation as possible. In networking, several factors can cause the signal to degrade. As you will see, all networking media use shielding and cancellation techniques to prevent signal degradation. However, the differences in the types of shielding and cancellation used in various networking media cause cables to differ in size, cost, and difficulty of installation.

In addition, networking media can employ different types of cable jackets. The jacket is the outside covering of the cable, usually made of some form of plastic, nonstick coating, or composite material. When designing a LAN, it is important to remember that networking media installed between walls, in an elevator shaft, or passing through an air-handling unit could become a torch capable of carrying fire from one part of a building to another. Moreover, plastic cable jackets can create toxic smoke when they burn. To guard against such occurrences, fire codes, building codes, and safety standards have been implemented that govern the type of cable jackets that can be used. Therefore, adherence to such codes must also be taken into consideration (along with such factors as cable size, speed, cost, and difficulty of installation) when determining what type of networking media to use in a LAN.

To understand this concept of selecting networking media more fully, think of two cities located several miles apart. Although they are several miles apart, the cities are connected to each other by means of roads. Some of the roads may be very basic in terms of their size and the types of materials used to construct them; an example of this would be an unimproved one-lane gravel road. Other roads may be larger in size and constructed of more sophisticated materials; an example of this would be a reinforced concrete four-lane superhighway.

If you were interested in taking a leisurely Sunday afternoon sightseeing drive from City A to City B, you might choose the unimproved one-lane gravel road for your trip. On the other hand, if you were an ambulance driver in City A attempting to deliver a critical patient to a hospital in City B, it would be foolhardy to follow the same route. Because it is faster, smoother, and wider, the four-lane superhighway could accommodate your needs as an ambulance driver, whereas the one-lane country road would have difficulty doing so. The cities are like two computers trying to communicate, and the roads are like networking media operating at the physical layer. As in the cities and roads example, the type of connecting material used by a network determines the amount of data that can travel across the network and its speed.

The Data Link Layer

As you learned in Chapter 1, "Networking and the OSI Reference Model," all data sent out on a network is from a source and is going to a destination. In addition, you learned that the function of the physical layer is to transmit data. After data is transmitted, the data link layer of the OSI model provides access to the networking media and physical transmission across the media, which enables the data to locate its intended destination on a network. In addition, the data link layer handles error notification, network topology, and flow control.

If you refer to the OSI model, you will see that the data link layer is adjacent to the physical layer. As you learned in Chapter 1, "Networking and the OSI Reference Model," the data link layer provides reliable transit of data across a physical link. This layer uses Media Access Control (MAC) addresses. In so doing, the data link layer is concerned with physical (as opposed to network, or logical) addressing, network topology, line discipline (how end systems will use the network link), error notification, ordered delivery of frames, and flow control. Moreover, the data link layer uses the MAC address to define a hardware or data link address in order for multiple stations to share the same medium and still uniquely identify each other. Before a data packet is exchanged with a directly connected device on the same LAN, the sending device needs to have a MAC address it can use as a destination address.

MAC Addresses

Every computer has a unique way of identifying itself. Every computer, whether it is attached to a network or not, has a unique physical address; no two physical addresses are ever alike. Referred to as the *MAC address*, the physical address is located on a *network interface card* (NIC), an example of which is shown in Figure 2-7. Thus, on a network, the NIC connects a device to the media. Each NIC, which is located in the data link layer of the OSI reference model, has a unique MAC address.

FIGURE 2-7
The physical address of a computer is located on a NIC, an example of which is shown here.

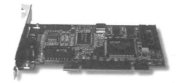

On a network, when one device wants to send data to another device, it can open a communication pathway to the other device by using the other device's MAC address. When data is sent out on a network by a source, it carries the MAC address of its intended destination. As this data travels along the networking media, the NIC in each device on the network checks whether its MAC address matches the physical destination address carried by the data packet. If no match is made, the NIC ignores the data packet and the data packet continues along the network to the next station.

However, when a match is made, the NIC makes a copy of the data packet and places the copy at the computer's data link layer. Although this copy has been made by the NIC and placed on the computer, the original data packet continues along the network, where other NICs will be able to look at it to determine whether a match can be made.

Network Interface Cards

NICs convert data packets into signals that they send out over the network. Before each NIC leaves the factory, it is assigned a physical address by the hardware manufacturer. This address is programmed into a chip on the NIC.

On most NICs, the MAC address is burned into ROM. When the NIC initializes, its address is copied into RAM. Because the MAC address is located on the NIC, if the NIC were replaced in a computer, the physical address of the station would change to that of the new NIC.

For example, imagine that you operate a motel. Room 207 has a lock called Lock A. Key A opens the door to Room 207. Room 410 has a lock called Lock F. Key F opens the door to Room 410. You decide to swap the locks on Rooms 207 and 410. After you have switched the two locks, Key A opens the door of Room 410, and Key F opens the door to Room 207. In this analogy, the locks are like NICs. When the NICs are swapped, the matching keys must also be changed. In this analogy, the keys are like the MAC addresses.

Summary

- The function of the physical layer is to transmit data.
- Several types of networking media may be used to connect computers:
  - Coaxial cable consists of a hollow outer cylindrical conductor that surrounds a single inner wire conductor.
  - UTP cable is a four-pair wire medium used in a variety of networks.
  - STP cable combines the techniques of shielding, cancellation, and twisting of wires.
  - Fiber-optic cable is a networking medium capable of conducting modulated light transmissions.
- Various criteria, such as rate of data transfer and expense, help determine which types of networking media should be used.
- The data link layer of the OSI model provides access to the networking media and physical transmission across the media, which enables the data to locate its intended destination on a network.
- The data link layer provides reliable transit of data across a physical link. This layer uses the MAC address, which is the physical address located on a NIC.
- NICs convert data packets into signals that they send out over the network. Each NIC is assigned a physical address by the hardware manufacturer.

Review Questions

1. What are all the physical connecting materials in a network called?

   A. Application media

   B. Educational media

   C. Networking media

   D. System media

2. What is one advantage of using fiber-optic cable in networks?

   A. It is inexpensive.

   B. It is easy to install.

   C. It is an industry standard and is available at any electronics store.

   D. It is capable of higher data rates than either coaxial or twisted-pair cable.

3. Which of the following best defines *networking media*?

   A. The cables and wires through which data passes

   B. The various physical environments through which transmission signals pass

   C. The computer systems and wires that make up a network

   D. Any hardware or software in a network

4. How is information stored on computers?

   A. As decimal numbers

   B. As binary numbers

   C. As electrons

   D. As words and pictures

5. The data link layer is which layer in the OSI model?

   A. Layer 1

   B. Layer 2

   C. Layer 3

   D. Layer 4

6. Which best describes the data link layer of the OSI model?

   A. It transmits data to other network layers.

   B. It provides services to application processes.

   C. It takes weak signals, cleans them, amplifies them, and sends them on their way across the network.

   D. It provides reliable transit of data across a physical link.

7. A NIC is located at which layer of the OSI model?

   A. The data link layer

   B. The physical layer

   C. The transmission layer

   D. The presentation layer

8. What is another name for a MAC address?

   A. Binary address

   B. Octadecimal address

   C. Physical address

   D. TCP/IP address

9. What does a NIC do?

   A. It establishes, manages, and terminates sessions between applications and manages data exchange between presentation layer entities.

   B. It provides network communication capabilities to and from a computer system.

   C. It provides services to application processes.

   D. It provides mechanisms for the establishment, maintenance, and termination of virtual circuits, transport fault detection, recovery, and information flow control.

10. How does a source device locate the destination for data on a network?

    A. The NIC at the destination identifies its MAC address in a data packet.

    B. A data packet stops at the destination.

    C. The NIC at the destination sends its MAC address to the source.

    D. The source sends a unique data packet to each MAC address on the network.

Objectives

After reading this chapter, you will be able to

- Identify and define networking devices
- Define and describe nodes
- Define and describe repeaters
- Define and describe signals
- Define and describe hubs
- Define and describe filters
- Define and describe ports
- Define and identify domains
- Define and describe bridges
- Define and describe routers

Chapter 3

Networking Devices

Introduction

In Chapter 2, "The Physical and Data Link Layers," you learned about the network functions that occur at the physical and data link layers of the OSI reference model. You learned about the different types of networking media that are used at the physical layer. These types of networking media include shielded twisted-pair cable, unshielded twisted-pair cable, coaxial cable, and fiber-optic cable. Finally, you learned that access to the networking media occurs at the data link layer of the OSI reference model. In particular, you learned about how data is able to locate its intended destination on a network.

You also learned that when one device wants to send data to another device, it can open a communication pathway to the other device by using its Media Access Control (MAC) address. When a source sends data out on a network, the data carries the MAC address of its intended destination. As the data travels along the networking media, the network interface card (NIC) in each device on the network checks to see whether its MAC address matches the physical destination address carried by the data packet. If no match is made, the NIC ignores the data packet and the data packet continues along the network to the next station.

However, when a match is made, the NIC makes a copy of the data packet and places it in the computer, where it resides at the data link layer. While this copy is made by the NIC and placed in the computer, the original data packet continues along the network, where other NICs are able to look at it to determine whether a match can be made.

Although sending out data to every device on a network might work for a relatively small network, it is easy to see that the larger a network is, the more traffic there is. This can present a serious problem because only one data packet can be on a cable at any one time. If there were only one cable interconnecting every device on a network, this could considerably slow down the flow of data over the network. In this chapter, you will learn how networking devices are able to control the amount of traffic on a network and speed up the flow of data over a network.

Networking devices are products used to connect networks. As computer networks grow in size and complexity, so do the networking devices used to connect them.

However, all networking devices share one or more common purposes:

- They allow a greater number of nodes to be connected to the network. A *node* is an endpoint of a network connection or a junction common to two or more lines in a network. Nodes can be processors, controllers, or workstations. Nodes vary in routing and other functional capabilities; they can be interconnected by links, and they serve as control points in the network. *Node* is sometimes used generically to refer to any entity that can access a network and is frequently used interchangeably with *device*.

- They increase the distance over which a network can extend.

- They localize traffic on the network.

- They can merge existing networks.

- They isolate network problems so that the problems can be diagnosed more easily.

The symbols shown in Figure 3-1 represent the following networking devices: repeaters, hubs, bridges, and routers. You will learn about these devices in this chapter.

FIGURE 3-1
Networking devices include repeaters, hubs, bridges, and routers.

 Repeater   Hub   Bridge   Router

Repeaters

Like networking media, repeaters are networking devices that exist at Layer 1, the physical layer, of the OSI reference model. To begin understanding how a repeater works, it is important to first understand that as data leaves a source and goes out over the network, it is transformed into either electrical or light impulses that pass along the networking media. These impulses are referred to as *signals*. When signals first leave a transmitting station, they are clean and easily recognizable. However, the longer the cable length, the weaker and more deteriorated the signals become as they pass along the networking media. For example, specifications for Category 5 twisted-pair Ethernet cable establish the maximum distance that signals can travel along a network as 100 meters. If a signal travels beyond that distance, there is no guarantee that a NIC will be able to read the signal. A repeater can provide a simple solution if this problem exists.

Using Repeaters to Increase the Extent of the Network

Repeaters can increase the distance over which a network can extend so that signals will not become unrecognizable to devices receiving them on the network. Repeaters take in weakened signals, clean them up, amplify them, and send them on their way along the network, thereby increasing the distance over which a network can operate.

For example, imagine that you are at a baseball game. You become hungry. You see the peanut vendor two sections away, so you stand up and yell, "Give me some peanuts!" The peanut vendor hears you but cannot understand what you said because he is too far away. You yell a second time, "Give me some peanuts!" This time, a man seated halfway between you and the peanut vendor hears you and repeats your message so that the peanut vendor can hear it. Because the man is closer to the peanut vendor and because he repeats the message loudly enough for the vendor, the peanut vendor is able to clearly hear your message. In this analogy, the man seated between you and the peanut vendor is like a repeater, and your message is like the signal carried on the networking media.

Using Repeaters to Increase the Number of Network Nodes

In networking, a common problem is that there are too many devices connected to a network. Signals become weaker and more deteriorated when there are too many devices attached to a network because each device attached to the network causes the signal to degrade slightly. Moreover, because a signal has to pass by too many stations or nodes, it can become so weak that it is unrecognizable to devices receiving it. However, a repeater can provide a simple solution if this problem exists as mentioned in the previous section. Repeaters take in weakened signals, clean them up, amplify them, and send them on their way along the network. You can therefore attach a greater number of nodes to a network.

Imagine that you have a popsicle that you want to give to your friend Tom. It is a very hot day. You must carry the popsicle the mile from your house to school, where Tom is waiting for you. As you walk to school, the popsicle melts and becomes smaller and smaller. By the time you reach the school, the popsicle has entirely melted. When you give the popsicle to Tom, all that remains is the stick, and Tom can no longer recognize what your gift to him once was.

The next day is also a very hot day; you leave your house to take a popsicle to your friend Tom at school a mile away. You walk a block and notice that the popsicle is beginning to melt. To prevent the popsicle from entirely melting, you stop at a freezer located at the corner. You place the popsicle in the freezer. The popsicle refreezes and becomes firm again. You take the popsicle out of the freezer and continue on your journey. Every time it begins to melt, you stop again and place it in a freezer located on the corner of each block. Eventually, you reach your destination, where you give your friend Tom his gift. Tom immediately recognizes what your gift is and begins to devour his treat.

Hubs

On a LAN, every workstation is connected to the network by means of some sort of transmission medium. Usually, each file server has only one NIC. Therefore, it would be impossible to connect every workstation directly to the file server. To solve this problem, LANs may use hubs, which are very common networking devices.

Generally speaking, the term *hub* is used instead of *repeater* when referring to the device that serves as the center of a network, as shown in Figure 3-2. The following are the most important properties of hubs:

- They amplify signals.
- They propagate signals through the network.
- They do not require filtering.
- They do not require path determination or switching.
- They are used as network concentration points.

FIGURE 3-2
A hub is a common networking device that serves as the center of a network.

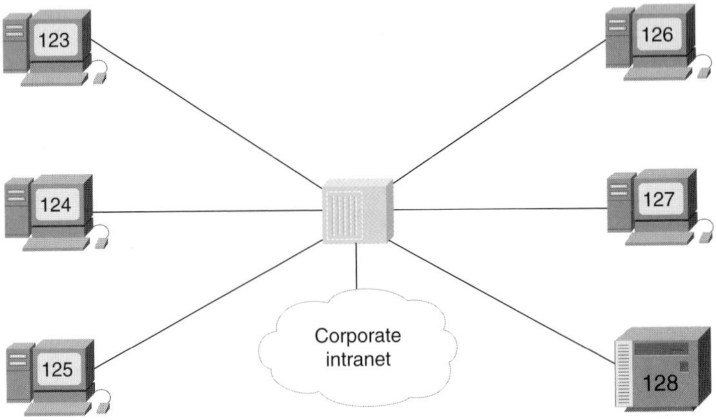

Hubs can also be understood to be hardware devices that contain multiple independent but connected modules of network equipment. In a LAN, where hubs act as multiport repeaters, they are sometimes referred to as *concentrators*. In such cases, hubs are used to split the networking media or provide for multiple connections.

The disadvantage of using a hub is that it can't filter network traffic. *Filtering* generally refers to a process or device that screens network traffic for certain characteristics, such as source address, destination address, or protocol, and determines whether to forward or discard that traffic based on the established criteria. On a hub, data arriving at one port gets sent out on all other ports. Consequently, a hub passes data to all other sections or segments of a network, regardless of whether the data needs to go there or not.

If there is only one cable interconnecting all the devices on a network or if segments of a network are only connected by nonfiltering devices such as hubs, more than one user may try to send data on the network at the same time. If more than one node attempts to transmit at the same time, a collision occurs. When a collision occurs, the data from each device hits each other and is damaged. The network area within which data packets originate and collide is called a *collision domain*. One way to solve the problems of too much traffic on a network and too many collisions is to use a bridge.

Bridges

Bridges operate at Layer 2, the data link layer, of the OSI reference model and are not required to examine upper-layer information. Therefore, a bridge eliminates unnecessary traffic and minimizes the chances of collisions occurring on a network by dividing it into segments and filtering traffic based on the station or MAC address.

Bridges filter network traffic by only looking at the MAC address. Therefore, they can rapidly forward traffic representing any network-layer protocol. Because bridges only look at MAC addresses, they are not concerned with protocols. Consequently, bridges are only concerned with passing packets, or not passing packets, based on their destination MAC addresses. The following are the important properties of bridges:

- They are more intelligent than hubs—that is, they can analyze incoming packets and forward (or drop) them based on addressing information.
- They collect and pass packets between two network segments.
- They control broadcasts to the network.
- They maintain address tables.

Figure 3-3 shows an example of a how a bridge is used.

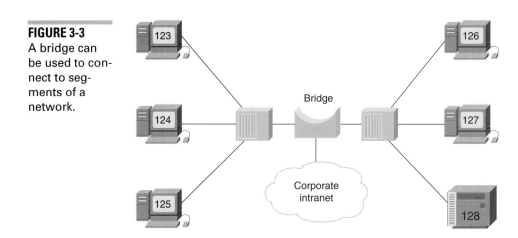

FIGURE 3-3
A bridge can be used to connect to segments of a network.

Imagine that Mrs. Jones has 30 students in her homeroom class. She knows which clubs each of her students belongs to because her homeroom seating chart includes this information next to each student's name. Every Monday morning a list of club announcements is delivered to each homeroom teacher so it can be read to students. This Monday, Mrs. Jones notices that the only announcement is for members of the high school marching band. She checks her seating chart list and sees that none of the students in her homeroom are members of the band. Therefore, Mrs. Jones does not read the announcement about the band to her homeroom students.

In this analogy, Mrs. Jones is like a bridge because she is filtering messages and deciding what will be forwarded to her students based on information regarding their club membership. In this example, club memberships shown next to each student's name on Mrs. Jones's seating chart are like the destination MAC addresses used by bridges.

In order to filter or selectively deliver network traffic, bridges build tables of all MAC addresses located on a network and other networks and maps them.

If data comes along the networking media, a bridge compares the destination MAC address carried by the data to MAC addresses contained in its tables. If the bridge determines that the destination MAC address of the data is from the same network segment as the source, as shown in Figure 3-4, it does not forward the data to other segments of the network. If the bridge determines that the destination MAC address of the data is not from the same network segment as the source, as shown in Figure 3-5, it forwards the data to all other segments of the network. Therefore, bridges can significantly reduce the amount of traffic between network segments by eliminating unnecessary traffic.

FIGURE 3-4
Bridges do not forward data to other segments of a network if the destination MAC address is from the same network. In this example, a data packet originates from Computer V and its destination is Computer Xc.

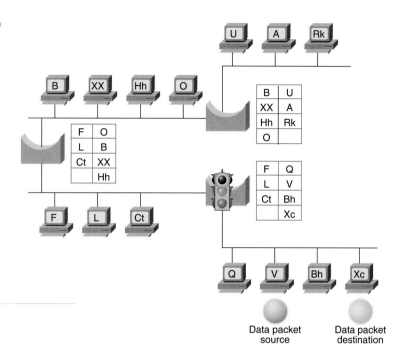

FIGURE 3-5
Bridges forward data to other segments of a network if the destination MAC address is not from the same network. In this example, a data packet originates from Computer V and its destination is Computer Hh.

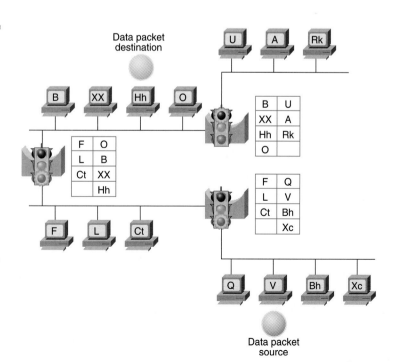

Routers

Routers are another type of internetworking device. As you learned earlier, bridges are primarily used to connect segments of a network. Routers are used to connect separate networks and to access the Internet.

Routers provide end-to-end routing by passing data packets and routing traffic between different networks based on network protocol or Layer 3 information. As shown in Figure 3-6, routers have the ability to make decisions about the best path for delivery of data on the network. The problem of excessive broadcast traffic can be solved by using a router because routers do not forward broadcast frames unless specifically told to do so.

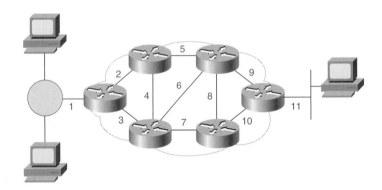

FIGURE 3-6
Routers use Layer 3 to determine the best path for delivery of data on the network, and they help contain broadcasts.

Routers differ from bridges in several respects. First, bridging occurs at Layer 2, the data link layer, whereas routing occurs at Layer 3, the network layer of the OSI reference model. Second, bridges use physical or MAC addresses to make data forwarding decisions. Routers use a different addressing scheme that occurs at Layer 3 to make forwarding decisions. They use network-layer addresses, which are referred to as Internet Protocol (IP), or logical, addresses, rather than MAC addresses. Because IP addresses are implemented in software and refer to the network a device is located on, sometimes these Layer 3 addresses are referred to as *protocol addresses* or *network addresses*. Physical, or MAC, addresses are usually assigned by the NIC manufacturer and are hard-coded into the NIC. IP addresses, on the other hand, are usually assigned by the network administrator.

For routing to be successful, each network must have a unique network number. As shown in Figure 3-7 and Table 3-1, this unique network number is incorporated into the IP address assigned to each device attached to the network.

FIGURE 3-7
A unique network number is incorporated into the IP address, which is assigned to each node attached to the network.

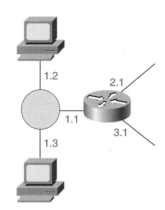

TABLE 3-1   Network and Node Addresses

Network Address	Node Address
1	1
	2
	3
2	1
3	1

For example, assume that you have a unique network called Network A, as shown in Figure 3-8, with four devices attached to that network. The IP addresses of these devices would be A1, A2, A3, and A4. Because the interface where the router connects to a network is considered to be part of that network, the port where a router connects to Network A would have the IP address A5.

FIGURE 3-8
Network A has
four devices
attached to it.

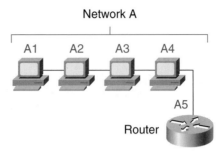

Network A

A1   A2   A3   A4

A5

Router

Assume that you have another unique network, called Network B, as shown in
Figure 3-9, with four devices attached to it and attached to the same router at
another of its interfaces. The IP addresses of the devices on this network would
be B1, B2, B3, and B4, and the IP address of the router's second interface
would be B5.

FIGURE 3-9
Network B
also has four
devices attach-
ed to it.

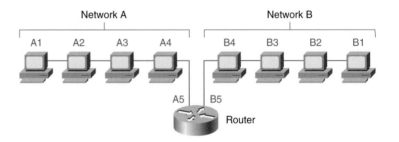

Network A   Network B

A1   A2   A3   A4   B4   B3   B2   B1

A5   B5

Router

Imagine that data is being sent from one network to another. The source network is Network A, and the destination network is Network B, and a router is
connected to Networks A, B, C, and D. When a logical grouping of information called a *frame* coming from a network reaches the router, the router performs the following functions:

1. The router strips off the data link header and trailer carried by the frame.
   The *data link header* is information that is attached to data when encapsulating that data for network transmission and contains the MAC
   addresses of the source and destination of the data. This allows the router
   to examine the network layer to determine the destination network.

2. The router consults its routing table, which keeps track of routes to particular network destinations, to determine out of which port it will need to send the data for it to reach its destination network.

Thus, in the example shown in Figure 3-10, the router would send the data from Network A to Network B from its port with the IP address B5. However, before actually sending the data out port B5, the router would encapsulate the data in the appropriate data link frame.

FIGURE 3-10
The router determines the path of the data sent from Network A to Network B with the IP address B5.

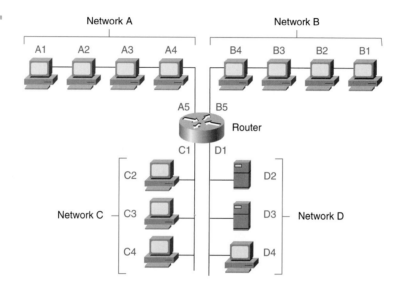

Summary

- Networking devices are products used to connect networks.
- Repeaters reshape, amplify, and re-time signals before sending them on along the network.
- The term *hub* is used instead of *repeater* when referring to the device that serves as the center of a network.
- The network area within which data packets originate and collide is called a *collision domain*.
- A bridge eliminates unnecessary traffic and minimizes the chances of collisions occurring on a network by dividing it into segments and filtering traffic based on the station or MAC address.
- Routers have the ability to make intelligent decisions as to the best path for delivery of data on the network.

Review Questions

1. Why are internetworking devices used?

   A. They allow a greater number of nodes, extend the network distance, and merge separate networks.

   B. They increase the speed of data transfer and reduce electromagnetic interference in buildings.

   C. They provide redundant pathways and thus prevent signal loss and corruption.

   D. They allow the connection of devices within an entire building.

2. Which of the following best describes a node?

   A. A device that determines the optimal path along which network traffic should be forwarded

   B. A device that establishes, manages, and terminates sessions between applications and manages data exchange between presentation-layer entities

   C. A device that synchronizes cooperating applications and establishes agreement on procedures for error recovery and control of data integrity

   D. An endpoint of a network connection or a junction common to two or more lines in a network that serve as control points

3. For which of the following problems can repeaters provide a simple solution?

   A. Too many types of incompatible equipment on the network

   B. Too much traffic on a network

   C. Too slow data transmission rates

   D. Too many nodes and/or not enough cable

4. Which of the following best defines signals?

   A. Electrical impulses representing data

   B. Amplification of data

   C. Conversion of data

   D. Officially specified rules or procedures

5. What is one disadvantage of using a hub?

   A. A hub cannot extend the network operating distance.

   B. A hub cannot filter network traffic.

   C. A hub cannot send weakened signals over a network.

   D. A hub cannot amplify weakened signals.

6. Which best describes *collision* in networking?

   A. The result of two nodes on a network transmitting individually

   B. The result of two nodes on a network transmitting simultaneously

   C. The result of two nodes on a network transmitting repeatedly

   D. The result of two nodes on a network not transmitting

7. Which best describes a collision domain?

   A. A network area within which data packets that have collided are propagated

   B. A network area that is bounded by bridges, routers, or switches

   C. A network area where routers and hubs are installed

   D. A network area where filters are applied

8. What happens if the bridge determines that the destination address carried by a data packet is from the same network segment as the source?

   A. It forwards the data to other segments of the network

   B. It does not forward the data to other segments of the network

   C. It passes data packets between two network segments

   D. It passes data packets between networks operating under different protocols

9. What does a router do?

   A. It matches information in the routing table with the data's destination IP address and sends incoming data to the correct subnetwork and host.

   B. It matches information in the routing table with the data's destination IP address and sends incoming data to the correct subnetwork.

C. It matches information in the routing table with the data's destination IP address and sends incoming data to the correct network.

D. It matches information in the routing table with the data's destination IP address and sends incoming data to the correct subnet.

10. What networking device can solve the problem of excessive broadcast traffic?

A. A bridge

B. A router

C. A hub

D. A filter

Objectives

After reading this chapter, you will be able to

- Describe the functionality of local-area networks (LANs)
- Describe the flow of traffic on a LAN using the Ethernet/802.3 standards
- Describe the overall purpose of wide-area networks (WANs)
- Identify the major components of a WAN
- Describe common data-link encapsulations associated with synchronous serial lines

Chapter 4

LANs and WANs

Introduction

In Chapter 3, "Networking Devices," you learned about networking devices, which can be used to filter traffic across a network and reduce large collision domains, which are areas where packets are likely to interfere with each other.

In this chapter, you will learn about LAN and WAN technologies, standards, and networking devices that operate at the physical, data link, and network layers of the OSI reference model.

LANs

LANs are high-speed, low-error data networks that cover a relatively small geographic area (up to a few thousand meters). LANs connect workstations, peripherals, terminals, and other devices in a single building or other geographically limited area. LANs provide multiple connected desktop devices (usually PCs) with access to high-bandwidth media. LANs connect computers and services to common Layer 1 media. As shown in Figure 4-1, LAN devices include

- *Bridges*—Connect LAN segments and help filter traffic
- *Hubs*—Concentrate LAN connection and allow use of twisted-pair copper media
- *Ethernet switches*—Offer full-duplex, dedicated bandwidth to segments or desktops
- *Routers*—Offer many services, including internetworking and broadcast control

FIGURE 4-1
LAN devices include bridges, hubs, Ethernet switches, and routers.

 Bridge

 Hub

 Ethernet switch

 Router

Ethernet, Fiber Distributed Data Interface (FDDI), and Token Ring are widely used LAN technologies that account for virtually all deployed LANs (see Figure 4-2). LAN standards specify cabling and signaling at the physical and data link layers of the OSI reference model. Because they are widely adhered to, this book covers the Ethernet and IEEE 802.3 LAN standards.

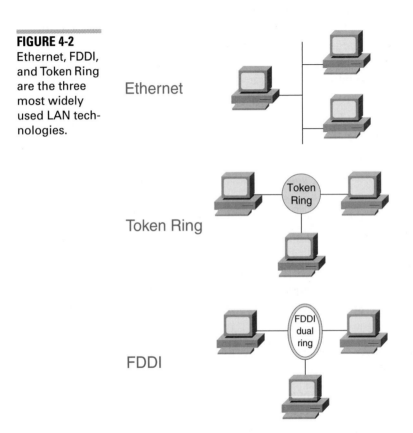

FIGURE 4-2
Ethernet, FDDI, and Token Ring are the three most widely used LAN technologies.

Ethernet and IEEE 802.3 LAN Standards

Ethernet was developed by Xerox Corporation's Palo Alto Research Center (PARC) in the 1970s. Ethernet is the most popular LAN standard today. There are millions of devices or nodes on Ethernet LANs. The early LANs required very little bandwidth to perform the simple network tasks required at that time—sending/receiving e-mail, transferring data files, and handling print jobs.

In 1980, the Institute of Electrical and Electronic Engineers (IEEE) released the IEEE 802.3 specification for which Ethernet was the technological basis.

Shortly thereafter, Digital Equipment Corporation, Intel Corporation, and Xerox Corporation jointly developed and released an Ethernet specification (Version 2.0) that is substantially compatible with IEEE 802.3. Together, Ethernet and IEEE 802.3 currently maintain the greatest market share of any LAN standard.

An Ethernet LAN is used to transport data between network devices, such as computers, printers, and file servers. Ethernet is known as a shared-medium technology; that is, all the devices are connected to the same delivery media. *Delivery media* refers to the method of transmitting and receiving data. For example, a handwritten letter can be sent (transmitted) using one of many delivery methods, such as the U.S. postal service, Federal Express, or fax. Electronic data can be transmitted via copper cable, thick coaxial cable, thin-net, wireless data transfer, and so on.

LANs and the Physical Layer

When it was developed, Ethernet was designed to fill the middle ground between long-distance, low-speed networks and specialized, computer-room networks carrying data at high speeds for very limited distances. Ethernet is well suited to applications in which a local communication medium must carry sporadic, occasionally heavy traffic at high-peak data rates.

The Ethernet and IEEE 802.3 standards define a bus-topology LAN that operates at a baseband signaling rate of 10 Mbps, which is referred to as 10Base. Figure 4-3 illustrates the combination of the three defined wiring standards in a network:

- *10Base2*—Known as thin Ethernet; allows network segments up to 185 meters on coaxial cable.
- *10Base5*—Known as thick Ethernet; allows network segments up to 500 meters on coaxial cable.
- *10BaseT*—Carries Ethernet frames on inexpensive twisted-pair wiring.

The 10Base5 and 10Base2 standards provide access for several stations on the same LAN segment. Stations are attached to the segment by a cable that runs from an attachment unit interface (AUI) in the station to a transceiver, which is called a media attachment unit (MAU), attached to the Ethernet coaxial cable. Because the 10BaseT standard provides access for a single station only, stations attached to an Ethernet LAN by 10BaseT are almost always connected to a hub or a LAN switch. In this arrangement, the hub or LAN switch is the same as an Ethernet segment.

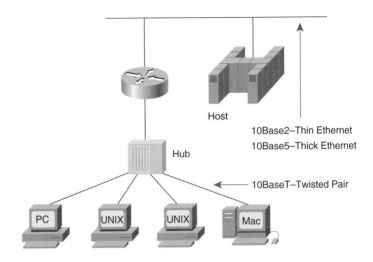

FIGURE 4-3
A network can use a combination of different Ethernet/802.3 access types.

Host

10Base2–Thin Ethernet
10Base5–Thick Ethernet

Hub

10BaseT–Twisted Pair

PC   UNIX   UNIX   Mac

LANs and the Data Link Layer

The Ethernet and 802.3 data link layers provide data transport across the physical link joining two devices. For example, as Figure 4-4 shows, the three devices can be directly attached to each other over the Ethernet LAN. The Macintosh on the left and the Intel-based PC in the middle show Media Access Control (MAC) addresses used by the data link layer. The router on the right also uses a MAC address for each of its LAN-side interfaces. To indicate the 802.3 interface on the router, you use the Cisco Internetwork Operating System (IOS) interface type abbreviation E followed by an interface number. For example, E0, as shown in Figure 4-4, is the 802.3 name of interface number 0.

FIGURE 4-4
A Cisco router's data link to Ethernet/802.3 uses an interface named E plus a number.

Mac   PC   0800.1234.1BC4

E0

0800.089c.34d5   0800.2006.1a56

Ethernet/802.3 Operation

In an Ethernet network, one node's transmission traverses the entire segment and is received and examined by every node. When the signal reaches the end of a segment, terminators absorb it to prevent it from going back onto the segment. Only one transmission is allowed on the LAN at any given time. For example, Figure 4-5 shows a linear bus network with Station A transmitting a packet addressed to Station D. This packet is received by all stations. Station D recognizes its MAC address and processes the frame. However, Stations B and C do not recognize their address and discard the frame.

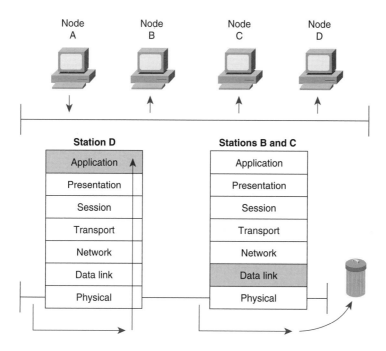

FIGURE 4-5
Station D recognizes its MAC address and processes the frame; Stations B and C do not recognize their addresses and discard the frame.

Ethernet/802.3 Broadcast

Broadcasting is a powerful tool that sends a single frame to many stations at the same time. Broadcasting uses a data-link destination address of all ones (FFFF.FFFF.FFFF in hexadecimal). As Figure 4-6 shows, if Station A transmits a frame with a destination address of all ones, Stations B, C, and D must all receive and pass the frame to their upper layers for further processing.

Broadcasting can seriously affect the performance of stations by interrupting them unnecessarily. For this reason, broadcasts should be used only when the MAC address of the destination is unknown or when the destination is all stations.

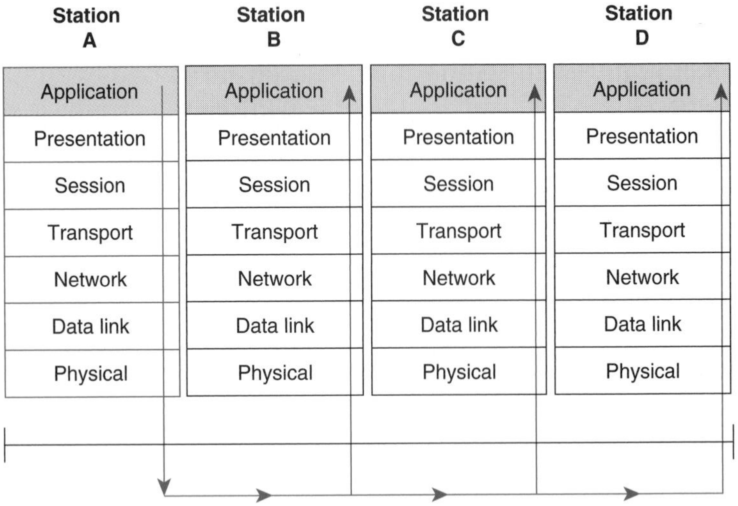

FIGURE 4-6
Broadcasting sends a single frame to many stations at the same time by using a data-link destination.

Station A	Station B	Station C	Station D
Application	Application	Application	Application
Presentation	Presentation	Presentation	Presentation
Session	Session	Session	Session
Transport	Transport	Transport	Transport
Network	Network	Network	Network
Data link	Data link	Data link	Data link
Physical	Physical	Physical	Physical

LANs and the Network Layer

Ethernet is a *shared-medium technology*, which means that all the devices on the network must listen to the transmissions on the network and contend, or negotiate, for the opportunity, or right, to transmit. This means that only one network transmission can occur at one time. There are some similarities between data traffic on a network and the traffic that occurs on a freeway, where drivers and their cars (devices) negotiate to use the freeway (media) by using turn signals, speed, and so on to move (transmit) data (passengers) from one location to another.

As you learned in Chapter 3, "Networking Devices," if more than one node attempts to transmit at the same time, a collision occurs. Consequently, the data from each device hits each other and is damaged. However, when a networking device determines that a collision has occurred, a *backoff* is issued by the device's network interface card (NIC). Because the retransmission delay is based on an algorithm, the length of this enforced retransmission delay is different for every device on the network, thus minimizing the likelihood of another collision. However, if traffic is very heavy on a network, repeated collisions cause repeated backoffs and considerably slow network traffic.

Carrier Sense Multiple Access/Collision Detection

Today, the term *standard Ethernet* refers to all networks using Ethernet (a shared-medium technology) that generally conform to Ethernet specifications, including IEEE 802.3. In order to use this shared-medium technology, Ethernet uses the Carrier Sense Multiple Access/Collision Detection (CSMA/CD) protocol to allow the networking devices to negotiate for the right to transmit.

CSMA/CD is an access method that allows only one station to transmit at a time on a shared medium. The goal of standard Ethernet is to provide a best-effort delivery service. Not all devices are able to transmit on an equal basis all the time because collisions can occur. However, standard Ethernet using CSMA/CD takes into consideration all the transmission requests and determines what devices can transmit and when they can transmit in order for all the devices to receive adequate service.

Stations on a CSMA/CD LAN can access the network at any time. Before sending data, CSMA/CD stations listen to the network to determine whether it is already in use. If it is in use, the station wishing to transmit waits. If the network is not in use, the station transmits. A collision occurs when two stations listen for network traffic, hear none, and transmit simultaneously. In this case, both transmissions are damaged and the stations must retransmit at some later time. Backoff algorithms determine when the colliding stations retransmit. CSMA/CD stations can detect collisions, so they know when they must retransmit.

As shown in Figure 4-7, CSMA/CD works in the following way: When a station wishes to transmit, it checks the network to determine whether another station is currently transmitting. If the network is not being used, the station proceeds with the transmission. While sending, the station monitors the network to ensure that no other station is transmitting. Two stations might start transmitting at approximately the same time if they determine that the network is available. If two stations send at the same time, a collision occurs, as illustrated in the upper half of Figure 4-7.

When a transmitting node recognizes a collision, it transmits a jam signal that causes the collision to last long enough for all other nodes to recognize it. All transmitting nodes then stop sending frames for a randomly selected time period, referred to as *backoff time*, before attempting to retransmit. If subsequent attempts also result in collisions, the node tries to retransmit up to 16 times before giving up.

The clocks in the nodes indicate different backoff times. If the two backoff times are sufficiently different, one station will succeed the next time it tries to retransmit. The backoff time doubles with each consecutive collision, up to the 10th retry, thereby reducing the chance of collision in subsequent transmits. From the 10th retry to the 16th retry, the stations do not increase the backoff time anymore, however; they keep it constant.

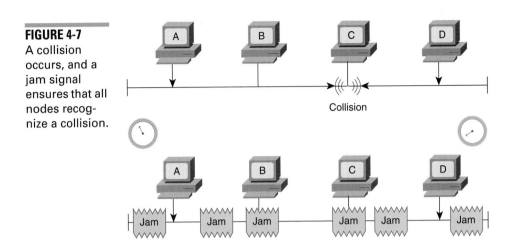

FIGURE 4-7
A collision occurs, and a jam signal ensures that all nodes recognize a collision.

WANs

WANs operate beyond a local LAN's geographic scope by using serial connections of various types to access bandwidth over wide-area geographies. They access bandwidth over wide-area geographies by using the services of carriers such as regional operating companies, Sprint, and MCI. Using these services to access bandwidth over wide-area geographies, WANs provide full-time and part-time connectivity and allow access over serial interfaces operating at different speeds.

WAN Devices

By definition, a WAN connects devices separated by wide areas. As shown in Figure 4-8, WAN devices include

- *Routers*, which offer many services, including internetworking and WAN interface ports
- *Switches*, which connect to WAN bandwidth for voice, data, and video communication
- *Modems*, which interface voice-grade services; channel service units/digital service units (CSU/DSUs), which interface T1/E1 services; terminal adapter/network termination 1 (TA/NT1) devices, which interface Integrated Services Digital Network (ISDN) services
- *Communication servers*, which concentrate dial-in and dial-out user communication

FIGURE 4-8
Common WAN devices include routers, WAN bandwidth switches, modems, and communication servers.

Router

WAN bandwidth switch

Modem CSU/DSU TA/NT1

Communication server

WAN Standards

WAN standards are defined and managed by a number of recognized authorities, including the following agencies:

- International Telecommunication Union-Telecommunication Standardization Sector (ITU-T), formerly the Consultative Committee for International Telegraph and Telephone (CCITT)
- International Organization for Standardization (ISO)
- Internet Engineering Task Force (IETF)
- Electronic Industries Association (EIA)

WAN standards typically describe both physical-layer and data-link-layer requirements.

WAN physical-layer protocols describe how to provide electrical, mechanical, operational, and functional connections for WAN services. These services are most often obtained from WAN service providers, such as regional operating companies, alternate carriers, and post, telephone, and telegraph agencies.

WAN data-link protocols describe how frames are carried between systems on a single data link. They include protocols designed to operate over dedicated point-to-point, multipoint, and multiaccess switched services, such as Frame Relay.

WANs and the Physical Layer

The WAN physical layer describes the interface between the data terminal equipment (DTE) and the data circuit-terminating equipment (DCE). The DTE is a device at the user end of a user-network interface that serves as a data source, destination, or both. The DCE provides a physical connection to the network, forwards traffic, and provides a clocking signal used to synchronize data transmission between DCE and DTE devices, as shown in Figure 4-9. Typically, the DCE is the service provider and the DTE is the attached device.

In this model, the services offered to the DTE are made available through a modem or CSU/DSU.

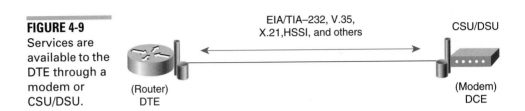

FIGURE 4-9
Services are available to the DTE through a modem or CSU/DSU.

Several physical-layer standards specify this interface:

- *EIA/TIA-232*—A common physical layer interface standard, developed by EIA and TIA, that supports unbalanced circuits at signal speeds of up to 64 kbps. It closely resembles the V.24 specification and is formerly known as RS-232.

- *EIA/TIA-449*—A popular physical-layer interface developed by EIA and TIA. Essentially, it is a faster (up to 2 Mbps) version of EIA/TIA-232 and capable of longer cable runs.

- *V.24*—An ITU-T standard for a physical-layer interface between DTE and DCE. V.24 is essentially the same as the EIA/TIA-232 standard.

- *V.35*—An ITU-T standard describing a synchronous physical-layer protocol used for communication between a network access device and a packet network. V.35 is most commonly used in the United States and in Europe, and is recommended for speeds up to 48 kbps.

- *X.21*—An ITU-T standard for serial communications over synchronous digital lines. The X.21 protocol is used primarily in Europe and Japan.

- *G.703*—An ITU-T electrical and mechanical specifications for connections between telephone company equipment and DTE using BNC connectors and operating at E1 data rates.

- *EIA-530*—Refers to two electrical implementations of EIA/TIA-449: RS-422 and RS-423.

WANs and the Data Link Layer

Several common data link encapsulations, which are shown in Figure 4-10, are associated with synchronous serial lines:

- HDLC (High-Level Data Link Control)
- Frame Relay

- PPP (Point-to-Point Protocol)
- ISDN

These encapsulations are discussed in the following sections.

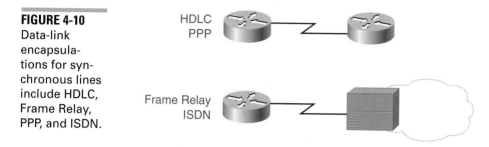

FIGURE 4-10
Data-link encapsulations for synchronous lines include HDLC, Frame Relay, PPP, and ISDN.

HDLC

HDLC is a bit-oriented synchronous data-link-layer protocol developed by the ISO. HDLC specifies a data encapsulation method on synchronous serial links using frame characters and checksums. HDLC is an ISO standard that might not be compatible between different vendors because of the way each vendor has chosen to implement it; therefore, is not a common data WAN implementation. HDLC supports both point-to-point and multipoint configurations.

Frame Relay

Frame Relay uses high-quality digital facilities. By using simplified framing with no error correction mechanisms, Frame Relay can send Layer 2 information very rapidly, compared to other WAN protocols. Frame Relay is an industry-standard, switched, data-link-layer protocol that handles multiple virtual circuits using HDLC encapsulation between connected devices. Frame Relay is more efficient than X.25, the protocol for which it is generally considered a replacement.

PPP

PPP provides router-to-router and host-to-network connections over synchronous and asynchronous circuits. PPP contains a protocol field to identify the network-layer protocol.

ISDN

ISDN is a set of digital services that transmits voice and data. ISDN is a communication protocol, offered by telephone companies, that permits telephone networks to carry data, voice, and other source traffic.

Summary

- A WAN is used to interconnect LANs that are separated by a large geographic area.
- A WAN operates at the OSI physical and data link layers.
- The WAN provides for the exchange of data packets between routers and the LANs that the routers support.
- The common data-link encapsulations associated with synchronous serial lines are
  - HDLC
  - Frame Relay
  - PPP
  - ISDN

Review Questions

1. Which of the following is *not* a major characteristic of a LAN?

    A. It operates over a wide geographic area.

    B. It provides multiple users with access to high-bandwidth media.

    C. It provides full-time connectivity to local services.

    D. It connects physically adjacent devices.

2. What is another name for 10Base5 cabling?

    A. Thick Ethernet

    B. Telephone wiring

    C. Thin Ethernet

    D. Coaxial Ethernet

3. What type of cabling medium is used for 10BaseT?

    A. Fiber-optic or unshielded twisted-pair cable

    B. Fiber-optic or coaxial cable

    C. Twisted-pair cable

    D. Coaxial cable

4. Which of the following is true about a CSMA/CD network?

    A. One node's transmission traverses the entire network and is received and examined by every node.

    B. Signals are sent directly to the destination if both the MAC and IP addresses are known by the source.

    C. One node's transmission goes to the nearest router, which sends it directly to the destination.

    D. Signals are always sent in broadcast mode.

5. Which best describes broadcasting?

    A. Sending a single frame to many stations at the same time

    B. Sending a single frame to all routers to simultaneously update their routing tables

    C. Sending a single frame to all routers at the same time

    D. Sending a single frame to all hubs and bridges at the same time

6. Which of the following best describes a WAN?

   A. Connects LANs that are separated by a large geographic area

   B. Connects workstations, terminals, and other devices in a metropolitan area

   C. Connects LANs within a large building

   D. Connects workstations, terminals, and other devices within a building

7. At which layers of the OSI reference model does a WAN operate?

   A. The physical and application layers

   B. The physical and data link layers

   C. The data link and network layers

   D. The data link and presentation layers

8. How do WANs differ from LANs?

   A. WANs typically exist in defined geographic areas.

   B. WANs provide high-speed multiple-access services.

   C. WANs use tokens to regulate network traffic.

   D. WANs use services of common carriers.

9. Which of the following best describes PPP?

   A. It uses high-quality digital facilities and is the fastest WAN protocol.

   B. It supports point-to-point and multipoint configurations and uses frame characters and checksums.

   C. It provides router-to-router and host-to-network connections over synchronous and asynchronous circuits.

   D. It is a digital service that transmits voice and data over existing telephone lines.

10. Which of the following best describes ISDN?

   A. It is a digital service that transmits voice and data over existing phone lines.

   B. It provides router-to-router and host-to-network connections over synchronous and asynchronous circuits.

   C. It uses high-quality digital facilities and is the fastest WAN protocol.

   D. It supports point-to-point and multipoint configurations and uses frame characters and checksums.

Objectives

After reading this chapter, you will be able to

- Understand IP addresses
- Understand that the binary numbering system is based on powers of 2
- Understand why IP addresses are written in dotted-decimal notation
- Understand that each network on the Internet has a unique network address
- Understand that each IP address has two parts
- Understand classes of network addresses
- Understand that each network has reserved IP addresses
- Understand what a subnet is and what a subnet address is

Chapter 5

IP Addressing

Introduction

As you learned in Chapter 3, "Networking Devices," networking devices are used to connect networks. You learned that repeaters reshape, amplify, and re-time signals before sending them along the network and that a hub is used instead of repeater as the device that serves as the center of a network.

In addition, you learned that the network area within which data packets originate and collide is called a *collision domain*. You also learned that a bridge eliminates unnecessary traffic and minimizes the chances of collisions occurring on a network by dividing the network into segments and filtering traffic based on the station or MAC address. Finally, you learned that routers have the ability to make intelligent decisions about the best path for delivery of data on the network.

In this chapter, you will learn about IP addressing and the three classes of networks in IP addressing schemes. You also will learn that some IP addresses have been set aside by ARIN and cannot be assigned to any network. Finally, you will learn about subnetworks and subnet masks and their IP addressing schemes.

Addressing Overview

As you learned in Chapter 2, "The Physical and Data Link Layers," MAC addresses exist at Layer 2 of the OSI reference model and, because most computer systems have one physical network connection, they have only a single MAC address. MAC addresses are typically unique for each network connection. Before a data packet is exchanged with a directly connected device on the same LAN, the sending device needs to have a MAC address it can use as a destination address. Therefore, locating computer systems on a network is an essential component of any network system. Various addressing schemes are used for this purpose, depending on the protocol family being used. In other words, AppleTalk addressing is different from Internet Protocol (IP) addressing, which in turn is different from Open System Interconnection (OSI) addressing, and so on.

In networking, there are two addressing schemes. You have already learned about one of these addressing schemes: MAC addressing. The second addressing scheme in networking is IP addressing. As its name implies, an IP address is based on the Internet Protocol. Every LAN must have its own unique IP address; an IP address is essential for internetworking over WANs to take place.

In an IP network environment, end stations communicate with servers or other end stations. This occurs because each node has an IP address, which is a unique 32-bit logical address. IP addresses exist at Layer 3, the network layer, of the OSI reference model. Unlike MAC addresses, which usually exist within a flat address space, IP addresses are usually hierarchical.

Each company listed on the network is seen as a single unique network that must be reached before an individual host within that company can be contacted. As shown in Figure 5-1, each company network has an address and the hosts that live on the network share the same network address, but each host is identified by the unique host address on the network.

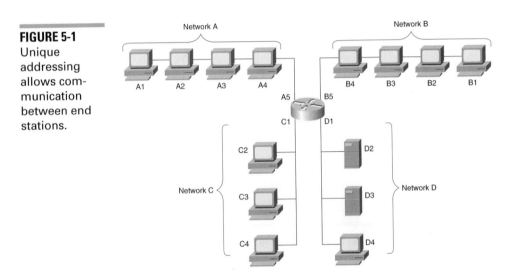

FIGURE 5-1
Unique addressing allows communication between end stations.

An IP address contains the address of the device itself as well as the address of the network on which the device is located. Therefore, if a device is moved from one network to a different network, the IP address of the device must change to reflect any such change that is made, as shown in Figures 5-2 through 5-5.

Because IP addresses are hierarchical addresses, such as phone numbers and zip codes, they provide a better way to organize computer addresses than MAC addresses, which are flat addresses, such as Social Security numbers. IP addresses can be set in software and, thus, are flexible. MAC addresses are burned into hardware. Both addressing schemes are important for efficient communications between computers.

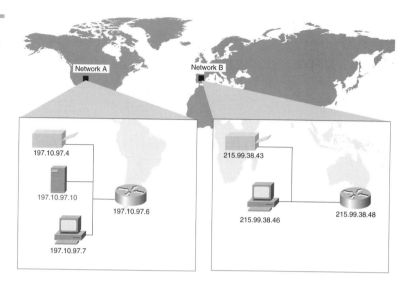

FIGURE 5-2
Network A has a server at address `197.10.97.10` that needs to be moved to Network B.

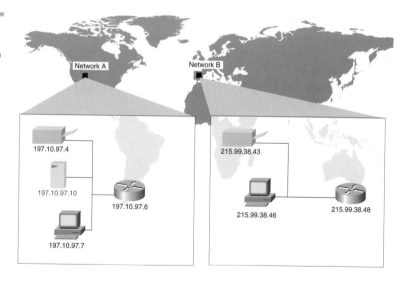

FIGURE 5-3
The file server at `197.10.97.10` is removed from Network A.

For example, IP addresses are like mail addresses, which describe a person's location by providing a country, a state, a zip code, a city, a street, a street number, and a name. One good example of a flat address space is the U.S. Social Security numbering system, in which each person has a single, unique Social Security number; the person can move around the country and obtain new logical addresses—the city, street, and zip code in which he or she lives—but keep the same Social Security number.

FIGURE 5-4
The server is shipped to a new location on another continent.

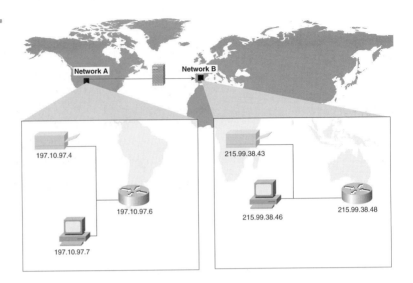

FIGURE 5-5
The file server is attached to Network B and is assigned a new IP address, `215.99.38.49`.

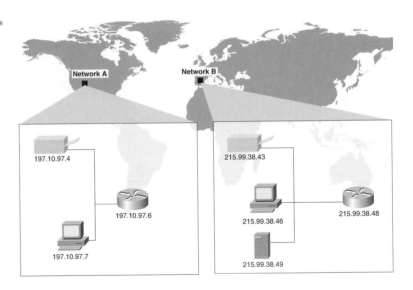

IP addressing makes it possible for data passing over the network media of the Internet to find its destination. The reason IP addresses are written as bits is so that the information they contain can be understood by computers. In order for data to pass along the media, it first must be changed to electrical impulses. When a computer receives these electrical impulses, it recognizes two things: the presence of voltage on the wire and the absence of voltage on the wire. Because only two things can be recognized by a computer, a binary math scheme, as shown in Figure 5-6, can be used to represent any data transmitted over the networking media. In such a scheme, the numbers 0 and 1 are used to communicate with computers.

FIGURE 5-6
Zeros and ones are used to represent data transmitted over the net-working media.

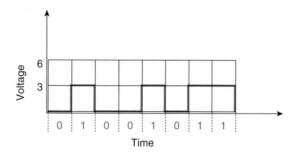

The Binary Numbering System

The numbering system most frequently used and the one you are probably most familiar with is the decimal numbering system. A decimal numbering system is based on powers of 10: 10^1, 10^2, 10^3, 10^4, and so on. 10^1 is the same as 10×1, or 10. 10^2 is the same as 10×10, or 100. 10^3 is the same as $10\times10\times10$, or 1,000. A binary numbering system is based on powers of the number 2: 2^1, 2^2, 2^3, 2^4, and so on.

An IP address is a 32-bit value written as four octets. This means that there are four groupings, each containing eight binary numbers consisting of ones and zeros. Thus, as shown in Figure 5-7, in an IP address expressed as 11000000.00000101.00100010.00001011, the first octet is the binary number 11000000, the second octet is the binary number 00000101, the third octet is the binary number 00100010, and the fourth octet is the binary number 00001011.

FIGURE 5-7
IP addresses are expressed as binary numbers consisting of ones and zeros.

Octet (8 bits) • Octet (8 bits) • Octet (8 bits) • Octet (8 bits)

$2^7 2^6 2^5 2^4 2^3 2^2 2^1 2^0 . 2^7 2^6 2^5 2^4 2^3 2^2 2^1 2^0 . 2^7 2^6 2^5 2^4 2^3 2^2 2^1 2^0 . 2^7 2^6 2^5 2^4 2^3 2^2 2^1 2^0$

11000000 00000101 00100010 00001011

EQUALS

192　•　5　•　34　•　11

Because the binary numbering system is based on powers of the number 2, each place in each octet represents a different power of 2. You begin on the right side of each binary number when assigning the power of 2 that will be used to represent each place in the binary number. To reach the binary number, you add the values in the octet. Thus, in the binary number of the first octet in Figure 5-7 (11000000), the following is true:

0 values of 2^0 (1) equals 0

0 values of 2^1 (2) equals 0

0 values of 2^2 (4) equals 0

0 values of 2^3 (8) equals 0

0 values of 2^4 (16) equals 0

0 values of 2^5 (32) equals 0

1 values of 2^6 (64) equals 64

1 values of 2^7 (128) equals 128

Therefore, binary 11000000 equals 192.

Binary IP Addressing

It is difficult enough to remember a number that is 8 digits long, let alone a number that is 32 digits long, such as the ones used in IP addresses. Therefore, a simpler way, using decimal numbers, has been devised to express the 32-bit numbers in IP addresses. It is called *dotted-decimal notation*.

In dotted-decimal notation, as shown in Figure 5-8, IP addresses, or dotted-decimal addresses, are expressed such that each number represents in decimal format 1 byte of the 4-byte IP address.

FIGURE 5-8
A 4-byte IP address contains four 1-byte octets.

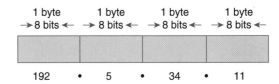

To convert the IP address 11000000.00000101.00100010.00001011 into this simpler format, begin by breaking it into 4 bytes, each containing 8 bits; in other words, divide the IP address number into four octets:

11000000
      00000101
           00100010
                00001011

Then, convert each of these 8-bit numbers into its decimal equivalent. As a result, the binary number 11000000.00000101.00100010.00001011 is equal to the dotted decimal number 192.5.34.11.

Classes of IP Addresses

The reason data can find its destination on the Internet is because each network connected to the Internet has a unique network number. To ensure that each network number on the Internet will always be unique and unlike that of any other number, an organization called the American Registry for Internet Numbers (ARIN) assigns to companies blocks of IP addresses based on the sizes of their networks. ARIN's Internet address is www.arin.net.

As shown in Figure 5-9, every IP address has two parts: the network number and the host number. The network number identifies the network to which a device is attached. The host number identifies a device's connection to that network.

FIGURE 5-9
The network number and the host number make up the IP address.

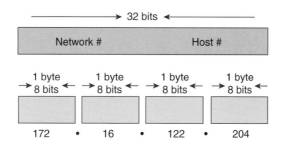

ARIN assigns three classes of IP addresses. It reserves Class A IP addresses for governments, Class B IP addresses for medium-size companies, and Class C IP addresses for everyone else.

When Class A IP addresses are written in binary format, as shown in Figure 5-10, the first bit is always 0. When Class B IP addresses are written in binary format, the first 2 bits are always 1 and 0. When Class C IP addresses are written in binary format, the first 3 bits are always 1, 1, and 0.

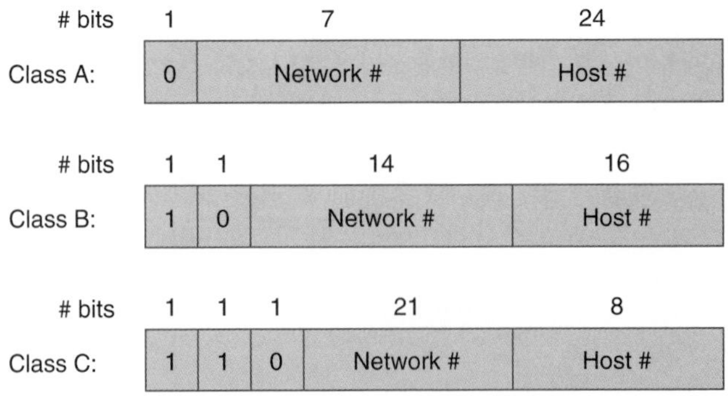

FIGURE 5-10
There are specific IP address bit patterns for Class A, B, and C IP addresses.

# bits	1	7	24
Class A:	0	Network #	Host #

# bits	1	1	14	16
Class B:	1	0	Network #	Host #

# bits	1	1	1	21	8
Class C:	1	1	0	Network #	Host #

Reserved Classes of Networks

Thus far, as shown in Figure 5-11, you have learned about three classes of network addresses that can be assigned by ARIN. In actuality, there are five classes of network addresses . However, only three of these—Classes A, B, and C network addresses—are used commercially. The other two classes of network addresses are reserved.

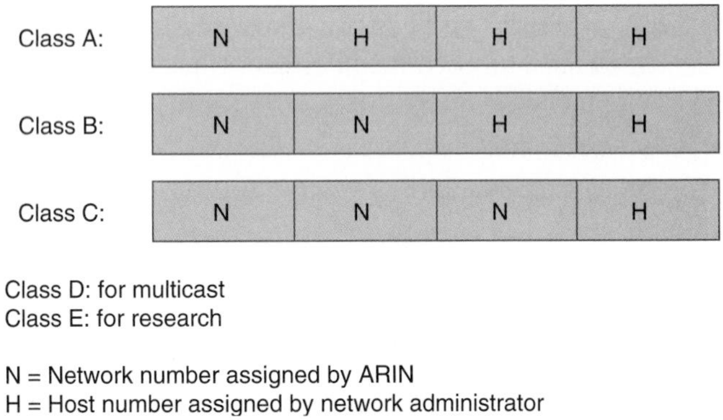

FIGURE 5-11
ARIN assigns three classes of IP addresses.

Class A:	N	H	H	H

Class B:	N	N	H	H

Class C:	N	N	N	H

Class D: for multicast
Class E: for research

N = Network number assigned by ARIN
H = Host number assigned by network administrator

It is possible for each octet in an IP address to total 255, as shown in Figure 5-12. However, decimal values could be assigned by ARIN to the first octet for any class network; the highest number listed was 223. You might have wondered why the highest value was only 223 and not 255, because there are 255 possible values for an octet. The reason is that ARIN reserves a number of addresses for multicast purposes and for experimental purposes; these numbers cannot be assigned to networks. Therefore, in IP addresses, the values 224 through 255 are not used in the first octet for networking purposes.

FIGURE 5-12
Each octet in
an IP address
can total 255.

128	64	32	16	8	4	2	1
2^7	2^6	2^5	2^4	2^3	2^2	2^1	2^0
1	1	1	1	1	1	1	1

$$128 + 64 + 32 + 16 + 8 + 4 + 2 + 1 = 255$$

In addition to these reserved IP addresses, any IP address that has all zeros in the host portion of the address is reserved, as is any address that has all ones in the host portion. The following sections cover both of these types of addresses in more depth.

In the examples used thus far, IP addresses have only been applied to devices attached to a network. There are times when you need to refer to all the devices on a network or, in other words, to the network itself. It would be cumbersome to write out IP addresses for all the devices on the network. You could use just two addresses with a hyphen between them to indicate that you are referring to all devices in a range of numbers, but that would be cumbersome, too. Instead, a shorter method to refer to the network has been devised. By convention, in IP addressing schemes, any IP address that ends in all binary zeros is reserved for the network address. Thus, in a Class A network, 113.0.0.0 would be the IP address of that network. Routers use a network's IP address when forwarding data on the Internet.

In a Class B network, the IP address 176.10.0.0 would be the network address. Note that decimal numbers fill the first two octets in a Class B network address. That is because both of those octets are assigned by ARIN and are network numbers. Only the last two octets have zeros. This is because numbers in those octets are host numbers reserved for devices attached to the network. Thus, in order to refer to all devices on the network—that is, to the network itself—the network address must have zeros in the last two octets. Because 176.10.0.0 is reserved for the network address (as shown in Figure 5-13), it will never be used as an IP address for any device attached to this network.

FIGURE 5-13
A reserved net-
work address
176.10.0.0 will
never be used
as an IP
address for any
device attached
to the network.

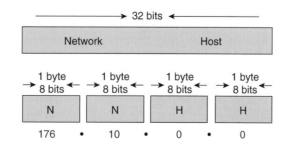

A broadcast occurs when a source sends out data to all devices on a network. So that all devices on the network will pay attention to such broadcasts, an IP address must be used that all devices will recognize and pick up. Typically, such IP addresses end in all binary ones. Thus, for the network used in Figure 5-13, Network 176.10.0.0, the broadcast address that would be sent out to all devices on that network would be 176.10.255.255.

When a frame (which is a kind of data) that is coming from one network reaches a router, the router performs several functions. First, the router strips off the data link header carried by the frame. The data link header contains the MAC addresses of the source and destination of the data. After this is done, the data link header allows the router to examine the network layer, which contains the IP destination network address. Next, the router consults its routing tables to determine which of its ports it will need to send the data out on in order for it to reach its destination network.

For transferal of data on the Internet, one network sees another as a single network and has no detailed knowledge of its internal structure. This helps keep routing tables small.

Internally, however, networks might view themselves quite differently. To provide extra flexibility for the network administrator, networks—particularly large networks—often are divided into smaller networks, called *subnetworks*. Usually, subnetworks are referred to simply as *subnets*. For example, it would be possible to break a Class B IP address into many subnets.

Subnet Addressing

As with the host number portion of Class A, Class B, and Class C addresses, subnet addresses are assigned locally. This is done usually by the network administrator. Like other IP addresses, each subnet address is unique. By using subnets, there is no change to how the outside world sees the network, but within the organization there is additional structure.

For example, the network 172.16.0.0 (shown in Figure 5-14) is subdivided or broken into four subnets: 172.16.1.0, 172.16.2.0, 172.16.3.0, and 172.16.4.0. Routers determine the destination network using the subnet address, limiting the amount of traffic on the other network segments.

FIGURE 5-14
Four subnets
make up
Network
172.16.0.0.

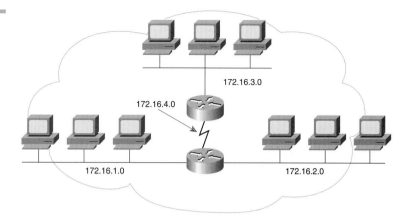

Network 172.16.0.0

From an addressing standpoint, as shown in Figure 5-15, subnets are an extension of the network number. Network administrators decide the size of subnets based on organization and growth needs.

FIGURE 5-15
Subnet
addressing
extends the
network num-
ber by creating
subnets.

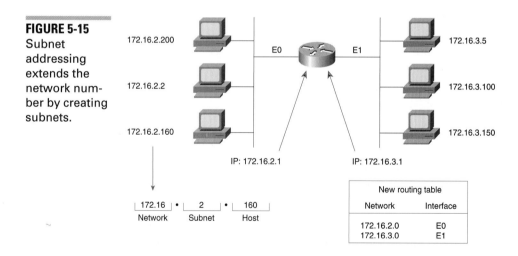

A subnet address includes a network number, a subnet number within the network, and a host number within the subnet. By providing this third level of addressing, subnets provide extra flexibility for the network administrator.

To create a subnet address, a network administrator "borrows" bits from the host field and designates them as the subnet field, as shown in Figure 5-16. Any number of bits can be borrowed, as long as 2 bits remain. Because there are only two octets in the host field of a Class B network, up to 14 bits can be borrowed to create subnetworks. A Class C network has only one octet in the host field. Therefore, only up to 6 bits can be borrowed in Class C networks to create subnetworks.

FIGURE 5-16

If there is 1 bit from the subnet mask under any field in the IP address, that bit is part of the network or subnetwork field.

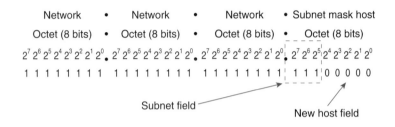

Each time a bit is borrowed from the host field, there is 1 bit fewer left in the octet that can be used for the host number. Thus, each time a bit is borrowed from the host field, the number of host addresses that can be assigned declines by a power of 2.

To see how this works, let's look at a Class C network. All 8 bits in the last octet are used for the host field. Therefore, there are 256, or 2^8, possible addresses available to start with.

Now, imagine that this Class C network is divided into subnetworks. If 1 bit is borrowed from the host field, the number of bits that can be used in host addresses declines to 7. If you were to write out all the possible combinations of zeros and ones that could occur in the remaining 7 bits, you would discover that the total number of possible hosts that can be assigned to each subnetwork declines to 128, or 2^7.

In the same Class C network, if 2 bits are borrowed from the host field, the number of bits that can be used for host addresses declines to 6. The total number of hosts that can be assigned to each subnetwork declines to 64, or 2^6.

Numbers in a Subnetwork That Are Reserved for Broadcasts

IP addresses ending in all binary ones are reserved for broadcasts. The same is true for subnetworks. To see why this is so, assume that you have a Class C network with the number 197.15.22.0 and that this network has been divided into eight subnetworks, as described in Table 5-1.

TABLE 5-1   The Last Octet in a Class C Network That Has Eight Subnets

Subnetwork	Binary Subnetwork Field Numbers	Range of Binary Host Field Numbers	Range of Decimal Host Field Numbers
First subnetwork	000	00000–11111	.0–.31
Second subnetwork	001	00000–11111	.32–.63
Third subnetwork	010	00000–11111	.64–.95
Fourth subnetwork	011	00000–11111	.96–.127
Fifth subnetwork	100	00000–11111	.128–.159
Sixth subnetwork	101	00000–11111	.160–.191
Seventh subnetwork	110	00000–11111	.192–.223
Eighth subnetwork	111	00000–11111	.224–.255

Next, look at the IP address 197.15.22.31 on that network. At first glance, this does not look like either a reserved network address or a reserved broadcast address. However, because the network has been divided into eight subnetworks, you know that the first 3 bits of the last octet have been borrowed to create the first subnetwork. This means that the last 5 bits are all that remain in the subnetwork's host field. Notice that all of the last 5 bits are expressed as binary ones. That means this IP address is a reserved broadcast address for the first subnetwork of network 197.15.22.0.

Numbers in a Subnetwork That Are Reserved for Subnetwork Numbers

IP addresses ending in all binary zeros are reserved for the network. The same is true for subnetworks. To see why this is so, again assume that you have a Class C network with the number 197.15.22.0 and that this network has been divided into the eight subnetworks (refer to Table 5-1).

Subnet Masking

Subnets are concealed from outside networks by using masks referred to as *subnet masks*. The function of a subnet mask is to tell devices which part of an address is the network number, including the subnet, and which part is the host.

Subnet masks use the same format as IP addressing. In other words, each is 32 bits long and divided into four octets. Subnet masks have all ones in the network and subnetwork portion, and all zeros in the host portion. By default, if no bits are borrowed, the subnet mask for a Class B network would be 255.255.0.0. However, if 8 bits were borrowed, the subnet mask for the same Class B network would be 255.255.255.0, as shown in Figures 5-17 and 5-18. However, because there are only two octets in the host field of a Class B network, up to 14 bits can be borrowed to create subnetworks. A Class C network has only one octet in the host field. Therefore, only up to 6 bits can be borrowed in Class C networks to create subnetworks.

FIGURE 5-17
If you borrow bits for a subnet mask, use host bits starting at the high-order bit position.

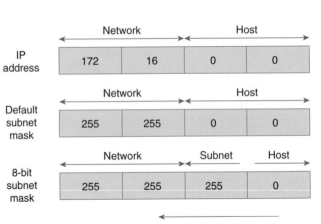

Subnet masks also use 32-bit-long IP addresses that always use all binary ones in the network and subnetwork portions of the address and all binary zeros in the host portion of the address. Thus, a Class B subnet mask address with 8 bits borrowed from the host field would be 255.255.255.0.

FIGURE 5-18
The decimal equivalent of bit patterns is used in an IP address.

128	64	32	16	8	4	2	1		
1	0	0	0	0	0	0	0	=	128
1	1	0	0	0	0	0	0	=	192
1	1	1	0	0	0	0	0	=	224
1	1	1	1	0	0	0	0	=	240
1	1	1	1	1	0	0	0	=	248
1	1	1	1	1	1	0	0	=	252
1	1	1	1	1	1	1	0	=	254
1	1	1	1	1	1	1	1	=	255

Now, imagine that you have a Class B network. This time, however, instead of borrowing all 8 bits of the third octet, only 7 bits are borrowed to create sub-networks. Using binary representation, in this example, the subnet mask would be 11111111.11111111.11111110.00000000. Therefore, 255.255.255.0 can no longer be used as the subnet mask.

The ANDing Operation

On the Internet, one network sees another network as a single network and has no detailed knowledge of its internal structure. Thus, it has no knowledge of whether the other network contains subnetworks.

For example, Cisco has a Class B network. Its network number is 131.108.0.0. Internally, Cisco's network is divided into subnetworks. However, outside networks are only aware that Cisco is a single network. Let's assume that a device on another network with the IP address 197.15.22.44 wants to send data to another device attached to Cisco's network with the IP address 131.108.2.2. The data is sent out over the Internet until it reaches the router that is attached to Cisco's network. The router's job is to determine which one of Cisco's subnetworks the data should be routed to.

To do this, the router looks at the data's destination IP address and determines which part is in the network field, which part is in the subnetwork field, and which part is in the host field. Remember that when the router looks at the data, it does not see the IP address as a decimal number. Instead, it sees the IP address as the binary number 10000011.01101100.00000010.00000010.

The router knows that Cisco's subnet mask address is 255.255.255.0. The router sees this number as 11111111.11111111.11111111.00000000. The subnet mask indicates that Cisco has borrowed 8 bits to create subnetworks. The router takes these two pieces of information—the destination IP address carried by the data and the subnet mask of Cisco's network—and logically ANDs them together bit by bit.

Whenever you logically AND a 1 and a 1 together, you get back what you started with. Whenever you logically AND anything with a 0, you get a 0 back. Therefore, when the router performs this ANDing operation, the host portion falls through. The router looks at what is left, which is the network number, including the subnetwork. The router then looks in its routing table and tries to match the network number, including the subnet, with an interface. When a match is made, the router knows which interface to use. Then the router sends the data to the correct interface and subnetwork destination IP address on Cisco's network.

To gain a better understanding of how the ANDing operation works, let's look at how a router would handle different subnet masks applied to the same network. Imagine that you have a Class B network with the network number 172.16.0.0. After assessing the needs of his network, the network administrator has decided to borrow 8 bits in order to create subnetworks. As you learned earlier, when 8 bits are borrowed to create subnets, the subnet mask is 255.255.255.0.

Someone outside the network sends data to the IP address 172.16.2.120. To determine where to send the data, the router ANDs this address with the subnet mask. When the two numbers are ANDed, the host portion of the address falls through. What is left is the network number, including the subnetwork. Thus, the data is being addressed to the device that is identified by the binary number 01111000.

Now, imagine that you have the same network, 172.16.0.0. This time, however, the network administrator has decided to borrow only 7 bits to create subnetworks. In binary notation, the subnet mask for this would be 11111111.11111111.11111110.00000000.

Subnet Planning

The network in Figure 5-19 has been assigned the Class C address 201.222.5.0. Assume that 20 subnets are needed, with 5 hosts per subnet. We can subdivide the last octet into a subnet and a host portion, and then determine what the subnet mask will be. Select a subnet field size that yields enough subnetworks. In this example, choosing a 29-bit mask allows 2^{21} subnets. The subnet addresses are all multiples of 8 (for example, `201.222.5.16`, `201.222.5.32`, and `201.222.5.48`).

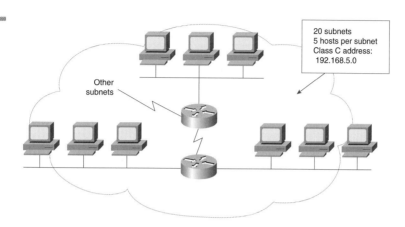

FIGURE 5-19
This network needs 20 subnets and 5 hosts per subnet.

20 subnets
5 hosts per subnet
Class C address:
192.168.5.0

Other subnets

The remaining bits in the last octet are used for the host field. The 3 bits of our example allow enough hosts to cover the required five hosts per wire. The host numbers will be 1, 2, 3, and so forth. The final host addresses are a combination of the network/subnet wire starting address plus each host value. The hosts on the `201.222.5.16` subnet would be addressed as `201.222.5.17`, `201.222.5.18`, `201.222.5.19`, and so forth. A host number of 0 is reserved for the wire address, and a host value of all ones is reserved because it selects all hosts—a broadcast.

A Class B Subnet Planning Example

Table 5-2 is an example of a table used for this subnet-planning example. Figure 5-20 shows the combining of an arriving IP address with the subnet mask to derive the subnet number.

TABLE 5-2   A Class B Network with Subnetting

Number of Bits for Subnets	Subnet Mask Number	Number of Subnets	Number of Hosts
2	255.255.192.0	2	16,382
3	255.255.224.0	6	8,190
4	255.255.240.0	14	4,094

TABLE 5-2   A Class B Network with Subnetting (Continued)

Number of Bits for Subnets	Subnet Mask Number	Number of Subnets	Number of Hosts
5	255.255.248.0	30	2,046
6	255.255.252.0	62	1,022
7	255.255.254.0	126	510
8	255.255.255.0	254	254
9	255.255.255.128	510	126
10	255.255.255.192	1,022	62
11	255.255.255.224	2,046	30
12	255.255.255.240	4,094	14
13	255.255.255.248	8,190	6
14	255.255.255.252	16,382	2

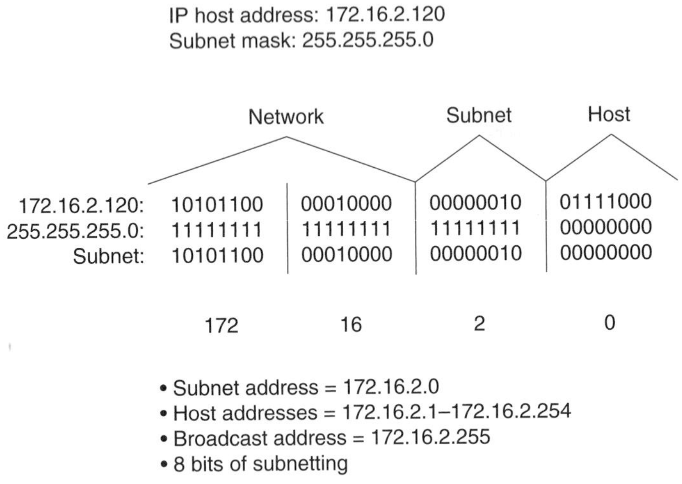

FIGURE 5-20
A Class B subnetting planning example with 8 bits of subnetting has up to 254 subnets and 254 host addresses.

IP host address: 172.16.2.120
Subnet mask: 255.255.255.0

	Network		Subnet	Host
172.16.2.120:	10101100	00010000	00000010	01111000
255.255.255.0:	11111111	11111111	11111111	00000000
Subnet:	10101100	00010000	00000010	00000000
	172	16	2	0

• Subnet address = 172.16.2.0
• Host addresses = 172.16.2.1–172.16.2.254
• Broadcast address = 172.16.2.255
• 8 bits of subnetting

A Class C Subnet Planning Example

Table 5-3 shows a Class C network, which is subnetted to provide 6 host addresses and 30 subnets; Figure 5-21 illustrates a Class C subnet planning example with a 5-bit subnet mask.

TABLE 5-3   An Example of a Class C Subnetted Network

Number of Bits	Subnet Mask Number	Number of Subnets	Number of Hosts
2	255.255.255.192	2	62
3	255.255.255.224	6	30
4	255.255.255.240	14	14
5	255.255.255.248	30	6
6	255.255.255.252	62	2

FIGURE 5-21
A Class C subnet planning example with 5 bits of subnetting has 30 subnets and 6 hosts.

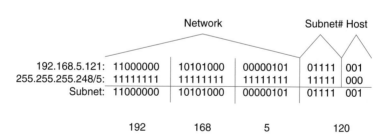

IP host address: 192.168.5.121
Subnet mask: 255.255.255.248

- Subnet address = 192.168.5.120
- Host addresses = 192.168.5.121–192.168.5.126
- Broadcast address = 192.168.5.127
- 5 bits of subnetting

Summary

- IP addresses are based on the Internet Protocol. IP addresses are unique 32-bit logical addresses that exist at Layer 3, the network layer, of the OSI reference model.

- An IP address contains the address of the device itself as well as the address of the network the device is located on.

- Because IP addresses are hierarchical addresses (such as phone numbers and zip codes), they provide a better way to organize computer addresses than MAC addresses, which are flat addresses, such as Social Security numbers.

- An IP address is a 32-bit value written as four octets, each containing 8 binary numbers consisting of ones and zeros.

- In dotted-decimal notation, IP addresses are expressed such that each number represents in decimal format 1 byte of the 4-byte IP address.

- ARIN reserves Class A IP addresses for governments throughout the world, Class B IP addresses for medium-size companies, and Class C IP addresses for everyone else. The other two classes of networks are reserved.

- Any IP address that has all zeros in the host portion of the address is reserved, as is any address that has all ones in the host portion.

- In order to provide extra flexibility for the network administrator, networks—particularly large ones—are often divided into smaller networks called subnetworks or subnets.

- Subnets are concealed from outside networks by using masks referred to as subnet masks.

Review Questions

1. How many bits are in an IP address?

   A. 4

   B. 8

   C. 16

   D. 32

2. The network number plays what part in an IP address?

   A. It specifies the network to which the host belongs.

   B. It specifies the identity of the computer on the network.

   C. It specifies which node on the subnetwork is being addressed.

   D. It specifies which networks the device can communicate with.

3. The host number plays what part in an IP address?

   A. It designates the identity of the computer on the network.

   B. It designates which node on the subnetwork is being addressed.

   C. It designates the network to which the host belongs.

   D. It designates which hosts the device can communicate with.

4. What decimal number equals the binary number 11111111?

   A. 8

   B. 128

   C. 254

   D. 255

5. What is a subnet?

   A. A part of a network that acts as a slave system to the main network

   B. A small network operating within a larger network that allows multiple types of devices to be networked

   C. A subdivision of a large network into smaller pieces

   D. A small network that maintains the database of all MAC addresses on the network

6. In the address 182.54.4.233, which portion is the subnet?

   A. 182

   B. 54

   C. 4

   D. 233

7. If a Class C network is subnetted with a mask of 255.255.255.192, how many usable subnets are created?

   A. 2

   B. 4

   C. 6

   D. 8

8. Given an IP host address of 192.168.5.121 and a subnet mask of 255.255.255.248, what is the network number of the host?

   A. 192.168.5.12

   B. 192.169.5.121

   C. 192.169.5.120

   D. 192.168.5.120

9. Which portion of the IP address 205.129.12.5 represents the host?

   A. 205

   B. 205.129

   C. 5

   D. 12.5

10. Which portion of the IP address 129.219.51.18 represents the network?

   A. 129.215

   B. 129

   C. 14.1

   D. 1

Objectives

After reading this chapter, you will be able to

- Describe ARP
- Describe ARP requests, ARP tables, ARP replies, and ARP request frames
- Describe why updated ARP tables are important
- Describe RARP
- Describe RARP servers, RARP requests, and RARP reply frames
- Identify which internetworking devices have ARP tables
- Define *default gateway*

Chapter 6

ARP and RARP

Introduction

In Chapter 5, "IP Addressing," you learned that on the Internet one network sees another as a single network and has no detailed knowledge of the other network's internal structure. Thus, a device on an outside network only sees the network number and host number of a device on another network. However, internally networks can view themselves as being a series of smaller networks called *subnetworks*. Thus, networks can see their IP addresses as being broken up into the network number, the subnetwork number, and the host number. Subnets use unique 32-bit subnet addresses that are created by borrowing bits from the host field. These subnet addresses are visible to other devices on the same network, but they are not visible to outside networks because subnetworks use subnet masks.

In this chapter, you will learn how devices on local-area networks (LANs) use Address Resolution Protocol (ARP) before forwarding data to a destination. You will learn what happens when a device on one network does not know the MAC address of a device on another network. You will learn that Reverse Address Resolution Protocol (RARP) is the protocol a device uses when it does not know its own IP address.

ARP

Protocols determine whether data is passed beyond the network layer to higher levels of the OSI reference model. Basically, for this to occur, the data packet must contain both a destination Media Access Control (MAC) address and a destination Internet Protocol (IP) address. If the data packet lacks one of these addresses, the data will not be passed to the upper levels. In this way, MAC addresses and IP addresses act as a sort of check and balance on each other.

When the source has determined the IP address for the destination, as illustrated in Figure 6-1, the source looks into its ARP table in order to locate the MAC address for the destination. If the source locates a mapping of the destination IP address to the destination MAC address in its table, it binds the IP address with the MAC address and uses them to encapsulate the data. As a result, as shown in Figure 6-2, the data packet is then sent out over the networking media to be picked up by the destination.

FIGURE 6-1
The source looks at its ARP table after it has determined the IP address for the destination.

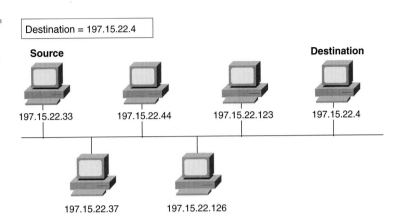

Destination = 197.15.22.4

FIGURE 6-2
The data is picked up by the destination after the IP and MAC addresses are bound and the data is encapsulated.

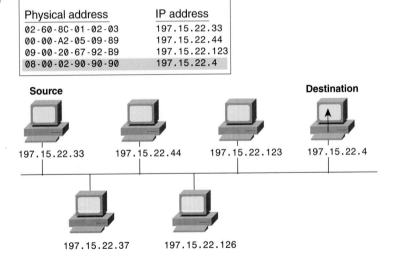

Physical address	IP address
02-60-8C-01-02-03	197.15.22.33
00-00-A2-05-09-89	197.15.22.44
09-00-20-67-92-B9	197.15.22.123
08-00-02-90-90-90	197.15.22.4

ARP Requests

In the example shown in Figure 6-3, a source device wants to send data to another device. The source knows the destination IP address but is unable to locate a MAC address for it in its own ARP table. As a result, if the destination is to retain the data and pass it along to the upper layers of the OSI reference model, the source must use both a destination MAC address and a destination IP address. Therefore, the device initiates a process called an *ARP request* that is designed to help it discover the destination MAC address. First, the device builds an ARP request packet and sends it to all devices on the network. To ensure that the ARP request packet will be seen by all devices on the network, the source uses a broadcast MAC address. The broadcast address that is used in a MAC addressing scheme results when all places are set to F. Thus, a MAC broadcast address would have the form FF-FF-FF-FF-FF-FF.

FIGURE 6-3
The source is unable to locate a MAC address for it in its own ARP table.

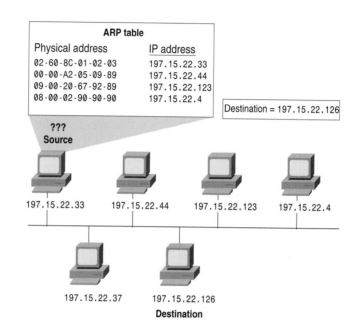

ARP requests are structured in a particular way. Because ARP functions at the lowest layers of the OSI reference model, the message containing the ARP request must be encapsulated within the hardware protocol frame. As shown in Figure 6-4, this can be represented by stating that the ARP request frame is divided into two parts: the frame header and the ARP message. In addition, the frame header can be further subdivided into a MAC header and an IP header, as shown in Figure 6-5.

FIGURE 6-4
An ARP request frame is divided into the frame header and the ARP message.

Frame header	ARP message What is your MAC address?

FIGURE 6-5
The frame header is sub-divided into a MAC header and an IP header.

MAC header		IP header		ARP request message
Destination	Source	Destination	Source	What is your MAC address?
FF-FF-FF-FF-FF-FF	02-60-8C-01-02-03	197.15.22.126	197.15.22.33	

ARP Replies

Because the ARP request packet is sent out in broadcast mode, all devices on the LAN receive the packet and then pass it up to the network layer to be examined. If the IP address of a device matches the destination IP address contained in the ARP request, the device responds by sending the source its MAC address. This is known as an *ARP reply*. In the example shown in Figure 6-3, where source 197.15.22.33 is asking for the MAC address of the destination with an IP address of 197.15.22.126, destination 197.15.22.126 would pick up the ARP request and respond with an ARP reply, which is shown in Figure 6-6, containing its MAC address.

FIGURE 6-6
The ARP reply structure includes the MAC header, the IP header, and the ARP reply message.

MAC header		IP header		ARP reply message
Destination	Source	Destination	Source	Here's my MAC address.
02-60-8C-01-02-03	08-00-02-89-90-80	197.15.22.33	197.15.22.126	

When the device that originated the ARP request receives the ARP reply, it extracts the MAC address from the MAC header and updates its ARP table. Now that the device has all the information it needs, the device can properly address its data with both a destination MAC address and a destination IP address. As shown in Figure 6-7, the device uses this new data frame structure to encapsulate the data before it sends it out over the network.

When the data arrives at the destination, a match is made at the data link layer. The data link layer strips off the MAC header and transfers the data to the next highest layer of the OSI reference model, the network layer. The network layer examines the data and finds that its IP address matches the destination IP address carried in the IP header of the data. The network layer strips off the IP header and transfers the data to the next highest layer, the transport layer (Layer 4). The process is repeated until the rest of the packet reaches the application where the data will be read.

FIGURE 6-7
Before data is sent out over the network, a new data frame structure is used to encapsulate the data.

MAC Header		IP Header		Data
Destination	Source	Destination	Source	
08-00-02-89-90-80	02-60-8C-01-02-03	197.15.22.126	197.15.22.33	

ARP Tables

Any device on the network that receives the broadcast ARP request sees the information supplied in the ARP request. Devices use the source information to update their ARP tables. If devices did not keep ARP tables, the process of issuing an ARP request and an ARP reply would have to take place each time a device wanted to send data to another device on the network. This would be extremely inefficient and could result in too much traffic on the network. To avoid this, each device maintains its own ARP table.

Some devices keep tables containing all the MAC addresses and IP addresses of other devices connected to the same LAN. These tables are simply a section of RAM memory on each device. They are called *ARP tables* because ARP is used to map IP addresses to MAC addresses (see Figure 6-8). For the most part, ARP tables are cached in memory and are maintained automatically. It is rare for a network administrator to modify a table entry manually. Each computer on a network maintains its own ARP table. Whenever a network device wants to send data on the network, it uses information provided by its ARP table to accomplish this.

FIGURE 6-8
Each computer on a network maintains an ARP table.

Physical address	IP address
02-60-8C-01-02-03	197.15.22.33
00-00-A2-05-09-89	197.15.22.44
09-00-20-67-92-89	197.15.22.123
08-00-02-90-90-90	197.15.22.4

ARP tables must periodically be updated so that they remain current. The process of updating ARP tables involves not only adding information, but deleting information as well. Because sending information across networks is dependent on the latest, most current information available, devices are set to delete any information contained in ARP tables that is older than a specified age. This process is known as *aging out*. To replace information that is purged from ARP tables, devices constantly update them with information obtained from their own ARP requests as well as requests coming from other devices on the LAN. The fact that ARP enables devices to maintain current, updated ARP tables helps to limit the amount of broadcast traffic on the local network.

RARP

You have already learned that IP addresses and MAC addresses must both be used before network devices can forward data to Layer 4, the transport layer, of the OSI reference model. In this way, IP addresses and MAC addresses act as checks and balances on each other.

So that the destination receiving the data packet will know who to respond to, the data packet must also carry both the source MAC address and the source IP address. But what happens when a source knows its MAC address but does not know its IP address? The protocol that a device uses when it does not know its own IP address is RARP. Like ARP, RARP binds MAC addresses to IP addresses so that network devices can use them to encapsulate data before sending it out on the network. As shown in Figure 6-9, devices using RARP require that a RARP server be present on the network to answer RARP requests.

RARP Requests

Imagine that a source device wants to send data to another device. However, the source knows its own MAC address but is unable to locate its own IP address in its ARP table. If the destination is to retain the data, pass it along to the higher layers of the OSI reference model, and respond to the device that originated the data, the source must include both its MAC address and IP address. Therefore, the source initiates a process called a *RARP request* that is designed to help it discover its IP address. First, the device builds a RARP request packet and sends it out on the network. To ensure that the RARP request will be seen by all devices on the network, the source uses a broadcast IP address.

FIGURE 6-9
To answer a
RARP request,
a RARP server
needs to be
present.

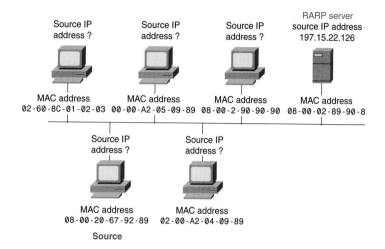

As shown in Figure 6-10, RARP requests have the same structure as ARP requests. Thus, RARP requests consist of a MAC header, an IP header, and the RARP request message. The only difference in a RARP packet format is that the MAC address for destination and source are both filled in, and the source IP address field is empty. Because it is being broadcast to all devices on the network, the destination IP address is set to all binary ones.

FIGURE 6-10
Structurally,
RARP and ARP
requests are
the same.

MAC header		IP header		RARP request message
Destination	Source	Destination	Source	What is my IP address?
00-40-33-2B-35-77	01-60-8C-01-02-03	11111111	?????????	

Because the RARP request frame is sent out in broadcast mode, all devices on the network see it. However, only a designated RARP server can respond to the RARP request. The designated RARP server replies by sending a RARP reply containing the IP address of the device that originated the RARP request.

RARP Replies

RARP replies have the same structure as ARP replies. A RARP reply contains a RARP reply message and is encapsulated in a MAC header and an IP header. When the device where the RARP request originated receives the RARP reply, it finds its own IP address. Figure 6-11 shows how this works for a situation in which a designated server with an IP address of 197.15.22.126 is responding to an IP request from a diskless workstation with a MAC address of 08-00-20-67-92-89.

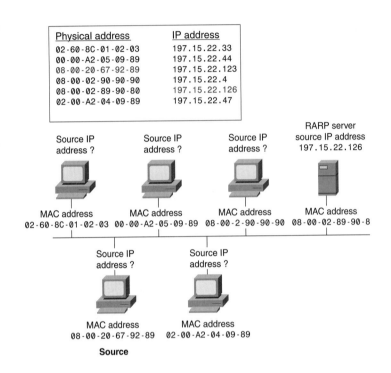

FIGURE 6-11
A RARP server responds to an IP request from a workstation with a MAC address of 08-00-20-67-92-89.

Physical address	IP address
02-60-8C-01-02-03	197.15.22.33
00-00-A2-05-09-89	197.15.22.44
08-00-20-67-92-89	197.15.22.123
08-00-02-90-90-90	197.15.22.4
08-00-02-89-90-80	197.15.22.126
02-00-A2-04-09-89	197.15.22.47

When the device that originated the RARP request receives the RARP reply, the device copies its IP address into its memory cache where it will reside for as long as the session lasts. However, when the terminal is shut down, this information disappears again. For as long as the session lasts, though, the diskless workstation that originated the RARP request can use the information it obtained in this manner to send and receive data on the network.

Routers and ARP Tables

Earlier, you learned that the port or interface where a router is connected to a network is considered to be part of that network. Therefore, as shown in Figure 6-12, the router interface connected to the network has an IP address for that network. Because routers, just like every other device on the network, send and receive data on the network, they build ARP tables that map IP addresses to MAC addresses.

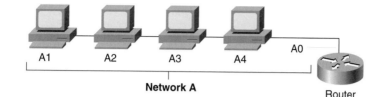

FIGURE 6-12
IP addresses are mapped to MAC addresses by ARP tables.

Routers can be connected to multiple networks or subnetworks. Generally, network devices map IP addresses and MAC addresses they see on a regular and repeated basis. In short, this means that a typical device contains mapping information pertaining only to devices on its own network. It knows very little about devices beyond its LAN. However, routers build tables that describe all networks connected to them. As a result, as shown in Figure 6-13, ARP tables kept by routers can contain IP addresses and MAC addresses of devices that are located on more than one network. In addition to mapping IP addresses to MAC addresses, router tables also map ports, as shown in Figure 6-14.

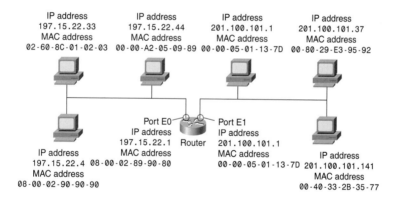

FIGURE 6-13
ARP tables are built by routers.

What happens if a data packet reaches a router destined for a network that the router is not connected to? In addition to IP addresses and MAC addresses of devices located on networks it is connected to, a router also possesses IP addresses and MAC addresses of other routers. As shown in Figure 6-15, a router uses these addresses to direct data toward its final destination. If a router receives a packet whose destination addresses are not in its routing table, it forwards the packet to the addresses of other routers, which presumably contain information about the destination host in their routing tables.

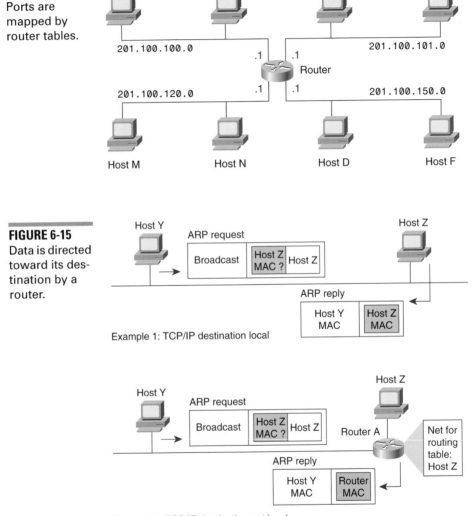

FIGURE 6-14
Ports are mapped by router tables.

FIGURE 6-15
Data is directed toward its destination by a router.

Example 1: TCP/IP destination local

Example 2: TCP/IP destination not local

Default Gateway

If the source resides on a network with a different network number than that of the desired destination, and if the source does not know the MAC address of the destination, it will have to use the services of a router in order for its data to reach the destination. When a router is used in this manner, it is called a *default gateway*. To obtain the services of the default gateway, the source encapsulates the data so that it contains the destination MAC address of the router. Because it wants the data delivered to a device and not the router, however, the source uses the destination IP address of the device and not that of the router in the IP header, which is depicted in Figure 6-16.

FIGURE 6-16
The destination IP address is used to deliver data.

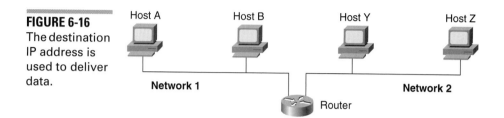

Host A to Host Z Data Packet

MAC header	IP header
Destination MAC address router	Destination IP address Host Z
Source MAC address Host A	Source IP address Host A

When the router picks up the data, it strips off the data link layer information used in the encapsulation. It passes the data up to the network layer, where it examines the destination IP address. Then, it compares the destination IP address with information contained in its routing tables. If the router locates the mapped destination IP address and MAC address and learns that the network the destination is located on is attached to one of its ports, it encapsulates the data with the new MAC address information and forwards it to the correct destination.

Summary

- All devices on the LAN are required to look at an ARP request, but only the device whose IP address matches the destination IP address carried in the ARP request must respond by providing its MAC address to the device that originated the request.
- If the IP address of a device matches the destination IP address contained in the ARP request, the device responds by sending the source its MAC address, which is known as the ARP reply.

- When a source is unable to locate the destination MAC address in its ARP table, it issues an ARP request in broadcast mode to all devices on the local network.

- When a device does not know its own IP address, it uses RARP.

- When the device that originated a RARP request receives a RARP reply, it copies its IP address into its memory cache, where it will reside for as long as the session lasts.

- Routers, like every other device on the network, send and receive data on the network, and build ARP tables that map IP addresses to MAC addresses.

- If the source resides on a network that has a different network number than the desired destination, and if the source does not know the MAC address of the destination, it will have to use the router as a default gateway for its data to reach the destination.

Review Questions

1. Which Internet protocol is used to map an IP address to a MAC address?

   A. TCP/IP

   B. RARP

   C. ARP

   D. AARP

2. Which of the following initiates an ARP request?

   A. A device that is unable to locate the destination IP address in its ARP table

   B. The RARP server, in response to a malfunctioning device

   C. A diskless workstation with an empty cache

   D. A device that is unable to locate the destination MAC address in its ARP table

3. Which of the following best describes an ARP table?

   A. A method to reduce network traffic by providing lists of shortcuts and routes to common destinations

   B. A way to route data within networks that are divided into sub-networks

   C. A protocol that performs an application-layer conversion of information from one stack to another

   D. A section of RAM on each device that maps IP addresses to MAC addresses

4. Which of the following best describes the ARP reply?

   A. The process of a device sending its MAC address to a source in response to an ARP request

   B. The route of the shortest path between the source and destination

   C. The updating of ARP tables through intercepting and reading messages traveling on the network

   D. The method of finding IP addresses based on the MAC address and used primarily by RARP servers

5. What are the two parts of the frame header called?

   A. The MAC header and the IP header

   B. The source address and the ARP message

   C. The destination address and the RARP message

   D. The request and the data packet

6. Why are current, updated ARP tables important?

   A. For testing links in the network

   B. For limiting the amount of broadcast

   C. For reducing network administrator maintenance time

   D. For resolving addressing conflicts

7. Why is a RARP request made?

   A. A source knows its MAC address but not its IP address.

   B. The data packet needs to find the shortest route between destination and source.

   C. The administrator needs to manually configure the system.

   D. A link in the network faults and a redundant system must be activated.

8. What is in a RARP request?

   A. A MAC header, an IP header, and the ARP request message

   B. A MAC header, a RARP header, and a data packet

   C. A RARP header and MAC and IP addresses

   D. A RARP header and an ARP trailer

9. Which of the following functions is unique to routers?

   A. They bind MAC and IP addresses.

   B. They receive broadcast messages and supply the requested information.

   C. They build ARP tables that describe all networks connected to them.

   D. They reply to ARP requests.

10. What happens if a router cannot locate a destination address?

   A. It consults the nearest name server that has a complete ARP table.

   B. It sends an ARP request to the RARP server.

   C. It locates the MAC address of another router and forwards the data to that router.

   D. It forwards the data packet to the nearest port, which queries the RARP server.

Objectives

After reading this chapter, you will be able to

- Define *topology*
- Describe how a bus topology works and list the advantages and disadvantages of using a bus topology
- Describe a star topology and list advantages and disadvantages of using a star topology
- Define *external terminators*
- Identify the characteristics of active and passive hubs
- Describe the characteristics of an extended star topology, identify maximum cabling lengths for a star topology, and describe how to extend the dimensions of a star topology
- Describe attenuation

Chapter 7

Topologies

Introduction

In Chapter 6, "ARP and RARP," you learned how devices on local-area networks (LANs) use Address Resolution Protocol (ARP) before forwarding data to a destination. You also learned what happens when a device on one network does not know the Media Access Control (MAC) address of a device on another network. In this chapter, you will learn about the topologies that are used to build networks.

Topology

In a LAN, workstations must be connected. If a file server is included in the LAN, it too is connected to the workstations. You have learned that networking media make this connection. The physical layout, which describes how a LAN is constructed, is called the *topology*. In this chapter, you will learn about three types of topologies: the bus topology, the star topology, and the extended star topology (see Figures 7-1 and 7-2).

FIGURE 7-1
A bus topology is typical of Ethernet LANs, including 10Base2 and 10Base5.

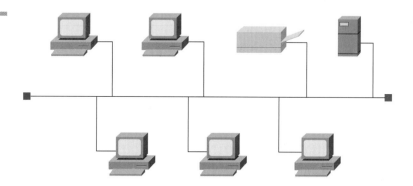

FIGURE 7-2
A star topology is typically used in Ethernet and Token Ring networks, where the center of the network is a hub, repeater, or concentrator.

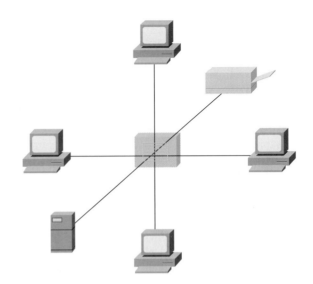

Bus Topology

A *bus topology* is one in which all devices on the LAN are attached to a linear networking medium. This linear networking medium is often referred to as the trunk line, bus, or highway. As shown in Figure 7-3, every device, such as workstations and servers, is independently attached to the common bus wire through some kind of connection. The bus wire must end in a terminating resistance, or terminator, which absorbs electrical signals so they don't bounce, or reflect, back and forth on the bus.

FIGURE 7-3
Electrical signals are absorbed in a bus wire by a terminator.

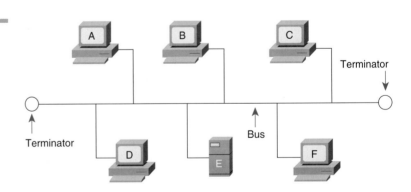

Signal Transmission over a Bus Topology

As shown in Figure 7-4, the signal travels in both directions from the source when a source transmits data over the networking media in a bus topology. These signals are made available to all devices on the LAN. As you have learned in previous lessons, each device checks the data as it passes. If the destination MAC address/destination IP address carried by the data does not match that of a device, the device ignores the data. However, if the destination MAC address/destination IP address carried by the data does match that of a device, the device copies the data and passes it up to the data link and network layers of the OSI reference model.

FIGURE 7-4

Data transmitted over a bus topology travels in both directions.

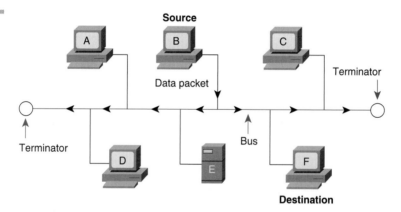

As you can see in Figure 7-4, each end of the cable has a terminator. When a signal reaches the end of the bus, it is absorbed by the terminator. This prevents signals from bouncing back and being received again by workstations attached to the bus.

In order to ensure that only one workstation transmits at a time, a bus topology uses collision detection because if more than one node attempts to transmit at the same time, a collision will occur. When a collision occurs, the data from each device impact with one another—that is, the voltage pulses from each device are both present on the common bus wire at the same time—and thus the data from both devices are damaged. The network area within which data packets originate and collide is called a *collision domain*. On a bus topology, when a network device detects that a collision has occurred, a backoff is issued by the network interface card (NIC). Because it is based on an algorithm, the length of this enforced retransmission delay is different for every device on the network, thus minimizing the likelihood of another collision.

Advantages and Disadvantages of a Bus Topology

A typical bus topology has a simple wiring layout that uses short lengths of networking media. Therefore, the cost of implementing this type of topology is usually low compared with that of other topologies. However, the low-cost implementation of this topology is offset by its high management costs. In fact, the biggest disadvantage of bus topology is that fault diagnosis and isolation of networking problems can be difficult because there are few points of concentration.

Because the networking medium does not pass through the nodes attached to it, if one device goes down on the network, it doesn't affect other devices on the network. Although this can be considered an advantage of bus topology, it is also offset by the fact that the single cable used in this type of topology can act as a single point of failure. In other words, if the networking medium used for the bus breaks, then none of the devices located along it will have the ability to transmit signals.

Star Topology

In LANs where the star topology is used, the networking media run from a central hub out to each device attached to the network. As shown in Figure 7-5, the physical layout of the star topology resembles spokes radiating from the hub of a wheel. As Figure 7-5 shows, a central point of control is used in a star topology. When a star topology is used, communication between devices attached to the LAN is via point-to-point wiring to the central link or hub.

FIGURE 7-5
A star topology resembles a hub-and-spokes configuration.

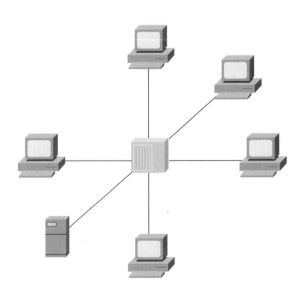

All network traffic in a star topology passes through the hub. Data is first sent to the hub, and then the hub directs data to the pathway of the device associated with the destination address carried by the data.

In a star topology, the hub can be either active or passive. If it is active, the hub not only connects the networking media, but it regenerates the signal and acts as a multiport repeater, which is sometimes referred to as a *concentrator*. By regenerating the signal, such active hubs enable data to travel over greater distances. By contrast, a passive hub simply connects networking media.

Advantages and Disadvantages of a Star Topology

Most LAN designers consider a star topology to be the easiest to design and install. This is because the networking media run directly out from a central hub to each workstation area. Another advantage of a star topology is ease of maintenance: The only area of concentration is the hub. In a star topology, the layout used for the networking media is easy to modify and problem diagnosis is relatively easy to perform. Moreover, workstations can be easily added to a network employing a star topology. If one run of networking media is broken or shorted, then only the device attached at that point is out of commission. However, the rest of the LAN will remain functional. In short, a star topology means greater reliability.

In some ways, a star topology's advantages can also be considered disadvantages. For example, although limiting one device per run of networking media can make diagnosis of problems easier, it also increases the amount of networking media required. This results in increased costs in setting up a star topology LAN. Moreover, the hub can make maintenance easier because all data has to pass through this central point; if the hub fails, however, the entire network fails also.

The Area Covered by a Star Topology

The maximum distance for a run of networking media, which is referred to as *horizontal cabling*, in the area extending from the wiring closet to a workstation, or the area that extends from the hub to any workstation, is 100 meters. This maximum distance for horizontal cabling is specified by the Electrical Industries Association (EIA) and the Telecommunications Industry Association (TIA). These two organizations jointly issue their list of standards, which you frequently see listed as the EIA/TIA standards. Specifically, the EIA/TIA-568B standard used for horizontal cabling for technical performance of the networking media has been and continues to be the most widely used.

In a star topology, each of the horizontal cabling runs can radiate from the hub, much like the spokes of a wheel; therefore, a LAN using this type of topology could cover a 200-meter by 200-meter area. As you can imagine, there are times when the area to be covered by a network exceeds what a simple star topology can accommodate. For example, envision a building that is 250 meters by 250 meters. A simple star topology that adhered to the horizontal cabling standard specified by EIA/TIA 568B could not provide complete coverage for a building with those dimensions. As indicated in Figure 7-6, workstations are located outside the area that can be covered by a star topology that adheres to EIA/TIA 568B specifications and, as depicted, they are not part of the LAN.

FIGURE 7-6

The maximum distance for a run of networking media from a hub to any workstation is 100 meters.

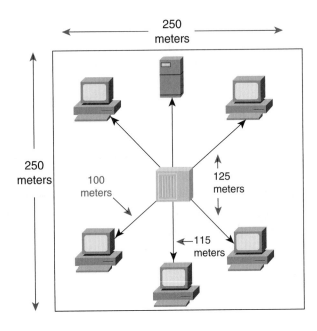

When signals first leave a transmitting station, they are clean and easily recognizable. However, as shown in Figure 7-7, the signals become more weak and deteriorate as they pass along the networking media—so the longer the cable length, the poorer the signals; this is referred to as *attenuation*. Therefore, if a signal travels beyond the maximum distance, there is no guarantee that, when it reaches a NIC, the NIC will be able to read the signal.

FIGURE 7-7
As signals pass along the networking media, they become weaker.

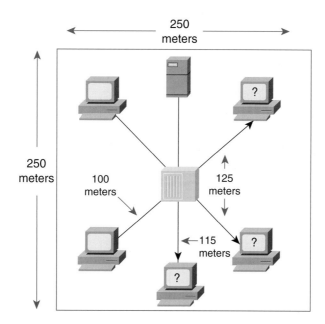

Extended Star Topology

If a simple star topology cannot provide enough coverage for the area to be networked, you can extend it by using internetworking devices that do not result in attenuation of the signal; the resulting topology is referred to as an *extended star topology.*

Again, imagine that you have a building that is 250 meters by 250 meters. In order for a star topology to be used effectively in this building, it must be extended. You don't do this by extending the horizontal cabling beyond the recommended maximum length. Instead, you use networking devices that do not degrade the signal.

Signals do not become unrecognizable to devices receiving them on the network if repeaters take in weakened signals, clean them up, amplify them, and send them on their way along the network. By using repeaters, as shown in Figure 7-8, you can extend the distance over which a network can reach. Repeaters work in tandem with the networking media and, therefore, they exist at the physical layer of the OSI reference model.

FIGURE 7-8
Repeaters can extend the distance over which a star topology can operate, as shown in this extended star topology network.

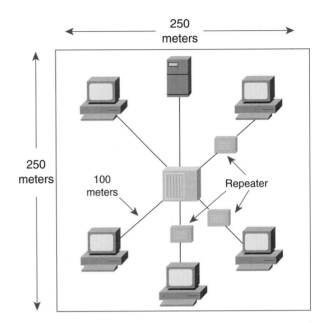

Summary

- A LAN's physical layout is called its topology.
- A bus topology is one in which all devices on the LAN are attached to a linear networking media. A typical bus topology has a simple wiring layout that uses short lengths of networking media.
- In LANs that us the star topology, the networking media run from a central hub out to each device attached to the network.
- The maximum distance for a run of networking media in a star topology is 100 meters.
- The star topology can be extended by using internetworking devices that prevent attenuation of the signal.

Review Questions

1. Which of the following best describes topology?

A. A connection of computers, printers, and other devices for the purpose of communications

B. The physical arrangement of network nodes and media within an enterprise networking structure

C. A network type that prevents collisions of data packets

D. A method for filtering network traffic to reduce the chance of bottlenecks and slowdowns

2. Which of the following best describes a star topology?

A. A LAN topology in which a central hub is connected by vertical cabling to other hubs that are dependent on it

B. A LAN topology in which transmissions from network stations propagate the length of the medium and are received by all other stations

C. A LAN topology in which endpoints on a network are connected to a common central switch by point-to-point links

D. A LAN topology in which central points on a network are connected to a common central switch by linear links

3. Which of the following best describes an extended star topology?

A. A LAN topology in which a central hub is connected by vertical cabling to other hubs that are dependent on it

B. A LAN topology in which transmissions from network stations propagate the length of the medium and are received by all other stations

C. A LAN topology in which endpoints on a network are connected to a common central switch by point-to-point links

D. A LAN topology in which central points on a network are connected to a common central switch by linear links

4. Which of the following best describes a terminator?

   A. A section of network with only one route in and out

   B. A device that quenches shorts before they reach expensive equipment

   C. A device placed at network dead ends to bounce signals back through the network

   D. A device that provides electrical resistance at the end of a transmission line to absorb signals

5. How is the signal transmitted over a bus topology?

   A. When a source transmits data over the networking media in a bus topology, the signal travels in a linear manner from the source.

   B. When a source transmits data over the networking media in a bus topology, the signal travels in both directions from the source.

   C. Signals on a bus topology are available only to the destination device on the LAN.

   D. When a source transmits data over the networking media in a bus topology, the signal travels in one direction from the source.

6. How is a backoff issued on a bus topology network?

   A. By the bridge closest to the collision

   B. By the terminator

   C. By the NIC in each device on the segment where the collision occurred

   D. By the route closest to the collision

7. What is one advantage to using a star topology?

   A. Great reliability

   B. Natural redundancy

   C. Low cost

   D. Requires minimum amount of networking media

8. What is the maximum distance that a star topology could cover?

   A. A 99-meter by 99-meter area

   B. A 100-meter by 100-meter area

   C. A 100-meter by 200-meter area

   D. A 200-meter by 200-meter area

9. What happens to the signal when horizontal cabling runs exceed the EIA/TIA 568B specified maximum length?

   A. The transmission is interrupted.

   B. The transmission is weakened.

   C. The transmission travels only the maximum distance and then stops.

   D. The workstations do not send a message to a point that exceeds the maximum distance.

10. What can you do if the dimensions of the building exceed the maximum cable length?

   A. Add a signal doubler.

   B. Add more cable.

   C. Add repeaters.

   D. Add another hub.

Objectives

After reading this chapter, you will be able to

- Identify and describe specific networking standards
- Describe Category 5 cable
- Describe an RJ45 jack, how it is used, and how it is mounted
- Describe punch tools
- Identify a wiring closet
- Define *MDF* and *IDF*
- Describe patch panels
- Describe cable testing
- Describe backbone cabling in an Ethernet LAN
- Explain the purpose of grounding computing devices
- Identify the causes of electrical noise
- Describe a surge suppressor
- Describe a UPS

Chapter 8

Structured Cabling and Electricity

Introduction

In Chapter 1, "Networking and the OSI Reference Model," you learned that because companies had deployed many different network technologies, it became difficult for networks using different specifications and implementations to communicate with each other. You learned that by creating the Open System Interconnection (OSI) model, the International Organization for Standardization (ISO) was providing vendors with a set of standards. You know that standards are sets of rules or procedures that are either widely used or officially specified and that they act as a type of blueprint to ensure greater compatibility and interoperability between the various types of network technologies that are produced by many companies around the world.

In this chapter, you will learn about other organizations that issue standards regarding specifications for the type of networking media used in local-area networks (LANs). You will also learn about structured cabling and electrical specifications used in LANs. In addition, you will learn about wiring and electrical techniques used in building networks.

Networking Media Standards

Until recently, there has been a somewhat confusing mix of standards governing networking media. Standards have ranged from those for fire and building codes to detailed electrical specifications. Other standards have focused on tests to ensure safety and performance. Early standards developed for networking media were largely proprietary standards developed by various companies. Later, numerous organizations and government bodies joined the movement to regulate and specify the type of cable that can be used.

For your studies, you will need to focus on the standards for networking media that are developed and issued by the Institute of Electrical and Electronic Engineers (IEEE), the Underwriters Laboratories (UL), the Electrical Industries Association (EIA), and the Telecommunications Industry Association (TIA). The latter two organizations jointly issue a list of standards, and frequently you see them listed as the EIA/TIA standards. In addition to these groups and organizations, local, state, county, and national government agencies issue specifications and requirements that can affect the type of cable used in a LAN.

EIA/TIA-568B Standards

Of all the organizations mentioned here, the EIA/TIA has had the greatest impact on networking media standards. The EIA/TIA standards were developed with the intent of identifying minimum requirements that would support multiproduct and multivendor environments. Moreover, these standards were developed to allow for planning and installation of LAN systems without knowledge of the specific equipment that is to be installed. Thus, the EIA/TIA standards allow the LAN designer options and room for expansion. Specifically, the EIA/TIA-568B standards for technical performance of the networking media have been and continue to be the most widely used.

The EIA/TIA standards address six elements of cabling for LAN systems: horizontal cabling, telecommunications closets, backbone cabling, equipment rooms, work areas, and entrance facilities. In this chapter, you will learn about horizontal cabling.

Horizontal Cabling

EIA/TIA-568B defines *horizontal cabling* as a networking medium that runs from the telecommunications outlet to the horizontal cross-connect. This element includes the networking medium that is run along a horizontal pathway, the telecommunications outlet or connector, the mechanical terminations in the wiring closet, and the patch cords or jumpers in the wiring closet. In short, horizontal cabling describes the networking medium that is used in the area extending from the wiring closet to a workstation. Figure 8-1 shows horizontal cabling typically run from the wiring closet to a single workstation.

FIGURE 8-1
Marking specified by UL for shielded twisted-pair (STP) and unshielded twisted-pair (UTP) cables.

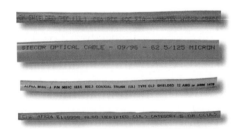

EIA/TIA-568B contains specifications governing cable performance. It calls for running two cables—one for voice and one for data—to each outlet. Of the two cables, one must be four-pair UTP for voice. The EIA/TIA-568B standard specifies five categories in these specifications: Category 1, Category 2, Category 3, Category 4, and Category 5 cable. Of these, only Category 3, Category 4, and Category 5 are recognized for use in LANs. Of these three categories, Category 5 is the one most frequently recommended and implemented in installations today.

Cabling Specifications

The networking media for the five categories of cable are the ones you have studied: STP, UTP, fiber-optic cable, and coaxial cable. For STP cable, the EIA/TIA-568B standard for horizontal cabling calls for two pairs of 150-ohm cable. For UTP, the standard calls for four pairs of 100-ohm cable, which is shown in Figure 8-2.

FIGURE 8-2
100-ohm UTP cable containing four pairs.

For fiber-optic cable, the standard calls for two fibers of 62.5/125-ohm multimode cable, which is shown in Figure 8-3. Although 50-ohm coaxial cable, which is shown in Figure 8-4, is a recognized type of networking media in EIA/TIA-568B, it is not recommended for new installation.

FIGURE 8-3
This 62.5/125-ohm multimode fiber-optic cable contains two fibers.

FIGURE 8-4
50-ohm coax-
ial cable is not
recommended
for new
installation.

According to EIA/TIA-568B, the maximum distance for cable runs in horizontal cabling is 90 meters, or 295 feet. This is true for all types of Category 5 UTP networking media. The standard also specifies that patch cords or cross-connect jumpers located at the horizontal cross-connect cannot exceed 6 meters, or 20 feet, in length. EIA/TIA-568B also allows 3 meters, or 9.8 feet, for patch cords that are used to connect equipment at the work area. The total length of the patch cords and cross-connect jumpers used in the horizontal cabling cannot exceed 10 meters, or 33 feet.

For the horizontal cabling component, EIA/TIA-568B requires a minimum of two telecommunications outlets or connectors at each work area. This tele-communications outlet/connector is supported by two cables. The first is a four-pair 100-ohm Category 3 or higher UTP cable, along with its appropriate connector (see Figure 8-5). The second can be any one of the following: a four-pair 100-ohm UTP cable and its appropriate connector; a 150-ohm STP cable; a coaxial cable and its appropriate connector; or a two-fiber 62.5/125-ohm optical fiber cable and its appropriate connector.

FIGURE 8-5
Category 5 UTP
cable and an
RJ45 jack.

Category 5
Unshielded Twisted Pair

RJ45 Jack

Telecommunications Outlet Jacks

EIA/TIA-568B specifies that an RJ45 jack is to be used for making the connection to a Category 5 UTP cable at the telecommunications outlet in a horizontal cabling scheme. The RJ45 jack contains color-coded slots. The wires are punched down into these slots to make an electrical connection. The jack also contains a female plug, which looks like a standard phone jack. However, the RJ45 jack has eight pins instead of the four found in a standard phone jack because it must accommodate four pairs of twisted wire found in Category 5 UTP.

Mounting an RJ45 Jack

The telecommunications outlet described in a horizontal cabling scheme is usually mounted on a wall. EIA/TIA-568B specifies two types of wall mounts that can be used to mount an RJ45 jack: surface mounting and flush mounting.

Surface-Mounted RJ45 Jacks

Surface-mounted jacks can be mounted to the wall by means of an adhesive-backed box. If you elect to use this method, be aware that once the boxes are mounted, they cannot be moved. This can be a factor if you anticipate changes in room use or configuration. Another method that can be used to surface mount RJ45 jacks is to use a screw-mounted box. In either method, the jack is simply inserted into the space provided for it by the box.

Many installers prefer to use surface-mounted RJ45 jacks because they are easier to install. Because they mount onto the surface of the wall, no cutting into the wall is required. This also means that they are faster to install. When labor costs are a factor in installing a LAN, this can become a consideration. Surface-mounted jacks may also be the only choice in some situations, such as in buildings with concrete block walls.

Flush-Mounted RJ45 Jacks

Before an RJ45 jack can be flush-mounted in a wall, several factors must be taken into consideration. For example, the techniques used to cut into drywall differ from those used to cut into plaster. Therefore, it is important to determine of what type of material the wall is made. You should also avoid placing jacks where they will interfere with trim located around doors or windows. Finally, you have to determine whether the jack will be mounted in a box or in a low-voltage mounting bracket.

If you are mounting a jack in drywall, select a position that is 12 to 18 inches above the floor. Then, bore a small hole in the location selected. After you have bored the hole, you will need to determine whether there are obstructions behind the spot selected. To do this, bend a piece of wire. Insert the wire in the hole and rotate it in a circle.

If you choose to place the jack on a wooden baseboard, avoid cutting the box opening in the bottom 2 inches of the baseboard. If you attempt to place the box in that location, the wall's bottom plate will block you from pushing the

> **HINT**
>
> Any time you will be working in walls, ceilings, or attics, it is important to remember to turn off power to all circuits going to or passing through the work area. If you are not sure what wires pass through the section of the building you will be working in, a good rule to follow is to shut off all power.

box that the jack is to be mounted in into the baseboard. Select the position where you want to place the box. Using the box as a template, trace its outline in the place you selected. Before attempting to saw around the outline, you will need to bore starter holes at each corner. Use either a keyhole saw or a jigsaw to cut from hole to hole.

After you have prepared an opening to receive the jack, you can mount it in the wall. If you are mounting the jack in a box, hold the cable and feed it through one of the slots into the box. Next, push the box into the wall opening. The box will be gripped to the wall surface when you tighten the screws at the top and bottom.

If you are mounting the jack in a low-voltage mounting bracket, put the bracket against the wall opening. The smooth side should be facing out. So that the bracket grips the wall, push the top and bottom flanges toward the back. Then, push the first one up and the other down. The bracket should now be securely mounted.

Wiring

NOTE

By *wiring sequence*, we mean which wire goes in which terminal.

A LAN's performance is closely linked to how good its connections are. When RJ45 jacks are used at the telecommunications outlet in a horizontal cabling scheme, the wiring sequence is critical for optimal network performance.

To understand how this works, let's look at an RJ45 jack, which is shown in Figure 8-5. The RJ45 jack is color coded; the colors, blue, green, brown, and orange, correspond to the wires found in each of the twisted pairs found in Category 5 UTP. To begin laying the wires, first strip the jacket from the end of the cable—approximately $1\frac{1}{2}$ to 2 inches. Try not to strip more of the cable jacket than is necessary. If too much of the jacket is stripped, the rate of data transmission will be slowed. Lay the wires in the center of the jack. While you work, be sure to keep the wires centered; if they become skewed, the rate of data transmission will be slowed. Also, make sure to keep the portion of the cable covered by the jacket within $\frac{1}{8}$ inch of the jack.

Next, separate each pair of twisted wires. Notice that the first color that appears on the left side of the jack is blue. Find the pair of wires that contains the blue wire. Untwist this pair of wires. Lay the blue wire in the slot to the left that is labeled in blue. Lay the second wire of this pair in the slot to the right that is labeled in blue and white. Next, notice that the color used to code the next slot on the right side of the jack is green. Locate the twisted pair that contains the green wire. Untwist this pair of wires until enough wire is free to work with. Lay the green wire in the slot to the right that is labeled in green.

Lay the second wire of this pair in the slot to the left that is labeled in green and white. Continue in this fashion until all the wires have been matched to their corresponding color-coded slots in the jack. After you have completed this step, you are ready to punch the wires down in the jack.

Punch Tools

To punch the wires down in the jack, you need to use a punch tool. A *punch tool* is a device that uses a spring-loaded action to push the wires between metal pins while it skins the sheath away from the wire. This ensures that the wire will make a good electrical connection with the pins inside the jack. The punch tool also cuts off any extra wire. When you use the punch tool, begin by positioning the blade on the outside of the jack. If you place the blade on the inside of the jack, you will cut the wire short of its connection point. If this happens, no electrical connection will be made.

After you have finished punching down all the wires, place the clips on the jack and tighten them. To snap the jack into its faceplate, push it in from the back side. When you do this, make sure the jack is right-side up. Next, attach the faceplate to either the box or bracket with screws. If you used a surface-mounted box, remember that it can hold a foot or two of excess cable. If you choose to store excess cable behind the box, you need to either slide the cable through its tie-wraps or uncover the raceway that covers it in order to work the rest of the excess cable back into the wall. If a flush-mounted jack is used, all you have to do is push the excess cable back into the wall.

Installing Cable

When you are connecting cable to jacks, remember to strip back only as much of the cable's jacket as is required to terminate the wires. The more wire that is exposed, the poorer the connection will be. This will result in signal loss. In addition, maintain the twists in each pair of wires as close as possible to the point of termination. It is the twisting of the wires that produces the cancellation needed to prevent radio and electromagnetic interference. For Category 4 UTP, the maximum amount of untwisting that is allowed is 1 inch. For Category 5 UTP, the maximum amount of untwisting that is allowed is $\frac{1}{2}$ inch.

If you must bend cable to route it, be sure to maintain a maximum bend radius of four times the diameter of the cable and never bend cable so that it exceeds a 90-degree angle. If multiple cables are run over the same path, use cable ties to cinch them together. When cable ties are needed to mount or secure cable, be sure to apply cable ties so that they can slide a little. Position ties at random intervals along the cable. Never secure the cable ties too tightly because it can damage the cable. When securing the cable ties, try to minimize the amount of jacket twisting. If cable is twisted too much, you can end up with torn cable

> **HINT**
>
> If you tilt the handle of the punch tool a little to the outside, it will cut better. If any wire remains attached after you have used the punch tool, simply twist the ends gently to remove them

jackets. Never allow the cable to be pinched or kinked. If this occurs, data will move more slowly and your LAN will operate at less than optimal capacity.

When handling the cable, avoid stretching it. If you exceed 25 pounds of pull, wires inside the cable can untwist. As you have learned, if wire pairs become untwisted, this can lead to interference and crosstalk. Above all, never cut corners with cable. It is important to leave ample slack. Remember, a few feet of extra cable is a small price to pay to avoid having to redo a cable run because of mistakes resulting in stretched cable. Most cable installers avoid this problem by leaving enough slack so that the cable can reach the floor and extend another 2 or 3 feet at both ends of the cable. Other installers follow the practice of leaving what is called a *service coil*: a few extra feet of cable left coiled up inside the ceiling or in another out-of-the-way location.

Use appropriate and recommended techniques for dressing and securing the cable, including using cable ties, cable support bars, wire management panels, and releasable Velcro straps. Never use a staple gun to position cables. Staples can pierce the jacket, causing loss of connection. Remember the do's and don'ts of installing cable, and see Figure 8-6 for a good example of well-installed cable.

FIGURE 8-6
You should use cable ties, cable support bars, wire management panels, and releasable Velcro straps for dressing and securing the cable.

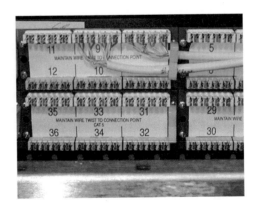

Documentation and Labeling

When you install cable, it is important to document the process. Therefore, as you install cable, be sure to make a *cut sheet*, which is a rough diagram that shows where cable runs are. It also indicates the numbers of the school rooms, offices, or other rooms where the cable runs go. Later, you can refer to this cut sheet so that corresponding numbers can be placed on all telecommunications outlets and at the patch panel in the wiring closet. You can use a page in your journal to document cable runs so that you have an additional layer of documentation for any cable installation.

EIA/TIA-606 specifies that a unique identifier must be given to each hardware termination unit. This identifier must be marked on each termination hardware unit or on its label. When identifiers are used at the work area, station terminations must be labeled on the faceplate, the housing, or the connector itself. Whether they are adhesive or insertable, all labels must meet legibility, defacement, and adhesion requirements, as specified in UL969.

Avoid labeling cabling, telecommunications outlets, and patch panels with such terms as "Mr. Zimmerman's math class" or "Mr. Snyder's chemistry class." This can lead to confusion years later if someone else needs to perform work involving the networking media. Instead, as shown in Figure 8-6, use labels that will remain understandable to someone years later.

Many network administrators incorporate room numbers in the labels they use. A letter is then assigned to each cable that is run to a room. Some labeling systems, particularly in very large networks, also incorporate color coding. For example, a blue label might be used to identify horizontal cabling at the wiring closet only, and a green label might be used to identify cabling at the work area.

To see how this works, imagine that four cables are run to room 1012. On a cut sheet, these cables would be labeled 1012A, 1012B, 1012C, and 1012D, as shown in Figure 8-7. The faceplates where cables 1012A, 1012B, 1012C, and 1012D connect to workstation patch cords would also be labeled to correspond with each cable, as shown in Figure 8-8.

FIGURE 8-7
This cut sheet shows cables labeled as 1012A, 1012B, 1012C, and 1012D.

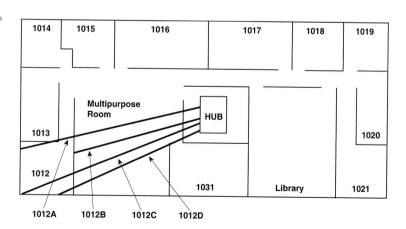

Cut Sheet Cabling Diagram

Where each cable connects at the patch panel in the wiring closet should also be labeled. Place connections at the patch panel so that labels can be arranged in ascending order. This will allow easy diagnosis and location of problems if they should arise later. Finally, the cable itself must be labeled at each end, as shown in Figure 8-6.

FIGURE 8-8
The faceplates where cables 1012A, 1012B, 1012C, and 1012D connect to workstation patch cords should be labeled to correspond with each cable. This figure shows the properly labeled 1012A faceplate.

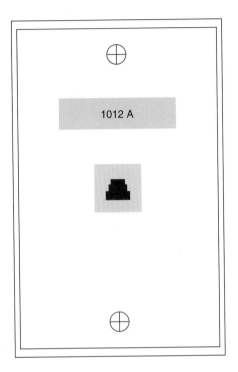

The Wiring Closet

Once you have successfully run cable in a horizontal cabling run, connections must be made in the wiring closet. A *wiring closet* is a specially designed room used for wiring a data or voice network. Because a wiring closet serves as a central junction point for the wiring and wiring equipment that is used for connecting devices in a LAN, it is at the center point of a star topology. Typically, the equipment found in a wiring closet can include patch panels, wiring hubs, bridges, switches, and routers, as shown in Figure 8-9.

Generally, the wiring closet must be large enough to accommodate the equipment and wiring located in it. Naturally, this varies with the size of the LAN and the types of equipment required to operate it. Equipment required for some small LANs might take up as little space as a large filing cabinet, whereas a large LAN could require a full-fledged computer room. Finally, the wiring closet must be large enough to accommodate future growth.

FIGURE 8-9
Central wiring connections for a data or voice network are made in the wiring closet.

EIA/TIA-569 specifies that there be a minimum of one wiring closet per floor and states that additional wiring closets should be provided for each area up to 1,000 square meters when the floor area served exceeds 1,000 square meters or the horizontal cabling distance exceeds 90 meters.

In large networks, it is not unusual to have more than one wiring closet. When this occurs, the topology is described as an extended star topology. Usually, when more than one wiring closet is required, one is designated as the main distribution facility (MDF) and all other wiring closets, referred to as intermediate distribution facilities (IDFs), are dependent on it.

If the wiring closet is to serve as the MDF, all cable leaving the room for IDFs and computer and communications rooms located on other floors of a building should be via 4-inch conduits or sleeved cores. Likewise, all such cable going into IDFs should be via the same 4-inch conduits or sleeved cores. The exact number of conduits required is determined by the amount of fiber-optic, UTP, and STP cable that must be supported in each wiring closet and computer or communications room.

Any location selected for a wiring closet must meet certain environmental requirements. Broadly speaking, these environmental requirements include sufficient power and heating, ventilation, and air-conditioning to maintain a room temperature of approximately 70 degrees Fahrenheit when all LAN equipment is fully functioning. In addition, the location selected should be secure from unauthorized access and meet all applicable building and safety codes.

All interior walls, or at least those on which equipment is to be mounted, should be covered with $\frac{3}{4}$-inch plywood that is raised from the underlying wall a minimum of $1\frac{3}{4}$ inch. If the wiring closet is to serve as the MDF for the building, the telephone point of presence (POP) may actually be located inside

NOTE

One thousand square meters equals 10,000 square feet. Ninety meters equals approximately 300 feet.

the room. In such instances, interior walls at the POP and behind the PBX should be covered from the floor to the ceiling with $\frac{3}{4}$-inch plywood, and a minimum of 15 feet of wall space should be provided for terminations and related equipment. In addition, fire-retardant paint that meets all applicable fire codes should be used to paint all interior walls. A wall switch to turn room lighting on and off should be located immediately inside the door. Because of the outside interference it generates, fluorescent lighting should be avoided.

Multiple Wiring Closets

An example where more than one wiring closet would probably be used is in a multibuilding campus that is networked. Backbone and horizontal cabling would be used in an Ethernet LAN in a multibuilding campus. In Figure 8-10, a central location on the campus has been used for the MDF. In this instance, the POP is located inside the MDF. The backbone, represented by dotted lines, runs from the MDF to each of the IDFs. The IDFs are located in each of the buildings on campus. In addition to the MDF, there is an IDF located in the main building so that all computers fall within a catchment area. Horizontal cabling running from the IDFs and MDFs to work areas is represented by the lines connecting the computer workstations to the IDFs and MDF.

FIGURE 8-10
A central location on a campus is used for the MDF.

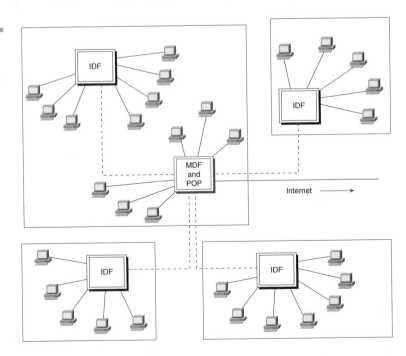

Backbone Cabling

Just as there is a special term (horizontal cabling) used by EIA/TIA-568 for the type of cabling that runs from the wiring closet to each work area, there is a special term for the type of cabling that connects wiring closets to each other when an extended star topology is used for an Ethernet LAN. EIA/TIA-568 refers to the type of cabling that connects wiring closets to each other as *backbone cabling*.

Backbone cabling consists of the backbone cabling runs; intermediate and main cross-connects; mechanical terminations; and patch cords used for backbone-to-backbone cross-connection. Included in this are the vertical networking media between wiring closets on different floors; networking media between the MDF and the POP; and networking media used between buildings in a multibuilding campus.

EIA/TIA-568 specifies four types of networking media that can be used for backbone cabling: 100-ohm UTP, 150-ohm STP, 62.5/125-micron optical fiber, and single-mode optical fiber. Although EIA/TIA-568 recognizes 50-ohm coaxial cable, generally it is not recommended for new installations and it is anticipated that it will be removed the next time the standard is revised. Most installations today use 62.5/125-micron fiber-optic cable as a matter of course for backbone cabling.

Patch Panels

In an Ethernet LAN using a star or an extended star topology, the horizontal cabling runs coming from the work areas are usually terminated at a patch panel. A *patch panel* is an interconnecting device through which horizontal cabling runs can be connected to other networking devices, such as hubs and repeaters. More specifically, a patch panel is a gathering of pin locations, as shown in Figure 8-6, and ports. Essentially, as shown in Figure 8-9, a patch panel acts as a switchboard where horizontal cabling coming from workstations can be connected to other workstations in a local-area network. In some instances, the patch panel will also provide locations where devices can be connected to a WAN or even to the Internet. This connection is described by EIA/TIA-568A as the *horizontal cross-connect*.

Patch panels can either be mounted on the wall in brackets, stand in racks, or reside in cabinets equipped with interior racks and doors. One used most commonly for mounting patch panels is the distribution rack. A *distribution rack* is a simple skeletal frame for holding equipment, such as patch panels, repeaters, hubs, and routers, that are used in the wiring closet. They range in height between 39 inches and 74 inches. The advantage of a distribution rack is that it allows easy access to both the front and the back of equipment. A floor plate is used to attach the distribution rack to the floor to ensure stability. Although a few companies currently market a 23-inch-wide rack, the standard since the 1940s has been the 19-inch rack.

Patch Panel Ports

To understand how a patch panel provides for the interconnection of horizontal cabling runs with other networking devices, let's look at how it is structured. Rows of pins much like those found in the RJ45 jack you have already worked with are located on one side of a patch panel. Just as on the RJ45 jack, these pins are color coded. To make electrical connections to the pins, you use a punch tool to punch down the wires, just as you do with the RJ45 jacks. As with RJ45 jacks, wire sequence is critical for optimal network performance. Therefore, when laying down the wires at the patch panel, make sure the colors of the wires correspond exactly to the colors indicated on the pin locations. Remember that different colored wires are not interchangeable.

Ports are located on the opposite side of the patch panel. As shown in Figure 8-11, these ports resemble the ports found on the faceplates at the telecommunications outlets in the work area. Like those RJ45 ports, the ports on patch panels take the same size plug. Patch cords that connect to the ports allow for the interconnection of computers and other networking devices, such as hubs, repeaters, and routers, that are also attached to the patch panel.

FIGURE 8-11
Ports are located on the front of a patch panel.

Patch Panel Wiring Structure

In any LAN system, connectors are the weakest links. If not properly installed, connectors can create electrical noise. Poor connections can also cause intermittent electrical contact between wires and pins. When this occurs, transmission of data on the network is disrupted or occurs at a much slower rate. Therefore, it pays to do it right. To ensure that cable is installed correctly, you should follow the EIA/TIA standards.

At the patch panel, it is important to lay down cable wires in ascending cable number order. (These are the cable numbers that were assigned to the cable when it was run from the work area to the wiring closet.) As you learned earlier, cable numbers correspond to the numbers of the rooms in which the workstations attached to the cable are located. Laying down the wires in ascending order at the patch panel allows for easy diagnosis and location of problems if they should arise later.

Use the cut sheet you prepared earlier to lay down the wires at the patch panel. Later, you can label the patch panel. As mentioned earlier, lay the wires down so that the colors of the wires correspond exactly to the colors indicated on the pin locations. As you work, it is important to remember to keep the end of the cable centered above its pin locations. If you are not careful to do this, the wires can become skewed, which will slow the rate of data transmission when your LAN is fully connected.

To avoid exposing too much wire, be sure to keep the jacket within $\frac{1}{4}$ inch of the pin locations you are working on. A good way to do this is to measure before you strip off the jacket. $1\frac{1}{2}$ to 2 inches should be sufficient to do the job. Remember that if too much wire is exposed, the rate of data transmission on the network will be slowed. Again, don't untwist the wire pairs more than necessary; not only do untwisted wires transmit data more slowly, but they can also lead to crosstalk.

Depending on what type of patch panel is used, you will use either a 110 or a Krone punch tool. The patch panel shown in the figures in this chapter is a 110. Check to see which tool you need to use before beginning work. The punch tool has a spring-loaded action, which allows the tool to do two jobs at the same time: As it pushes a wire between two metal pins, skinning the sheath from the wires so that it makes an electrical connection with the pins, the punch tool's blade also cuts off any extra wire.

When you use a punch tool, be sure to position it so that its blade is on the side away from where the wire enters each pin location. If you fail to take this precaution, you will cut the wire so that it falls short of where it should make an electrical connection.

Cable Testing

As you learned earlier, the foundation of the OSI reference model is the networking media; every other layer of that model depends on and is supported by the networking media. You read that a network is only as reliable as its cabling, and you learned that many experts consider it to be the most important component in any network.

Therefore, after the networking media has been installed, it is important to determine how good your network's cables are. Even with a great investment in the best-quality cable, connectors, patch panels, and other equipment, poor installation practices can prevent your network from operating at its optimal level. Therefore, you should test the entire installation when it is in place.

When testing your network, you should follow these steps:

1. Break the system into logically conceived functional elements.

2. Note any symptoms.

3. Based on the symptoms you observe, determine what is the most likely dysfunctional element.

4. Use substitution or additional testing to discover whether the likely element is, in fact, dysfunctional.

5. If the element suspected of being dysfunctional proves not to be the problem, proceed to the next most likely element you suspect.

6. When the dysfunctional element is found, repair it if possible.

7. If it is not possible to repair the dysfunctional element, replace it.

The IEEE and EIA/TIA have established standards that allow you to evaluate whether your network is operating at an acceptable level after installation has been completed. Provided that your network passes this test and has been certified as meeting the standards, you can use the network's initial operating level as an established baseline.

Knowing this baseline measurement is important because the need to test does not end just because your network installation has been certified as meeting the standards. You will want to continue testing your network periodically to ensure optimal network performance. You can do this by comparing recorded measurements taken when the system was known to be operating properly against current measurements. A significant drop from the baseline measurement is an indication that something is wrong with the network.

Repeated testing of your network and comparison against its baseline will help you spot specific problems and allow you to track degradation caused by aging, poor maintenance practices, weather, or other factors. You might think that testing cable is a simple matter of substituting one cable for another. However, this does not provide certain proof of anything because a common problem can affect all cables on a LAN. For this reason, it is recommended that you use a cable tester to measure network performance. *Cable testers* are handheld devices that can be used to certify that the cable meets the required IEEE and EIA/TIA standards. Cable testers vary in the types of testing functions they provide. Some can provide printouts; others can be attached to a PC to create a data file.

Cable Testers

Cable testers have a wide range of features and capabilities. Therefore, the list of things cable testers can measure provided here is intended to give you a general overview of the features that are available. You need to determine what features will best meet your needs and make your selection accordingly.

Generally, cable testers can perform tests that measure the overall capability of a cable run. This includes determining cable distance, locating bad connections, providing wire maps for detecting crossed pairs, measuring signal attenuation, detecting near-end crosstalk, detecting split pairs, performing noise level tests, and tracing cable behind walls.

It is important to measure the distance of the cable because the overall length of the runs of cable can affect the ability of devices on the network to share the networking media. As you have already learned, cable that exceeds the maximum length specified by EIA/TIA-568A causes signal degradation.

Cable testers referred to as *time domain reflectometers (TDRs)* measure the distance to open-ended or shorted cable. The TDR does this by sending an electrical pulse down the cable. The device then times the signal's reflection back from the end of the cable. Distance readings provided using this technique can be expected to be accurate to within 2 feet.

When UTP cable is used for a LAN installation, distance measurements can be used to determine whether the connections at the patch panel and at the telecommunications outlets are good. To understand how this works, you must understand more about how the TDR works.

When it measures distance on a cable, the TDR sends an electrical signal that is reflected when it encounters the most distant open connection. Imagine that this device is used to determine which connections in a cable run are faulty. Begin by attaching the device to the patch cord at the patch panel. If the TDR reports the distance to the patch panel instead of the distance to a further point, then you will know you have a connection problem. The same procedure can be used at the opposite end of the cable to measure through the RJ45 jack located at the telecommunications outlet.

Wire Maps

Cable testers use a feature called *wire map* to indicate which wire pairs connect to what pins on lugs and sockets. This test is used to show whether an installer properly connected wires to a plug or jack or whether this was done in reverse order. Wires connected in reverse order are referred to as *crossed pairs*. This is a common problem that is unique to UTP cable installations. As shown in Figures 8-12 and 8-13, when crossed pairs are detected in UTP LAN cabling systems, the connection is not good. Where the crossed pairs have been detected, the wiring will have to be redone.

FIGURE 8-12
This wiring is correct.

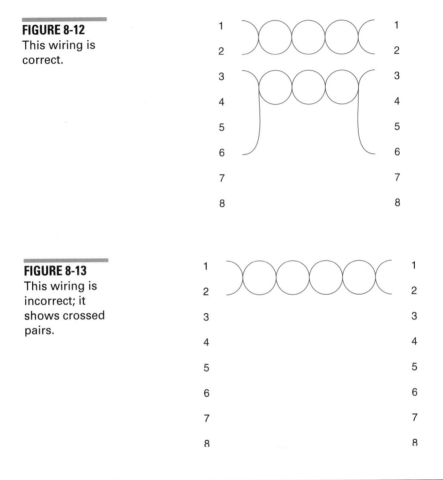

FIGURE 8-13
This wiring is incorrect; it shows crossed pairs.

Electricity

When it reaches a building, electricity is carried to workstations, servers, and networking devices via wires concealed in walls, floors, and ceilings. Consequently, inside these buildings, alternating current (AC) power line noise is all around. If not properly addressed, power line noise can present problems for a network.

In fact, as you will discover the more you work with networks, AC line noise coming from a nearby video monitor or hard disk drive can be enough to create errors in a computer system. It does this by burying the desired signals and preventing a computer's logic gates from detecting the leading and trailing edges of the square signal waves. This problem can be further compounded when a computer has a poor ground connection.

Grounding

In electrical equipment that also has a safety ground connection, the safety ground wire is always connected to any exposed metal parts of the equipment. In computer equipment, motherboards and computing circuits are electrically connected to the chassis and, therefore, to the safety grounding wire. This ground is used to dissipate static electricity.

The purpose of connecting the safety ground to exposed metal parts of the computing equipment is to prevent such metal parts from becoming energized with a hazardous voltage resulting from a wiring fault inside the device.

An example of a wiring fault that could occur in a networking device is an accidental connection between the hot wire and the chassis. If such a fault were to occur, the safety ground wire connected to the device would serve as a low-resistance path to the earth ground. When properly installed, the low-resistance path provided by the safety ground wire offers sufficiently low reistance and sufficient current-carrying capacity to prevent the buildup of hazardous high voltages. Moreover, because the circuit now directly links the hot connection to earth, any time electrical current is passed via this path into the ground, it will cause protective devices such as circuit breakers to activate. By interrupting the circuit to the transformer, circuit breakers stop the flow of electrons, thus eliminating the hazard of electrical shock.

Large buildings frequently require more than one earth ground. Separate earth grounds for each building are also required in multibuilding campuses. Unfortunately, the earth ground between buildings is almost never the same. Separate earth grounds for the same building can also vary. When ground wires in separate locations have slightly different potential (voltage) to the common and hot wires, it can present a serious problem.

To understand this, assume that the ground wire for Building A has a slightly different potential to the common and hot wires than the ground wire for Building B. Therefore, the outside cases of computer devices located in Building A have a different potential (voltage) from the outside cases of computer equipment located in Building B. If a circuit is established linking computer devices in Building A to those in Building B, electrical current will flow from the negative source to the positive source and anyone coming into contact with any device on that circuit could receive a nasty shock. In addition, this errant potential voltage has the ability to severely damage delicate computer memory chips.

When everything works correctly and according to IEEE standards, there should be no voltage difference between the networking media and the chassis of a networking device. However, things don't always work as intended. For example, if there is a faulty ground wire connection to an outlet, there can be lethal voltages between the LAN's UTP cabling and the chassis of a networking device.

Most network installers today recommend the use of fiber-optic cable for backbone cabling to link wiring closets on different floors of the same building as well as between separate buildings. The reason for this is simple: It is not uncommon for floors of the same building to be fed by different power transformers. Different power transformers can have different earth grounds, causing the problems just discussed. Nonconducting optical fibers eliminate this problem.

Signal Reference Grounds

When a computer attached to a network receives data in the form of digital signals, it must have some way of recognizing the signals. It does this by measuring and comparing the 3- to 5-volt signals it receives to a reference point called the *signal reference ground*. To function correctly, the signal reference ground must be close to a computer's digital circuits. Engineers have accomplished this by designing a ground plane into circuit boards. The computer's cabinet is used as a common point of connection for the circuit board ground planes to establish the signal reference ground. (Signal reference ground establishes the zero volts line in the figures in this section that show signals.)

Ideally, the signal reference ground should be completely isolated from the electrical ground. Isolation would keep AC power leakage and voltage spikes off the signal reference ground. However, engineers have not found it practical to isolate the signal reference ground in this manner. Instead, the chassis of a computing device serves as the signal reference ground and as the AC power line ground.

Because there is a link between the signal reference ground and the power ground, problems with the power ground can lead to interference with the data system. Such interference can be difficult to detect and trace. Usually, however, it stems from the fact that electrical contractors and installers don't care about the length of the neutral and ground wires that lead to each electrical outlet. Unfortunately, when these wires are long, they can act as an antenna for electrical noise. This noise interferes with the digital signals a computer must be able to recognize.

The Effects of Electrical Noise Digital Signals

To understand how electrical noise affects digital signals, imagine that you want to send data represented by the binary number 1011001001101 over the network. The computer converts the binary number to a digital signal. Figure 8-14 shows what the digital signal for 1011001001101 looks like.

FIGURE 8-14
This is the digital signal for 1011001001101

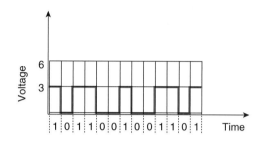

This digital signal is sent over the networking media to the destination. The destination happens to be near an electrical outlet that is fed by long neutral and ground wires. These wires act as an antenna for electrical noise. Figure 8-15 shows what electrical noise looks like. Because the destination computer's chassis is used for both the earth ground and the signal reference ground, this noise interferes with the digital signal that the computer receives. Figure 8-16 shows what happens to the signal when it is combined with electrical noise. Instead of reading the signal as 1011001001101, because of the electrical noise on top of the signal, the computer reads the signal as 1011000101101, as shown in Figure 8-17.

FIGURE 8-15
This graph shows an electrical noise signal.

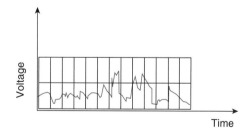

To avoid the problem of electrical noise, it is important to work closely with your electrical contractor and the power company. This will enable you to get the best and shortest electrical ground. One way to do this is to investigate the costs of getting a single power transformer dedicated to your LAN installation area. If you can afford this option, you will be able to control the attachment of other devices to your power circuit. Restricting how and where such devices as motors or high-current electrical heaters attach, you can eliminate much of the electrical noise generated by them.

FIGURE 8-16
Noise interferes with the digital signal that the computer receives.

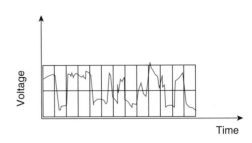

FIGURE 8-17
Because of the electrical noise on top of the signal, the computer reads the signal as 1011000101101.

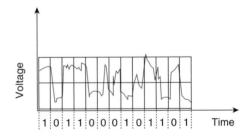

When working with your electrical contractor, you should ask that separate power distribution panels, known as *breaker boxes,* be installed for each office area. Because the neutral wires and ground wires from each outlet come together in the breaker box, taking this step will increase your chances of shortening the length of the signal ground. Although installing individual power distribution panels for every cluster of computers will increase the up-front cost of your power wiring, it will reduce the length of the ground wires and limit several kinds of signal-burying electrical noise.

Surge Suppressors

Surge suppressors are an effective means of addressing the problems of surges and spikes. In addition, it is important that all devices on a network be protected by surge suppressors. Typically, surge suppressors are mounted on a wall power socket to which a networking device is connected. This type of surge suppressor has circuitry that is designed to prevent surges and spikes from damaging the networking device. A surge suppressor protects the networking device by redirecting excess voltages that occur during spikes and surges to a ground. Simply put, a surge suppressor is a device that is capable of absorbing very large currents without damage.

When surge suppressors located in close proximity to networking devices divert large voltages onto the common ground, this can create a large voltage differential between networking devices. As a result, these devices can experience loss of data or, in some instances, damaged circuits.

To avoid these problems, instead of installing individual surge suppressors at each workstation, you should use commercial-quality surge suppressors. These should be located at each power distribution panel rather than in close proximity to networking devices, as shown in Figure 8-18. By placing a commercial-grade surge suppressor near the power panel, you can reduce the impact on the network of voltage surges and spikes diverted to ground.

FIGURE 8-18
A surge suppressor should be located at each power distribution panel.

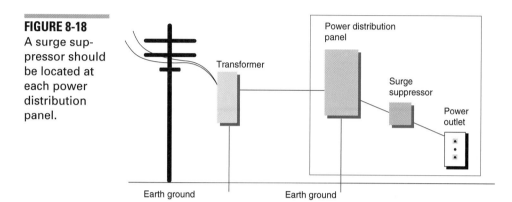

Power Outages

Power outages occur when something, such as a lightning strike, creates a power overload and trips a circuit breaker. Because circuit breakers are designed to automatically reset, they can work from the surrounding power grid to where the source of a short is located in order to reestablish power.

Longer power outages can occur, however. Usually, this happens when some event, such as a severe storm or flood, causes physical disruption of the power transmission system. Unlike short power outages, repairing this type of disruption in service is usually dependent on service crews.

Generally speaking, an uninterruptable power supply (UPS) is designed to handle only short-duration power outages. (You'll learn more about UPSs in the next section.) If a LAN requires uninterrupted power, even during power outages of several hours' duration, then a generator is needed to supplement the backup provided by a UPS.

Uninterruptable Power Supplies

Sags and brownouts are power outages that are of relatively short duration. The problem of sags and brownouts can best be addressed through the use of UPSs. The extent to which a UPS must be provided for a LAN depends on factors such as how much the budget allows, the types of services the LAN must provide its users, how frequently a region can expect to experience such outages, and the typical length and duration of power outages when they occur.

At a minimum, every network file server should be provided with power backup. If power wiring hubs are required, then they must also be supported with power backup. Finally, in extended star topology networks where inter-networking devices such as bridges and routers are used, power backup must be provided to them as well in order to avoid failures in the system. Where possible, power backup should also be provided for all work areas. As every network administrator knows, it does little good to have an operational server and wiring system if he cannot ensure that computers will not go down before users can save their spreadsheets and word processing files.

Generally, a UPS consists of batteries, a battery charger, and a power inverter. The function of the inverter is to convert low-level direct current (DC) voltage of the batteries into the AC voltage normally supplied by the power line to net-working devices. The battery charger is designed to keep the batteries in peak condition during periods when the power line system is functioning normally. As a general rule of thumb, the bigger the batteries in a UPS, the longer the period of time it will be able to support your networking devices during power outages.

A number of vendors have developed UPSs. You will find that these differ in the following ways: the power storage capacity of the batteries, the power delivery capability of the inverter, and whether the inverter is designed to oper-ate all the time or only when the input voltage reaches a specific level. Gener-ally, the more features a UPS has, the more it costs.

Typically, UPS devices that offer fewer features and cost less money are used as standby power systems only. This means that they monitor the power line. If and when a problem occurs, the UPS switches over to the inverter powered by its batteries. The time needed for this switch to occur is referred to as the *transfer time*. Usually, the transfer time lasts for only a few milliseconds. Because the transfer time is of such short duration, this does not usually present a problem for most modern computers, which are designed to coast on their own power supplies for at least a hundred milliseconds.

UPS devices that offer more features and cost more money typically operate online. This means that they constantly supply power from inverters powered by their batteries. While they do this, their batteries continue charging from the power line. Because their inverters supply freshly generated AC, such UPS devices have the added benefit of ensuring that no spikes from the power line reach the networking devices it serves. If and when the AC power line goes down, however, the UPS's batteries smoothly switch from recharging to providing power to the inverter. Consequently, this type of UPS effectively reduces the needed transfer time to zero.

Other UPS products fall into a hybrid category. Although they appear to be online systems, they don't run their inverters all the time. Because of these differences, be sure to investigate the features of any UPS you plan to incorporate as part of a LAN installation.

In any event, a good UPS should be designed to communicate with the file server. This is important so that the file server can be warned to shut down files when the UPS's battery power nears its end. Additionally, a good UPS reports when the server starts to run on battery power and supplies this information to any workstation running on the network after the power outage has occurred.

Summary

- EIA/TIA standards govern the type of networking media that can be used in the horizontal cabling of LANs.

- Any time you install cable, it is important to document what you have done.

- A wiring closet is a specially designed room used for wiring a data or voice network.

- Backbone cabling consists of the backbone cabling runs; intermediate and main cross-connects; mechanical terminations; and patch cords used for backbone-to-backbone cross-connection.

- The IEEE and the EIA/TIA have established standards that allow you to evaluate whether your network is operating at an acceptable level after installation has been completed.

- Cable testers can perform tests that measure the overall capability of a cable run. Cable testers use a feature called wire map to indicate which wire pairs connect to what pins on lugs and sockets.

- If not properly addressed, AC power line noise can present problems for a network.

- The purpose of connecting the safety ground to exposed metal parts of computing equipment is to prevent such metal parts from becoming energized with a hazardous voltage resulting from a wiring fault inside the device.

- Surge suppressors are an effective means of addressing the problems of surges and spikes.

- The problem of sags and brownouts can best be addressed through the use of UPSs.

Review Questions

1. Which grade of UTP cabling described in the EIA/TIA-568B standard is the one most frequently recommended and implemented in installations today?

    A. Category 2

    B. Category 3

    C. Category 4

    D. Category 5

2. What type of fiber-optic cable is required by the EIA/TIA-568B standard for horizontal cabling?

    A. Two-pair 100-ohm cable

    B. Two-pair 150-ohm cable

    C. Two fibers of 62.5/125-ohm multimode cable

    D. Four fibers of 62.5/125-ohm multimode cable

3. What kind of jack must be used for making a connection to a Category 5 UTP cable in a horizontal cabling scheme?

    A. RJ45

    B. TIA 74

    C. UTP 55

    D. EIA 45

4. Why is a punch tool used?

    A. To test the network connection

    B. To securely fasten cable to drop ceiling supports

    C. To attach labels to cables

    D. To make a good electrical connection between the cable and the jack

5. What is the cut sheet used for?

    A. To keep cables orderly and unkinked

    B. To place appropriate numbers on telecommunications outlets and on the patch panel

C. To solve problems associated with crosstalk by consulting the appropriate table entry

D. To translate codes from IEEE to EIA and vice versa

6. What is the difference between an MDF and an IDF?

   A. The MDF contains the primary network server and the major networking devices, and the IDF contains only the necessary additional routers and repeaters.

   B. The MDF is on the lowest floor in a multifloor network, and the IDF is on upper floors.

   C. The MDF has all the bridges, hubs, routers, and ports needed for the network, and the IDF holds any needed repeaters.

   D. The MDF is the primary communications room and the central point in the network, and the IDF is the secondary communications room dependent on the MDF.

7. Which best describes a patch panel's function?

   A. It serves as a temporary fix to network problems.

   B. It acts as a hub for temporary short-term networks often found at conventions and shows.

   C. It acts as a switchboard where horizontal cabling from workstations can be connected to other workstations to form a LAN.

   D. It serves as the center of a Token Ring network and controls the passing and redemption of tokens.

8. What do patch cords do?

   A. They cross-connect computers wired to the patch panel, which allows the LAN to function.

   B. They serve as temporary fixes to network cabling problems.

   C. They connect cabling together when changes in network configuration occur.

   D. They allow the network administrator to reconfigure a LAN with a minimum of new cabling runs.

9. What is the purpose of grounding computing equipment?

   A. To prevent metal parts from becoming energized with a hazardous voltage resulting from a wiring fault inside the device

   B. To connect the safety ground to exposed metal parts of the computing equipment so that minor surges in power can be diverted

   C. To forestall the possibility that a power surge may corrupt the motherboard or the RAM

   D. To prevent any power surge that might harm the end user from traveling through the computer

10. Which best describes a UPS?

   A. It is a device that absorbs excess line voltage caused by lightning strikes.

   B. It is a backup device that provides power during a power failure.

   C. It is a device that allows you to avoid rewiring the network when power fluctuations are continual.

   D. It is a device that powers the multipath connection between computers.

Objectives

After reading this chapter, you will be able to

- Describe the application, presentation, session, and transport layers
- Describe the process of establishing a connection with a peer system
- Describe how to use flow control
- Describe windowing and its processes
- Describe the process of acknowledgment and identify acknowledgment techniques and their purposes

The Application, Presentation, Session, and Transport Layers

Introduction

In Chapter 8, "Structured Cabling and Electricity," you learned about structured cabling and electrical specifications used in local-area networks (LANs). In addition, you learned about wiring and electrical techniques used in building networks.

In this chapter, you will learn about the four upper layers of the Open System Interconnection (OSI) reference model: the application, presentation, session, and transport layers. This chapter briefly explains the functions of the application, presentation, and session layers, and the specific applications for which these layers are responsible. The transport layer is covered in the most detail; we look at how data is transmitted between the sender and the receiver. Finally, this chapter describes the functions and processes used at the transport layer to provide reliable delivery of data as well as to provide effective control of traffic flow.

The Application Layer

In the context of the OSI reference model, the application layer (Layer 7) supports the communicating component of an application. As depicted in Figure 9-1, computer applications can require only information that resides on the computer in which the applications are operating. Several types of computer applications are listed in Figure 9-1. Netscape Navigator and Internet Explorer are probably the most familiar ones.

A word processor might incorporate a file transfer component that allows a document to be transferred electronically over a network. This file transfer component qualifies the word processor as an application in the OSI context and belongs in Layer 7 of the OSI reference model. Web browsers, such as Netscape Navigator and Internet Explorer, also have data transfer components. An example of this is when you go to a Web site: The Web pages are transferred to your computer.

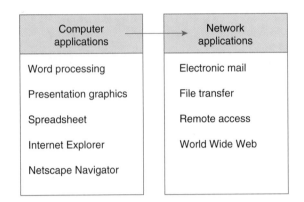

FIGURE 9-1
The communicating component of an application is supported by the application layer.

The OSI application layer includes actual applications as well as application service elements (ASEs). ASEs allow easy communication from applications to lower layers. The three most important ASEs are association control service element (ACSE), remote operations service element (ROSE), and reliable transfer service element (RTSE). ACSE associates application names with one another in preparation for application-to-application communication. ROSE implements a generic request–reply mechanism that permits remote operations in a manner similar to that of remote-procedure calls (RPCs). RTSE aids reliable delivery by making session-layer constructs easy to use.

Five common OSI applications are

- *Common Management Information Protocol (CMIP)*—Provides network management capabilities. Like SNMP and NetView, CMIP allows exchange of management information between end systems and management stations (which are also end systems).

- *Directory services (DSs)*—Derived from the Consultative Committee for International Telegraph and Telephone (CCITT; now referred to as the International Telecommunication Union Telecommunication Standardization Sector [ITU-T]) X.500 specification, this service provides distributed database capabilities useful for upper-layer node identification and addressing.

- *File Transfer, Access, and Management (FTAM)*—Provides file transfer service. In addition to classical file transfer, for which FTAM provides numerous options, FTAM also offers distributed file access facilities in the spirit of NetWare from Novell, Inc., or Network File System (NFS) from Sun Microsystems, Inc.

- *Message handling systems (MHSs)*—Provides an underlying transport mechanism for electronic messaging applications and other applications desiring store-and-forward services. Although they accomplish similar purposes, MHS is not the same as Novell's NetWare MHS.

- *Virtual Terminal Protocol (VTP)*—Provides terminal emulation. In other words, it allows a computer system to appear to a remote end system as if it were a directly attached terminal. With VTP, users can, for example, run remote jobs on mainframes.

The Presentation Layer

Layer 6 of the OSI reference model, the presentation layer, is typically a pass-through protocol for information from adjacent layers. This allows communication between applications on diverse computer systems in a manner that's transparent to the applications.

The presentation layer provides code formatting and conversion. Code formatting is used to make sure that applications have meaningful information to process. If necessary, this layer can translate between different data formats.

The presentation layer is not only concerned with the format and representation of data. It is also concerned with the data structure programs use. Thus, Layer 6 arranges how data will be organized when it is transferred.

To see how this works, imagine that you have two systems. One system uses extended binary coded decimal interchange code (EBCDIC), such as IBM mainframe, and the other uses American Standard Code for Information Interchange (ASCII; most other computer manufacturers) to represent data. When the two systems need to communicate, the presentation layer is needed to convert and translate between the two different formats.

Another function handled at the presentation layer is the encryption of data. Encryption is used when there is a need to protect information as it is being transmitted from unauthorized receivers. To accomplish this task, processes and codes located in the presentation layer must convert the data. Still other routines located in the presentation layer compress text and convert graphic images into bit streams so they can be transmitted across a network.

Presentation-layer standards also guide how graphic images are presented. As shown in Figure 9-2, PICT, a picture format used to transfer QuickDraw graphics between Macintosh and PowerPC programs, can be used. Another presentation format that can be used is the tagged image file format (TIFF). Typically, TIFF is used for high-resolution bitmapped images. Still another presentation-layer standard that can be used for graphic images is from the Joint Photographic Experts Group; in common day-to-day usage, you see this standard simply referred to as JPEG.

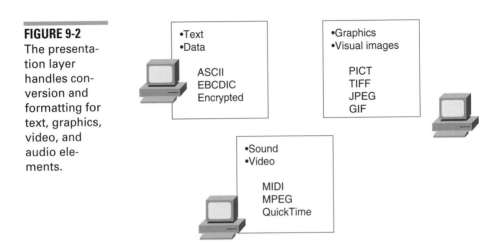

FIGURE 9-2
The presentation layer handles conversion and formatting for text, graphics, video, and audio elements.

Still other presentation-layer standards guide the presentation of sound and movies. Included in these standards are the Musical Instrument Digital Interface (MIDI) for digitized music; the Motion Picture Experts Group's standard (MPEG) for the compression and coding of motion video for CDs, digital storage, and bit rates up to 1.5 Mbps; and QuickTime, a standard that handles audio and video for Macintosh and PowerPC programs.

The Session Layer

The OSI session layer (Layer 5) protocol turns the data streams provided by the four lower layers into sessions by implementing various control mechanisms. These mechanisms include accounting, conversation control (that is, determining who can talk when), and session parameter negotiation.

The session layer establishes, manages, and terminates sessions between applications. Essentially, as shown in Figure 9-3, the session layer coordinates service requests and responses that occur when applications communicate between different hosts. Session conversation control is implemented by use of a token, the possession of which provides the right to communicate. The token can be requested, and end systems can be given priorities that provide for unequal token use.

FIGURE 9-3
When applications communicate between different hosts, the session layer coordinates service requests and responses.

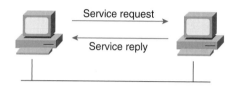

•Network File System (NFS)
•Structured Query Language (SQL)
•Remote-Procedure Call (RPC)
•X Window system
•AppleTalk Session Protocol (ASP)
•DNA Session Control Protocol (SCP)

Service request

Service reply

The Transport Layer

The transport layer defines end-to-end connectivity between host applications. Transport services include four basic services:

- They segment upper-layer applications.
- They establish end-to-end operations.
- They send segments from one end host to another end host.
- They ensure data reliability.

The transport layer, Layer 4, assumes that it can use the network as a "cloud," as shown in Figure 9-4, to send data packets from sender source to receiver destination. The cloud contains issues such as "Which of several paths is best for a given route?" We can start to see the role that routers perform in this process.

FIGURE 9-4
The network is used as a cloud to send data packets.

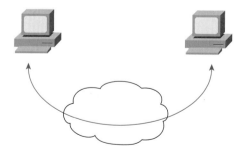

The transport-layer data stream provides transport services from the host to the destination. Services such as these are sometimes referred to as *end-to-end services*. The transport-layer data stream is a logical connection between the endpoints of a network.

Flow Control

As the transport layer sends its data segments, it can also ensure the integrity of the data. One method of doing this is called *flow control*. Flow control avoids the problem of a host at one side of the connection overflowing the buffers in the host at the other side. Overflows can present serious problems because they can result in the loss of data.

Transport-layer services also allow users to request reliable data transport between hosts and destinations. To obtain such reliable transport of data, a connection-oriented relationship is used between the communicating end systems. Reliable transport can accomplish the following:

- Ensure that segments delivered will be acknowledged to the sender.
- Provide for retransmission of any segments that are not acknowledged.
- Put segments back into their correct sequence at the destination.
- Provide congestion avoidance and control.

Establishing a Connection with a Peer System

In the OSI reference model, multiple applications can share the same transport connection. As shown in Figure 9-5, transport functionality is accomplished segment-by-segment. This means that different applications can send data segments on a first-come, first-served basis. Such segments can be intended for the same destination or for many different destinations.

FIGURE 9-5
Multiple applications can share the same transport connection.

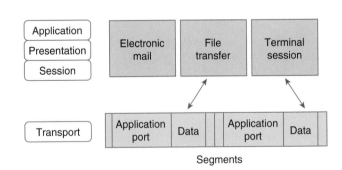

Segments

To see how this works, imagine that you are sending an e-mail message with attached files to someone else on the network. One of the attached files is in Microsoft Word. The other file is in Excel.

When you send your e-mail, software in your device sets a port number for each software application used before transmission begins. It includes extra bits that encode the message type, originating program, and protocols used. As each application used in the e-mail message sends a data stream segment, it uses the previously defined port number. When the destination device receives the data stream, it separates and sorts the segments so that the transport layer can pass the data to the correct destination application. In this way, the data from your Excel file is received and read by the Excel program on the destination device and the Word file is received and read by the Word program on the destination device.

One user of the transport layer must establish a connection-oriented session with its peer system. For data transfer to begin, both the sending and receiving applications inform their respective operating systems that a connection will be initiated. One machine places a call that must be accepted by the other. Protocol software modules in the two operating systems communicate by sending messages across the network to verify that the transfer is authorized and that both sides are ready.

After all synchronization has occurred, a connection is said to be established and the transfer of data begins. During transfer, the two machines continue to communicate with their protocol software to verify that data is received correctly.

Figure 9-6 shows a typical connection between sending and receiving systems. The first handshake requests synchronization. The second and third handshakes acknowledge the initial synchronization request, as well as synchronize connection parameters in the opposite direction. The final handshake segment is an acknowledgment used to inform the destination that both sides agree that a connection has been established. After the connection has been established, data transfer begins.

When data transfer is in progress, congestion can occur for two reasons. First, a high-speed computer might be able to generate traffic faster than a network can transfer it. Second, if many computers simultaneously need to send datagrams to a single destination, that destination can experience congestion, although no single source caused the problem.

FIGURE 9-6
A typical connection between sending and receiving systems.

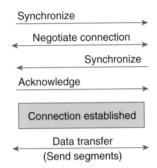

When datagrams arrive too quickly for a host or gateway to process, they are stored in memory temporarily. If the traffic continues, the host or gateway eventually exhausts its memory and must discard additional datagrams that arrive.

Instead of allowing data to be lost, the transport function can issue a "not ready" indicator to the sender. Acting like a stop sign, this indicator signals the sender to stop sending data. When the receiver can handle additional data, the receiver sends a "ready" transport indicator, which is like a go signal. As shown in Figure 9-7, when it receives this indicator, the sender can resume segment transmission.

Windowing

In the most basic form of reliable connection-oriented data transfer, data packets must be delivered to the recipient in the same order in which they were transmitted. The protocol fails if any data packets are lost, damaged, duplicated, or received in a different order. The basic solution is to have a recipient acknowledge the receipt of every data segment.

If the sender has to wait for an acknowledgment after sending each segment, throughput is low. Because time is available after the sender finishes transmitting the data packet and before the sender finishes processing any received acknowledgment, the interval is used for transmitting more data. The number of data packets the sender is allowed to have outstanding without having received an acknowledgment is known as the *window.*

The Transport Layer

157

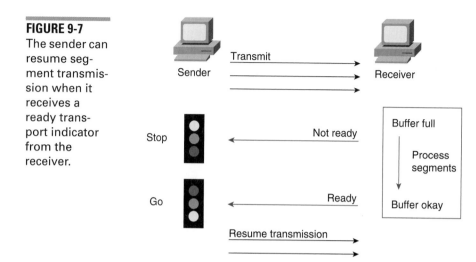

FIGURE 9-7
The sender can resume segment transmission when it receives a ready transport indicator from the receiver.

Windowing is a method of controlling the amount of information transferred end-to-end. Some protocols measure information in terms of the number of packets; others, such as TCP/IP, measure information in terms of the number of bytes.

In Figure 9-8, the sender and receiver are workstations. With a window size of 1, the sender waits for an acknowledgment for every data packet transmitted. With a window size of 3, the sender can transmit three data packets before expecting an acknowledgment.

Acknowledgment

Reliable delivery guarantees that a stream of data sent from one machine will be delivered through a data link to another machine without duplication or data loss. Positive acknowledgment with retransmission is one technique that guarantees reliable delivery of data streams. Positive acknowledgment requires a recipient to communicate with the source, sending back an acknowledgment message when it receives data. The sender keeps a record of each data packet it sends and waits for an acknowledgment before sending the next data packet. The sender also starts a timer when it sends a segment, and it retransmits a segment if the timer expires before an acknowledgment arrives.

Figure 9-9 shows the sender transmitting data packets 1, 2, and 3. The receiver acknowledges receipt of the packets by requesting packet 4. The sender, upon receiving the acknowledgment, sends packets 4, 5, and 6. If packet 5 does not arrive at the destination, the receiver acknowledges with a request to re-send packet 5. The sender re-sends packet 5 and must receive an acknowledgment to continue with the transmission of packet 7.

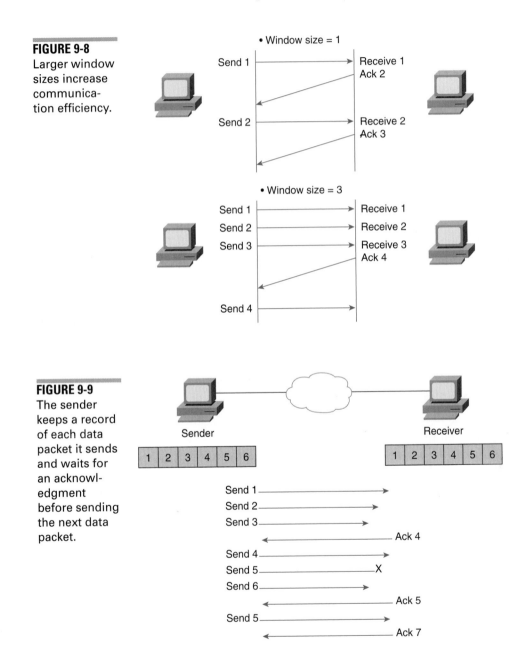

FIGURE 9-8
Larger window sizes increase communication efficiency.

FIGURE 9-9
The sender keeps a record of each data packet it sends and waits for an acknowledgment before sending the next data packet.

Summary

- Each of the upper levels performs its own functions and depends on lower-layer services.

- All four upper layers—transport (Layer 4), session (Layer 5), presentation (Layer 6), and application (Layer 7)—can encapsulate data in end-to-end segments:

  — The application layer supports the communicating component of an application.

  — The presentation layer formats and converts network application data to represent text, graphics, images, video, and audio.

  — Session-layer functions coordinate communication interactions between applications.

  — The transport layer assumes that it can use the network as a cloud to send data packets from sender source to receiver destination.

- Reliable transport-layer functions include

  — Flow control

  — Establishing a connection with a peer system

  — Windowing

  — Acknowledgment

Review Questions

1. What are the four upper layers of the OSI reference model?

   A. Application, presentation, session, and transport

   B. Application, session, network, and physical

   C. Physical, data link, network, and transport

   D. Physical, network, transport, and application

2. Which layer of the OSI reference model supports communication between programs such as e-mail, file transfer, and Web browsers?

   A. The application layer

   B. The presentation layer

   C. The session layer

   D. The transport layer

3. Which best describes flow control?

   A. A method to manage limited bandwidth

   B. A method of connecting two hosts synchronously

   C. A method to ensure data integrity

   D. A method to check data for viruses prior to transmission

4. Which layer of the OSI reference model handles flow control and error recovery?

   A. The application layer

   B. The presentation layer

   C. The transport layer

   D. The network layer

5. Which of the following best describes segmentation?

   A. It breaks data into smaller packets for faster transmission.

   B. It switches hosts from send mode to receive mode continuously during peak traffic periods.

   C. It allows multiple applications to share a transport connection.

   D. It transfers data from the presentation layer to the network layer for encoding and encapsulation.

6. Which of the following controls the amount of information transferred end-to-end and helps enable TCP reliability?

    A. Broadcasting

    B. Windowing

    C. Error recovery

    D. Flow control

7. Which layer of the OSI reference model can translate between different data formats, such as ASCII and EBCDIC?

    A. The application layer

    B. The presentation layer

    C. The session layer

    D. The transport layer

8. Which of the following best describes the function of the presentation layer?

    A. It establishes, manages, and terminates applications.

    B. It supports communication between programs, such as e-mail, file transfer, and Web browsers.

    C. It provides transport services from the host to the destination.

    D. It translates between different data formats, such as ASCII and EBCDIC.

9. ASCII, encryption, QuickTime, and JPEG are all typical of which layer?

    A. The presentation layer

    B. The transport layer

    C. The application layer

    D. The session layer

10. Which layer of the OSI reference model establishes, manages, and terminates communication between applications?

    A. The application layer

    B. The presentation layer

    C. The session layer

    D. The transport layer

Objectives

After reading this chapter, you will be able to

- Describe the function of the application layer in TCP/IP
- Describe the function of the transport layer in TCP/IP
- Describe the function of the network layer in TCP/IP
- Describe ICMP
- Describe ARP
- Describe RARP
- Describe why TCP is a reliable protocol
- Describe why UTP is an unreliable system

Chapter 10

TCP/IP

Introduction

In Chapter 9, "The Application, Presentation, Session, and Transport Layers," you learned about the four upper layers of the OSI reference model. In addition, you learned about the function and processes used at the transport layer to provide reliable delivery of data as well as effective control of traffic flow. In this chapter, you will learn about Transmission Control Protocol/Internet Protocol (TCP/IP) and its operation to ensure communication across any set of interconnected networks.

An Overview of TCP/IP

The TCP/IP suite of protocols was developed as part of the research done by the Defense Advanced Research Projects Agency (DARPA). It was originally developed to provide communication through DARPA. Now, TCP/IP is the *de facto* standard for internetwork communications and serves as the transport protocol for the Internet, enabling millions of computers to communicate globally.

This book focuses on TCP/IP for several reasons:

- TCP/IP is a universally available protocol that you likely will use at work.
- TCP/IP is a useful reference for understanding other protocols because it includes elements that are representative of other protocols.
- TCP/IP is important because the router uses it as a configuration tool.

The TCP/IP Protocol Stack

Internet protocols can be used to communicate across any set of interconnected networks. They are equally well-suited for LAN and WAN communication. The Internet Protocol suite includes not only Layers 3 and 4 specifications (such as IP and TCP), but also specifications for such common applications as e-mail, remote login, terminal emulation, and file transfer.

The TCP/IP protocol stack maps closely to the lower layers of the Open System Interconnection (OSI) reference model, as shown in Figure 10-1. TCP/IP supports all standard physical and data-link protocols.

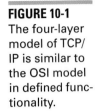

FIGURE 10-1
The four-layer model of TCP/IP is similar to the OSI model in defined functionality.

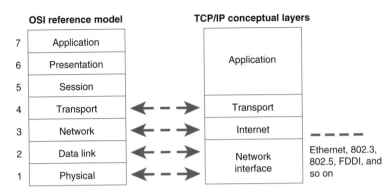

TCP/IP information is transferred in a sequence of datagrams. One message may be transmitted as a series of datagrams that are reassembled into the message at the receiving location.

TCP/IP and the Application Layer

As shown in Figure 10-2, application-layer protocols exist for file transfer, e-mail, and remote login. Network management is also supported at the application layer.

FIGURE 10-2
Some applications, such as Trivial File Transfer Protocol (TFTP) and Simple Network Management Protocol (SNMP), can reside on routers.

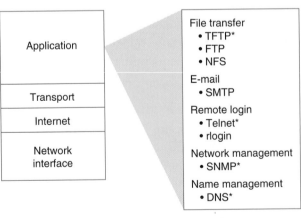

TCP/IP and the Transport Layer

The transport layer performs two functions:

- Flow control, which is provided by sliding windows
- Reliability, which is provided by sequence numbers and acknowledgments

As shown in Figure 10-3, two protocols are provided at the transport layer:

- TCP is a connection-oriented, reliable protocol. It is responsible for breaking messages into segments, reassembling them at the destination station, resending anything that is not received, and reassembling messages from the segments. TCP supplies a virtual circuit between end-user applications.

- User Datagram Protocol (UDP) is connectionless and "unreliable." Although UDP is responsible for transmitting messages, no software checking for segment delivery is provided at this layer; hence the description "unreliable."

FIGURE 10-3
Application developers can select a connection-oriented (TCP) or connectionless (UDP) transport.

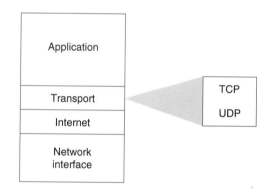

TCP Segment Format

Figure 10-4 shows the fields in the TCP segment, which are defined as follows:

- *Source Port*—Number of the calling port
- *Destination Port*—Number of the called port
- *Sequence Number*—Number used to ensure correct sequencing of the arriving data
- *Acknowledgment Number*—Next expected TCP octet
- *HLEN*—Number of 32-bit words in the header
- *Reserved*—Set to zero
- *Code Bits*—Control functions (such as setup and termination of a session)
- *Window*—Number of octets that the sender is willing to accept

- *Checksum*—Calculated checksum of the header and data fields
- *Urgent Pointer*—Indicates the end of the urgent data
- *Option*—One currently defined: maximum TCP segment size
- *Data*—Upper-layer protocol data

FIGURE 10-4
The TCP segment format includes 12 fields.

Number of bits	16	16	32	32	4	6	6
	Source Port	Destination Port	Sequence Number	Acknowledgment Number	HLEN	Reserved	Code Bits

16	16	16	0 or 32	
Window	Checksum	Urgent Pointer	Option	Data

Port Numbers

Both TCP and UDP use port (or socket) numbers to pass information to the upper layers, as illustrated in Figure 10-5. Port numbers are used to keep track of different conversations crossing the network at the same time.

FIGURE 10-5
Port numbers indicate the upper-layer protocol that is using the transport.

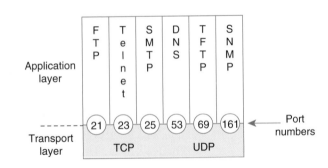

Application software developers agree to use well-known port numbers that are defined in RFC 1700. For example, any conversation bound for the FTP application uses the standard port number 21, as shown in Figure 10-5.

Conversations that do not involve an application with a well-known port number are assigned port numbers randomly chosen from within a specific range instead. As shown in Table 10-1, these port numbers are used as source and destination addresses in the TCP segment.

TABLE 10-1   Reserved TCP and UDP Port Numbers

Decimal	Keyword	Description
0	—	Reserved
1–4	—	Unassigned
5	rje	Remote job entry
7	echo	Echo
9	discard	Discard
11	users	Active users
13	daytime	Daytime
15	netstat	Who is up or netstat
17	quote	Quote of the day
19	chargen	Character generator
20	ftp-data	File Transfer Protocol (data)
21	ftp	File Transfer Protocol
23	telnet	Terminal connection
25	smtp	Simple Mail Transfer Protocol
37	time	Time of day
39	rlp	Resource Location Protocol
42	nameserver	Host name server
43	nicname	Who is
53	domain	Domain Name Server
67	bootps	Bootstrap protocol server
68	bootpc	Bootstrap protocol client
69	tftp	Trivial File Transfer Protocol
75	—	Any private dial-out service
77	—	Any private RJE service
79	finger	Finger

TABLE 10-1   Reserved TCP and UDP Port Numbers (Continued)

Decimal	Keyword	Description
123	ntp	Network Time Protocol
133–159	—	Unassigned
160–223	—	Reserved
224–241	—	Unassigned
242–255	—	Unassigned

Some ports are reserved in both TCP and UDP, but applications might not be written to support them. Port numbers have the following assigned ranges:

- Numbers below 255 are for public applications.
- Numbers from 255 to 1,023 are assigned to companies for salable applications.
- Numbers above 1,023 are unregulated.

An end system uses a port number to select the proper application. As shown in Figure 10-6, an originating source port number—usually some number greater than 1,023—is dynamically assigned by the source host.

FIGURE 10-6
The source port and destination do not need to be the same.

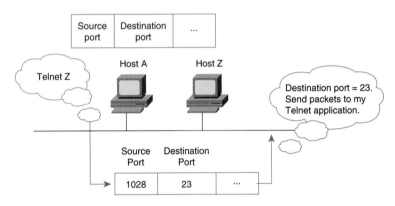

The TCP Three-Way Handshake/Open Connection

For a connection to be established or initialized, the two TCPs use processes or end stations instead of TCPs and must synchronize on each other's initial sequence numbers (ISNs). Sequence numbers are used to track the order of communication and to ensure that there are no missing pieces of data that require multiple packets. The initial sequence number is the starting number used when a TCP connection is established. Exchanging beginning sequence numbers during the connection sequence ensures that lost data can be recovered if problems occur later.

Synchronization is accomplished by exchanging segments carrying the ISNs and a control bit called *SYN*, which stands for *synchronize*. (Segments carrying the SYN bit are also called SYNs.) Successful connection requires a suitable mechanism for choosing an initial sequence and a slightly involved handshake to exchange the ISNs.

Synchronization requires that each side send its own ISN and receive a confirmation and ISN from the other side of the connection. Each side must receive the other side's ISN and send a confirming acknowledgment (ACK) in a specific order, outlined in the following steps:

1. A→B SYN—My sequence number is X.
2. A←B ACK—Your sequence number is X.
3. A←B SYN—My sequence number is Y.
4. A→B ACK—Your sequence number is Y.

Because the second and third steps can be combined in a single message, the exchange is called a three-way handshake/open. As illustrated in Figure 10-7, both ends of a connection are synchronized with a three-way handshake/open connection sequence.

FIGURE 10-7
Data cannot be exchanged until the three-way handshake has been successfully completed.

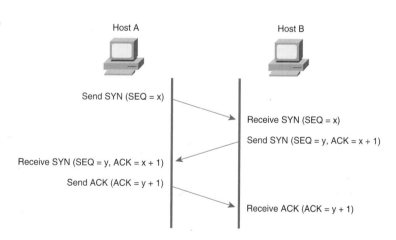

This sequence is like two people talking. The first person wants to talk to the second, so she says, "I would like to talk with you" (SYN). The second person responds, "Good, I want to talk with you" (SYN, ACK). The first person says, "Fine—let's talk" (ACK).

A three-way handshake is necessary because sequence numbers are not tied to a global clock in the network and TCPs may use different mechanisms for picking the ISN. The receiver of the first SYN has no way of knowing if the segment was an old delayed one unless it remembers the last sequence number used on the connection, which is not always possible, and so it must ask the sender to verify this SYN.

At this point, either side can begin communicating, and either side can break the communication because TCP is a peer-to-peer (balanced) communication method.

TCP Simple Acknowledgment and Windowing

Window size refers to the number of segments that can be transmitted while awaiting an acknowledgment. After a host transmits the window-size number of bytes, it must receive an acknowledgment before any more messages can be sent.

The window size determines how much data the receiving station can accept at one time. With a window size of 1, each segment must be acknowledged before another segment is transmitted. This results in inefficient host use of bandwidth.

The purpose of windowing is to improve flow control and reliability. Unfortunately, with a window size of 1, you see a very inefficient use of bandwidth, as shown in Figure 10-8.

The TCP Sliding Window

To govern the flow of data between devices, TCP uses a flow control mechanism. The receiving TCP reports a window to the sending TCP. This window specifies the number of bytes, starting with the acknowledgment number, that the receiving TCP is currently prepared to receive, as shown in Figure 10-9.

TCP uses expectational acknowledgments, meaning that the acknowledgment number refers to the octet expected next. The *sliding* part of *sliding window* refers to the fact that the window size is negotiated dynamically during the TCP session. A sliding window results in more efficient host use of bandwidth because a larger window size allows more data to be transmitted pending acknowledgment.

TCP Sequence and Acknowledgment Numbers

TCP provides sequencing of segments with a forward reference acknowledgment. Each datagram is numbered before transmission. At the receiving station, TCP reassembles the segments into a complete message. If a sequence number is missing in the series, that segment is retransmitted. Segments that are not acknowledged within a given time period result in retransmission.

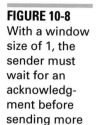

FIGURE 10-8
With a window size of 1, the sender must wait for an acknowledgment before sending more data.

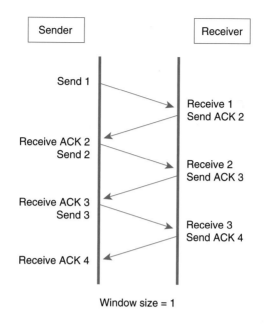

Window size = 1

FIGURE 10-9
A larger window increases flow efficiency.

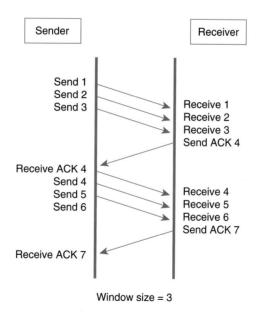

Window size = 3

The sequence and acknowledgment numbers are directional, which means that the communication occurs in both directions. Figure 10-10 illustrates the communication going in one direction. The sequence and acknowledgments take place with the sender on the left. In addition, TCP provides full-duplex communication and, as a result, acknowledgments provide reliability.

FIGURE 10-10
The receiver asks for the next datagram in the sequence.

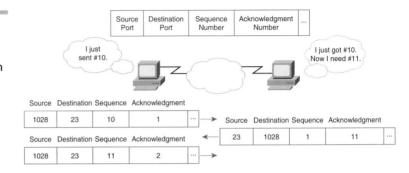

UDP Segment Format

UDP uses no windowing or acknowledgments. Application-layer protocols can provide reliability. UDP is designed for applications that do not need to put together sequences of segments.

Protocols that use UDP include TFTP, SNMP, Network File System (NFS), and Domain Name System (DNS). As you can see in Figure 10-11, a UDP header is relatively small.

FIGURE 10-11
UDP has no sequence or acknowledgment fields.

Number of bits	16	16	16	16	
	Source Port	Destination Port	Length	Checksum	Data...

TCP/IP and the Internet Layer

The Internet layer of the TCP/IP stack corresponds to the network layer of the OSI model. Each layer is responsible for getting packets through an internetwork using software addressing.

As shown in Figure 10-12, several protocols operate at the TCP/IP Internet layer, which corresponds to the OSI network layer:

- IP provides connectionless, best-effort delivery routing of datagrams. It is not concerned with the content of the datagrams. Instead, it looks for a way to move the datagrams to their destinations.

- Internet Control Message Protocol (ICMP) provides control and messaging capabilities.
- Address Resolution Protocol (ARP) determines the data link layer address for known IP addresses.
- Reverse Address Resolution Protocol (RARP) determines network addresses when data link layer addresses are known.

FIGURE 10-12
The OSI network layer corresponds to the TCP/IP Internet layer.

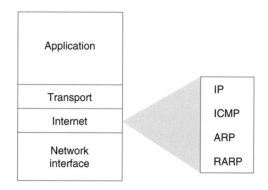

IP Datagram

Figure 10-13 illustrates the format of an IP datagram. An IP datagram contains an IP header and data, and is surrounded by the Media Access Control (MAC) layer header and MAC layer trailer.

FIGURE 10-13
The IP header is variable in length because of the IP Options field.

Number of bits	4	4	8	16	16	3	13	8
	VERS	HLEN	Type of Service	Total Length	Identification	Flags	Frag Offset	TTL

8	16	32	32	var	
Protocol	Header Checksum	Source IP Address	Destination IP Address	IP Options	Data...

Field definitions within this IP datagram are as follows:

- *VERS*—Version number.
- *HLEN*—Header length, in 32-bit words.
- *Type of Service*—How the datagram should be handled.
- *Total Length*—Total length (header plus data).
- *Identification, Flags, and Frag Offset*—Provide fragmentation of datagrams to allow differing MTUs in the Internet.

- *TTL*—The Time To Live countdown field. Every station must decrement this number by one or by the number of seconds it holds onto the packet. When the counter reaches zero, the TTL expires and the packet is dropped. TTL keeps packets from endlessly wandering the Internet in search of non-existent destinations.

- *Protocol*—Upper-layer (Layer 4) protocol sending the datagram. The Protocol field determines the Layer 4 protocol being carried within an IP datagram. Although most IP traffic uses TCP, other protocols can use IP. Each IP header must identify the destination Layer 4 protocol for the datagram. Transport-layer protocols are given numbers, as shown in Figure 10-14, in a manner similar to that used for port numbers. IP includes the protocol number in the protocol field.

- *Header Checksum*—Integrity check on the header.

- *Source IP Address and Destination IP Address*—32-bit IP addresses that identify the end devices involved in the communication.

- *IP Options*—Network testing, debugging, security, and others.

FIGURE 10-14
The Protocol field determines the destination upper-layer protocol.

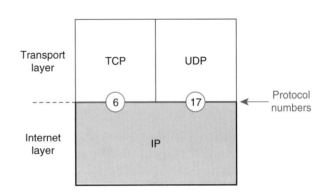

ICMP

ICMP is implemented by all TCP/IP hosts. ICMP messages are carried in IP datagrams and are used to send error and control messages.

ICMP uses the following types of defined messages, some of which are shown in Figure 10-15:

- Destination unreachable
- Time exceeded
- Parameter problem
- Source quench
- Redirect

- Echo
- Echo reply
- Timestamp
- Timestamp reply
- Information request
- Information reply
- Address request
- Address reply

Other messages exist that are not included on this list.

FIGURE 10-15
ICMP provides error and control mechanisms.

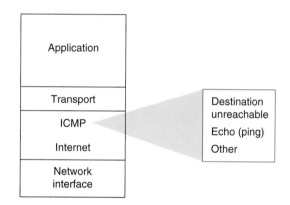

ICMP Testing

If a router receives a packet that it is unable to deliver to its ultimate destination, the router sends an ICMP host unreachable message to the source. An echo request is what a router would originally send to the destination router. As shown in Figures 10-16 and 10-17, the message might be undeliverable because there is no known route to the destination, and an echo reply is a successful reply to a `ping` command. However, results could include other ICMP messages, such as unreachables and timeouts.

ARP

ARP is used to resolve or map a known IP address to a MAC sublayer address to allow communication on a multiaccess medium such as Ethernet. To determine a destination address for a datagram, the ARP cache table is checked. If the address is not in the table, ARP sends a broadcast, looking for the destination station. Every station on the network receives the broadcast.

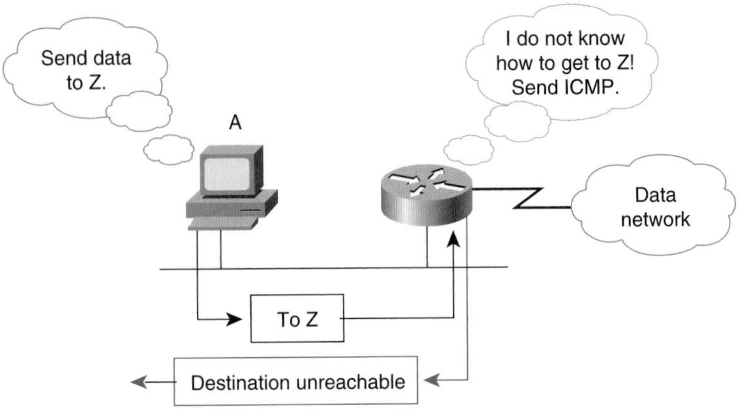

FIGURE 10-16
ICMP indicates that the desired destination is unreachable.

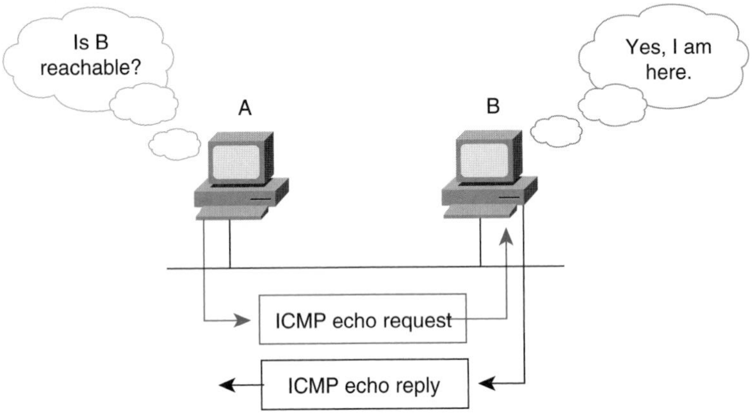

FIGURE 10-17
An echo request is generated by the `ping` command.

The term *local ARP* is used to describe resolving an address when both the requesting host and the destination host share the same media or wire. As shown in Figure 10-18, prior to issuing the ARP, the subnet mask is consulted. In the case shown in Figure 10-18, the mask determines that the nodes are on the same subnet.

RARP

RARP relies on the presence of a RARP server with a table entry or other means to respond to RARP requests (see Figure 10-19). On the local segment, RARP can be used to initiate a remote operating system load sequence.

FIGURE 10-18
ARP is used to get the MAC address.

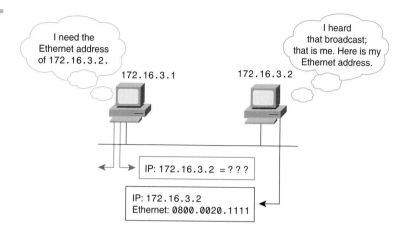

FIGURE 10-19
RARP is used to obtain an IP address using an RARP request.

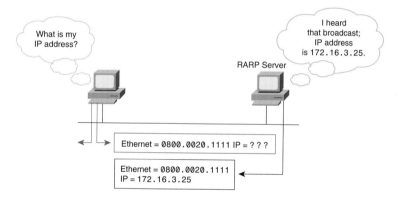

Summary

- The TCP/IP protocol stack maps closely to the lower layers of the OSI reference model and has the following components:
    - Protocols to support file transfer, e-mail, remote login, and other applications
    - Reliable and unreliable transports
    - Connectionless datagram delivery at the network layer
- Application protocols exist for file transfer, e-mail, and remote login. Network management is also supported at the application layer.

- The transport layer performs two functions:
  - Flow control, which is provided by sliding windows
  - Reliability, which is provided by sequence numbers and acknowledgments
- The TCP/IP Internet layer corresponds to the OSI network layer.
- ICMP provides control and message functions at the network layer. ICMP is implemented by all TCP/IP hosts.
- ARP is used to resolve or map a known IP address to a MAC sublayer address to allow communication on a multiaccess medium such as Ethernet.
- RARP relies on the presence of a RARP server with a table entry or other means to respond to RARP requests.

Review Questions

1. Which of the following best describes TCP/IP?

   A. It is a suite of protocols that can be used to communicate across any set of interconnected networks.

   B. It is a suite of protocols that allows LANs to connect into WANs.

   C. It is a suite of protocols that allows for data transmission across a multitude of networks.

   D. It is a suite of protocols that allows different devices to be shared by interconnected networks.

2. Which of the following best describes the purpose of TCP/IP protocol stacks?

   A. They map closely to the OSI reference model's upper layers.

   B. They support all standard physical and data link protocols.

   C. They transfer information in a sequence of datagrams.

   D. They reassemble datagrams into complete messages at the receiving location.

3. Which of the following is one of the protocols found in the transport layer?

   A. UCP

   B. UDP

   C. TDP

   D. TDC

4. What is the purpose of port numbers?

   A. They keep track of different conversations crossing the network at the same time.

   B. Source systems use them to keep a session organized and to select the proper application.

   C. End systems use them to dynamically assign end users to a particular session, depending on their application use.

   D. Source systems generate them to predict destination addresses.

5. Why are TCP three-way handshake/open connections used?

    A. To ensure that lost data can be recovered if problems occur later

    B. To determine how much data the receiving station can accept at one time

    C. To provide efficient use of bandwidth by users

    D. To change binary `ping` responses into information in the upper layers

6. What does a TCP sliding window do?

    A. It makes the window larger so more data can come through at once, which results in more efficient use of bandwidth.

    B. The window size slides to each section of the datagram to receive data, which results in more efficient use of bandwidth.

    C. It allows the window size to be negotiated dynamically during the TCP session, which results in more efficient use of bandwidth.

    D. It limits the incoming data so that each segment must be sent one-by-one, which is an inefficient use of bandwidth.

7. UDP segments use what protocols to provide reliability?

    A. Network-layer protocols

    B. Application-layer protocols

    C. Internet protocols

    D. Transmission Control Protocols

8. What is the purpose of ICMP testing?

    A. To determine whether messages reach their destination and, if they don't, to determine possible reasons why they did not

    B. To make sure that all activity on the network is being monitored

    C. To determine whether the network was set up according to the model

    D. To determine whether the network is in control mode or user mode

9. Assuming the MAC is not in the ARP table, how does a sender find out the destination's MAC address?

    A. It consults its routing table.

    B. It sends a message to all the addresses, searching for the address.

    C. It sends out a broadcast message to the entire LAN.

    D. It sends out a broadcast message to the entire network.

10. Which of the following best describes window size?

A. The maximum size of the window that software can have and still process data rapidly

B. The number of messages that can be transmitted while awaiting an acknowledgment

C. The size of the window, in picas, that must be set ahead of time so data can be sent

D. The size of the window opening on a monitor, which is not always equal to the monitor size

Objectives

After reading this chapter, you will be able to

- Identify the parts in a network address
- Understand distance-vector routing
- Understand link-state routing
- Understand hybrid routing
- Compare the processes used by routers to update routing tables and the problems and solutions encountered when updating routers due to topography changes

Chapter 11

The Network Layer and Routing

Introduction

In Chapter 10, "TCP/IP," you learned about Transmission Control Protocol/Internet Protocol (TCP/IP) and its operation to ensure communication across any set of interconnected networks.

In this chapter, you will learn about the router's use and operations in performing the key internetworking function of the Open System Interconnection (OSI) reference model's network layer, Layer 3. In addition, you will learn the difference between routing and routed protocols and how routers track distance between locations. Finally, you will learn about distance-vector, link-state, and hybrid routing approaches and how each resolves common routing problems.

Cisco Router Configuration

Routers are devices that implement the network service. They provide interfaces for a wide range of links and subnetworks at a wide range of speeds. Routers are active and intelligent network nodes and, thus, can participate in managing the network. Routers manage networks by providing dynamic control over resources and supporting the tasks and goals for networks: connectivity, reliable performance, management control, and flexibility.

In addition to the basic switching and routing functions, routers have implemented a variety of value-added features that help to improve the cost-effectiveness of the network. These features include sequencing traffic based on priority and traffic filtering.

Typically, routers are required to support multiple protocol stacks, each with its own routing protocols, and to allow these different environments to operate in parallel. In practice, routers also incorporate bridging functions and can serve as a limited form of hub. In this chapter, you will learn about operations and techniques for configuring Cisco routers to operate the protocols and many of the media shown in Figure 11-1.

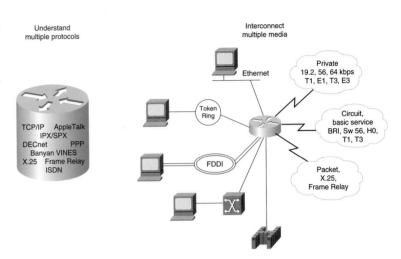

FIGURE 11-1
Cisco router configuration of multiple protocols is used to interconnect multiple media.

Network Layer Basics

The network layer interfaces to networks and provides the best end-to-end packet delivery services to its user, the transport layer. The network layer sends packets from the source network to the destination network.

In this section, you will learn about the general performance of the network layer, including how it determines and communicates the chosen path to a destination, how protocol addressing schemes work and vary, and how routing protocols work.

Network Layer Path Determination

Which path should traffic take through the cloud of networks? Path determination occurs at the network layer. The path determination function enables a router to evaluate the available paths to a destination and to establish the best handling method for a packet.

Routing protocols use network topology information when evaluating network paths. This information can be configured by the network administrator or collected through dynamic processes running in the network.

The network layer interfaces to networks and provides best-effort end-to-end packet delivery services to its user, the transport layer. The network layer sends packets from the source network to the destination network based on the IP routing table.

After the router determines which path to use, it can proceed with switching the packet: Taking the packet it accepted on one interface and forwarding it to another interface or port that reflects the best path to the packet's destination.

The Communicate Path

To be truly practical, a network must consistently represent the paths available between routers. As Figure 11-2 shows, each line between the routers has a number that the routers use as a network address. These addresses must convey information that can be used by a routing process. This means that an address must have information about the path of media connections the routing process uses to pass packets from a source toward a destination.

FIGURE 11-2
Addresses represent the path of media connections.

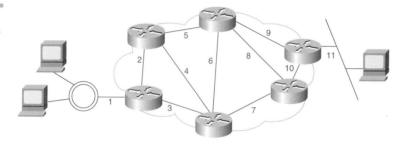

Using these addresses, the network layer can provide a relay connection that interconnects independent networks. The consistency of Layer 3 addresses across the entire internetwork also improves the use of bandwidth by preventing unnecessary broadcasts. Broadcasts invoke unnecessary process overhead and waste capacity on any devices or links that do not need to receive the broadcast.

By using consistent end-to-end addressing to represent the path of media connections, the network layer can find a path to the destination without unnecessarily burdening the devices or links on the internetwork with broadcasts.

Addressing: The Network and the Host

The network address consists of a network portion and a host portion used by the router within the network cloud. Both are needed to deliver packets from source to destination.

The router uses the network address to identify the source or destination network of a packet within a network. Figure 11-3 shows three network numbers—1.1, 2.1, and 3.1—emanating from the router.

FIGURE 11-3
A network address consists of a network portion and a host portion.

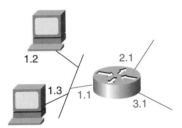

Network	Host
1	1 2 3
2	1
3	1

For some network-layer protocols, this relationship is established by a network administrator who assigns network addresses according to an internetwork addressing plan. For other network-layer protocols, assigning addresses is partially or completely dynamic.

Most network-protocol addressing schemes use some form of a host or node address. For example, in Figure 11-3, three hosts are shown sharing the network number 1.

Routing Using Network Addresses

Routers generally relay a packet from one data link to another. To relay a packet, a router uses two basic functions: a path determination function and a switching function.

Figure 11-4 illustrates how routers use addressing for routing and switching functions. The network portion of the address is used to make path selections, and the node portion of the address refers the router port to the path.

A router is responsible for passing the packet to the next network along the path. The router uses the network portion of the address to make path selections.

FIGURE 11-4
The network portion of the address is used to make path selections.

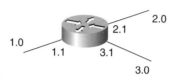

Destination network	Direction and router port
1.0	← 1.1
2.0	→ 2.1
3.0	↘ 3.1

The switching function allows a router to accept a packet on one interface and forward it on a second interface. The path determination function enables the router to select the most appropriate interface for forwarding a packet. The node portion of the address refers to a specific port on the router that leads to an adjacent router in that direction.

Routed Versus Routing Protocols

Confusion often exists between the similar terms *routing protocol* and *routed protocol*, as illustrated in Figure 11-5. The following provides some clarification:

- *Routed protocols*—Any network protocol that provides enough information in its network layer address to allow a packet to be forwarded from host to host based on the addressing scheme. Routed protocols define the format and use of the fields within a packet. Packets generally are conveyed from end system to end system. The Internet Protocol (IP) is an example of a routed protocol.

- *Routing protocol*—Supports a routed protocol by providing mechanisms for sharing routing information. Routing protocol messages move between routers. A routing protocol allows the routers to communicate with other routers to update and maintain tables. Examples of routing protocols are Routing Information Protocol (RIP), Interior Gateway Routing Protocol (IGRP), Enhanced Interior Gateway Routing Protocol (EIGRP), and Open Shortest Path First (OSPF).

FIGURE 11-5
A routed protocol is used to direct traffic and a routing protocol is used between routers to maintain tables.

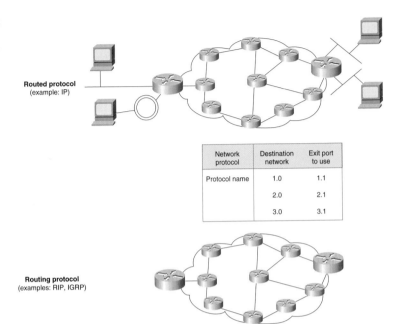

Network protocol	Destination network	Exit port to use
Protocol name	1.0	1.1
	2.0	2.1
	3.0	3.1

Network-Layer Protocol Operations

When a host application needs to send a packet to a destination on a different network, a data-link frame is received on one of a router's interfaces. The network layer examines the header to determine the destination network and then references the routing table that associates networks to outgoing interfaces, as shown in Figure 11-6.

The packet is again encapsulated in the data-link frame for the selected interface and queued for delivery to the next hop in the path.

This process occurs each time the packet switches through another router. At the router connected to the network containing the destination host, the packet is again encapsulated in the destination LAN's data-link frame type and delivered to the destination host.

Multiprotocol Routing

Routers are capable of supporting multiple independent routing protocols and maintaining routing tables for several routed protocols concurrently. This capability allows a router to deliver packets from several routed protocols over the same data links. (See Figure 11-7.)

FIGURE 11-6
Each router provides its services to support upper-layer functions.

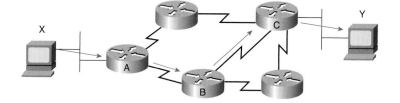

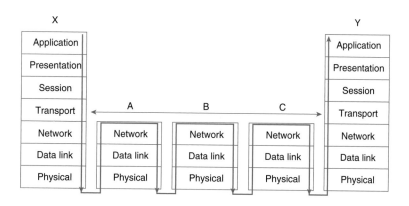

FIGURE 11-7
Routers pass traffic from all routed protocols over the network.

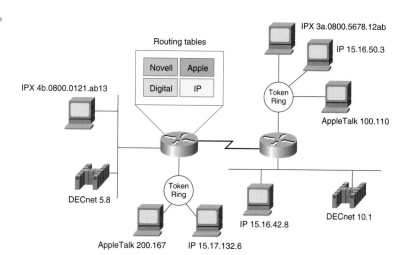

Static Versus Dynamic Routes

Static knowledge is administered manually: A network administrator enters it into the router's configuration. The administrator must manually update this static route entry whenever a network topology change requires an update.

Dynamic knowledge works differently. After the network administrator enters configuration commands to start dynamic routing, route knowledge is updated automatically by a routing process whenever new information is received from the network. Changes in dynamic knowledge are exchanged between routers as part of the update process.

A Static Route Example

Static routing has several useful applications that involve a network administrator's special knowledge about network topology. One such application is security. Dynamic routing tends to reveal everything known about a network. For security reasons, it might be appropriate to hide parts of a network. Static routing allows an internetwork administrator to specify what is advertised about restricted partitions.

When a network is accessible by only one path, a static route to the network can be sufficient. This type of partition is called a *stub network*. Configuring static routing to a stub network avoids the overhead of dynamic routing. (See Figure 11-8.)

FIGURE 11-8
Static routing entries can eliminate the need to allow route updates across the WAN link.

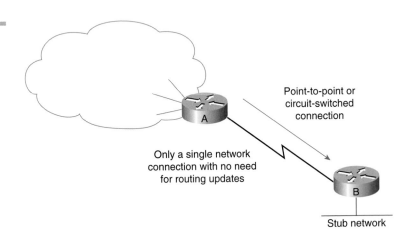

Point-to-point or circuit-switched connection

Only a single network connection with no need for routing updates

Stub network

A Default Route Example

Figure 11-9 shows a use for a *default route*—a routing table entry that is used to direct frames for which the next hop is not explicitly listed in the routing table. Default routes can be set as the result of the administrator's static configuration.

FIGURE 11-9
A default route is used if the next hop is not explicitly listed in the routing table.

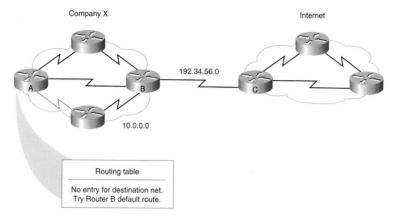

Routing table

No entry for destination net.
Try Router B default route.

In this example, Company X routers possess specific knowledge of the topology of the Company X network, but not of other networks. Maintaining knowledge of every other internetwork accessible by way of the Internet cloud is unnecessary and unreasonable, if not impossible.

Instead of maintaining specific network knowledge, each router in Company X is informed by the default route that it can reach any unknown destination by directing the packet to the Internet.

Adapting to Topology Changes

The network shown in Figure 11-10 adapts differently to topology changes depending on whether it uses statically or dynamically configured knowledge.

FIGURE 11-10
Dynamic routing enables routers to automatically use backup routes whenever necessary.

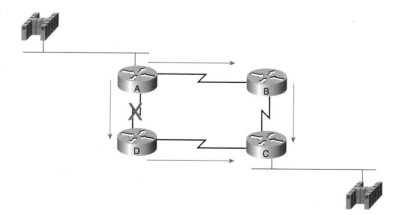

Static routing allows the routers to properly route a packet from network to network. The router refers to its routing table and follows the static knowledge there to relay the packet to Router D. Router D does the same and relays the packet to Router C. Router C delivers the packet to the destination host.

But what happens if the path between Router A and Router D fails? Obviously, Router A will not be able to relay the packet to Router D with a static route. Until Router A is manually reconfigured to relay packets by way of Router B, communication with the destination network is impossible.

Dynamic routing offers more automatic flexibility. According to the routing table generated by Router A, a packet can reach its destination over the preferred route through Router D. However, a second path to the destination is available by way of Router B. When Router A recognizes that the link to Router D is down, it adjusts its routing table, making the path through Router B the preferred path to the destination. The routers continue sending packets over this link.

When the path between Routers A and D is restored to service, Router A can once again change its routing table to indicate a preference for the counterclockwise path through Routers D and C to the destination network.

Dynamic routing protocols can also redirect traffic between different paths in a network.

Dynamic Routing Operations

The success of dynamic routing depends on two basic router functions:

- Maintenance of a routing table
- Timely distribution of knowledge—in the form of routing updates—to other routers (see Figure 11-11)

FIGURE 11-11
Routing protocols maintain and distribute routing information.

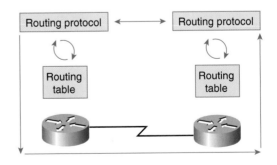

Dynamic routing relies on a routing protocol to share knowledge. A routing protocol defines the set of rules used by a router when it communicates with neighboring routers. For example, a routing protocol describes

- How updates are sent
- What knowledge is contained in these updates
- When to send this knowledge
- How to locate recipients of the updates

Representing Distance with Metrics

When a routing algorithm updates the routing table, its primary objective is to determine the best information to include in the table. Each routing algorithm interprets *best* in its own way. The algorithm generates a number—called the *metric*—for each path through the network. Typically, the smaller the metric number, the better the path. (See Figure 11-12.)

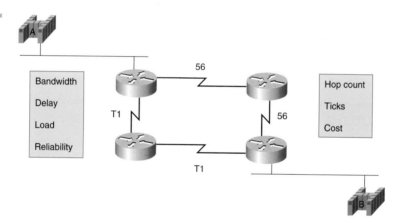

FIGURE 11-12
A variety of metrics can be used to define the best path.

Metrics can be calculated based on a single characteristic of a path. You can calculate more complex metrics by combining several characteristics. As shown in Figure 11-13, several path characteristics are used in metric calculations.

The metrics most commonly used by routers follow:

- *Hop count*—The number of routers a packet must go through to reach a destination. The lower the hop count, the better the path. Path length is used to indicate the sum of hops to a destination.
- *Bandwidth*—The data capacity of a link. For instance, normally, a T1 link at 1.544 Mbps is preferable to a 64-kbps leased line.
- *Delay*—The length of time required to move a packet from source to destination.

- *Load*—The amount of activity on a network resource such as a router or link.

- *Reliability*—The error rate of each network link.

- *Ticks*—The delay on a data link using IBM PC clock ticks (approximately 55 milliseconds).

- *Cost*—The arbitrary value, usually based on bandwidth, dollar expense, or other measurement, that is assigned by a network administrator.

FIGURE 11-13
In order to calculate metrics, several path characteristics are used.

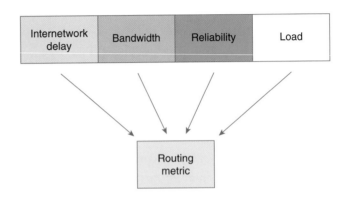

Routing Protocols

Most routing algorithms can be classified into three basic algorithms—distance-vector, link-state, and hybrid routing—as shown in Figure 11-14:

- The distance-vector routing approach determines the direction (vector) and distance to any link in the network.

- The link-state (also called shortest path first) approach re-creates the exact topology of the entire network (or at least the partition in which the router is situated).

- The hybrid approach combines aspects of the link-state and distance vector algorithms.

The following sections cover procedures and problems for each of these routing algorithms and present techniques for minimizing the problems.

The routing algorithm is fundamental to dynamic routing. Whenever the topology of the network changes because of growth, reconfiguration, or failure, the network knowledge base must also change; this disrupts routing.

FIGURE 11-14
Distance-vector, link-state, and hybrid routing represent most routing algorithms.

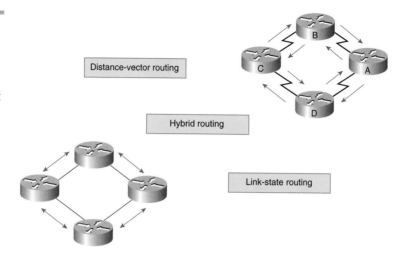

The knowledge needs to reflect an accurate, consistent view of the new topology. When all routers use a consistent view of network topology, *convergence* occurs. When all routers in an internetwork are operating with the same knowledge, the internetwork is said to have *converged*. The process and time required for router reconvergence varies from one routing protocol to another. Fast convergence is a desirable network feature because it reduces the amount of time that routers have outdated knowledge for making routing decisions that could be incorrect, wasteful, or both.

Distance-Vector Routing Algorithms

Distance-vector–based routing algorithms (also known as *Bellman-Ford algorithms*) periodically pass copies of a routing table from router to router. Regular updates between routers communicate topology changes.

Each router receives a routing table from its neighbor. For example, in Figure 11-15, Router B receives information from Router A. Router B adds a distance-vector number (such as a number of hops) that increases the distance vector, and then passes the routing table to its other neighbor, Router C. This same step-by-step process occurs in all directions between routers that are neighbors.

In this way, the algorithm accumulates network distances so that it can maintain a database of network topology information. Distance-vector algorithms do not allow a router to know the exact topology of an internetwork.

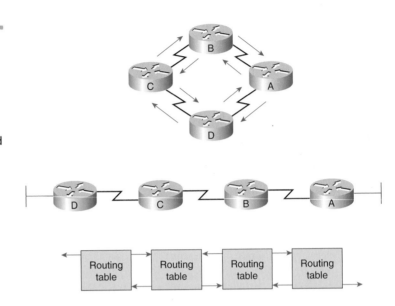

FIGURE 11-15
Distance-vector routers periodically pass copies of their routing table to neighbor routers and accumulate distance vectors.

Distance-Vector Network Discovery

Each router using distance-vector routing begins by identifying, or *discovering*, its own neighbors. In Figure 11-16, the port to each directly connected network is shown as having a distance of 0.

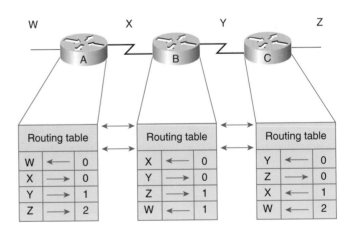

FIGURE 11-16
Distance-vector routers discover the best path to the destination from each neighbor.

As the distance-vector network discovery process proceeds, routers discover the best path to destination networks based on information from each neighbor.

For example, Router A learns about other networks based on information it receives from Router B. Each of these other network entries in the routing table has an accumulated distance vector to show how far away that network is in the given direction.

Distance-Vector Topology Changes

When the topology in a distance-vector protocol network changes, routing table updates must occur. As with the network discovery process, topology change updates proceed step-by-step from router to router, as shown in Figure 11-17.

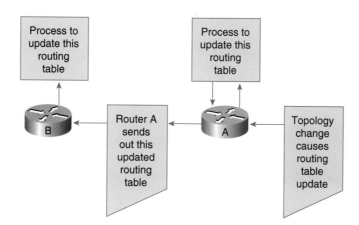

FIGURE 11-17
Updates proceed step-by-step from router to router.

Distance-vector algorithms call for each router to send its entire routing table to each of its adjacent neighbors. Distance-vector routing tables include information about the total path cost (defined by its metric) and the logical address of the first router on the path to each network it knows about.

Problem: Routing Loops

Routing loops can occur if the network's slow convergence on a new configuration causes inconsistent routing entries. Figure 11-18 illustrates how a routing loop can occur:

1. Just before the failure of Network 1, all routers have consistent knowledge and correct routing tables. The network is said to have converged. Assume for the remainder of this example that Router C's preferred path to Network 1 is by way of Router B, and Router C has a distance of 3 to Network 1 in its routing table.

2. When Network 1 fails, Router E sends an update to Router A. Router A stops routing packets to Network 1, but Routers B, C, and D continue to route because they have not yet been informed about the failure. When Router A sends out its update, Routers B and D stop routing to Network1; however, Router C is still not updated. To Router C,

Network 1 is still reachable via Router B. This would be the new pre-ferred route with a metric of three hops.

3. Now Router C sends a periodic update to Router D, indicating a path to Network 1 by way of Router B. Router D changes its routing table to reflect this good, but incorrect, information, and propagates the information to Router A. Router A propagates the information to Routers B and E, and so on. Any packet destined for Network 1 now loops from Router C to B to A to D, and back to C.

FIGURE 11-18
Router A updates its table to reflect the new but erroneous hop count.

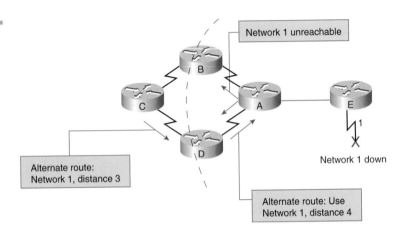

Problem: Counting to Infinity

Let's continue using our example from the previous section. The invalid updates about Network 1 continue to loop until some other process can stop the looping. This condition, called *count to infinity*, continuously loops packets around the network, despite the fundamental fact that the destination Network 1 is down. While the routers are counting to infinity, the invalid information allows a routing loop to exist.

Without countermeasures to stop the process, the distance vector of hop count increments each time the packet passes through another router (see Figure 11-19). These packets loop through the network because of wrong information in the routing tables.

Solution: Defining a Maximum

Distance-vector routing algorithms are self-correcting, but the routing loop problem can require a count to infinity first. To avoid this prolonged problem, distance-vector protocols define *infinity* as some maximum number. This number refers to a routing metric (for example, a simple hop count).

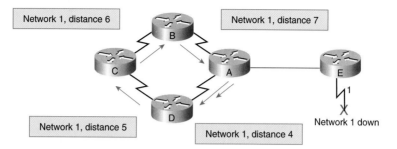

FIGURE 11-19
Routing loops
increment the
distance vector.

With this approach, the routing protocol permits the routing to loop until the
metric exceeds its maximum allowed value. Figure 11-20 shows this defined
maximum as 16 hops; for hop-count distance vectors, a maximum of 15 hops
is commonly used. In any case, when the metric value exceeds the maximum,
Network 1 is considered unreachable.

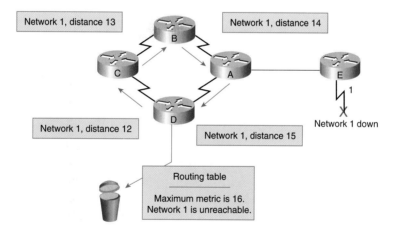

FIGURE 11-20
You can specify
a maximum
distance vec-
tor as infinity.

Solution: Split Horizon

One way to eliminate routing loops and speed up convergence is through the
technique called *split horizon*. The logic behind split horizon is that it is never
useful to send information about a route back in the direction from which the
information originally came.

Another possible source for a routing loop occurs when incorrect information
sent back to a router contradicts the correct information it sent. Here is how
this problem occurs:

1. Router A passes an update to Router B and Router D indicating that Network 1 is down. However, Router C transmits an update to Router B indicating that Network 1 is available at a distance of 4 by way of Router D.

2. Router B concludes incorrectly that Router C still has a valid path to Network 1, although at a much less favorable metric. Router B sends an update to Router A, advising A of the "new" route to Network 1.

3. Router A now determines that it can send to Network 1 by way of Router B; Router B determines that it can send to Network 1 by way of Router C; and Router C determines that it can send to Network 1 by way of Router D. Any packet introduced into this environment will loop between routers.

Split horizon attempts to avoid this situation. As shown in Figure 11-21, if a routing update about Network 1 arrives from Router A, Router B or D cannot send information about Network 1 back to Router A. Split horizon thus reduces incorrect routing information and reduces routing overhead.

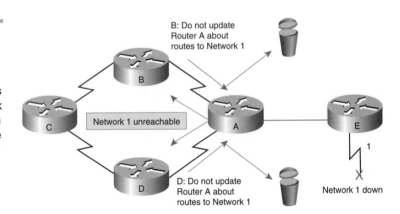

FIGURE 11-21
Split horizon ensures that information about a route is never sent back in the direction from which the original packet came.

Solution: Hold-Down Timers

Hold-down timers are used to prevent regular update messages from inappropriately reinstating a route that may have gone bad. You can avoid the count-to-infinity problem by using hold-down timers, which work as follows:

1. When a router receives an update from a neighbor, indicating that a previously accessible network is now inaccessible, the router marks the route as inaccessible and starts a hold-down timer, as shown in Figure 11-22. If an update indicating that the network is again accessible is received from the same neighbor at any time before the hold-down timer expires, the router marks the network as accessible and removes the hold-down timer.

2. If an update arrives from a different neighboring router with a better metric than originally recorded for the network, the router marks the network as accessible and removes the hold-down timer.

3. If at any time before the hold-down timer expires an update is received from a different neighboring router with a poorer metric, the update is ignored. Ignoring an update with a poorer metric when a hold-down is in effect allows more time for the knowledge of a disruptive change to propagate through the entire network.

FIGURE 11-22
A router keeps an entry for the network down state, allowing time for other routers to re-compute for this topology change.

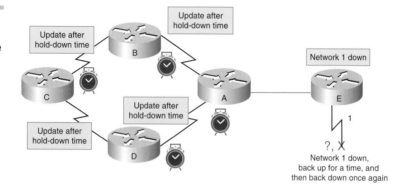

Link-State Routing Algorithms

The second basic algorithm used for routing is the link-state algorithm. Link-state routing algorithms, also known as *shortest path first (SPF) algorithms*, maintain a complex database of topology information. Whereas the distance-vector algorithm has nonspecific information about distant networks and no knowledge of distant routers, a link-state routing algorithm maintains full knowledge of distant routers and how they interconnect.

Link-state routing uses link-state advertisements (LSAs), a topological database, the SPF algorithm, the resulting SPF tree, and a routing table of paths and ports to each network (see Figure 11-23). The following sections cover these processes and databases in more detail.

Engineers have implemented the link-state concept in OSPF routing. RFC 1583 contains a description of OSPF link-state concepts and operations.

Link-State Network Discovery

Link-state network discovery mechanisms are used to create a common picture of the entire network. All link-state routers share this view of the network. This is similar to having several identical maps of a town. In Figure 11-24, four networks (W, X, Y, and Z) are connected by three link-state routers.

FIGURE 11-23
The link-state algorithm updates topology information on all other routers.

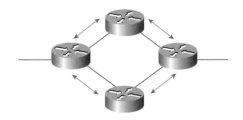

Link-state advertisement packets

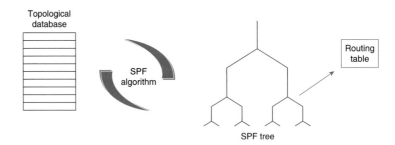

FIGURE 11-24
In link-state routing, routers calculate the shortest path to destinations in parallel.

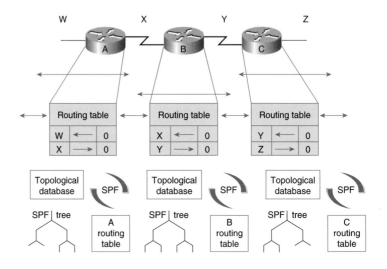

Network discovery for link-state routing uses the following processes:

1. Routers exchange LSAs with each other. Each router begins with directly connected networks for which it has direct information.

2. Next, the routers, in parallel with one another, construct a topological database consisting of all the LSAs from the internetwork.

3. The SPF algorithm computes network reachability, determining the shortest path to each of the other networks in the link-state protocol internetwork. The router constructs this logical topology of shortest paths as an SPF tree, with itself as root. This tree expresses paths from the router to all destinations.

4. The router lists its best paths and the ports to these destination networks in the routing table. It also maintains other databases of topology elements and status details.

Link-State Topology Changes

Link-state algorithms rely on routers having a common view of the network. As shown in Figure 11-25, whenever a link-state topology changes, the routers that first become aware of the change send information to other routers or to a designated router that all other routers can use for updates. This entails the sending of common routing information to all routers in the network. To achieve convergence, each router does the following:

- Keeps track of its neighbors: the neighbor's name, whether the neighbor is up or down, and the cost of the link to the neighbor.

- Constructs an LSA packet that lists its neighbor router names and link costs. This includes new neighbors, changes in link costs, and links to neighbors that have gone down.

- Sends out the LSA packet so that all other routers receive it.

- When it receives an LSA packet, records the LSA packet in its database so that it can store the most recently generated LSA packet from each other router.

- Using accumulated LSA packet data to construct a complete map of the network topology, the router proceeds from this common starting point to rerun the SPF algorithm and compute routes to every network destination.

Each time an LSA packet causes a change to the link-state database, the link-state algorithm recalculates the best paths and updates the routing table. Then every router takes the topology change into account as it determines the shortest paths to use for packet switching.

FIGURE 11-25
Update processes proceed using the same link-state update.

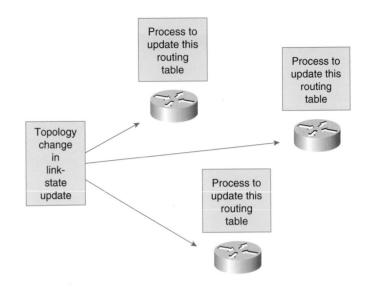

Link-State Concerns

As shown in Figure 11-26, there are two main link-state concerns:

■ *Processing and memory requirements*—Running link-state routing protocols in most situations requires that routers use more memory and perform more processing. Network administrators must ensure that the routers they select are capable of providing these resources for routing.

Routers keep track of their neighbors and the networks they reach through other routing nodes. For link-state routing, memory must hold information from various databases, the topology tree, and the routing table.

Computing the shortest path requires a processing task proportional to the number of links in the internetwork multiplied by the number of routers in the network.

■ *Bandwidth requirements*—During the initial discovery process, all routers using link-state routing protocols send LSA packets to all other routers. This action floods the internetwork as routers make their peak demand for bandwidth and temporarily reduces the bandwidth available for routed traffic that carries user data.

After this initial flooding, link-state routing protocols generally require only internetwork bandwidth to send infrequent or event-triggered LSA packets that reflect topology changes.

FIGURE 11-26

The two main link-state concerns are processing and memory required for link-state routing and bandwidth consumed for the link-state flood.

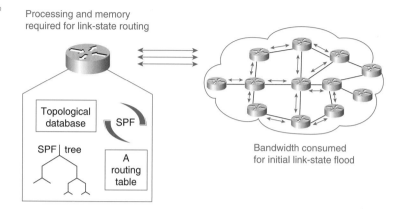

Processing and memory required for link-state routing

Topological database

SPF

SPF tree

A routing table

Bandwidth consumed for initial link-state flood

Problem: Link-State Updates

The most complex and important aspect of link-state routing is making sure all routers get all the LSA packets necessary. Routers with different sets of LSAs calculate routes based on different topological data. As shown in Figure 11-27, routes become unreachable as a result of the disagreement among routers about a link. Here is an example of inconsistent path information:

- Suppose that Network 1 between Routers C and D goes down. As discussed earlier, both routers construct an LSA packet to reflect this unreachable status.

- Soon afterward, Network 1 comes back up; another LSA packet reflecting this next topology change is needed.

- If the original "Network 1, Unreachable" message from Router C uses a slow path for its update, that update comes later. This LSA packet can arrive at Router A after Router D's "Network 1, Back Up Now" LSA.

- With unsynchronized LSAs, Router A can face a dilemma about which SPF tree to construct: Does it use paths containing Network 1 or without Network 1, which was most recently reported as unreachable?

If LSA distribution to all routers is not done correctly, link-state routing can result in invalid routes.

Scaling up with link-state protocols on very large internetworks can expand the problem of faulty LSA packet distribution.

If one part of the network comes up first with other parts coming up later, the order for sending and receiving LSA packets will vary. This variation can alter and impair convergence. Routers might learn about different versions of the topology before they construct their SPF trees and routing tables. On a large network, parts that update more quickly can cause problems for parts that update more slowly.

FIGURE 11-27
Unsynchro-
nized updates
and inconsis-
tent path deci-
sions make
routers
unreachable.

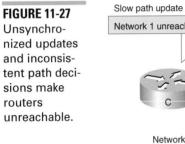
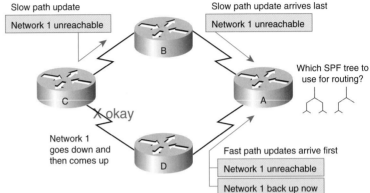

Solution: Link-State Mechanisms

Link-state routing has several techniques for preventing potential problems arising from resource requirements and link-state packet (LSP) distribution:

- A network administrator can reduce the periodic distribution of LSPs so that updates occur only after some long, configurable duration. Reducing the rate of periodic updates does not interfere with LSP updates triggered by topology changes.

- LSP updates can go to a multicast group rather than a flood to all routers. On interconnected LANs, you can use one or more designated routers as the targeted depository for LSP transmissions. Other routers can use these designated routers as a specialized source of consistent topology data.

- In large networks, you can set up a hierarchy made up of different areas. A router in one area of the hierarchical domain does not need to store and process LSPs from other routers not located in its area.

- For problems of LSP coordination, link-state implementations can allow for LSP time stamps, sequence numbers, aging schemes, and other related mechanisms to help avoid inaccurate LSP distribution or uncoordinated updates.

Comparing Distance-Vector Routing and Link-State Routing

You can compare distance-vector routing to link-state routing in several key areas (see Table 11-1):

- Distance-vector routing gets all topological data from the routing table information of its neighbors. Link-state routing obtains a wide view of the entire internetwork topology by accumulating all necessary LSAs.

- Distance-vector routing determines the best path by adding to the metric value it receives as tables move from router to router. For link-state routing, each router works separately to calculate its own shortest path to destinations.

- With most distance-vector routing protocols, updates for topology changes come in periodic table updates. These tables pass from router to router, usually resulting in slower convergence.

- With link-state routing protocols, updates are usually triggered by topology changes. Relatively small LSAs passed to all other routers usually result in faster time to converge on any internetwork topology change.

TABLE 11-1   Distance Vector and Link-State Operational Qualities

Distance-Vector	Link-State
Views network topology from neighbor's perspective	Gets common view of entire network topology
Adds distance vectors from router to router	Calculates the shortest path to other routers
Frequent, periodic updates, slow convergence	Event-triggered updates, fast convergence
Passes copies of routing table to neighbor routers	Passes link-state routing updates to other routers

Balanced Hybrid Routing

An emerging third type of routing protocol combines aspects of distance-vector and link-state routing, as shown in Figure 11-28. This third type is called *balanced hybrid routing*.

The balanced hybrid routing protocol uses distance vectors with more accurate metrics to determine the best paths to destination networks. However, it differs from most distance-vector protocols by using topology changes to trigger routing database updates.

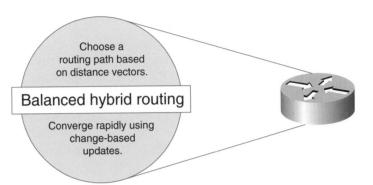

FIGURE 11-28
Hybrid routing shares attributes of distance-vector and link-state routing.

The balanced hybrid routing type converges more rapidly, like the link-state protocols. However, it differs from these protocols by using fewer resources, such as bandwidth, memory, and processor overhead. Examples of balanced hybrid protocols are OSI's Intermediate System-to-Intermediate System (IS-IS) routing and Cisco's Enhanced IGRP.

Basic Routing Processes

Regardless of whether a network uses distance-vector or link-state routing mechanisms, its routers must perform the same basic routing functions. The network layer must relate to and interface with various lower layers. Routers must be capable of seamlessly handling packets encapsulated into different lower-level frames without changing the packets' Layer 3 addressing.

LAN-to-LAN Routing

Figure 11-29 shows an example of network-layer interfacing in LAN-to-LAN routing. In this example, packet traffic from Source Host 4 on Ethernet Network 1 needs a path to Destination Host 5 on Network 2. The LAN hosts depend on the router and its consistent network addressing to find the best path.

When the router checks its routing table entries, it discovers that the best path to destination Network 2 uses Outgoing Port To0, the interface to a Token Ring LAN.

Although the lower-layer framing must change as the router switches packet traffic from the Ethernet on Network 1 to the Token Ring on Network 2, the Layer 3 addressing for source and destination remains the same. In Figure 11-29, the destination address remains Network 2, Host 5, despite the different lower-layer encapsulations.

FIGURE 11-29
The router uses the destination network address contained in the packet to look up a route.

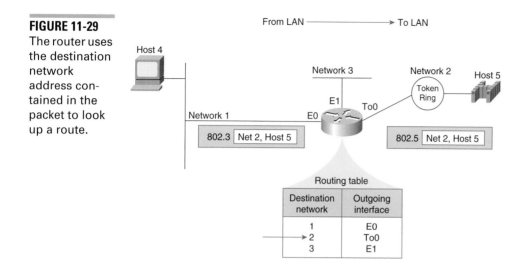

LAN-to-WAN Routing

The network layer must relate to and interface with various lower layers for LAN-to-WAN traffic. As an internetwork grows, the path taken by a packet might encounter several relay points and a variety of data-link types beyond the LANs. For example, in Figure 11-30, a packet from the top workstation at address 1.3 must traverse three data links to reach the file server at address 2.4 shown on the bottom.

The routed communications follow these basic steps:

1. The workstation sends a packet to the file server by encapsulating the packet in a Token Ring frame addressed to Router A.

2. When Router A receives the frame, it removes the packet from the Token Ring frame, encapsulates it in a Frame Relay frame, and forwards the frame to Router B.

3. Router B removes the packet from the Frame Relay frame and forwards the packet to the file server in a newly created Ethernet frame.

4. When the file server at address 2.4 receives the Ethernet frame, it extracts and passes the packet to the appropriate upper-layer process.

The routers enable LAN-to-WAN packet flow by keeping the end-to-end source and destination addresses constant while encapsulating the packet at the port to a data link that is appropriate for the next hop along the path.

FIGURE 11-30
Routers maintain the end-to-end address information as they forward the packet.

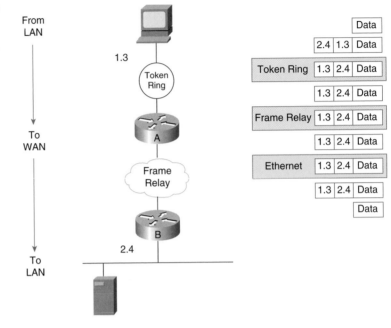

Summary

- Internetworking functions of the network layer include network addressing and best path selection for traffic.

- Routed protocols direct user traffic, whereas routing protocols work between routers to maintain path tables.

- Network discovery for distance-vector routing involves exchange of routing tables; one possible problem is slow convergence.

- For link-state routing, routers calculate the shortest paths to other routers; one possible problem is inconsistent updates.

- Balanced hybrid routing uses attributes of both link-state and distance-vector routing, applying paths to several protocols.

Review Questions

1. Which of the following best describes one function of Layer 3, the network layer, in the OSI model?

    A. It is responsible for reliable network communication between nodes.

    B. It is concerned with physical addressing and network topology.

    C. It determines which is the best path for traffic to take through the network.

    D. It manages data exchange between presentation-layer entities.

2. What function allows routers to evaluate available routes to a destination and to establish the preferred handling of a packet?

    A. Data linkage

    B. Path determination

    C. SDLC interface protocol

    D. Frame Relay

3. How does the network layer send packets from the source to the destination?

    A. By using an IP routing table

    B. By using ARP responses

    C. By referring to a name server

    D. By referring to the bridge

4. What are the two parts of an address that routers use to forward traffic through a network?

    A. Network address and host address

    B. Network address and MAC address

    C. Host address and MAC address

    D. MAC address and subnet mask

5. Which of the following best describes a routed protocol?

    A. It provides enough information to allow a packet to be forwarded from host to host.

    B. It provides information necessary to pass data packets up to the next highest network layer.

C. It allows routers to communicate with other routers to maintain and update address tables.

D. It allows routers to bind MAC and IP addresses together.

6. Which of the following best describes a routing protocol?

   A. A protocol that accomplishes routing through the implementation of an algorithm

   B. A protocol that specifies how and when MAC and IP addresses are bound together

   C. A protocol that defines the format and use of fields within a data packet

   D. A protocol that allows a packet to be forwarded from host to host

7. What is one advantage of distance-vector algorithms?

   A. They are not likely to count to infinity.

   B. You can implement them easily on very large networks.

   C. They are not prone to routing loops.

   D. They are computationally simple.

8. Which of the following best describes a link-state algorithm?

   A. It re-creates the exact topology of the entire internetwork.

   B. It requires minimal computations.

   C. It determines distance and direction to any link on the internetwork.

   D. It uses little network overhead and reduces overall traffic.

9. Why do routing loops occur?

   A. Slow convergence occurs after a modification to the internetwork.

   B. Split horizons are artificially created.

   C. Network segments fail catastrophically and take other network segments down in a cascade effect.

   D. Default routes were never established and initiated by the network administrator.

10. Which of the following best describes balanced hybrid routing?

    A. It uses distance vectors to determine best paths but topology changes trigger routing table updates.

    B. It uses distance-vector routing to determine best paths between topology during high-traffic periods.

    C. It uses topology to determine best paths but does frequent routing table updates.

    D. It uses topology to determine best paths but uses distance vectors to circumvent inactive network links.

Objectives

After reading this chapter, you will be able to

- Identify the commands and process of programming a router
- Describe user mode
- Describe privileged mode
- Describe help
- Describe editing
- Describe when, why, and how to review a command history

Chapter 12

The Router User Interface and Modes

Introduction

In Chapter 11, "The Network Layer and Routing," you learned about the router's use and operations in performing the key internetworking function of the Open System Interconnection (OSI) reference model network layer. In this chapter, you will learn about the network administrator's role in operating a router to ensure efficient and effective delivery of data on a network with routers.

An Overview of the User Interface

You can configure Cisco routers from the user interface that runs on the router console or terminal. You also can configure Cisco routers using remote access. You must log in to the router before you can enter an EXEC command.

For security purposes, Cisco routers have two levels of access to commands:

- *User mode*—Typical tasks include those that check the router status. In this mode, router configuration changes are not allowed.
- *Privileged mode*—Typical tasks include those that change the router configuration.

Logging In to a Router: The Cisco Internetwork Operating System (IOS)

When you first log in to a router, you see a user-mode prompt, which looks like this:

```
Router>
```

Commands available at this user level are a subset of the commands available at the privileged level. For the most part, these commands allow you to display information without changing router configuration settings.

To access the full set of commands, you must first enable privileged mode; your prompt shows as a pound sign (#) while you are in this mode. From the privileged level, you also can access global configuration mode and the other specific configuration modes, including interface, subinterface, line, router, route-map, and several additional configuration modes (see Listing 12-1).

Listing 12-1 Logging In to and Out of the Router

```
Router con0 is now available.

Press RETURN to get started.


User Access Verification
Password:
Router>
Router> enable
Password:
Router#
Router# disable
Router>
Router> exit
```

To log out of the router, type **exit**.

User-Mode Commands

NOTE

Throughout this chapter, note that screen output varies with your specific Cisco IOS software level and router configuration.

Typing a question mark (?) at the user-mode prompt or the privileged-mode prompt displays a handy list of commonly used commands. When you use the **?** command at the Router> prompt, as follows, you get a list of the user-mode commands, which are shown in Table 12-1:

```
Router> ?
```

TABLE 12-1   User-Mode Commands

Command	Description
access-enable	Creates a temporary access list entry
atmsig	Executes ATM signaling commands
cd	Changes current device
clear	Resets functions
connect	Opens a terminal connection
dir	Lists files on a given device
disable	Turns off privileged commands
disconnect	Disconnects an existing network connection
enable	Turns on privileged commands
exit	Exits EXEC
help	Gets a description of the interactive help system
lat	Opens a LAT connection

TABLE 12-1   User-Mode Commands (Continued)

Command	Description
`lock`	Locks the terminal
`login`	Logs in as a particular user
`logout`	Exits from EXEC mode
`mrinfo`	Requests neighbor and version information from a multicast router
`mstat`	Shows statistics after multiple multicast traceroutes
`mtrace`	Traces the reverse multicast path from destination to source
`name-connection`	Names an existing network connection
`pad`	Opens an X.29 PAD connection
`ping`	Sends echo messages
`ppp`	Starts IETF Point-to-Point Protocol (PPP)
`pwd`	Displays current device
`resume`	Resumes an active network connection
`rlogin`	Opens an rlogin connection
`show`	Shows running system information
`slip`	Starts Serial-Line IP (SLIP)
`systat`	Displays information about terminal lines
`telnet`	Opens a Telnet connection
`terminal`	Sets terminal line parameters
`tn3270`	Opens a TN3270 connection
`traceroute`	Sets a traceroute to the destination
`tunnel`	Opens a tunnel connection
`where`	Lists active connections
`x3`	Sets X.3 parameters on PAD
`xremote`	Enters XRemote mode

NOTE

Anywhere in Cisco IOS software where the -- More -- prompt appears, you can resume output of the next available screen by pressing the Spacebar. To display the next line, press the Return key (or, on some keyboards, the Enter key). Press any other key to return to the prompt.

NOTE

The privileged EXEC command set also includes those commands contained in user EXEC mode.

The screen displays 22 lines at one time. So sometimes you will get the -- More -- prompt at the bottom of the display. It indicates that multiple screens are available as output; that is, more commands follow.

Privileged-Mode Commands

Type `enable` (or the abbreviation `ena`) to get into privileged EXEC mode:

```
Router> ena
Password:
```

You must also enter a password. Typing a question mark (?) at the user prompt or the privileged prompt

```
Router# ?
```

displays a much larger list of commands. Table 12-2 show some of these commands.

TABLE 12-2   Privileged-Mode Commands

Command	Description
access-enable	Creates a temporary access list entry
access-template	Creates a temporary access list entry
appn	Sends a command to the APPN subsystem
atmsig	Executes ATM signaling commands
bfe	Sets manual emergency modes
calendar	Manages the hardware calendar
cd	Changes the current device
clear	Resets functions
clock	Manages the system clock
cmt	Starts or stops FDDI connection management functions
configure	Enters configuration mode
connect	Opens a terminal connection
copy	Copies configuration or image data
debug	Uses debugging functions (see also undebug)
delete	Deletes a file
dir	Lists files on a given device

TABLE 12-2   **Privileged-Mode Commands (Continued)**

Command	Description
`disable`	Turns off privileged commands
`disconnect`	Disconnects an existing network connection
`enable`	Turns on privileged commands
`erase`	Erases Flash or configuration memory
`exit`	Exits from EXEC mode
`format`	Formats a device
`help`	Gets a description of the interactive help system
`lat`	Opens a LAT connection
`lock`	Locks the terminal
`login`	Logs in as a particular user
`logout`	Exits EXEC mode
`mbranch`	Traces the multicast route down the tree branch
`mrbranch`	Traces the reverse multicast up the tree branch
`mrinfo`	Requests neighbor and version information from a multicast router
`mstat`	Shows statistics after multiple multicast traceroutes
`mtrace`	Traces reverse multicast path from destination source
`name-connection`	Names an existing network connection
`ncia`	Starts/stops NCIA server
`pad`	Opens an X.29 PAD connection
`ping`	Sends echo messages
`ppp`	Starts IETF Point-to-Point Protocol (PPP)
`pwd`	Displays current device
`reload`	Halts and performs a cold return
`resume`	Resumes an active network connection

TABLE 12-2   Privileged-Mode Commands (Continued)

Command	Description
rlogin	Opens an rlogin connection
rsh	Executes a remote command
sdlc	Sends SDLC test frames
send	Sends a message over tty lines
setup	Runs the setup command facility
show	Shows running system information
slip	Starts Serial-Line IP (SLIP)
squeeze	Squeezes a device
start-chat	Starts a chat script on a line
systat	Displays information about terminal lines
tarp	Targets ID Resolution Process (TARP) commands
telnet	Opens a Telnet connection
terminal	Sets terminal line parameters
test	Tests subsystems, memory, and interfaces
tn3270	Opens a TN3270 connection
traceroute	Sets a traceroute to the destination
tunnel	Opens a tunnel connection
undebug	Disables debugging functions (see also debug)
undelete	Undeletes a file
verify	Verifies the checksum of a Flash file
where	Lists active connections
which-route	Does an OSI route table lookup and displays results
write	Writes running configuration to memory, network, or terminal
x3	Sets X.3 parameters on PAD
xremote	Enters XRemote mode

Help Functions

Suppose you want to set the router clock. If you do not know the command to do so, use the **help** command, the output of which is shown in Listing 12-2, to check the syntax for setting the clock.

Listing 12-2 Help Functions

```
Router# clok
Translating "CLOK"
% Unknown command or computer name, or unable to find computer address

Router# cl?
clear   clock

Router# clock
% Incomplete command.

Router# clock ?
set     Set the time and date

Router# clock set
% Incomplete command

Router# clock set ?
Current Time ( hh : mm : ss )
```

The **help** output in Listing 12-2 shows that the **set** keyword is required. Next, check the syntax for entering the time and enter the current time using hours, minutes, and seconds, as shown in Listing 12-3.

Listing 12-3 Syntax Checking and Command Prompting

```
Router# clock set 19:56:00% Incomplete command.

Router# clock set 19:56:00 ?
<1-31>     Day of the month
MONTH      Month of the year

Router# clock set 19:56:00 04 8
                              ^
% Invalid input detected at the '^' marker

Router# clock set 19:56:00 04 August
% Incomplete command.

Router# clock set 19:56:00 04 August ?
<1993-2035>   Year
```

As shown in Listing 12-3, the system indicates that you need to provide additional information to complete the command. Press Ctrl-P (or the up arrow) to repeat the previous command entry automatically. Then add a space and a question mark (?) to reveal the additional arguments. Now you can complete the command entry.

The caret symbol (^) and help response indicate an error. To list the correct syntax, reenter the command up to the point where the error occurred and then enter a question mark (?). Enter the year, using the correct syntax, and press Return to execute the command.

Note that the user interface provides syntax checking by placing a caret symbol (^) where the error has occurred. The ^ appears at the point in the command string where you have entered an incorrect command, keyword, or argument. The error location indicator and interactive help system allow you to find and correct syntax errors easily.

Using Editing Commands

The user interface includes an enhanced editing mode that provides a set of editing key functions. Enhanced editing mode is automatically enabled with the current software release; however, you can disable it and revert to the editing mode of previous software releases. You also might want to disable enhanced editing if you have written scripts that do not interact well when enhanced editing is enabled.

Use the key sequences listed in Table 12-3 to move the cursor around on the command line for corrections or changes.

TABLE 12-3   Editing Commands

Command	Description
Ctrl-A	Moves to the beginning of the command line
Ctrl-E	Moves to the end of the command line
Esc-B	Moves back one word
Ctrl-F	Moves forward one character
Ctrl-B	Moves back one character
Esc-F	Moves forward one word

The editing command set provides a horizontal scrolling feature for commands that extend beyond a single line on the screen. When the cursor reaches the right margin, the command line shifts 10 spaces to the left. You cannot see the first 10 characters of the line, but you can scroll back and check the syntax at the beginning of the command.

To scroll back, press Ctrl-B or the left arrow key repeatedly until you are at the beginning of the command entry, or press Ctrl-A to return directly to the beginning of the line.

Reviewing a Command History

The user interface provides a history, or record, of commands you have entered. This feature is particularly useful for recalling long or complex commands or entries. As shown in Table 12-4, the command history feature allows you to complete the following tasks:

- Set the command history buffer size
- Recall commands
- Disable the command history feature

TABLE 12-4 Command History Commands

Command	Description
Ctrl-P or up arrow key	Recalls last (previous) command
Ctrl-N or down arrow key	Recalls most recent command
`show history`	Shows command buffer
`terminal history` [`size` *number-of-lines*]	Sets command buffer size
`no terminal editing`	Disables advanced editing features
`terminal editing`	Reenables advanced editing
Tab	Completes the entry

By default, command history is enabled and the system records 10 command lines in its history buffer. To change the number of command lines the system will record during the current terminal session, you use the `terminal history size` or `history size` command. The maximum number of commands you can include in the history is 256.

To recall commands in the history buffer beginning with the most recent command, press Ctrl-P or the up arrow key. Repeat the key sequence to recall successively older commands.

To return to more recent commands in the history buffer after recalling commands with Ctrl-P or the up arrow, press Ctrl-N or the down arrow key. Repeat the key sequence to recall successively more recent commands.

After you enter the unique characters for a command, press the Tab key, and the interface will finish the entry for you.

On most laptop computers, you may also have additional select and copy facilities available. You can copy a previous command string, and then paste or insert it as your current command entry and press Return.

Ctrl-Z backs you out of configuration mode.

Summary

- You can configure Cisco routers from the user interface that runs on the router console or terminal.
- For security purposes, Cisco routers have two levels of access to commands: user mode and privileged mode.
- Using a user interface to a router, you can
  - Log in with a user password
  - Enter privileged mode with the `enable` password
  - Disable or quit
- You can use advanced help features to perform the following:
  - Command completion and prompting
  - Syntax checking
- The user interface includes an enhanced editing mode that provides a set of editing key functions.
- The user interface provides a history, or record, of commands you have entered.

Review Questions

1. What are the two modes of access to router commands for Cisco routers?

    A. User and privileged

    B. User and guest

    C. Privileged and guest

    D. Guest and anonymous

2. Which mode do you use to make router configuration changes on Cisco routers?

    A. User

    B. Privileged

    C. Administrator

    D. Root

3. What does it mean if you see a greater-than symbol (>) on a Cisco router user interface?

    A. You are in login mode.

    B. You are in help mode.

    C. You are in user mode.

    D. You are in privileged mode.

4. Which of the following is the privileged mode prompt for Cisco router user interfaces?

    A. #

    B. >

    C. <

    D. ¦#

5. Which mode gives you access to a list of commonly used commands if ? is typed on a Cisco router user interface?

    A. Guest

    B. Privileged only

    C. User only

    D. User and privileged

6. What does the -- More -- prompt at the bottom of a screen on a Cisco router user interface mean?

   A. Multiple screens are available as output.

   B. Additional detail is available in the manual pages.

   C. Multiple entries are required in the command.

   D. Additional conditions must be stated.

7. Which keystroke(s) automatically repeats the previous command entry on a Cisco router user interface?

   A. Left arrow

   B. Right arrow

   C. Ctrl-R

   D. Ctrl-P

8. What happens if you press the up arrow key in a Cisco router user interface?

   A. You see a list of all users logged in to the router.

   B. You list the last command you typed.

   C. You print the screen.

   D. You pause the current process.

9. What happens if you type **?** in a Cisco router user interface?

   A. You see a list of all users logged in to the router.

   B. You list the last command you typed.

   C. You enter the help system.

   D. You find out which mode you are currently in.

10. What happens if you type **show ?** at the router prompt?

   A. You get a list of the users currently on the router.

   B. You get a list of all active connections and their status.

   C. You get a list of the most recent router table.

   D. You get a list of the subcommands that are available within the **show** command.

Objectives

After reading this chapter, you will be able to

- Describe router configuration components
- Describe router modes
- Use forms of the `show` command to examine the status of a router
- Use CDP commands to get information about neighboring networks and routers
- Use the `telnet` command to test the application layer
- Use `ping`, `trace`, and `show ip route` commands to test the network layer
- Use the `show interfaces serial` command to test the physical and data link layers

Chapter 13

Displaying Router Configuration Information

Introduction

In Chapter 12, "The Router User Interface and Modes," you learned about the network administrator's role in operating a router to ensure efficient and effective delivery of data on a network with routers. In this chapter, you will learn the correct procedures and commands to access a router, examine and maintain its components, and test its network connectivity.

Configuration Components and Router Modes

In this section, you will learn about the router components that play a key role in the configuration process. Knowing which components are involved in the configuration process gives you a better understanding of how the router stores and uses your configuration commands. Being aware of the steps that take place during router initialization will help you determine what and where problems may occur when you start up your router.

External Configuration Sources

The router can be configured from many external locations, as shown in Figure 13-1:

- Upon initial installation, it can be configured from the console terminal, which is a computer connected to the router through the console port.
- It can be connected via modem using the auxiliary port.
- Once installed on the network, it can be configured from virtual terminals 0 through 4.
- Configuration files can also be downloaded from a TFTP server on the network.

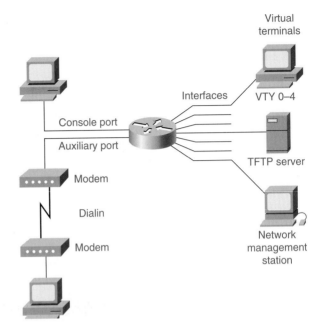

FIGURE 13-1
Configuration information can come from many sources.

Internal Configuration Components

The internal architecture of the Cisco router supports components that play an important role in the startup process, as shown in Figure 13-2. Internal configuration components are as follows:

- *RAM/DRAM*—Stores routing tables, ARP cache, fast-switching cache, packet buffering (shared RAM), and packet hold queues. RAM also provides temporary and/or running memory for the router's configuration file while the router is powered on. RAM content is lost when you power down or restart. Lastly, RAM also contains the copy of the Cisco Internetwork Operating System (IOS).

- *NVRAM*—Nonvolatile RAM (NVRAM) stores the router's backup configuration file. NVRAM content is retained when you power down or restart.

- *Flash*—Erasable, reprogrammable ROM. Flash memory holds the operating system image and microcode. Flash memory allows you to update software without removing and replacing chips on the processor. Flash content is retained when you power down or restart. Multiple copies of Cisco IOS software can be stored in Flash memory. Finally, Flash memory can also hold configuration files and boot images.

- *ROM*—Contains power-on diagnostics, a bootstrap program, and operating system software. To perform software upgrades, remove and replace pluggable chips on the CPU.

■ *Interfaces*—Network connections through which packets enter and exit the router. Interfaces are on the motherboard or on separate interface modules.

FIGURE 13-2
The internal configuration components include several elements.

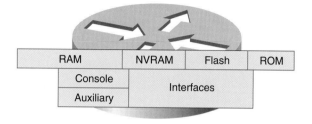

RAM for Working Storage

RAM is the working storage area for the router. When the router is turned on, a bootstrap program is executed from ROM. This program performs some tests, and then loads the Cisco IOS software into memory. The command executive, or EXEC, is one part of the Cisco IOS software. EXEC receives and executes commands you enter for the router.

As shown in Figure 13-3, the router also stores an active configuration file and tables of network maps and routing address lists. The configuration file can be displayed on a remote or console terminal. A saved version of this file is stored in NVRAM. The saved file is accessed and loaded into main memory each time the router initializes. The configuration file contains global, process, and interface information that directly affects the operation of the router and its interface ports.

The operating system image cannot be displayed on the terminal screen. The image is usually executed from the main RAM and loaded from one of several input sources. The operating software is organized into routines that handle the tasks associated with different protocols, movement of data, management of tables and buffers, routing of updates, and execution of user commands.

Router Modes

Whether accessed from the console or by a Telnet session through an auxiliary port, the router can be placed in several modes. The Cisco IOS user interface provides access to command modes, each of which provides different functions:

■ *User EXEC mode*—This is a look-only mode in which the user can view some information about the router but cannot change anything. This mode uses the Router> prompt.

■ *Privileged EXEC mode*—This mode supports the debugging and testing commands, detailed examination of the router, manipulation of configuration files, and access to configuration modes. It uses the Router# prompt.

FIGURE 13-3
An active configuration file is stored in the router.

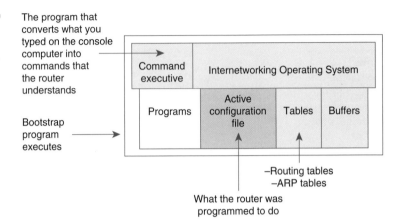

The program that converts what you typed on the console computer into commands that the router understands

Bootstrap program executes

–Routing tables
–ARP tables

What the router was programmed to do

- *Setup mode*—This mode presents an interactive prompted dialog at the console that helps the new user create a first-time basic configuration.

- *Global configuration mode*—This mode implements powerful one-line commands that perform simple configuration tasks. It uses the `Router(config)#` prompt.

- *Other configuration modes*—These modes provide more complicated multiple-line configurations. These modes use the `Router(config-mode)#` prompt.

- *RXBOOT mode*—This maintenance mode can be used, among other things, to recover lost passwords.

Examining Router Status by Using Router Status Commands

In this section, you will learn basic commands that you can issue to determine the current status of a router. These commands help you obtain vital information you need when monitoring and troubleshooting router operations.

It is important to be able to monitor the health and state of your router at any given time. Cisco routers have a series of commands that allow you to determine whether the router is functionally correct or where problems have occurred, as shown in Figure 13-4.

Router status commands are shown in Table 13-1.

FIGURE 13-4
Many commands are available to monitor router configuration.

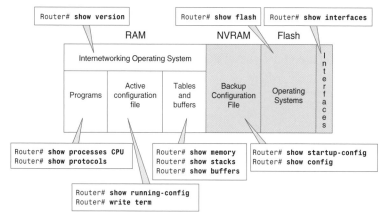

TABLE 13-1   Router Status Commands

Command	Description
show version	Displays the configuration of the system hardware, the software version, the names and sources of configuration files, and the boot images, and displays the reason for the last system reboot.
show processes	Displays information about the active processes.
show protocols	Displays the configured protocols. This command shows the status of any configured Layer 3 (network layer) protocol.
show memory	Shows statistics about the router's memory, including memory free pool statistics.
show stacks	Monitors the stack use of processes and interrupt routines.
show buffers	Provides statistics for the buffer pools on the router.
show flash	Shows information about the Flash memory device.
show running-config (write term on Cisco IOS Release 10.3 or earlier)	Displays the active configuration file.

continues

TABLE 13-1   Router Status Commands (Continued)

Command	Description
`show startup-config` (`show config` on Cisco IOS Release 10.3 or earlier)	Displays the backup configuration file.
`show interfaces`	Displays statistics for all interfaces configured on the router.

NOTE

The commands **write term** and **show config** used with Cisco IOS Release 10.3 and earlier have been replaced by new commands. These commands continue to perform their normal functions in the current release but are no longer documented. Support for these commands will cease in a future release. You know that you are looking at the active configuration file when you see the words Current Configuration at the top. You know that you are looking at the backup configuration file when you see a message at the top telling you how much nonvolatile memory has been used.

The `show running-config` and `show startup-config` Commands

The `show running-config` command (see Listing 13-1) and the `show startup-config` command (see Listing 13-2) are among the most frequently used Cisco IOS software EXEC commands because they allow an administrator to see the current running configuration on the router or the image size and startup configuration commands the router will use on the next restart.

Listing 13-1 The `show running-config` Command

```
Router# show running-config
Building configuration...

Current configuration:
!
version 11.1
!
      -- More --
```

Listing 13-2 The `show startup-config` Command

```
Router# show startup-config
Using 1108 out of 130048 bytes
!
version 11.2
!
Hostname router

      -- More --
```

The `show interfaces` Command

The `show interfaces` command displays configurable parameters and real-time statistics related to serial interfaces (see Listing 13-3).

Listing 13-3 The `show interfaces` Command

```
Router# show interfaces
Serial0is up, line protocol is up
Hardware is MK5025
Internet address is 183.8.64.129, subnet mask is 255.255.255.128
MTU 1500 bytes, BW 56 kbit, DLY 20000 usec, rely 255/255. load 9/255
Encapsulation HDLC, loopback not set, keepalive set (10 sec)
Last input 0:00:00, output 0:00:01, output hang never
Last clearing of show interfaces counters never
```

```
Output queue 0/40, 0 drops, input queue 0/75, 0 drops
Five minute input rate 1000 bits/sec, 0 packets/sec
331885 packets input, 62400237 bytes, no buffer
Received 230457 broadcasts, 0 runts, 0 giants
3 input errors, 3 CRC, 0 frame, 0 overrun, 0 ignored, 0 abort
403591 packets output, 66717279 bytes, 0 underruns
0 output errors, 0 collisions, 8 interface resets, 0 restarts
45 carrier transitions
```

The `show version` Command

The `show version` command displays information about the Cisco IOS software version that is currently running on the router (see Listing 13-4).

Listing 13-4 The `show version` Command

```
Router# show version
Cisco Internetwork Operating System Software
IOS (tm) 4500 Software (C4500-J-M). Version 11.2
Copyright (c) 1986-1996 by Cisco Systems, Inc.
Compiled Fri 28-Jun-96  16:32 by rbeach
Image text-base: 0x600088A0, data-base: 0x6076E000

ROM: System Bootstrap, Version 5.1(1) RELEASE SOFTWARE (fc1)
ROM: 4500-XBOOT Bootstrap Software, Version 10.1(1) RELEASE SOFTWARE (fc1)

router uptime is 1 week, 3 days, 32 minutes
System restarted by reload
System image file is c4500-j-mz, booted via tftp from 171.69.1.129

-- More --
```

The `show protocols` Command

You use the `show protocols` EXEC command to display the protocols configured on the router. This command shows the global and interface-specific status of any configured Level 3 protocols (for example, IP, DECnet, IPX, and Apple-Talk). (See Listing 13-5.)

Listing 13-5 The `show protocols` Command

```
Router# show protocols
Globalvalues:
Internet Protocol routing is enabled
DECNET routing is enabled
XNS routing is enabled

Vines routing is enabled
AppleTalk routing is enabled
Novell routing is enabled
-- More--
Ethernet0 is up, line protocol is up
Internet address is 183.8.126.2, subnet mask is 255.255.255.128
Decnet cost is 5
XNS address is 3010.aa00.0400.0284
CLNS enabled
Vines metric is 32
AppleTalk address is 3012.93, zone ld-e0
Novell address is 3010.aa00.0400.0284
-- More --
```

Gaining Access to Other Routers by Using Cisco Discovery Protocol

Cisco Discovery Protocol (CDP) provides a single proprietary command that enables network administrators to access a summary of what the configurations look like on other directly connected routers. CDP runs on the data link layer, connecting lower physical media and upper-network-layer protocols, as shown in Figure 13-5. Because CDP operates at this level, CDP devices that support different network-layer protocols can learn about each other. (Remember that the data link address is the same as the MAC address.)

FIGURE 13-5
CDP enables discovery on multiprotocol networks.

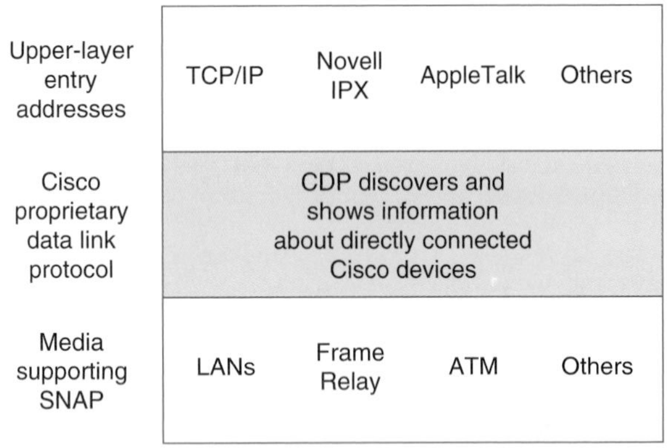

Upper-layer entry addresses	TCP/IP	Novell IPX	AppleTalk	Others
Cisco proprietary data link protocol	CDP discovers and shows information about directly connected Cisco devices			
Media supporting SNAP	LANs	Frame Relay	ATM	Others

When a Cisco device running Cisco IOS Release 10.3 or later boots up, CDP starts up automatically. CDP can then automatically discover neighboring Cisco devices running CDP. Discovered devices extend beyond those having TCP/IP. CDP discovers directly connected Cisco devices regardless of which Layer 3 and 4 protocol suite they run.

Showing CDP Neighbor Entries

The primary use of CDP is to discover platforms and protocols on your neighboring devices. Use the `show cdp neighbors` command to display the CDP updates on the local router.

Figure 13-6 shows an example of how CDP delivers its benefits to a system manager. Each router running CDP exchanges with its neighbors information about any protocol entries it knows. The administrator can display the results of this CDP information exchange on a console connected to a router configured to run CDP on its interfaces.

FIGURE 13-6
The command
`show cdp neighbors`
displays the results of the CDP discovery process.

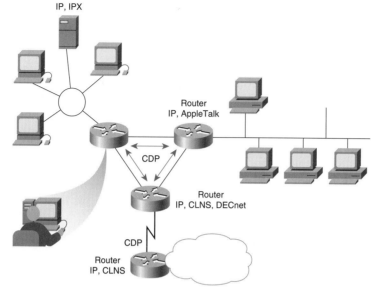

The network manager uses a `show` command to display information about the networks directly connected to the router. CDP provides information about each CDP neighbor device. Values include the following:

- *Device identifiers*—For example, the router's configured host name and domain name (if any).
- *Address list*—At least one protocol for SNMP, up to one address for each protocol supported.
- *Port identifier*—Such as Ethernet 0, Ethernet 1, Serial 0, and so on.
- *Capabilities list*—If, for example, the device acts as a source route bridge as well as a router.
- *Version*—Information such as that provided by the local command `show version`.
- *Platform*—The device's hardware platform; for example, Cisco 7000.

Notice that the router at the bottom of Figure 13-6 is not directly connected to the router of the administrator's console. To obtain CDP information about this device, the administrator would need to Telnet to a router directly connected to this target.

A CDP Configuration Example

CDP begins automatically upon a device's system startup. The CDP function normally starts by default when a Cisco product boots up with Cisco IOS Release 10.3 or later.

Although CDP runs by default, you must explicitly enable it on the device's interface by using the command `cdp enable`. For example, Figure 13-7 shows the `cdp enable` command that you use on the E0 and S0 interfaces on the router named Router A. This command begins CDP's dynamic discovery function on the device's interfaces. Only directly connected neighbors exchange CDP frames. A router caches any information it receives from its CDP neighbors. If a subsequent CDP frame indicates that any of the information about a neighbor has changed, the router discards the older information and replaces it with newer information.

FIGURE 13-7
The `cdp enable` command enables CDP on each interface.

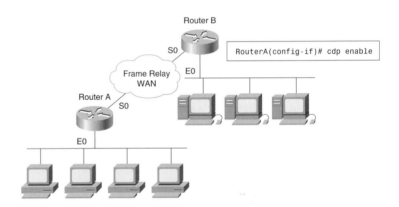

Use the command `show cdp interface`, as shown in Listing 13-6, to display the values of the CDP timers, the interface status, and the encapsulation used by CDP for its advertisement and discovery frame transmission. Default values for timers set the frequency between CDP updates and for aging CDP entries. These timers are set automatically at 60 seconds and 180 seconds, respectively. If the device receives a more recent update or if this holdtime value expires, the device must discard the CDP entry.

Listing 13-6 The `show cdp interface` Command

```
routerA# show cdp interface
Serial0 is up, line protocol is up, encapsulation is Frame Relay
  Sending CDP packets every 60 seconds
  Holdtime is 180 seconds
Ethernet0 is up, line protocol is up, encapsulation is ARPA
  Sending CDP packets every 60 seconds
  Holdtime is 180 seconds
```

Showing CDP Entries for a Device

You use the command **show cdp entry** *device-name*, as shown in Listing 13-7, to display a single cached CDP entry. Notice that output from this command includes all the Layer 3 addresses present in the neighbor Router B—an administrator can see the IP addresses of the targeted CDP neighbor (Router B) with the single command entry on Router A.

Listing 13-7 The show cdp entry *device-name* **Command**

```
routerA#show cdp entry routerB
- - - - - - - - - - - - - - - - - - - - - - - - - - -
Device ID: routerB
Entry address(es):
  IP address: 198.92.68.18
Platform: 2501. Capabilities: Router
Interface: Ethernet0, Port ID (outgoing port): Ethernet0
Holdtime: 155 sec

Version
IOS (tm) GS Software (GS3), 11.2(13337)[asastry 161]
Copyright (c) 1986-1996 by Cisco Systems, Inc.
Compiled Tue 14-May-96 1:04
```

The holdtime value indicates how long ago the CDP frame arrived with this information. The command includes abbreviated version information about Router B. CDP was designed and implemented as a very simple, low-overhead protocol. A CDP frame can be small yet retrieve a lot of useful information about neighboring routers.

Showing CDP Neighbors

You use the command **show cdp neighbors**, as shown in Listing 13-8, to display the CDP updates received on the local router. Notice that for each local port, the display shows the following:

- The neighbor device ID
- The local port type and number
- The decremental holdtime value in seconds
- The neighbor's device capability code
- The hardware platform of the neighbor
- The neighbor's remote port type and number

Listing 13-8 The `show cdp neighbors` Command

```
routerA#show cdp neighbors
Capability Codes: R - Router, T - Trans Bridge,
                  B - Source Route Bridge,
                  S - Switch, H - Host, I - IGMP

Device ID    Local Interface   Holdtime   Capability   Platform   Port ID
routerB        Eth 0             151          R           2501      Eth 0
routerB        Ser 0             165          R           2501      Ser 0

routerA#show cdp neighbors detail
----------------
Device ID: routerB
Entry address(es):
  IP address: 198.92.68.18
Platform: 2501, Capabilities: Router
Interface: Ethernet0, Port ID (outgoing port): Ethernet0
Holdtime: 143 sec
```

To display this information as well as information like that from `show cdp entry`, you use the optional `show cdp neighbors detail`.

Basic Networking Testing

Addressing problems are the most common problems that occur on IP networks. It is important to test your address configuration before continuing with further configuration steps. Basic testing of a network should proceed in sequence from one OSI reference model layer to the next. Each test presented in this section focuses on network operations at a specific layer of the OSI model. As shown in Figure 13-8, `telnet`, `ping`, `trace`, `show ip route`, and `show interfaces` are commands that allow you to test your internetwork.

FIGURE 13-8

You use the `telnet`, `ping`, and `trace` commands to verify your configuration.

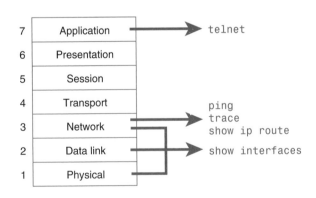

Testing the Application Layer by Using `telnet`

Another way to learn about a remote router is to connect to it. Telnet, a virtual terminal protocol that is part of the TCP/IP protocol suite, is a simple application that allows you to connect to the router. You can set a connection between the router and a connected device. Telnet allows you to verify the application-layer software between source and destination stations. This is the most complete test mechanism available. A router can have up to five simultaneous incoming Telnet sessions.

Let's begin testing by initially focusing on upper-layer applications. As shown in Figure 13-9, the `telnet` command provides a virtual terminal so that administrators can use Telnet operations to connect with other routers running TCP/IP.

FIGURE 13-9
You can test the application layer by using `telnet`.

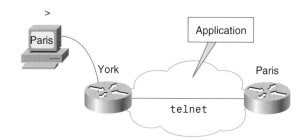

Let's determine whether the remote router can be accessed. For example, your success running Telnet to connect from the router York to the router Paris provides a basic test of the network connecting the two. If we can remotely access another router through Telnet, then at least we know that one TCP/IP application can reach the remote router. A successful Telnet connection indicates that the upper-layer application (and the services of lower layers as well) functions properly.

If we can Telnet to one router but not to another router, it is likely that the Telnet failure is caused by specific addressing, naming, or access permission problems. These problems can exist on our router or on the router that failed as a Telnet target. The next step is to try `ping`. This command lets you test end-to-end at the network layer.

Testing the Network Layer with the `ping` Command

As an aid to diagnosing basic network connectivity, many network protocols support an echo protocol, which is a test to determine whether protocol packets are being routed.

The `ping` command sends a packet to the destination host and then waits for a reply packet from that host, as shown in Figure 13-10. Results from this echo protocol can help evaluate the path-to-host reliability, delays over the path, and whether the host can be reached or is functioning. For a `ping` to work, your router needs to know not only how to get to the destination but that the destination router or device knows how to get to the source.

FIGURE 13-10
The `ping` command tests IP network connectivity.

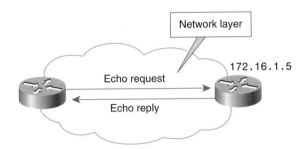

In Listing 13-9, the `ping` target `172.16.1.5` responds successfully to all five datagrams sent. An exclamation point (!) indicates each successful echo. If you instead receive one or more periods (.) on your display, the application on your router has timed out waiting for a given packet echo from the `ping` target. The `ping` user EXEC command can be used to diagnose basic network connectivity. The formal term for the `ping` process is Internet Control Message Protocol (ICMP).

Listing 13-9 The `ping` Command
```
Router> ping 172.16.1.5
Type escape sequence to abort.
Sending 5, 100 byte ICMP Echos to 172.16.1.5, timeout is 2 seconds:
!!!!!
Success rate is 100 percent, round-trip min/avg/max = 1/3/4 ms
Router>
```

Testing the Network Layer with the `trace` Command

The `trace` command is the ideal tool for finding where data is being sent in your network. The `trace` command uses the same technology as the `ping` command, except that instead of testing end-to-end connectivity, `trace` tests each step along the way and enables you to see the possible end-to-end path, as shown in Figure 13-11. This operation can be performed at either the user or privileged EXEC levels. The `trace` command takes advantage of the error messages generated by routers when a packet exceeds its Time To Live (TTL) value. The `trace` command sends several packets and displays the round-trip time for each. The benefit of the `trace` command is that it tells which router in the path is the last one to be reached. This is called *fault isolation*.

FIGURE 13-11
The **trace** command shows interface addresses used to reach the destination.

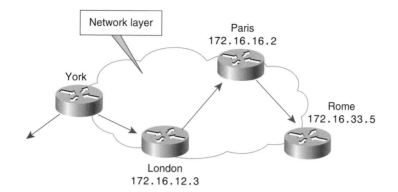

In Listing 13-10, we are tracing the path from York to Rome. Along the way, the path must go through London and Paris. If one of these routers had been unreachable, we would have seen three asterisks (***) instead of the name of the router.

Listing 13-10 The trace Command

```
York# trace ROME
Type escape to abort.
Tracing the route to Rome (172.16.33.5)
  1 LONDON (172.16.12.3) 1000 msec 8 msec 4 msec
  2 PARIS (172.16.16.2) 8 msec 8msec 8msec
  3 ROME (172.16.35.5) 8msec 8msec 4msec

York#
```

Using the show ip route Command to Test the Network Layer

The router offers some powerful tools that allow you to actually look at the routing table—the directions that the router uses to determine how it will direct traffic across the network.

The next basic test also focuses on the network layer. You use the **show ip route** command to determine whether a routing table entry exists for the target network. Listing 13-11 shows that Rome (131.108.33.0) is reachable to Paris (131.108.16.2) via the Enternet1 interface.

Listing 13-11 The show ip route Command

```
Paris# show ip route

Codes:  I - IGRP derived, R - RIP derived, O - OSPF derived
        C - connected, S - static, E - EGP derived, B - BGP derived
        i - IS-IS derived, D - EIGRP derived
        * - candidate default route, IA - OSPF inter area route
        E1 - OSPF external type 1 route, E2 - OSPF external type 2 route
        L1 - IS-IS level-1 route, L2 - IS-IS level -2 route
        EX - EIGRP external route
```

```
Gateway of last resort is not set

I    144.253.0.0 [100/1300] via 133.3.32.2. 0:00:22 Ethernet1
     131.108.0.0 is subnetted (mask is 255.255.255.0), 3 subnets
I      131.108.33.0 [100/180771] via 131.108.16.2, 0:01:29, Ethernet1
C      131.108.12.0 is directly connected, Ethernet1
C      101.108.16.0 is directly connected, Ethernet0
I    219.100.103.0 [100/1200] via 133.3.32.2, 0:00:22, Ethernet1
```

Using the `show interfaces serial` Command to Test the Physical and Data Link Layers

As shown in Figure 13-12, the interface has two pieces, physical (hardware) and logical (software):

- The hardware—such as cables, connectors, and interfaces—must make the actual connection between the devices.

- The software is the messages—such as keepalive messages, control information, and user information—that are passed between adjacent devices. This information is data being passed between two connected router interfaces.

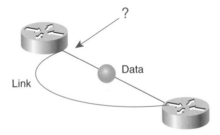

FIGURE 13-12
You use the `show inter-faces serial` command to test the physical and data link layers.

When you test the physical and data link layers, you ask these questions:

- Is there a Carrier Detect signal? Is the physical link between devices good?
- Are the keepalive messages being received? Can data packets be sent across the physical link?

One of the most important elements of the `show interfaces serial` command output is display of the line and data-link protocol status. Figure 13-13 indicates the key summary line to check and the status meanings.

The line status in this example is triggered by a Carrier Detect signal, and refers to the physical-layer status. However, the line protocol, triggered by keepalive frames, refers to the data-link framing.

FIGURE 13-13
You use the
**show inter-
faces serial**
command to
identify line
and protocol
problems.

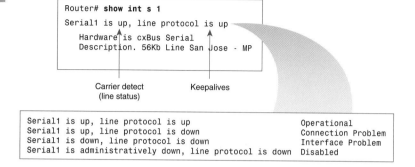

```
Router# show int s 1
Serial1 is up, line protocol is up
   Hardware is cxBus Serial
   Description. 56Kb Line San Jose - MP
```

        Carrier detect   Keepalives
        (line status)

```
Serial1 is up, line protocol is up                        Operational
Serial1 is up, line protocol is down                      Connection Problem
Serial1 is down, line protocol is down                    Interface Problem
Serial1 is administratively down, line protocol is down   Disabled
```

Clearing show interfaces Counters

The router tracks statistics that provide information about the interface. You use the **show interfaces** command to display the statistics, which reflect router operation since the last time the counters were cleared, as shown in the top boldface line in Listing 13-12. In this example, the counters were last cleared two weeks and four days ago. You use the **clear counters** command to reset the counters to zero. By starting from zero, you get a clearer picture of the current status of the network.

Listing 13-12 The show interfaces Command
```
Router# show interfaces serial 1

Serial1 is up, line protocol is up

   Hardware is cxBus Serial
   Description: 56Kb Line San Jose - MP
   Internet address is 150.136.190.203, subnet mask is 255.255.255.0
   MTU 1500 bytes, BW 56 Kbit, DLY 20000 usec, rely 255/255, load 1/255
   Encapsulation HDLC, loopback not set, keepalive set (10 sec)
   Last input 0:00:07, output 0:00:00, output hang never
   Last clearing of show interfaces counters 2w4d
   Output queue 0/40, 0 drops; input queue 0/75, 0 drops
   Five minute input rate 0 bits/sec, 0 packets/sec
   Five minute output rate 0 bits/sec, 0 packets/sec
      16263 packets input, 1347238 bytes, no buffer
      Received 13983 broadcasts, 0 runts, 0 giants
      2 input errors, 0 CRC, 0 frame, 0 overrun, 0 ignored, 2 abort
      0 input packets with dribble condition detected
      22146 packets output, 2383680 bytes, 0 underruns
      0 output errors, 0 collisions, 2 interface resets, 0 restarts
      1 carrier transitions
```

Summary

- The router is made up of configurable components and has modes for examining, maintaining, and changing the components.
- `show` commands are used for examination.
- You use CDP to show entries about neighbors.
- You can gain access to other routers by using Telnet.
- You should test network connectivity layer by layer.
- Testing commands include `ping` and `trace`.

Review Questions

1. Which of the following describes a location from which a router is configured?

    A. Once installed on the network, a router can be configured from virtual terminals.

    B. Upon initial configuration, a router is configured from the virtual terminals.

    C. Once installed on the network, a router can be configured via modem from the console terminal.

    D. Upon initial configuration, a router is configured via modem by using the auxiliary port.

2. Which of the following router components has these characteristics: holds the operating system and microcode, retains its contents when you power down or restart, and allows software updates without replacing chips?

    A. NVRAM

    B. RAM/DRAM

    C. Flash

    D. ROM

3. Which of the following does *not* correctly describe the function of a router status command?

    A. `show version`—Displays configuration of the system hardware, the names and sources of configuration files, and the boot images.

    B. `show memory`—Displays statistics about the router's memory, including memory free pool statistics.

    C. `show buffers`—Displays statistics for the buffer pools on the router.

    D. `show interfaces`—Displays statistics for all interfaces configured on the router.

4. Which of the following describes a function of the `show startup-config` command?

    A. It allows an administrator to see the current running configuration on the router.

    B. It displays a message, showing how much nonvolatile memory has been used.

C. It allows an administrator to see the reason for the last system reboot.

D. It displays this message: `Current Configuration`.

5. The `show interfaces serial` command can display which of the following lines of information?

A. `IOS (tm) 4500 Software (C4500-J-M), Experimental Version 11.2`

B. `DECNET routing is enabled`

C. `Serial1 is up, line protocol is up`

D. `System image file is "c4500-j-mz"`

6. Why would you use the `show cdp neighbors` command?

A. To get a snapshot view of the routers in the network

B. To get an overview of the routers that are directly connected to the network

C. To get the IP addresses for neighboring routers

D. To build a routing table for all routers in the network neighborhood

7. What four important pieces of information do you receive after issuing a `ping` command?

A. The size and quantity of ICMP packets; the timeout duration; the success rate; and the minimum, average, and maximum roundtrip times.

B. The quantity of ICMP packets; the timeout duration; the success rate; and the minimum, average, and maximum roundtrip times.

C. The size and quantity of ICMP packets; the MAC address; the success rate; and the minimum, average, and maximum roundtrip times.

D. The quantity of ICMP packets; the timeout duration; the transfer rate; and the minimum, average, and maximum roundtrip times.

8. What information does testing a network by using the `trace` command provide?

A. It determines whether the line protocol is operational.

B. It determines whether a routing table entry exists for the target network.

C. It maps every router that a packet goes through to reach its destination.

D. It determines whether upper-layer applications are functioning properly.

9. What information does testing a network by using the `show interfaces serial` command provide?

A. It displays line and data-link protocol status.

B. It displays how the router directs traffic across the network.

C. It displays the path that packets follow across the network.

D. It displays the names of routers on the network.

10. Which command is entered to display the router's active configuration file?

A. `show running-config`

B. `show config term`

C. `show version`

D. `show backup-config`

Objectives

After reading this chapter, you will be able to

- Describe the startup sequence
- Use startup commands
- Describe the system configuration dialog
- Describe the setup of global parameters
- Describe the setup of interface parameters
- Describe the setup and use of script review

Router Startup and Setup Configuration

Introduction

In Chapter 13, "Displaying Router Configuration Information," you learned the correct procedures and commands to access a router, examine and maintain its components, and test its network connectivity. In this chapter, you will learn how to start a router for the first time by using the correct commands and startup sequence to do an initial configuration of a router. In addition, this chapter explains the startup sequence of a router and the setup dialog that the router uses to create an initial configuration file.

Startup Routines for Cisco Internetwork Operating System (IOS)

The startup routines for Cisco IOS software are used for starting router operations. The router must deliver reliable performance by connecting the user networks it was configured to serve. To do this, the startup routines must

- Make sure the router comes up with all its hardware tested
- Find from memory and load the Cisco IOS software that the router uses for its operating system
- Find from memory and apply the configuration statements about the router, including protocol functions and interface addresses

The router makes sure that it comes up with tested hardware. When a Cisco router powers up, it performs a power-up self-test. During this self-test, the router executes diagnostics from read-only memory (ROM) on all modules. These diagnostics verify the basic operation of the CPU, memory, and network interface ports. After verifying the hardware functions, the router proceeds with software initialization.

The Startup Sequence

After the power-up self-test on the router, the following events, illustrated in Figure 14-1, occur when the router initializes:

1. The generic bootstrap loader executes from ROM on the CPU card. A *bootstrap* is a simple, preset operation to load instructions that in turn cause

other instructions to be loaded into memory, or cause entry into other configuration modes.

2. The operating system source can be located in several places. The location is determined from the Boot field of the configuration register. If the Boot field indicates a Flash or network load, boot system commands in the configuration file indicate the exact location of the image.

3. The operating system image is loaded. Then the operating system determines the hardware and software components and lists the results on the console terminal.

4. The saved configuration file in nonvolatile random-access memory (NVRAM) is loaded into main memory and executed one line at a time. These configuration commands start routing processes, supply addresses for interfaces, set media characteristics, and so on.

5. If no valid configuration file exists in NVRAM, the operating system executes a question-driven initial configuration routine referred to as the *system configuration dialog*. This mode is also called the *setup dialog*.

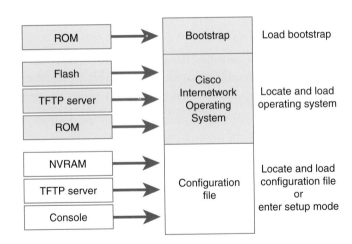

FIGURE 14-1
After the power-up self-test on the router, a start-up sequence is initiated.

Commands Relating to Startup

Setup is not intended as the mode for entering complex protocol features in the router. Instead, setup is used to bring up a minimal configuration. Rather than use setup, network administrators use various config-mode commands for most router configuration tasks.

Listing 14-1 lists the startup commands for routers running Release 10.3 or earlier. The top two commands in Listing 14-1 display the backup and active configuration files. The `erase startup-config` command deletes the backup configuration file in NVRAM. The `reload` command reloads the router, causing it to run through the entire configuration process. The last command is used to enter setup mode from the privileged EXEC prompt.

Listing 14-1 Startup Commands for Use with Routers Running Release 10.3 or Earlier

```
Router# show startup-config
        (show config) *

Router# show running-config
        (write term) *

Router# erase startup-config
        (write erase) *

Router# reload

Router# setup
```

Setup: The System Configuration Dialog

One routine for initial configuration is setup mode. The main purpose of setup mode, which is depicted in Listing 14-2, is to quickly bring up a minimal configuration for any router that cannot find its configuration from some other source.

Listing 14-2 The Setup Mode

```
#setup

-- System Configuration Dialog --

At any port you may enter a question mark '?' for help.
Use ctrl-c to abort configuration dialog at any prompt.
Default settings are in square brackets '[]'.

Continue with configuration dialog? [yes].

First, would you like to see the current interface summary? [yes]

Interface     IP-Address     OK?   Method   Status   Protocol
TokenRing0    unassigned     NO    not set  down     down
Ethernet0     unassigned     NO    not set  down     down
Serial0       unassigned     NO    not set  down     down
Fddi0         unassigned     NO    not set  down     down
```

For many of the prompts in the system configuration dialog of the `setup` command facility, default answers appear in square brackets ([]) following the question. Pressing the Return (or Enter) key allows you to use the defaults. If the system was previously configured, the defaults that appear are the currently configured values. If you are configuring the system for the first time, the

> **NOTE**
>
> The commands `show config`, `write term`, and `write erase` used with Cisco IOS Release 10.3 and earlier have been replaced by new commands. The commands that have been replaced continue to perform their normal functions in the current release but are no longer documented. Support for these commands will cease in a future release.

factory defaults are provided. If there is no factory default, as in the case of passwords, nothing is displayed after the question mark (?).

At this point, you can choose not to continue with the system configuration dialog and can exit by entering **no** at the prompt. To begin the initial configuration process, enter **yes**. You can press Ctrl+C to terminate the process and start over at any time. If a -- More -- prompt appears, press the Spacebar to continue.

Setup Global Parameters

A prompt appears on your monitor, as illustrated in Listing 14-3. It indicates that you are to enter the global parameters that you set for your router. These parameters are the configuration values you decided on. The first global parameter requires you to set the router host name, which will precede the Cisco IOS prompts for all configuration modes. At initial configuration, the router name default is shown between the square brackets as [Router]. You use the global parameters shown in Listing 14-3 to set the various passwords used on the router.

Listing 14-3 The Prompt at Which You Enter the Global Parameters for Your Router

```
Configuring global parameters:

  Enter host name [Router]

The enable secret is a one-way cryptographic secret used
instead of the enable password when it exists.

  Enter enable secret[<Use current secret>]

  Enter enable password[san-fran]:
%Please choose a password that is different from the enable secret
  Enter enable password[san-fran].
  Enter virtual terminal password [san-fran]:
  Configure SNMP Network Management? [no]:
```

You must enter an enable secret password. When you enter a string of password characters for the prompt Enter enable secret, the characters are processed by Cisco-proprietary encryption. This can enhance the security of the password string. Whenever anyone lists the contents of the router configuration file, this enable password appears as a meaningless string of characters. Setup recommends, but does not require, that the enable password be different from the enable secret password.

When you are prompted for global parameters at the console, as displayed in Listing 14-4, you need to use the configuration values you have determined for your router to enter the global parameters at the prompts. When you answer yes to a prompt, additional questions may appear about that protocol.

Listing 14-4 The Prompts for Global Parameters at the Console

```
Configure IP? [yes]:
  Configure IGRP routing? [yes]:
    Your IGRP autonomous system number [1]: 200
Configure DECnet? [no]:
Configure XNS? [no]:
Configure Novell? [no]: yes
Configure Apollo? [no]:
Configure AppleTalk? [no]: yes
    Multizone networks? [no]: yes
Configure Vines? [no]:
Configure bridging? [no]:
```

Setup Interface Parameters

When you are prompted for parameters for each installed interface, as shown in Listing 14-5, you need to use the configuration values you have determined for your interface to enter the interface parameters at the prompts.

Listing 14-5 The Prompts for Parameters for Each Installed Interface

```
Configuring interface parameters:

Configuring interface TokenRing0:
Is this interface in use? [yes]:
Tokenning ring speed (4 or 16)? [16]:
Configure IP on this interface? [no]: yes
IP address for this interface: 172.16.92.67
Number of bits in subnet field [0]:
Class B network is 172.16.0.0, 0 subnet bit; mask is 255.255.0.0
Configure Novell on this interface? [no]: yes
Novell network number [1]:

Configure interface Serial0:
Is this interface in use? [yes]:
Configure IP on this interface? [yes]
Configure IP unnumbered on this interface? [no]:
IP address for this interface: 172.16.97.67
Number of bits in subnet field [0]:
Class B network is 172.16.0.0, 0 subnet bits; mask is 255.255.0.0
Configure Novell on this interface? [yes]: no

Configuring Interface Serial 1:
Is this interface in use? [yes]: no
```

Setup Script Review and Use

When you complete the configuration process for all installed interfaces on your router, the **setup** command program displays the configuration that was created, which is depicted in Listing 14-6. The **setup** command program asks whether you want to use this configuration. If you answer yes, the configuration is executed and saved to NVRAM. If you answer no, the configuration is not saved, and the process begins again. There is no default for this prompt; you must answer either yes or no. After you have answered yes to this last question, your system is ready to use. If you want to modify the configuration you have just established, you must manually configure it.

Listing 14-6 The `setup` Command Program Displaying the Configuration That Was Created

```
The following configuration command script was created:
hostname router
enable secret 5 $ 1Sg772S
enable password san-fran
enable password san-fran
line vty 0 4
password san-fran
snmp-server community
!
ip routing
no decnet routing
no xns routing
no apollo routing
appletalk routing
no cins routing
no vines
no bridge
no mop enabled

Interface Ethernet
Ip address 172.16.92.67 255.255.0.0
network 1
no mop enabled
!
interface Serial0
Ip address 172.16.97.67 255.255.0.0

Interface Serial1
shutdown
!
end

Use this configuration? [yes/no]: yes
[OK]
Use the enabled mode 'configure' command to modify this configuration.
```

The script tells you to use configuration mode to change the configuration file after setup has been used. The script file generated by **setup** is additive: You can turn on features with **setup,** but you cannot turn them off. Also, **setup** does not support many of the advanced features of the router or features that require a more complex configuration.

Summary

- The router initializes by loading a bootstrap, the operating system, and a configuration file.
- If the router cannot find a configuration file, the router enters setup mode.
- The router stores a backup copy of the new configuration from setup mode in NVRAM.

Review Questions

1. Which of the following is the correct order of steps in the Cisco router system startup routine?

    A. (1) Locate and load operating system; (2) load bootstrap; (3) test hardware; (4) locate and load configuration file

    B. (1) Test hardware; (2) load bootstrap; (3) locate and load operating system; (4) locate and load configuration file

    C. (1) Load bootstrap; (2) locate and load configuration file; (3) test hardware; (4) locate and load operating system

    D. (1) Test hardware; (2) load bootstrap; (3) locate and load configuration file; (4) locate and load operating system

2. Which of the following is an important function of the power-up self-test?

    A. To determine the router hardware and software components and list them on the console terminal

    B. To cause other instructions to be loaded into memory

    C. To execute diagnostics that verify the basic operation of router hardware

    D. To start routing processes, supply addresses for interfaces, and set up media characteristics

3. Which of the following is an important result of the Cisco IOS software loading onto a router?

    A. Determining the router hardware and software components and listing them on the console terminal

    B. Causing other instructions to be loaded into memory

    C. Executing diagnostics that verify the basic operation of router hardware

    D. Starting routing processes, supplying addresses for interfaces, and setting up media characteristics

4. Which of the following is an important result of the configuration file loading onto a router?

   A. Determining the router hardware and software components and listing them on the console terminal

   B. Causing other instructions to be loaded into memory

   C. Executing diagnostics that verify the basic operation of router hardware

   D. Starting routing processes, supplying addresses for interfaces, and setting up media characteristics

5. What is the function of the `erase startup-config` command?

   A. It deletes the backup configuration file in NVRAM.

   B. It deletes the bootstrap image from Flash memory.

   C. It deletes the current Cisco IOS software from NVRAM.

   D. It deletes the current running configuration from Flash memory.

6. What is the function of the `reload` command?

   A. It loads a backup configuration file from a TFTP server.

   B. It saves the new Cisco IOS software to Flash memory.

   C. It reboots the router.

   D. It loads the new configuration file in NVRAM.

7. When is router setup mode executed?

   A. After the saved configuration file is loaded into main memory

   B. When the network administrator needs to enter complex protocol features on the router

   C. When the router begins software initialization

   D. When the router cannot find a valid configuration file

8. Which of the following correctly describes a procedure for setup of router global and interface parameters on a router?

   A. A default parameter is shown in square brackets at every prompt.

   B. The router host name must be set.

   C. An `enable secret` password can be set, but is not required.

   D. For each installed interface, a series of questions must be answered.

9. Why might you want to issue `show startup-config` and `show running-config` commands?

    A. It's time to update the Cisco IOS software and you need to kill certain router processes before proceeding.

    B. To determine the time since the router booted and the current register setting.

    C. The router suddenly isn't working right and you want to compare the initial state to the present state.

    D. To find out where the Cisco IOS software booted from and which version is being used.

10. What file(s) would you find in NVRAM?

    A. Cisco IOS software and configuration files

    B. Configuration files

    C. A backup copy of Cisco IOS software

    D. A limited version of Cisco IOS software and registry files

Objectives

After reading this chapter, you will be able to

- Describe how to locate configuration files and generate router configuration information
- Describe the purpose and function of router modes
- Describe user EXEC mode
- Describe privileged EXEC mode
- Describe global mode
- Describe specific configuration modes
- Describe password configuration
- Describe router identification

Chapter 15

Router Configuration

Introduction

In Chapter 14, "Router Startup and Setup Configuration," you learned how to start a router when it is used the first time by using the correct commands and startup sequence to do an initial configuration of a router. In this chapter, you will learn to use router modes and configuration methods to update a router's configuration file with current and prior versions of Cisco Internetwork Operating System (IOS) software.

Router Configuration Overview

A router uses the following information from the configuration file when it starts up:

- Cisco IOS software version
- Router identification
- Boot file locations
- Protocol information
- Interface configurations

The configuration file contains commands to customize router operation. As you learned in Chapter 14, if there is no configuration file available, the system configuration dialog setup guides you through the process of creating one.

Working with 11.0 or Later Configuration Files

Router configuration information can be generated by several means. The privileged EXEC **configure** command can be used to configure from either a virtual (remote) terminal or the console terminal, allowing you to enter changes to an existing configuration at any time. The privileged EXEC **configure** command can also be used to load a configuration from a network Trivial File Transfer Protocol (TFTP) server, allowing you to maintain and store configuration information at a central site.

Figure 15-1 illustrates the configuration command summary, which consists of the commands shown in Table 15-1.

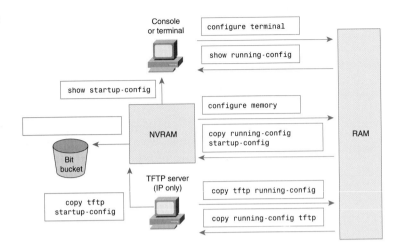

FIGURE 15-1
You use these commands for routers running Release 11.0 or later.

TABLE 15-1   **The Configuration Command Summary for Routers Running Release 11.0 or Later**

Command	Description
`configure terminal`	Configures the router manually from the console terminal.
`configure memory`	Loads configuration information from nonvolatile random-access memory (NVRAM).
`copy tftp running-config`	Loads configuration information from a network TFTP server.
`show running-config`	Displays the current configuration in RAM.
`copy running-config startup-config`	Stores the current configuration in RAM into NVRAM.
`copy running-config tftp`	Stores the current configuration in RAM on a network TFTP server.
`show startup-config`	Displays the saved configuration, which is the contents of NVRAM.
`erase startup-config`	Erases the contents of NVRAM.

Working with Pre-11.0 Configuration Files

The commands shown in Figure 15-2 are used with Cisco IOS Release 10.3 and earlier and have been replaced by new commands. The commands that have been replaced continue to perform their normal function in the current release but are no longer documented. Support for these commands will cease in a future release.

FIGURE 15-2
The configuration commands used with Cisco IOS Release 10.3 and earlier.

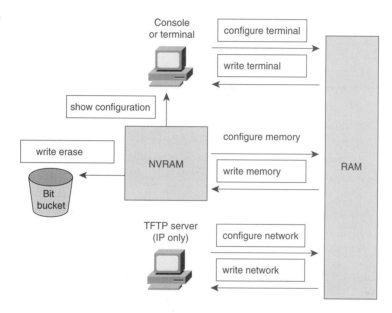

Using a TFTP Server

A current copy of the configuration can be stored on a TFTP server. You use the `copy running-config tftp` command, as shown in Listing 15-1, to store the current configuration in RAM on a network TFTP server. To do so, complete the following tasks:

1. Enter the `copy running-config tftp` command.

2. Enter the IP address of the host in which you want to store the configuration file.

3. Enter the name you would like to assign to the configuration file.

4. Confirm your choices by answering yes.

Listing 15-1 The `copy running-config tftp` Command

```
tokyo# copy running-config tftp
Remote host []? 131.108.2.155
Name of configuration file to write [tokyo-config]? tokyo.2
Write file tokyo.2 to 131.108.2.155? [confirm] y
Writing tokyo.2 !!!!!! [OK]
tokyo#
```

You can configure the router by loading the configuration file stored on one of your network servers. To do so, complete the following tasks:

1. Enter configuration mode by entering the `copy tftp running-config` command, as shown in Listing 15-2.

2. At the system prompt, select a host or network configuration file. The network configuration file contains commands that apply to all routers and terminal servers on the network. The host configuration file contains commands that apply to one router in particular.

3. At the system prompt, enter the optional IP address of the remote host from which you are retrieving the configuration file. In this example, the router is configured from the TFTP server at IP address 131.108.2.155. At the system prompt, enter the name of the configuration file or accept the default name. The filename convention is UNIX-based. The default filename is *hostname*-config for the host file and *network*-config for the network configuration file. In the DOS environment, the server filenames are limited to eight characters plus a three-character extension (for example, *router*.cfg). Confirm the configuration filename and the server address that the system supplies. In Listing 15-2, notice that the router prompt changes to tokyo immediately. This is evidence that the reconfiguration happens as soon as the new file is downloaded.

Listing 15-2 The `copy tftp running-config` Command

```
Router# copy tftp running-config
Host or network configuration file [host]?
IP address of remote hose [255.255.255.255]? 131.108.2.155
Name of configuration file [Router-config]? tokyo.2
Configure using tokyo.2 from 131.108.2.155? [confirm] y
Booting tokyo.2 from 131.108.2.155:!! [OK-874/16000 bytes]
tokyo.2
```

Using NVRAM with Release 10.3

The commands shown in Listing 15-3 manage the contents of NVRAM (see Table 15-2).

Listing 15-3 NVRAM Commands that Are Used with Cisco IOS Release 10.3 and Earlier

```
Router# configure memory
[OK]
Router#

Router# write erase
[OK]
Router#

Router# write memory
[OK]
Router#
```

```
Router# show configuration

Using 5057 out of 32768 bytes
!
enable-password san-fran
!
interface Ethernet 0
ip address 131.108.100.5 255.255.255.0
!

   -- More --
```

**TABLE 15-2   Commands Used to Manage the Contents of NVRAM in Cisco IOS
Release 11.x**

Command	Description
`configure memory`	Loads configuration information from NVRAM.
`erase startup-config`	Erases the contents of NVRAM.
`copy running-config startup-config`	Stores the current configuration in RAM (that is, the running configuration) into NVRAM (as the startup configuration).
`show startup-config`	Displays the saved configuration, which is the contents of NVRAM.

Using NVRAM with 11.0 Cisco IOS Releases

The commands shown in Listing 15-4 are used with Cisco IOS Release 10.3
and earlier. These commands have been replaced by new commands. The commands that have been replaced continue to perform their normal function in
the current release, but are no longer documented. Support for these commands will cease in a future release.

Listing 15-4 Release 11.x Commands that Manage the Contents of NVRAM

```
Router# configure memory
[OK]
Router#

Router# erase startup-config
[OK]
Router#

Router# copy running-config startup-config
[OK]
Router#

Router# show startup-config
```

```
Using 5057 out of 32768 bytes
!
enable-password san-fran
!
interface Ethernet 0
ip address 131.108.100.5 255.255.255.0
!

    -- More --
```

An Overview of Router Modes

The EXEC mode interprets the commands you type and carries out the corresponding operations. You must log in to the router before you can enter an EXEC command. There are two EXEC modes; the EXEC commands available at the user mode are a subset of the EXEC commands available at the privileged mode. From the privileged level, you can also access global configuration mode and specific configuration modes, some of which are shown in Figure 15-3 and listed in Table 15-3.

FIGURE 15-3
You use these router modes to configure a router.

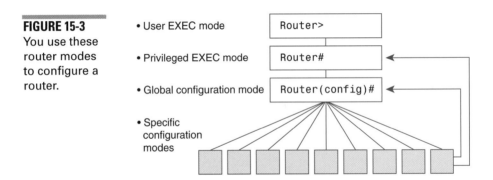

- User EXEC mode — Router>
- Privileged EXEC mode — Router#
- Global configuration mode — Router(config)#
- Specific configuration modes

TABLE 15-3   Configuration Modes and Prompts

Configuration Mode	Prompt
Interface	Router(config-if)#
Subinterface	Router(config-subif)#
Controller	Router(config-controller)#
Map-list	Router(config-map-list)#
Map-class	Router(config-map-class)#
Line	Router(config-line)#
Router	Router(config-router)#

TABLE 15-3   Configuration Modes and Prompts (Continued)

Configuration Mode	Prompt
IPX-router	Router(config-ipx-router)#
Route-map	Router(config-route-map)#

If you type **exit**, the router backs out one level, eventually allowing you to log out. In general, typing **exit** from one of the specific configuration modes returns you to global configuration mode. Pressing Ctrl-Z causes you to leave configuration mode completely and returns the router to privileged EXEC mode.

Configuration Modes

Global configuration mode commands apply to features that affect the system as a whole. They are used for systemwide configurations requiring one-line commands. In addition, global configuration mode commands include commands to enter other configuration modes, which are used for other configurations requiring multiple-line commands. You use the privileged EXEC command **configure**, as shown in Listing 15-5, to enter global configuration mode. When you enter this command, EXEC prompts you for the source of the configuration commands.

Listing 15-5 The Privileged EXEC Command configure
```
Router# configure terminal
Router(config)# (commands)
Router(config)# exit
Router#

Router# configure terminal
Router(config)# router protocol
Router(config-router)# (commands)
Router(config-router)# exit
Router(config)# interface type port
Router(config-if)# (commands)
Router(config-if)# exit
Router(config)# exit
Router#
```

You can then specify the terminal, NVRAM, or a file stored on a network server as the source. The default is to type commands from the terminal console. Pressing the Return key begins this configuration method. Commands to enable a particular routing or interface function begin with global configuration commands:

- To configure a routing protocol, which is indicated by the prompt Router(config-router)# in Listing 15-6, you first enter a global router protocol command type.

Listing 15-6 Configuring a Routing Protocol

```
Router# configure terminal
Router(config)# router protocol

Router(config-router)# (commands)
Router(config-router)#
```

- To configure an interface, which is indicated by the prompt Router(config-if)# in Listing 15-7, you first enter the global interface type and number command.

Listing 15-7 Configuring an Interface

```
Roter# configure terminal
Router(config)# interface type port
Router(config-if)# (commands)
Router(config-if)# exit
```

After entering commands in any of these modes, you finish with the command exit.

IP Routing Protocol Mode

After a routing protocol is enabled by a global command, the router configuration mode prompt Router(config-router)# is displayed, as shown in Listing 15-8. You type a question mark (?) to list the router configuration commands.

Listing 15-8 The Router Configuration Mode Prompt After a Routing Protocol Is Enabled

```
Router(config)# router?
bgp       Border Gateway Protocol (BGP)
egp       Exterior Gateway Protocol (EGP)
eigrp     Enhanced Interior Gateway Routing Protocol (EIGRP)
igrp      Interior Gateway Routing Protocol (IGRP)
isis      ISO IS-IS
iso-igrp  IGRP for OSI networks
mobile    Mobile routes
odr       On Demand stub Routes
ospf      Open Shortest Path First (OSPF)
rip       Routing Information Protocol (RIP)
static    Static routes

Router(config)# router rip
Router(config-router)# ?
Router configuration commands
default-information    Control distribution of default information
default-metric        Set metric of redistributed routes
distance              Define an administrative distance
distribute-list       Filter networks in routing updates
exit                  Exit from routing protocol configuration mode

-- More --
```

Interface Configuration Mode

Because all router interfaces are automatically in the administratively down mode, many features are enabled on a per-interface basis. Interface configuration commands modify the operation of an Ethernet, a Token Ring, or a serial port. In addition, interface subcommands always follow an interface command because the interface command defines the interface type.

In the following command the *type* argument includes **serial**, **ethernet**, **token ring**, and others:

```
Router(config)# interface type port
Router(config)# interface type slot/port
```

The following command is used to administratively turn off the interface:

```
Router(config-if)# shutdown
```

The following command is used to turn on an interface that has been shut down:

```
Router(config-if)# no shutdown
```

The following command is used to quit the current interface configuration mode:

```
Router(config-if)# exit
```

Interface Configuration Examples

The following commands are associated with interfaces:

```
Router(config)# interface serial 1/0
Router(config-if)# bandwidth 56
Router(config-if)# clockrate 56000
```

On serial links, one side must provide a clocking signal. This is provided by data communications equipment (DCE), such as a channel service unit/data service unit (CSU/DSU). On the other side of the link is data terminal equipment (DTE). By default, Cisco routers are DTE devices but, in some cases, they can be used as DCE devices.

If you are using an interface to provide clocking, you must specify a rate with the **clockrate** command. The **bandwidth** command overrides the default bandwidth that is displayed in the **show interfaces** command and is used by some routing protocols, such as Interior Gateway Routing Protocol (IGRP).

The following command is used to configure the primary interface:

```
Router(config)# interface serial 0
Router(config-if)# int & 0.1 point-to-point
Router(config-if)# int & 0.2 point-to-point
```

The following commands are associated with Cisco 4000 series routers:

```
Router(config)# interface ethernet 2
Router(config-if)# media-type 10baset
```

On a Cisco 4000 router, there are two connections on the outside of the box for Ethernet interfaces: an attachment unit interface (AUI) connector and a 10BaseT connector. The default is AUI, so you must specify media-type 10BaseT if you want to use the other connection.

Configuration Methods

In this section, you will learn the commands associated with the Cisco IOS configuration methods:

- Release 11.x configuration
- Pre-11.0 release configuration
- Password configuration
- Router identification configuration

Release 11.x Configuration Methods

The commands shown in Figure 15-4 are used with Cisco IOS Release 11.0 and later. Figure 15-4 shows you a way to

- Enter configuration statements
- Save the changes to a backup the router will use when it starts up
- Examine the changes you have made
- If necessary, modify or remove configuration statements

FIGURE 15-4
You use these configuration commands with Release 11.x configuration methods.

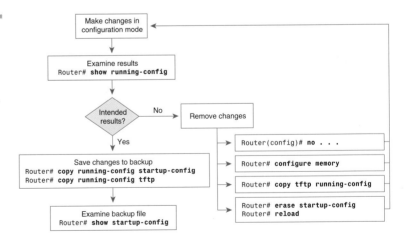

Pre-11.0 Release Configuration

The commands shown in Figure 15-5 are used with Cisco IOS Release 10.3 and earlier. They have been replaced by new commands. The commands that have been replaced continue to perform their normal functions in the current release but are no longer documented. Support for these commands will cease in a future release.

FIGURE 15-5
You use these commands for routers running Cisco IOS Release 10.3 and earlier.

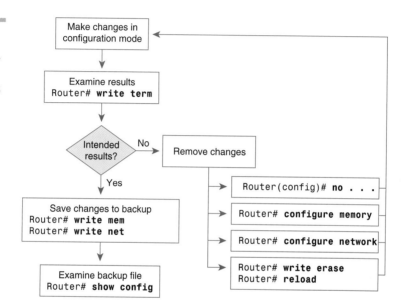

Password Configuration

You can secure your system by using passwords to restrict access. Passwords can be established both on individual lines and to the privileged EXEC mode:

- The **line console 0** command establishes a password on the console terminal:

```
Router(config)# line console 0
Router(config-line)# login
Router(config-line)# password cisco
```

- The **line vty 0 4** command establishes password protection on incoming Telnet sessions:

```
Router(config)# line vty 0 4
Router(config-line)# login
Router(config-line)# password cisco
```

- The **enable password** command restricts access to privileged EXEC mode:

```
Router(config)# enable password san-fran
```

■ The `enable secret` password from the system configuration dialog to set up global parameters uses a Cisco-proprietary encryption process to alter the password character string. Passwords can be further protected from display through the use of the `service password-encryption` command. The encryption algorithm does not match the Data Encryption Standard (DES):

```
Router(config)# service password-encryption
        (set passwords here)
Router(config)# no service password-encryption
```

Router Identification Configuration

The configuration of network devices determines the network's behavior. To manage device configurations, you need to list and compare configuration files on running devices, store configuration files on network servers for shared access, and perform software installations and upgrades.

One of the first basic tasks is to name your router. The name of the router is considered to be the host name and is the name displayed by the system prompt. If no name is configured, the system default router name is Router. You can name the router in global configuration mode. In the example shown in Figure 15-6, the router name is set to Tokyo.

FIGURE 15-6
The identification of the router can be set in global configuration mode.

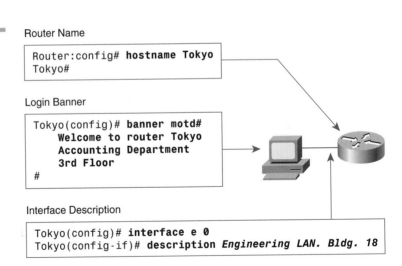

Router Name

```
Router:config# hostname Tokyo
Tokyo#
```

Login Banner

```
Tokyo(config)# banner motd#
    Welcome to router Tokyo
    Accounting Department
    3rd Floor
#
```

Interface Description

```
Tokyo(config)# interface e 0
Tokyo(config-if)# description Engineering LAN. Bldg. 18
```

You can configure a message-of-the-day banner to be displayed on all connected terminals. This banner is displayed at login and is useful for conveying messages that affect all network users, such as impending system shutdowns. To configure this message, use the `banner motd` command in global configuration mode.

Summary

- The router uses information from the configuration file when it starts up.
- Configuration files can come from the console, NVRAM, or a TFTP server.
- The commands used with Cisco IOS Release 10.3 and earlier have been replaced by new commands.
- EXEC mode interprets the commands you type and carries out the corresponding operations.
- A router has several modes:
  - Privileged mode is used for copying and managing entire configuration files.
  - Global configuration mode is used for one-line commands and commands that change the entire router.
  - Other configuration modes are used for multiple command lines and detailed configurations.
- You can secure your system by using passwords to restrict access.
- The configuration of network devices determines the network's behavior.

Review Questions

1. Which of the following is *not* a function of the privileged EXEC `configure` command?

   A. To configure a router from a virtual terminal

   B. To configure a TFTP server from a virtual terminal

   C. To configure a router from the console terminal

   D. To load a configuration from a network TFTP server

2. What is the function of the `configure memory` router command?

   A. It loads configuration information from NVRAM.

   B. It erases the contents of NVRAM.

   C. It stores in NVRAM the current configuration in RAM.

   D. It displays the configuration saved in NVRAM.

3. What is the function of the `copy running-config startup-config` router command?

   A. It loads configuration information from NVRAM.

   B. It erases the contents of NVRAM.

   C. It stores in NVRAM the current configuration in RAM.

   D. It displays the configuration saved in NVRAM.

4. If you want to completely back out of configuration mode, which of the following must you enter?

   A. `exit`

   B. `no config-mode`

   C. Ctrl-E

   D. Ctrl-Z

5. If you are planning to configure an interface, what prompt should be on the router?

   A. `router(config)#`

   B. `router(config-in)#`

   C. `router(config-intf)#`

   D. `router(config-if)#`

6. Which of the following is a correct order for the process of configuring a router? (Assume that you have already made router changes in configuration mode.)

A. (1) Save changes to backup, (2) decide whether the changes are your intended results, (3) examine the results, and (4) examine the backup file.

B. (1) Examine the results, (2) decide whether the changes are your intended results, (3) save the changes to backup, and (4) examine the backup file.

C. (1) Decide whether the changes are your intended results, (2) examine the backup file, (3) save the changes to backup, and (4) examine the results.

D. (1) Examine the results, (2) save the changes to backup, (3) decide whether the changes are your intended results, and (4) examine the backup file.

7. Which of the following is a command that can be used to save router configuration changes to a backup?

A. `Router# copy running-config tftp`

B. `Router# show running-config`

C. `Router# config mem`

D. `Router# copy tftp running-config`

8. Which of the following is *not* a command to remove router configuration changes?

A. `Router(config)# no ...`

B. `Router# config mem`

C. `Router# copy running-config startup-config`

D. `Router# copy tftp running-config`

9. Which of the following correctly describes password configuration on routers?

A. All passwords are established in privileged EXEC mode.

B. All passwords alter the password character string.

C. A password can be established on all incoming Telnet sessions.

D. The `enable password` command restricts access to user EXEC mode.

10. Which of the following does *not* describe password configuration on routers?

A. Passwords can be established in every configuration mode.

B. A password can be established on any console terminal.

C. The `enable secret` password uses an encryption process to alter the password character string.

D. All password establishment begins in global configuration mode.

Objectives

After reading this chapter, you will be able to

- Describe the process used to locate Cisco Internetwork Operating System (IOS) software

- Identify the commands to locate information about Cisco IOS software

- Describe how to specify a fall-back system for booting Cisco IOS software

- Describe how to use a Trivial File Transfer Protocol (TFTP) server to load software onto the router

- Describe the process for checking the router to see whether it can handle software

- Describe the process and commands for creating and loading a software image backup

- Describe how to read naming conventions

Chapter 16

Sources for Cisco IOS Software

Introduction

In Chapter 15, "Router Configuration," you learned to use router modes and configuration methods to update a router's configuration file with current and prior versions of Cisco IOS software. In this chapter, you will learn to use a variety of Cisco IOS software source options, execute commands to load Cisco IOS software onto the router, maintain backup files, and upgrade Cisco IOS software. In addition, you will learn about the functions of the configuration register and how to determine what version of the file you have. This chapter also describes how to use a TFTP server as a software source.

Locating Cisco IOS Software

The default source for Cisco IOS software depends on the hardware platform, but most commonly the router looks to the configuration commands saved in nonvolatile random-access memory (NVRAM). Cisco IOS software offers several alternatives: You can specify other sources where the router should look for software, or the router can use its own fallback sequence as necessary to load software.

As depicted in Figure 16-1, the settings in the configuration register enable the following alternatives for where the router will bootstrap Cisco IOS software:

- You can specify enabled config-mode `boot system` commands to enter fallback sources for the router to use in sequence. Save these statements in NVRAM to use during the next startup with the command `copy running-config startup-config`. The router will use these commands as needed, in sequence, when it restarts.
- If NVRAM lacks `boot system` commands that the router can use, the router will fall back and use default Cisco IOS in Flash memory.
- If Flash memory is empty, the router will try its next TFTP alternative. The router uses the configuration register value to form a filename from which to boot a default system image stored on a network server.

FIGURE 16-1
Settings in the configuration register enable alternatives for where the router will bootstrap Cisco IOS software.

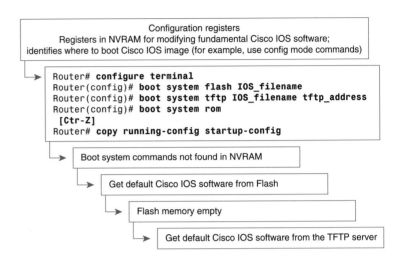

Configuration Register Values

The order in which the router looks for system bootstrap information depends on the boot field setting in the configuration register. You can change the default configuration register setting with the enabled config-mode command `config-register`. You use a hexadecimal number as the argument to this command:

```
Router# configure terminal
Router(config)# config-register 0x10F
 [Ctrl-Z]
```

In this example, the configuration register is set so that the router will examine the startup file in NVRAM for boot system options. The configuration register is a 16-bit register in NVRAM. The lowest 4 bits of the configuration register (bits 3, 2, 1, and 0) form the boot field. To change the boot field and leave all other bits set to their default values, follow these guidelines (see Table 16-1):

- Set the configuration register value to `0x100` if you need to enter the ROM monitor, which is primarily a programmer's environment. From the ROM monitor, boot the operating system manually by using the `b` command at the ROM monitor prompt. (This value sets the boot field bits to `0-0-0-0`.)

- Set the configuration register to `0x101` to configure the system to boot automatically from ROM. (This value sets the boot field bits to `0-0-0-1`.)

- Set the configuration register to any value from `0x102` to `0x10F` to configure the system to use the boot system commands in NVRAM. This is the default. (These values set the boot field bits to `0-0-1-0` through `1-1-1-1`.)

To check the boot field setting—for example, to verify the `config-register` command—you use the `show version` command.

TABLE 16-1 `config-register` **Values**

Value	Description
0x100	Use ROM monitor mode (manually boot using the **b** command).
0x101	Automatically boot from ROM (default if router has no Flash).
0x102 to 0x10F	Examine NVRAM for boot system commands (0x2 is the default if the router has Flash).

The show version Command

The `show version` command displays information about the Cisco IOS software version that is currently running on the router. This includes the boot field setting. In the example illustrated in Listing 16-1, the Cisco IOS version and descriptive information is highlighted on the second output line. The listing shows an experimental version of Release 11.2. The line

```
System image file is "c4500-f-mz", booted via tftp from 171.69.1.129
```

shows the system image name. You will learn about Cisco IOS software Release 11.2 image naming conventions later in this chapter. For now, notice the portion of the filename that indicates that this image is for a Cisco 4500 platform.

Listing 16-1 The show version Command

```
Router# show version
Cisco Internetwork Operating System Software
IOS (tm) 4500 Software (C4500-J-M),
    Experimental Version 11.2(19960626:214907) ]
Copyright (c)1986-1006 by Cisco Systems, Inc.
Compiled Fri 28-Jun-96  16.32 by rbeach
Image text-base: 0x600088A0, data-base: 0x6076E000

ROM: System Bootstrap, Version 5.1(1) [daveu 1], RELEASE SOFTWARE (fc1)
ROM: 4500-XBOOT Bootstrap Software, Version 10.1(1), RELEASE SOFTWARE (fc1)

router uptime is 1 week, 3 days, 32 minutes
System restarted by reload
System image file is "c4500-f-mz", booted via tftp from 171.69.1.129

Cisco 4500 (R4K) processor (revision 0x00) with 32768K/16384K bytes of memory
Processor board ID 01217941
R4600 processor, implementation 32, Revision 1.0
G.703/E1 software, Version 1.0
Bridging software
SuperLAT software copyright 1990 by Meridian Technology Corp.
```

```
X.25 software, Version 2.0, NET2, BFE and GOSIP compliant
TN3270 Emulation software (copyright 1994 by TGV Inc.)
Primary Rate ISDN software, Version 1.0
2 Ethernet/IEEE 802.3 interfaces.
48 Serial network interfaces.
2 Channelized t1/PRI ports.
128K bytes of non-volatile configuration memory.
8192K bytes of processor board System flash (Read/Write)
4096K bytes of processor board Boot flash (Read/Write)
```

As it continues to output, the `show version` command displays information about the type of platform on which the version of Cisco IOS software is currently running.

Bootstrap Options in Software

You can enter multiple boot system commands to specify the fallback sequence for booting Cisco IOS software. The following three examples show boot system entries that specify that a Cisco IOS image will load first from Flash memory, next from a network server, and finally from ROM:

NOTE

You will not see evidence of any config-register setting in output from either the **show running-config** or **show startup-config** commands.

- *Flash memory*—Using this approach, you can copy a system image without changing electrically erasable programmable read-only memory (EEPROM). Information stored in Flash memory is not vulnerable to the network failures that can occur when loading system images from TFTP servers:

```
Router# configure terminal
Router(config)# boot system flash gsnew-image
 [Ctrl-Z]
Router# copy running-config startup-config
```

- *Network server*—To provide for a backup in case Flash memory becomes corrupted, you can specify that a system image should be loaded from a TFTP server:

```
Router# configure terminal
Router(config)# boot system tftp test exe 172.16.13.111
 [Ctrl-Z]
Router# copy running-config startup-config
```

- *ROM*—If Flash memory is corrupted and the network server fails to load the image, booting from ROM is the final bootstrap option in software. However, the system image in ROM will likely be a subset of Cisco IOS software that lacks the protocols, features, and configurations of full Cisco IOS software. It may also be an older version of Cisco IOS software if you have updated software since you purchased the router:

```
Router# configure terminal
Router(config)# boot system rom
 [Ctrl-Z]
Router# copy running-config startup-config
```

The command `copy running-config startup-config` saves the command in NVRAM. The router executes the `boot system` commands as needed, in the order in which they were originally entered in configuration mode.

Preparing for TFTP

Production internetworks usually span wide areas and contain multiple routers. These geographically distributed routers need a source or backup location for software images. Using a TFTP server allows image and configuration uploads and downloads over the network.

The TFTP server can be another router, or it can be a host system. The TFTP server could be a workstation running UNIX. The host could also be a laptop computer running DOS or Windows. The TFTP host can be any system with TFTP loaded and operating that is able to contain files on the TCP/IP network.

You will be copying software between the TFTP host and Flash memory in the router. To prepare for using the TFTP server, you must check for the following preliminary conditions:

- Check the router to make sure you can see and write into Flash. Verify that the router has sufficient room in Flash to accommodate the Cisco IOS software image:

  ```
  Router# show flash
  4096 kbytes of flash memory on embedded flash (in XX).

  file    offset     length       name
  0       0x40       1204637      xk09140z
    [903848/2097152 bytes free]
  ```

- Check the TFTP server to make sure you can access it over the TCP/IP network. You can use the `ping` command as one method to check this:

  ```
  Router# ping tftp-address
  ...
  !!!!!
  ```

- Check the TFTP server to make sure you know the file or file space for the Cisco IOS software image. For upload and download operations, you need to specify a path or filename:

  ```
  ls gs7-j-mz. 112-0.11
  ```

It is efficient to perform these preparation steps because they help ensure a successful file copy. If you rush into the file copy itself, chances are good that the copy will fail and you will have to begin troubleshooting the cause of the copy failure.

The show flash **Command**

You use the **show flash** command to verify that you have sufficient memory on your system for the Cisco IOS software you want to load. In the following example, the router has 4 MB of Flash, all of it free:

```
Router# show flash
4096K bytes of flash memory sized on embedded flash
File name/status
 0  mater/California//i11/bin/gs7-j-mz.112-0.11 [deleted]
 [0/4194304 bytes free/total]
```

Compare this with the length of the Cisco IOS software image. Sources for this image size may include the software order document or output from the configuration software application on the Cisco Connection Online (CCO) World Wide Web site.

If there is insufficient free memory, you will not be able to copy or load the image. If that obstacle occurs, you can either try to obtain a smaller Cisco IOS software image or increase the memory available on the router.

Cisco IOS Naming Conventions

Cisco products have expanded beyond the generic router to include many platforms at all ends of the network product spectrum. To optimize how Cisco IOS software operates on these various platforms, Cisco is working to develop many different Cisco IOS software images. These images accommodate the various platforms, available memory resources, and feature set needs customers have for their network devices.

With Cisco IOS Release 11.2, the naming convention for Cisco IOS software involves the following three parts, which are depicted in Table 16-2:

- The first part of the image name contains the platform on which the image runs.
- The second part of the image name identifies the special capabilities of the image. A letter or series of letters identifies the feature sets supported in the image.
- The third part of the image name specifies where the image runs and whether it has been zip compressed.

The Cisco IOS software naming conventions, name part field meaning, image content, and other details are subject to change. Refer to your sales representative, distribution channel, or CCO for updated details.

TABLE 16-2   Naming Conventions for Cisco IOS Release 11.2

Naming Example	Hardware Product Platform	Feature Capability	Run Location Compressed Status
cpa25-cg-l	CiscoPro 2500 (cpa25)	Comm-server/ Remote Access Server, ISDN (cg)	Relocatable, not compressed (l)
igs-inr-l	Cisco ICG, 25xx, and 3xxx (igs)	IP subset, Novell IPX, and IBM base option (inr)	Relocatable, not compressed (l)
c4500-aj-m	Cisco 4500 and 4700 (c4500)	APPN and Enterprise subset for low-end/midrange (aj)	RAM, not compressed (m)
gs7-k-mz	Cisco 7000 and 7010 (gs7)	Enterprise for high-end range (k)	RAM, zip compressed (mz)

Creating a Software Image Backup

You can copy a system image back to a network server. This copy of the system image can serve as a backup copy and can be used to verify that the copy in Flash is the same as the original disk file. Listing 16-2 and Figure 16-2 use the **show flash** command to learn the name of the system image file (xk09140z) and the **copy flash tftp** command to copy the system image to a TFTP server.

Listing 16-2 The show flash and copy flash tftp Commands

```
Router# show flash
4096 bytes of flash memory on embedded flash (in XX).

file    offset    length       name
0       0x40      1204637      xk09140z
  [903848/2097152 bytes free]

Router# copy flash tftp
IP address of remote host [255.255.255.255]? 172.16.13.111
filename to write on tftp hose? c4500-i
writing C4500-l !!!!!!!!!!!!!!!!!!!!!!!!!!!!!!!!!!!!!!!!!
successful tftp write.
Router#
```

The files can be renamed during transfer.

FIGURE 16-2
You can use
the show flash
command to
learn the name
of the system
image file
(xk09140z) and
the copy flash
tftp command
to copy the
system image
to a TFTP
server.

In this example, an administrator is backing up the current image to the TFTP server. One scenario for this upload to the server would be to provide a fallback copy of the current image prior to updating the image with a new version. Then, if the new version has trouble, the administrator can download the backed-up image and return to the image that was running before the update attempt.

Upgrading the Image from the Net

After you have provided for a backup copy of the current Cisco IOS software image, proceed to load a new image. Download the new image from the TFTP server by using the command copy tftp flash. Listing 16-3 and Figure 16-3 show that the copy tftp flash command begins operation by requesting the IP address of the remote host that will act as a TFTP server.

Listing 16-3 The copy tftp flash Command
```
Router# copy tftp flash
IP address or name of remote host [255.255.255.255]? 172.16.13.111
Name of tftp filename to copy into flash []? c4500-aj-m
copy C4500-AJ-M from 172.16.13.111 into flash memory? [confirm] <Return>
xxxxxxxx bytes available for writing without erasure.
erase flash before writing? [confirm] <Return>
Clearing and initializing flash memory [please wait] ####...##
Loading from 172.16.13.111: !!!!!!!!!!!!!!!!!!!!!!!!!!!!!
!!!!!!! (text omitted) [OK - 324572/524212 bytes]
Verifying checksum...
VVVVVVVVVVVVVVVVVVVVVVVVVVVVVVVVVVVVVVVVVVVVVVVVVVVV
VVVVVVVVV (text omitted)
Flash verification successful. Length = 1804637, checksum = 0xA5D3
```

Next, you are prompted for the name of the update image. By preparing for this, you can enter the correct and appropriate filename of the update image as it is named on the TFTP server.

FIGURE 16-3
The **copy tftp flash** command begins operation by requesting the IP address of the remote host that will act as a TFTP server.

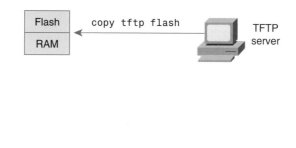

Following an opportunity to confirm your entries, the procedure asks whether you are willing to erase Flash. This makes room for the new image. Often, there is not sufficient Flash memory for more than a single Cisco IOS image. You have the option of erasing the existing Flash memory before writing to it. If no free Flash memory space is available, or if the Flash memory has never been written to, the erase routine is usually required before new files can be copied. The system informs you of these conditions and prompts you for a response.

Each exclamation point (!) means that one User Datagram Protocol (UDP) segment has successfully transferred. The series of vs indicates successful check run verification of a segment.

You use the **show flash** command to view the file and to compare its size with that of the original on the server before changing the **boot system** commands to use the updated image. Following a successful copy, the **reload** command boots the router as specified with the boot system using the updated image.

Loading a Software Image Backup

If you need to load the backup Cisco IOS version, you use the **copy tftp flash** command. With this variation of the command, you can download the image that you previously uploaded to the TFTP server.

After you enter the **copy tftp flash** command, as shown in Listing 16-4, the system prompts you for the IP address (or name) of the TFTP server.

Listing 16-4 The `copy tftp flash` **Command**

```
Router# copy tftp flash
IP address or name of remote host [255.255.255.255]? 172.16.13.111
Name of tftp filename to copy into flash []? c4500-i
copy C4500-I already exists; it will be invalidated!
Copy C4500-I from 172.16.13.111 into flash memory? [confirm] <Return>
xxxxxxxx bytes available for writing without erasure.
erase flash before writing? [confirm] <Return>
Clearing and initializing flash memory [please wait] ####...##
Loading from 172.16.13.111: !!!!!!!!!!!!!!!!!!!!!!!!!!!!!
!!!!!!! (text omitted) [OK - 324572/524212 bytes]
Verifying checksum...
vvvvvvvvvvvvvvvvvvvvvvvvvvvvvvvvvvvvvvvvvvvvvvvvvvvvvvvvv
vvvvvvvvvv (text omitted)
Flash verification successful. Length = 1204637, checksum = 0x95D9
```

This can be another router serving ROM or Flash system software images. You are then prompted for the filename of the software image. Listing 16-4 shows sample output from copying a system image named C4500-I into Flash memory.

If you attempt to copy into Flash memory a file that is already there, a prompt tells you that a file with the same name already exists. This file is deleted when you copy the new file into Flash. The first copy of the file still resides within Flash memory but is rendered unusable in favor of the newest version. It will be listed with the *[deleted]* tag when you use the **show flash** command.

If you abort the copy process, the newer file is marked *[deleted]* because the entire file was not copied and, therefore, is not valid. In this case, the original file still resides within Flash memory and is available to the system.

Summary

- The default source for Cisco IOS software depends on the hardware platform but, most commonly, the router looks to the configuration commands saved in NVRAM.

- The **show version** command displays information about the Cisco IOS software version that is currently running on the router.

- You can enter multiple boot system commands to specify the fallback sequence for booting Cisco IOS software. Routers can boot Cisco IOS software from Flash, the TFTP server, and ROM.

- You use the **show flash** command to verify that you have sufficient memory on your system for the Cisco IOS software you want to load.

- With Cisco IOS Release 11.2, the naming convention for Cisco IOS contains the following three parts:
  - The platform on which the image runs
  - The special capabilities of the image
  - Where the image runs and whether it has been zip compressed
- You can copy a system image back to a network server. This copy of the system image can serve as a backup copy and can be used to verify that the copy in Flash is the same as the original disk file.
- You can download a new image from the TFTP server by using the command `copy tftp flash`.
- If you need to load the backup Cisco IOS version, you can use a variation of the `copy tftp flash` command to download the image you previously uploaded to the TFTP server.

Review Questions

1. Which of the following is the sequence used by the router for automatic fallback to locate the Cisco IOS software?

   A. (1) Flash, (2) NVRAM, (3) TFTP server

   B. (1) NVRAM, (2) TFTP server, (3) Flash

   C. (1) NVRAM, (2) Flash, (3) TFTP server

   D. (1) TFTP server, (2) Flash, (3) NVRAM

2. Which of the following does *not* describe configuration register settings for Cisco IOS bootstrapping?

   A. The order in which the router looks for system bootstrap information depends on the boot field setting.

   B. You change the configuration register setting with the command `config-register.`

   C. You use a hexadecimal number when setting the configuration register boot field.

   D. Use the `show running-config` command to check the boot field setting.

3. Which of the following is *not* displayed by the Cisco IOS `show version` command?

   A. Statistics for configured interfaces

   B. The type of platform running the Cisco IOS software

   C. The configuration register setting

   D. The Cisco IOS version

4. Which of the following is *not* part of specifying the fallback sequence to boot the Cisco IOS software?

   A. Boot system commands are entered from global configuration mode.

   B. One boot system command is used to specify the entire fallback sequence.

   C. The command `copy running-config startup-config` saves boot system commands to NVRAM.

   D. Boot system commands are executed as needed during fallback in the order in which they were entered.

5. Which of the following correctly describes preparing to use a TFTP server to copy software to Flash memory?

  A. The TFTP server must be another router or a host system, such as a UNIX workstation or a laptop computer.

  B. The TFTP host must be a system connected to an Ethernet network.

  C. The name of the router containing the Flash memory must be identified.

  D. The Flash memory must be enabled.

6. Which of the following is the fastest way to make sure the TFTP server is reachable prior to trying to transfer a Cisco IOS image file?

  A. `trace` the TFTP server.

  B. `ping` the TFTP server.

  C. `telnet` to the TFTP server.

  D. Call the TFTP server administrator.

7. Why do you need to determine the file size of the Cisco IOS image on the TFTP server before transferring it to your router?

  A. To check that there is enough space in Flash to store the file

  B. To verify that the file is the correct Cisco IOS version for your router

  C. To complete a TFTP operation

  D. To calculate the download time for the file and, thus, the amount of time the router will be out of service

8. Why do you create a Cisco IOS software image backup?

  A. To verify that the copy in Flash is the same as the copy in ROM.

  B. To provide a fallback copy of the current image prior to copying the image to a new router.

  C. To create a fallback copy of the current image as part of the procedures during recovery from system failure.

  D. To create a fallback copy of the current image prior to updating with a new version.

9. Which of the following has a limited version of Cisco IOS software?

  A. ROM

  B. Flash

C. TFTP server

D. ROM monitor

10. What is the command you need to issue if you want to upgrade an old version of the Cisco IOS by downloading a new image from the TFTP server?

A. boot system tftp 131.21.11.3

B. copy tftp flash***

C. show flash

D. tftp ios.exe

Objectives

After reading this chapter, you will be able to

- Describe TCP/IP addresses, host addresses, and broadcast addresses
- Describe the format of IP addresses
- Understand the process used to configure IP addresses, including
  - Logical network addresses
  - Network masks
- Describe name server configuration
- Describe display commands
- Describe the verification of IP addresses by using
  - `telnet`
  - `ping`
  - `trace`

Chapter 17

Configuring Router Interfaces with IP Addresses

Introduction

In Chapter 16, "Sources for Cisco IOS Software," you learned to use a variety of Cisco Internetwork Operating System (IOS) software source options, execute commands to load Cisco IOS software onto the router, maintain backup files, and upgrade Cisco IOS software. In this chapter, you will learn the details of IP address classes, network and mode addresses, and subnet masking. In addition, you will learn the basic concepts you need to understand before configuring an IP address.

TCP/IP Address Overview

In a TCP/IP environment, end stations communicate with servers or other end stations. This occurs because each node using the TCP/IP protocol suite has a unique 32-bit logical address known as the *IP address*.

Often traffic is forwarded through the internetwork based on the name of an organization rather than an individual person or host. If names are used instead of addresses, each name must be translated to the numeric address before the traffic can be delivered. The location of the organization dictates the path the data follows through the internetwork.

Each company listed on the internetwork has a unique 32-bit logical address. This address is seen as a single unique network that must be reached before an individual host within that company can be contacted. Each company network has an address; the hosts that live on that network share that same network address, but each host is identified by the unique host address on the network. (See Figure 17-1.)

FIGURE 17-1
A unique 32-bit logical address must be reached before an individual host within a company can be contacted.

Concepts of IP Address Configuration

In this section, you will learn basic concepts you need to understand before configuring an IP address. By examining various network requirements, you can select the correct class of address and define how to establish IP subnets.

Host Addresses

Each device or interface must have a nonzero host number. A host address of all ones is reserved for an IP broadcast into that network, as shown in Figure 17-2. A value of zero means "this network" or "the wire itself" (for example, 172.16.0.0). A value of zero was also used for IP broadcasts in some early TCP/IP implementations, although it is rarely found now. The routing table (shown in Table 17-1) contains entries for network or wire addresses; it usually does not contain any information about hosts.

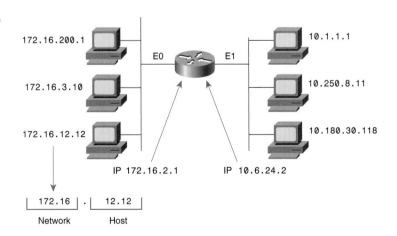

FIGURE 17-2
All hosts must have non-zero IP addresses.

TABLE 17-1   **A Routing Table that Contains Entries for Network Addresses**

Network	Interface
172.16.0.0	E0
10.0.0.0	E1

An IP address with a subnet address on an interface achieves three purposes:

- It enables the system to process the receipt and transmission of packets.
- It specifies the device's local address.
- It specifies a range of addresses that share the cable with the device.

A Subnetting Example

Figure 17-3 and Table 17-2 show a small network with assigned interface addresses, subnet masks, and the resulting subnet numbers. The number of bits in each subnet mask is indicated by the /8 following the mask.

FIGURE 17-3
Interface addresses, subnet masks, and the resulting subnet numbers are assigned to a network.

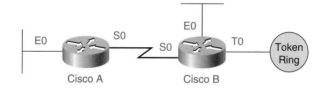

TABLE 17-2   **Network Assignment**

Interface Address	Subnet Mask	Subnet Number
Cisco A		
E0: 172.16.2.1	255.255.255.0/8	172.16.2.0
S0: 172.16.1.1	255.255.255.0/8	172.16.1.0
Cisco B		
S0: 172.16.1.2	255.255.255.0/8	172.16.1.0
E0: 172.31.4.1	255.255.255.0/8	172.31.4.0
T0: 172.31.16.1	255.255.255.0/8	172.31.16.0

Broadcast Address

Broadcasting is supported on the Internet. Broadcast messages are those you want every host on the network to see. The broadcast address is formed by using an IP address of all ones.

The Cisco IOS software supports two kinds of broadcasts: directed broadcasts and flooded broadcasts. Flooded broadcasts (represented by the address 255.255.255.255) are not propagated, but are considered local broadcasts, as illustrated in Figure 17-4. Broadcasts directed into a specific network are allowed and are forwarded by the router. These directed broadcasts contain all ones in the host portion of the address.

FIGURE 17-4
You can broadcast locally or to a subnet.

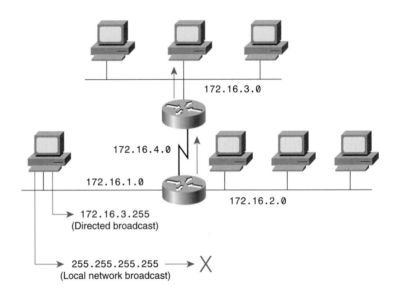

172.16.3.0

172.16.4.0

172.16.1.0

172.16.2.0

→ 172.16.3.255
(Directed broadcast)

→ 255.255.255.255 ⟶ X
(Local network broadcast)

IP Address Configuration

You use the **ip address** command as follows to establish the logical network address of this interface:

```
Router(config-if)# ip address ip-address subnet-mask
```

where *ip-address* is a 32-bit dotted-decimal number and *subnet-mask* is a 32-bit dotted-decimal number; ones indicate positions that must match and zeros indicate positions that do not match. The **ip address** command assigns an address and a subnet mask and starts IP processing on an interface.

You use the **term ip** *netmask-format* command as follows to specify the format of network masks for the current session:

```
Router(config)# term ip netmask-format
```

This command sets the format of the network mask (see Table 17-3). Format options for the network mask are

- Bit count
- Dotted decimal (the default)
- Hexadecimal.

TABLE 17-3   IP Address Commands

Command Level	Command	Purpose
Router (config-if) #	**ip address** *ip-address subnet mask*	Assigns an address and subnet to an interface; starts IP processing.
Router #	Term ip netmask-format {bit-count/decimal/hexadecmimal}	Sets format of network mask for current session.
Router (confi-if) #	ip netmask-format {bitcount/ decimal/hexadecimal}	Sets format of network mask for a specific line.

IP Host Names

The Cisco IOS software maintains a table of host names and their corresponding addresses, also called *host name–to–address mapping*. Telnet uses host names to identify network devices (hosts). The router and other network devices must be able to associate host names with IP addresses to communicate with other IP devices.

The **ip host** command makes a static name-to-address entry in the router's configuration file (see Table 17-4).

TABLE 17-4   The ip host Command

ip host Command	Description
name	Any name you prefer to describe the destination.
tcp-port-number	An optional number that identifies the TCP port to use when using the host name with an EXEC connect or Telnet command. The default is port23 for Telnet.
address	An IP address or addresses where the device can be reached.

The following command defines static host name–to–IP address mapping:

```
Router(config)# ip host name [tcp-port-number] address [address]...
ip host tokyo 1.0.0.5 2.0.0.8
ip host kyoto 1.0.0.4
```

where `1.0.0.5 2.0.0.8` defines two network addresses to the host `tokyo` and `1.0.0.4` defines `kyoto` as a name equivalent for the address `1.0.0.4`.

Name Server Configuration

The `ip name-server` command defines which hosts can provide the name service. A maximum of six IP addresses can be specified as name servers in a single command.

```
Router(config)# ip name-server server-address1 [[server-address2] ...server-address6]
```

To map domain names to IP addresses, you must identify the host names; then specify a name server and enable the Domain Name System (DNS). Any time the operating system software receives a command or an address it does not recognize, it refers to DNS for the IP address of that device.

Name-to-Address Schemes

Each unique IP address can have a host name associated with it. The Cisco IOS software maintains a cache of host name–to–address mappings for use by EXEC commands. This cache speeds the process of converting names to addresses.

IP defines a naming scheme that allows a device to be identified by its location in IP. A name such as `ftp.cisco.com` identifies the domain of the File Transfer Protocol (FTP) for Cisco. To keep track of domain names, IP identifies a name server that manages the name cache.

DNS is enabled by default with a server address of `255.255.255.255`, which is a local broadcast. As shown here, the `no ip domain-lookup` command turns off name-to-address translation in the router:

```
Router(config)# no ip domain-lookup
```

This means that the router will not forward DNS broadcast packets.

Displaying Host Names

The `show hosts` command, which is shown in Listing 17-1, is used to display a cached list of host names and addresses.

Listing 17-1 The `show hosts` Command
```
Router# show hosts
Default domain is not set
Name/address lookup uses static mappings
```

```
Host        Flags         Age   Type   Address(es)
TOKYO       (perm, OK)    5     IP     144.253.100.200  133.3.13.2
                                       133.3.5.1   133.3.10.1
S           (perm, OK)    **    IP     172.16.100.156
LUBBOCK     (perm, OK)    5     IP     183,8.128.12   153.50.3.2
AMARILLO    (perm, OK)    **    IP     153.50.129.200   153.50.3.1
BELLEVUE    (perm, OK)    **    IP     144.253.100.201   153.50.193.2
                                       153.50.65.1   153.50.33.1
BOSTON      (perm, OK)    **    IP     144.253.100.203   192.3.63.129
                                       192.3.63.33   192.3.63.65
CHICAGO     (perm, OK)    5     IP     183.8.0.129   183.8.128.130
                                       183.8.64.130
Router      (perm, OK)    **    IP     144.253.100.202   183.8.128.2
                                       183.8.128.129   183.8.64.129
FARGO       (perm, OK)    **    IP     183.8.0.130   183.8.64.100
HARTFORD    (perm, OK)    **    IP     192.3.63.196   192.3.63.34
                                       192.3.63.66
HOUSTON     (perm, OK)    **    IP     153.50.129.1   153.50.65.2
--More --
```

Table 17-5 shows output from the **show hosts** command, which you can use to obtain specific information about a host name entry.

TABLE 17-5   **show hosts Command Output**

show hosts Fields	Description
Host	Names of learned hosts
Flag	Descriptions of how information was learned and its current status
perm	Manually configured in a static host table
temp	Acquired from DNS use
OK	Entry is current
EX	Entry has aged out or expired
Age	Time, measured in hours, since software referred to the entry
Type	Protocol field
Address(es)	Logical addresses associated with the name of the host

Verifying Address Configuration

Addressing problems are the most common problems that occur on IP networks. It is important to verify your address configuration before continuing with further configuration steps. These three commands allow you to verify address configuration in your network:

- **telnet**—Verifies the application-layer software between source and destination stations. This is the most complete test mechanism available.
- **ping**—Uses Internet Control Message Protocol (ICMP) to verify the hardware connection and the logical address of the network layer. This is a very basic testing mechanism.
- **trace**—Uses Time To Live (TTL) values to generate messages from each router used along the path. This is very powerful in its ability to locate failures in the path from the source to the destination.

The telnet Command

The **telnet** command is a simple command that you use to see whether you can connect to the router. If you cannot Telnet to the router but you can **ping** the router, you know the problem lies in the upper-layer functionality at the router. At this point, you may want to reboot the router and Telnet to it again.

The ping Command

The **ping** command sends ICMP echo packets and is supported in both user and privileged EXEC modes. In the following example, one **ping** timed out, as reported by the dot (.), and four were successfully received, as shown by the exclamation points (!):

```
Router> ping 172.16.101.1
Type escape sequence to abort.
Sending 5 100-byte ICMP echoes to 172.16.10.1. timeout is 2 seconds:
.!!!!
Success rate is 80 percent, round-trip min/avg/max = 6/6/6 ms
Router>
```

The responses in Table 17-6 may be returned by the **ping** test.

TABLE 17-6   The ping Command for Testing IP Network Connectivity

Character	Definition
!	Successful receipt of an echo reply
.	Timed out waiting for datagram reply
U	Destination unreachable error
C	Congestion-experienced packet
I	ping interrupted (for example, Ctrl-Shift-6 X)
?	Packet type unknown
&	Packet TTL exceeded

The Extended `ping` Command

The extended `ping` command is supported only from privileged EXEC mode. As shown in Listing 17-2, you can use the extended command mode of the `ping` command to specify the supported Internet header options. To enter the extended mode, enter **y** at the `Extended commands` prompt.

Listing 17-2 The Extended `ping` Command, Which Is Supported Only from Privileged EXEC Mode

```
Router# ping
Protocol [ip]:
Target IP address: 192.168.101.162
Repeat count [5]:
Datagram size [100]:
Timeout in seconds [2]:
Extended commands [n]: y
Source address:
Type of service [0]:
Set DF bit in IP header? [no]: yes
Data pattern [0xABCD]:
Loose, Strict, Record, Timestamp, Verbose [non]:
Sweep range of sizes [n]:
Type escape sequence to abort.
Sending 5 100-byte ICMP echoes to 192.168.101.162. timeout is 2 seconds:
!!!!!
Success rate is 100 percent (5/5), roundrobin min/avg/max = 24/26/28 ms
Router#
```

The `trace` Command

When you use the `trace` command, shown in Listing 17-3, host names are shown if the addresses are translated dynamically or via static host table entries. The times listed represent the time required for each of three probes to return.

Listing 17-3 The `trace` Command

```
Router# trace aba.nyc.mil
Type escape sequence to abort.
Tracing the route to aba.nyc.mil (26.0.0.73)

1. debris.cisco.com (172.16.1.6) 1000 msec 8 msec 4 msec
2. barmet-gw.cisco.com (172.16.16.2) 8 msec 4 msec 4 msec
3. external-a-gateway.stanford.edu (192.42.110.225) 8 msec 4 msec 4 msec
4. bb2.su.barmet.net (131.119.254.6) 8 msec 8 msec 8 msec
5. su.arc.barmet.net (131.119.3.8) 12 msec 12 msec 8 msec
6. moffett-fld-mb.in.mil (192.52.195.1) 216 msec 120 msec 132 msec
7. aba.nyc.mil (26.0.0.73) 412 msec * 664 msec
```

When the trace reaches the target destination, an asterisk (*) is reported at the display. This normally is caused by the receipt of a port-unreachable packet and the timeout in response to the probe packet. Other responses include those shown in Table 17-7.

> **NOTE**
>
> `trace` is supported by Internet Protocol (IP), Connectionless Network Service (CLNS), Virtual Integrated Network Service (VINES), and AppleTalk.

TABLE 17-7   trace Command Responses

Response	Definition
!H	The probe was received by the router but not forwarded, which is usually due to an access list.
P	The protocol was unreachable.
N	The network was unreachable.
U	The port was unreachable.
*	Timed out.

Summary

- In a TCP/IP environment, end stations communicate with servers or other end stations. This occurs because each node using the TCP/IP protocol suite has a unique 32-bit logical address known as the *IP address*.

- An IP address with a subnet address on an interface achieves three purposes:
  — It enables the system to process the receipt and transmission of packets.
  — It specifies the device's local address.
  — It specifies a range of addresses that share the cable with the device.

- Broadcast messages are those you want every host on the network to see.

- You use the **ip address** command to establish the logical network address of this interface.

- The **ip host** command makes a static name-to-address entry in the router's configuration file.

- The **ip name-server** command defines which hosts can provide the name service.

- The **show hosts** command is used to display a cached list of host names and addresses.

- **telnet, ping,** and **trace** commands can be used to verify IP address configuration.

Review Questions

1. Which of the following best describes the function of a broadcast address?

   A. It sends a message to a single network destination.

   B. It copies messages and sends them to a specific subset of network addresses.

   C. It sends a message to all nodes on a network.

   D. It sends a message to every node to which the router has access.

2. What is the purpose of using the `trace` command?

   A. It is the most complete test mechanism available.

   B. It is a very basic testing mechanism.

   C. It adds the IP address and the DNS to the router table.

   D. It locates failures in the path from the source to the destination.

3. What is the purpose of the `ip name-server` command?

   A. It defines which hosts can provide the name service.

   B. It defines a naming scheme that allows a device to be identified by its location.

   C. It identifies which TCP port to use when using the host name.

   D. It generates messages from each router used along a datagram's path.

4. If you want to map a domain name to an IP address, what is the first thing you must do?

   A. Identify the host names.

   B. Specify a name server.

   C. Enable the DNS.

   D. Refer to the DNS for the IP address of that device.

5. What is the purpose of the `no ip domain-lookup` command?

   A. It defines which hosts can provide the name service.

   B. It defines a naming scheme that allows a device to be identified by its location.

C. It turns on name-to-address translation in the router.

D. It turns off name-to-address translation in the router.

6. Which of the following best describes the function of the `show hosts` command?

   A. It identifies the subnet mask being used at the destination site.

   B. It maintains a cache of host name–to–address mappings for use by EXEC commands.

   C. It is used to display a cached list of host names and addresses.

   D. It shows the host name for the IP address.

7. What is the function of the `telnet` command?

   A. It verifies the application-layer software between source and destination stations.

   B. It verifies the hardware connection and the logical address of the network layer.

   C. It generates messages from each router used along the path.

   D. It shows how many hours have passed since the software referred to the entry.

8. What is the function of the `ping` command?

   A. It verifies the application-layer software between source and destination stations.

   B. It uses ICMP to verify the hardware connection and the logical address of the network layer.

   C. It assigns values to generate messages from each router used along the path.

   D. It gives descriptions of how information was sent and its current status.

9. Which command would you use to set up static `name-to-address` entries in the router's configuration file?

   A. `ip perm`

   B. `ip route`

   C. `ip name`

   D. `ip host`

10. Which of the following best describes the function of the extended command mode of the `ping` command?

   A. It is used to specify the supported Internet header options.

   B. It is used to specify the time frame for the `ping` return.

   C. It is used to diagnose why a `ping` was delayed or not returned.

   D. It is used to trace the datagram as it passes through each router.

Objectives

After reading this chapter, you will be able to

- Describe initial router configuration mode—setup mode
- Describe an IP routing table
- Describe static routing commands
- Describe default routing commands
- Describe dynamic routing commands, including RIP and IGRP

Chapter 18

Router Configuration and Routing Protocols: RIP and IGRP

Introduction

In Chapter 17, "Configuring Router Interfaces with IP Addresses," you learned the process of configuring Internet Protocol (IP) addresses. In this chapter, you will learn about the initial configuration of the router to enable the IP routing protocols of Routing Information Protocol (RIP) and Interior Gateway Routing Protocol (IGRP) and monitoring IP.

Initial Router Configuration

After testing the hardware and loading the Cisco IOS system image, a router finds and applies the configuration statements. These entries provide the router with details about router-specific attributes, protocol functions, and interface addresses. However, if the router faces a beginning condition where it is unable to locate a valid startup configuration file, it enters an initial router configuration mode called the *setup mode*.

With the setup mode command facility (the `setup` command), you can answer questions in the system configuration dialog. This facility prompts you for basic configuration information. The answers you enter allow the router to use a sufficient but minimal-feature router configuration that includes

- An inventory of interfaces
- An opportunity to enter global parameters
- An opportunity to enter interface parameters
- A setup script review
- An opportunity to indicate whether you want the router to use this configuration

After you approve setup-mode entries, the router uses the entries as a running configuration. The router also stores the configuration in nonvolatile RAM (NVRAM) as a new startup configuration file. You can start using the router. For additional protocol and interface changes, you use the enable mode and enter the command `configure`.

The Initial IP Routing Table

Initially, as shown in Figure 18-1, a router must refer to entries about networks or subnets that are directly connected. Each interface must be configured with an IP address and mask. The Cisco IOS software learns about this IP address and mask information from configuration information that is input from some source. The initial source of addressing is the person who types it into a configuration.

FIGURE 18-1
Routers maintain an address-to-port association table.

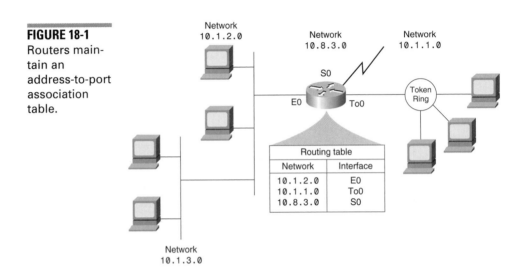

In this section, you will start up your router in a beginning condition, a state that lacks another source for startup configuration. This condition on the router will permit you to use the setup mode command facility and answer prompts for basic configuration information. The answers you enter include address-to-port commands to set up router interfaces for IP.

Routers learn paths to destinations three different ways:

- *Static route*—The static route is manually defined by the system administrator as the only path to the destination. It is useful for controlling security and reducing traffic. (See Figure 18-2.)
- *Default route*—The default route is manually defined by the system administrator as the path to take when no route to the destination is known. (See Figure 18-3.)
- *Dynamic route*—The router learns of paths to destinations by receiving periodic updates from other routers.

FIGURE 18-2
A fixed route to address reflects the administrator's knowledge.

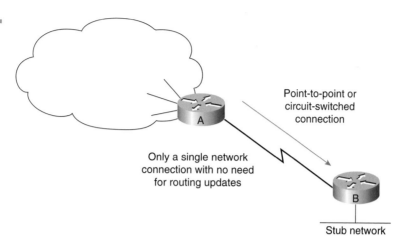

Point-to-point or circuit-switched connection

Only a single network connection with no need for routing updates

Stub network

FIGURE 18-3
The default route is used if the next hop is not explicitly stated in the routing table.

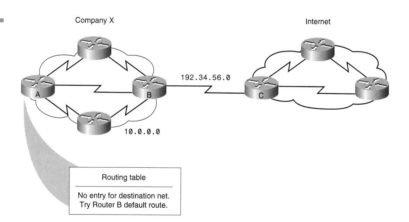

Company X

Internet

192.34.56.0

10.0.0.0

Routing table
No entry for destination net.
Try Router B default route.

Static Route Configuration

Static routes are user-defined routes that cause packets moving between a source and a destination to take a specified path. The **ip route** command sets up a static route by using the following syntax:

ip route network [mask] {address ¦ interface} [distance]

The parameters have the following meanings:

network	Destination network or subnet
mask	Subnet mask
Ethernet 0	Name of interface to use to get to the destination address

address	IP address of next hop router
interface	Name of interface to use to get to destination network
distance	The administrative distance

The administrative distance is a rating of the trustworthiness of a routing information source expressed as a numeric value from 0 to 255. The higher the number, the lower the trustworthiness rating. For example, an administrative distance of 253 would have an extremely untrustworthy rating.

A static route allows manual configuration of the routing table. No dynamic changes to this table entry occur as long as the path is active.

A static route may reflect some special knowledge of the networking situation known to the network administrator. Manually entered administrative distance values for static routes are usually low numbers. Routing updates are not sent on a link if only defined by a static route, thereby conserving bandwidth.

A Static Route Example

The example shown in Figure 18-4 includes the following values:

ip route 172.16.1.0	Specifies a static route to the destination subnetwork.
255.255.255.0	Subnet mask indicates that 8 bits of subnetting are in effect.
172.16.2.1	IP address of next hop router in the path to the destination.

FIGURE 18-4
Router A is configured with a static router to 172.16.1.0.

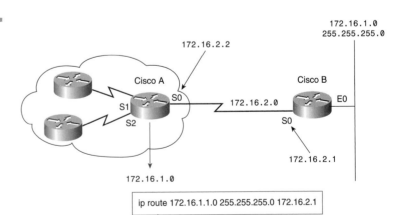

ip route 172.16.1.0 255.255.255.0 172.16.2.1

The assignment of a static route to reach the stub network 172.16.1.0 is proper for Cisco A because there is only one way to reach that network. The assignment of a static route from Cisco B to the cloud networks is also possible. However, a static route assignment is required for each destination network, so a default route may be more appropriate.

Default Route Configuration

A router might not know the routes to all other networks. To provide complete routing capability, the common practice is to use some routers as default routers and give the remaining routers default to those routers.

The `ip default-network` command establishes a default route by using the following syntax:

```
ip default-network network-number
```

where *network-number* is equal to the IP network number or subnet number defined as the default.

When an entry for the destination network does not exist in the routing table, the packet is sent to the default network. The default network must exist in the routing table. Default routes keep the length of routing tables shorter.

You use the default network number when you need a route but have only partial information about the destination network. Because the router does not have complete knowledge about all destination networks, it can use a default network number to indicate the direction to take for unknown network numbers.

A Default Route Example

In the example shown in Figure 18-5, the global command `ip default-network` `192.168.17.0` defines the Class C network 192.168.17.0 as the destination path for packets that have no routing table entry. Router A could need a firewall for routing updates. The Company X administrator does not want updates coming in from the public network. Router A may need a mechanism to group those networks that will share Company X's routing strategy. One such mechanism is an autonomous system number.

An *autonomous system* consists of routers, run by one or more operators, that present a consistent view of routing to the external world.

The Network Information Center assigns a unique 16-bit autonomous system number to each enterprise. A routing protocol such as Cisco's IGRP requires that you specify this unique, assigned autonomous system number in your configuration.

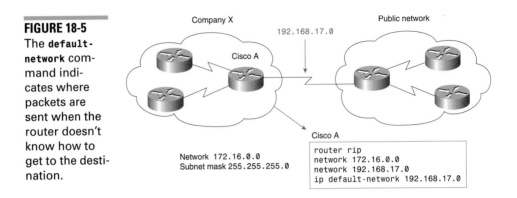

FIGURE 18-5
The **default-network** command indicates where packets are sent when the router doesn't know how to get to the destination.

Interior or Exterior Routing Protocols

As shown in Figure 18-6, an exterior routing protocol such as Border Gateway Protocol (BGP) is used to communicate between autonomous systems. An interior routing protocol such as RIP is used within a single autonomous system.

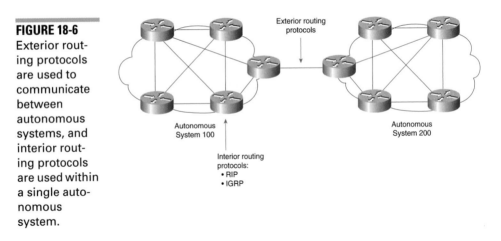

FIGURE 18-6
Exterior routing protocols are used to communicate between autonomous systems, and interior routing protocols are used within a single autonomous system.

At the Internet layer of the TCP/IP suite of protocols, a router can use the IP routing protocol to accomplish routing through the implementation of a specific routing algorithm. Examples of the IP routing protocols include

- *RIP*—A distance-vector routing protocol
- *IGRP*—Cisco's distance-vector routing protocol
- *Open Shortest Path First (OSPF)*—A link-state routing protocol
- *Enhanced IGRP*—A balanced hybrid routing protocol

This chapter focuses on the first two of these protocols.

IP Routing Configuration Tasks

The selection of IP as a routing protocol involves the setting of both global and interface parameters, as shown in Figure 18-7.

Global tasks include

- Selecting a routing protocol—either RIP or IGRP.
- Assigning IP network numbers without specifying subnet values.

The interface task is to assign network/subnet addresses and the appropriate subnet mask.

FIGURE 18-7
A router can use more than one routing protocol if desired.

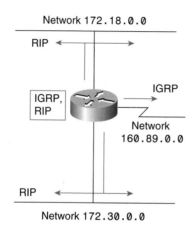

Network 172.18.0.0

RIP

IGRP, RIP

IGRP

Network 160.89.0.0

RIP

Network 172.30.0.0

Dynamic routing uses broadcasts and multicasts to communicate with other routers. The routing metric helps routers find the best path to each network or subnet.

Dynamic Routing Configuration

Two primary commands are used to configure dynamic routing: **router** and **network**. The **router** command starts a routing process by first defining an IP routing protocol; its form is as follows:

```
Router(config)# router protocol [keyword]
```

Then, the **network** command is needed for each IP routing process:

```
Router(config-router)# network network-number
```

The parameters specify the following:

`protocol`	Either RIP, IGRP, OSPF, or Enhanced IGRP.
network	Such as autonomous system, which is used with those protocols that require an autonomous system, such as IGRP. The **network** command is required because it allows the routing process to determine which interfaces will participate in the sending and receiving of routing updates.
`network-number`	A directly connected network.

The network number must be based on the Network Information Center network numbers, not subnet numbers or individual addresses.

RIP

RIP was originally specified in RFC 1058. Key characteristics of RIP include the following:

- It is a distance-vector routing protocol.
- Hop count is used as the metric for path selection (see Figure 18-8).
- The maximum allowable hop count is 15.
- Routing updates are broadcast every 30 seconds by default.

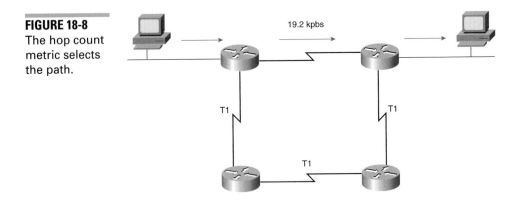

FIGURE 18-8
The hop count metric selects the path.

The **router rip** command selects RIP as the routing protocol:

```
Router(config)# router rip
```

The **network** command assigns a Network Information Center–based address to which the router is directly connected:

```
Router(config-router)# network network-number
```

The routing process associates interfaces with the proper addresses and begins packet processing on the specified networks.

A RIP Configuration Example

In the example shown Figure 18-9,

- `router rip` selects RIP as the routing protocol.
- `network 1.0.0.0` specifies a directly connected network.
- `network 2.0.0.0` specifies a directly connected network.

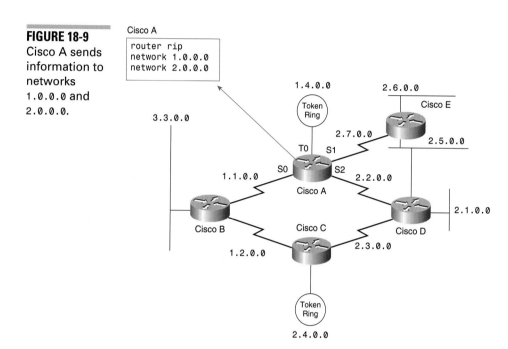

FIGURE 18-9
Cisco A sends information to networks 1.0.0.0 and 2.0.0.0.

The Cisco A router interfaces connected to networks `1.0.0.0` and `2.0.0.0` send and receive RIP updates. These routing updates allow the router to learn the network topology.

Monitoring IP

The `show ip protocol` command is used to view RIP information. As shown in Listing 18-1, this command displays values about routing timers and network information associated with the entire router.

Listing 18-1 The `show ip protocol` Command Observing RIP's Behavior

```
Router> show ip protocol
Routing Protocol is rip
  Sending updates every 30 seconds, next due in 13 seconds
  Invalid after 180 seconds, hold down 180, flushed after 240
  Outgoing update filter list for all interface is not set
  Incoming update filter list for all interface is not set
  Redistributing: rip
  Routing for Networks:
    183.8.0.0
    144.253.0.0
  Routing Information Sources:
  Gateway              Distance        Last Update
    183.8.128.12          120          0:00:14
    183.8.64.130          120          0:00:19
    183.8.128.130         120          0:00:03
  Distance: (default is 120)
```

You use this information to identify a router that you suspect of delivering bad routing information.

A router sends updated routing table information every 30 seconds. (This interval is configurable.) It has been 17 seconds since it sent its last update, and the next one will be sent in 13 seconds. The router is injecting routes for the networks listed following the `Routing for Networks` line.

Displaying the IP Routing Table

The `show ip route` command, as shown in Listing 18-2, displays the contents of the IP routing table. The routing table contains entries for all known networks and subnetworks and contains a code that indicates how that information was learned.

Listing 18-2 The `show ip route` Command Displaying the Local Routing Table

```
Router> show ip route
Codes: C - connected, S - static, R - RIP, M - mobile, B - BGP
       D - EIGRP, EX - EIGRP external, O - OSPF, IA - OSPF inter area
       E1 - OSPF external type 1, E2 - OSPF external type 2, E-EGP
       i - IS-IS, L1 - IS-IS level 1, L2 - IS-IS level 2
       * - candidate default

Gateway of last resort is not set

     144.253.0.0 is subnetted (mask is 255.255.255.0), 1 subnets
C       144.253.100.0 is directly connected. Ethernet1
R    133.3.0.0
R    153.50.0.0 [120/1] via 183.8.128.12, 00:00:09, Ethernet0
     183.8.0.0 is subnetted (mask is 255.255.255.128), 4 subnets
R       183.8.0.128 [120/1] via 183.8.128.130.00, 00:00:17, Serial0
                     [120/1] via 183.8.64.130, 00:00:17, Serial1
C       183.8.128.0 is directly connected, Ethernet0
C       183.8.64.128 is directly connected, Serial1
C       183.8.128.128 is directly connected, Ethernet0
R    192.3.63.0
```

The values are defined as follows:

- c indicates a network that was configured with the **network** command.
- R indicates an entry learned through RIP.
- via refers to the router that informed you about this route.
- The 00:00:09 timer value means that RIP updates are every 9 seconds.
- The administrative distance is 120.
- The hop count to 153.50.0.0 is 1.

IGRP

IGRP is a distance-vector routing protocol developed by Cisco. IGRP sends routing updates at 90-second intervals that advertise networks for a particular autonomous system.

The following are some key characteristics of IGRP:

- Versatility to automatically handle indefinite, complex topologies.
- Flexibility for segments having different bandwidth and delay characteristics.
- Scalability to function in very large networks.

The IGRP routing protocol uses a combination of variables to determine a composite metric, as shown in Figure 18-10.

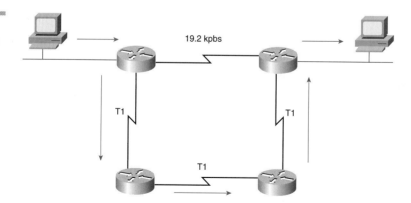

FIGURE 18-10
With IGRP, the composite metric selects the path, and speed is the primary consideration.

IGRP's metric does not have RIP's hop-count limitation. It includes the following components:

- Bandwidth
- Delay
- Load
- Reliability
- Maximum transmission unit (MTU)

The `router igrp` command selects IGRP as a routing protocol:

```
Router(config)# router igrp autonomous-system
```

The parameter specifies the following:

`autonomous-system`	Identifies the IGRP router processes that will share routing information.

The `network` command specifies any directly connected networks to be included:

```
Router(config-router)# network network-number
```

The parameter specifies the following:

`network-number`	Specifies a directly connected network: a Network Information Center network number, not a subnet number or individual address.

An IGRP Configuration Example

In the example shown in Figure 18-11,

- `router igrp 109` selects IGRP as the routing protocol for autonomous system 109.
- `network 1.0.0.0` specifies a directly connected network.
- `network 2.0.0.0` specifies a directly connected network.

IGRP is selected as the routing protocol for autonomous system 109. All interfaces connected to networks `1.0.0.0` and `2.0.0.0` process IP traffic.

The `show ip protocol` Command

The `show ip protocol` command, as shown in Listing 18-3, displays parameters, filters, and network information about the entire router. The algorithm used to calculate the routing metric for IGRP is also shown in this display. It defines the value of the K1 through K5 metrics and the maximum hop count.

FIGURE 18-11
You use *router igrp* and *network* commands to create an IGRP router.

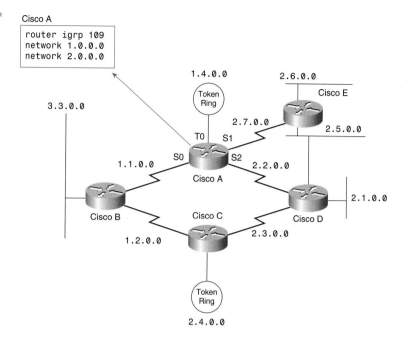

```
Cisco A
router igrp 109
network 1.0.0.0
network 2.0.0.0
```

Listing 18-3 The `show ip protocols` **Command**

```
Router> show ip protocol
Routing Protocol is igrp 300
  Sending updates every 90 seconds, next due in 55 seconds
  Invalid after 270 seconds, hold down 280, flushed after 360
  Outgoing update filter list for all interfaces is not set
  Incoming update filter list for all interfaces is not set
  Default networks flagged in outgoing updates
  Default networks accepted from incoming updates
  IGRP metric weight K1=1, K2=0, K3=1, K4=0, K5=0
  IGRP maximum hopcount 100
  IGRP maximum metric variance 1
  Redistributing igrp 300
  Routing for Networks:
    183.8.0.0
    144.253.0.0
  Routing Information Sources
    Gateway           Distance     Last Update
    144.253.100.1     100          0:00:52
    183.8.128.12      100          0:00:43
    183.8.64.130      100          0:01:02
  Distance: (default is 100)
-- More --
```

The show ip interfaces **Command**

The **show ip interfaces** command, as shown in Listing 18-4, displays the status and global parameters associated with an interface. The Cisco IOS software automatically enters a directly connected route in the routing table if the interface is one through which software can send and receive packets. Such an interface is marked "up." If the interface is unusable, it is removed from the routing table. Removing the entry allows implementation of backup routes, if they exist.

Listing 18-4 The show ip interfaces Command
```
Router> show ip interfaces
Ethernet0 is up, line protocol is up
  Internet address is 183.8.128.2, subnet mask is 255.255.255.128
  Broadcast address is 255.255.255.255
  Address determined by non-volatile memory
  MTU is 1500 bytes
  Helper address is not set
  Directed broadcast forwarding is enabled
  Outgoing access list is not set
  Inbound access list is not set
  Proxy ARP is enabled
  Security level is default
  Split horizon is enabled
  ICMP redirects are always sent
  ICMP unreachables are always sent
  ICMP mask replies are never sent
  IP fast switching enabled
  IP fast switching on the same interface is disabled
  IP SSE switching is disabled
  Router Discovery is disabled
  IP output packet accounting is disabled
  IP access violation accounting is disabled
  TCP/IP header compression is disabled
  Probe proxy name replies are disabled
  -- More --
```

The show ip route **Command**

The **show ip route** command, as shown in Listing 18-5, displays the contents of an IP routing table. The table contains a list of all known networks and subnets and the metrics associated with each entry. Note that, in this example, the information was derived from IGRP or from direct connections.

Listing 18-5 The show ip route Command
```
Router> show ip route
Codes: C - connected, S - static, I - IGRP, R - RIP, M - mobile, B - BGP
       D - EIGRP, EX - EIGRP external, O - OSPF, IA - OSPF inter area
       E1 - OSPF external type 1, E2 - OSPF external type 2, E-EGP
       i - IS-IS, L1 - IS-IS level 1, L2 - IS-IS level 2
       * - candidate default

Gateway of last resort is not set
```

```
     144.253.0.0 is subnetted (mask is 255.255.255.0). 1 subnets
C    144.253.100.0 is directly connected, Ethernet1
I    133.3.0.0 [100/1200] via 144.253.100.200, 00:00:57, Ethernet1
I    153.50.0.0 [100/1200] via 183.8.128.12, 00:00:05, Ethernet0
     183.8.0.0 is subnetted (mask is 255.255.255.128), 4 subnets
I    183.8.0.128 [100/180671] via 183.8.64.130, 00:00:27, Serial1
     [100/180671] via 183.8.128.130, 00:00:27, Serial0
C    183.8.128.0 is directly connected, Ethernet0
C    183.8.64.128 is directly connected, Serial1
C    183.8.128.128 is directly connected, Serial0
I    172.16.0.0 [100/1200] via 144.253.100.1, 00:00:55, Ethernet1
I    192.3.63.0 [100/1300] via 144.253.100.200, 00:00:58, Ethernet1
```

The debug ip rip Command

The **debug ip rip** command, as shown in Listing 18-6, displays RIP routing updates as they are sent and received. In this example, an update is sent by 183.8.128.130. It reported on three routers, one of which is inaccessible because its hop count is greater than 15. Updates were then broadcast through 183.8.128.2.

Listing 18-6 The debug ip rip Command

```
Router# debug ip rip
RIP Protocol debugging is on
Router#
RIP: received update from 183.8.128.130 on Serial0
     183.8.0.128 in 1 hops
     183.8.64.128 in 1 hops
     0.0.0.0 in 16 hops (inaccessible)
RIP: received update from 183.8.64.140 on Serial1
     183.8.0.128 in 1 hops
     183.9.128.128 in 1 hops
     0.0.0.0 in 16 hops (inaccessible)
RIP: received update from 183.8.128.130 on Serial0
     183.8.0.128 in 1 hops
     183.8.64.128 in 1 hops
     0.0.0.0 in 16 hops (inaccessible)
RIP: sending update to 255.255.255.255 via Ethernet0 (183.8.128.2)
     subnet 183.8.0.128, metric 2
     subnet 183.8.64.128, metric 1
     subnet 183.8.128.128, metric 1
     default 0.0.0.0, metric 16
     network 144.253.0.0, metric 1
RIP: sending update to 255.255.255.255 via Ethernet1 (144.253.100.202)
     default 0.0.0.0, metric 16
     network 153.50.0.0, metric 2
     network 183.8.0.0, metric 1
```

Summary

- Initially, a router must refer to entries about networks or subnets that are directly connected.
- Routers learn paths to destinations three different ways:
  — Static routes
  — Default routes
  — Dynamic routes
- The `ip route` command sets up a static route.
- The `ip default-network` command establishes a default route.
- Routers can be configured to use one or more IP routing protocols, such as RIP and IGRP.

Review Questions

1. What kind of entries does a router initially refer to?

A. Entries about networks or subnets that are directly connected

B. Entries it has learned about from the Cisco IOS software

C. Entries whose IP address and mask information are known

D. Entries it has learned about from other routers

2. Which of the following best describes a static route?

A. A routing table entry that is used to direct frames for which a next hop is not explicitly listed in the routing table

B. A route that is explicitly configured and entered into the routing table and takes precedence over routes chosen by dynamic routing protocols

C. A route that adjusts automatically to network topology or traffic changes

D. A route that adjusts involuntarily to direct frames within a network topology

3. Which of the following best describes a default route?

A. A routing table entry that is used to direct frames for which a next hop is not explicitly listed in the routing table

B. A route that is explicitly configured and entered into the routing table

C. A route that adjusts automatically to network topology or traffic changes

D. A route that adjusts involuntarily to direct frames within a network topology

4. What are exterior routing protocols used for?

A. To transmit between nodes on a network

B. To deliver information within a single autonomous system

C. To communicate between autonomous systems

D. To set up a compatibility infrastructure between networks

5. What are interior routing protocols used for?

   A. They are used to set up a compatibility infrastructure between networks.

   B. They are used to communicate between autonomous systems.

   C. They are used to transmit between nodes on a network.

   D. They are used within a single autonomous system.

6. Which of the following is a global task?

   A. Addressing IP network numbers by specifying subnet values

   B. Selecting a routing protocol—RIP or IGRP

   C. Assigning network/subnet addresses and the appropriate subnet mask

   D. Setting up a routing metric to find the best path to each network

7. What metric does RIP use to determine the best path for a message to travel on?

   A. Bandwidth

   B. Hop count

   C. Varies with each message

   D. Administrative distance

8. You suspect that one of the routers connected to your network is sending bad routing information. What command can you use to check?

   A. `router(config)#` **`show ip protocol`**

   B. `router#` **`show ip protocol`**

   C. `router>` **`show ip protocol`**

   D. `router(config-router)#` **`show ip protocol`**

9. Why would you display the IP routing table?

   A. To set the router update schedule

   B. To identify destination network addresses and next-hop pairs

   C. To trace where datagrams are coming from

   D. To set the parameters and filters for the router

10. If you wanted to learn which routing protocol a router was configured with, what command structure would you use?

   A. `router>` `show router protocol`

   B. `router(config)>` `show ip protocol`

   C. `router(config)#` `show router protocol`

   D. `router>` `show ip protocol`

Objectives

After reading this chapter, you will be able to

- Identify the functions of various types of audits
- Identify the purpose of a network map
- Identify network software management tools and their functions
- Identify characteristics and functions of SNMP and CMIP
- Identify methods needed to troubleshoot a network
- Identify the purpose of network performance evaluation

Chapter 19

Network Management

Introduction

In this book, you have learned how to design and build networks. You have learned how to select, install, and test cable, and you have learned to determine where wiring closets will be located. But network design and implementation are only part of what you need to know. You must also know how to maintain the network and keep it functioning at an acceptable level. This means that you must know how to troubleshoot problems when they arise. In addition, you must know when it is necessary to expand or change the network's configuration in order to meet the changing demands placed on it. In this chapter, you will begin to learn about managing a network by using techniques such as documenting, auditing, monitoring, and evaluating.

The First Steps in Managing a Network

After a network has been implemented successfully and is in operation might seem like the perfect time to relax. A smart network administrator knows that is exactly the wrong approach to take. Instead, what you should be doing is documenting the network. Knowing how the network is supposed to work will make your job easier when problems occur. So instead of relaxing, use the time when the network is operating smoothly to perform an audit of the network. In fact, you will need to perform five types of audits on the network: an inventory audit, a facility audit, an operational audit, an efficiency audit, and a security audit. All these types of audits are described in this chapter. You can begin inventory and facility audits almost immediately. Information for the operational, efficiency, and security audits can and should be obtained after the network has begun to function because these audits require data that can only be provided through monitoring and analysis of the network's behavior and performance.

Inventory Audits

An *inventory audit* allows you to take stock of all the network's hardware and software. Ideally, this information should be obtained when the hardware and software is purchased and before it is set up. This will save you time and effort and will reduce the amount of inconvenience experienced by network end users.

An inventory audit of the network's hardware should include the device's serial number, the type of device, and the name of the individual using the device. It should also list the settings on the various workstations and networking devices. Some network administrators find it useful to keep hardware inventory information directly attached to each networking device. Others prefer to store the information in either a written or a computerized database, where it is easily accessible to network support staff.

An inventory audit of the network's software applications should include the types of software used, the number of users for each application, and the operating requirements of each application. During the inventory audit, you should also make sure that the number of users for each software application does not surpass the number of licenses your site possesses.

Facility Audits

A *facility audit* allows you to note where everything is. It should include the cabling, workstations, printers, and internetworking devices (such as hubs, bridges, and routers). In short, it should provide detailed information about the location of all the network's components. Ideally, all this information should have been recorded on a working version of a document called a *cut sheet* at the time the network was installed. When the audit is complete, it is time to transfer the information you recorded on the cut sheets to a set of the building's blueprints.

Network Maps

After you have conducted the inventory and facility audits, you should use the information you have gathered to generate a *network map*, which looks similar to a blueprint. The map should include the physical location and layout of all devices attached to the network and the applications that run on them. It should also include the IP and MAC addresses of each device. Finally, the network map should include the distances of each cabling run between nodes on the network. The completed network map should be kept near the location selected for network administration and monitoring.

When monitoring programs and devices report a problem with a network's physical components, they often indicate the location of the problem, such as a break or short, by providing you with its distance from where the monitoring device is located. In other instances, the monitoring program provides you with the address of the device or devices where a problem is occurring. Obviously, locating and solving the problem is greatly facilitated if you have the information you need, which is shown in Figure 19-1, readily available.

FIGURE 19-1
Information about a network should show the address of the device or devices where a problem might be occurring.

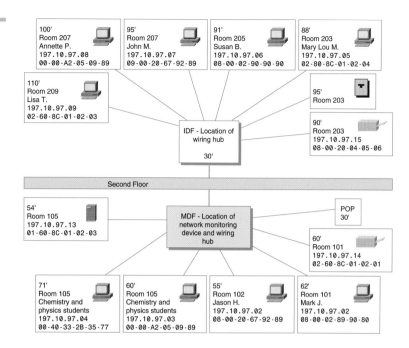

The inventory and facility audits should be done as quickly as possible. These audits should be performed before the network begins providing services to its customers. Having the information provided by these audits at hand will let you troubleshoot problems more rapidly and effectively later, when they do occur.

Operational Audits

An *operational audit* allows you to view the day-to-day activity on the network. It requires the use of specialized software and hardware. In addition to a network monitor, an operational audit may also include the use of such devices as a network analyzer, a time domain reflectometer, breakout boxes, power meters, and an oscillator. Devices such as network monitors and analyzers use specialized software to perform their functions.

Together, all this hardware and software allows the network administrator to keep track of network traffic by counting the number of packets sent, the number of times packets must be retransmitted, packet size, and how the network is being used. Simply stated, these devices and the software they use allow you to detect such events as shorts and breaks in the cable, noise on the networking media, and network bottlenecks.

Of the hardware management tools mentioned here, the ones used most frequently to provide information needed for operational, efficiency, and security audits are network monitors and analyzers. A more detailed discussion of these two devices is provided later in the chapter. For now, it is sufficient that you know these devices are usually centrally located where they can be easily accessed by authorized support personnel.

Network Software Management Tools

Vendors provide a variety of network software management tools. These tools are designed to monitor the nodes on the network, monitor levels of network traffic, watch for network bottlenecks, keep track of software metering, and collect diagnostic information. Most of these applications support vendor-specific types of information and follow one of two network management protocols: Simple Network Management Protocol (SNMP) or Common Management Information Protocol (CMIP). Both of these management protocols use a concept known as the Management Information Base (MIB). Simply put, an MIB contains information, tests, equations, and controls to which all resources on a network conform. Although both SNMP and CMIP share the same mission and use the MIB concept, their methods of retrieving network information differ greatly. In some instances, this may affect which protocol you choose to use in monitoring your network.

SNMP

First released by the U.S. Department of Defense and the developers of TCP/IP in 1988, SNMP is the most used and well known of the network software management tools.

To retrieve network information, SNMP uses a technique called *MIB collection*. This means that it goes from one network device to another, polling them about their status. Then, as shown in Figure 19-2, it copies information regarding each device's status as well as each device's local MIB.

One advantage of SNMP is that devices on the network do not have to be smart enough to report when a problem occurs. SNMP's polling takes care of that task for them. However, in large networks that have many devices and resources attached to them, SNMP's polling technique can be a disadvantage because it contributes significantly to network traffic. This can actually slow the network.

FIGURE 19-2
SNMP uses a technique called *MIB collection* to retrieve network information by polling network devices.

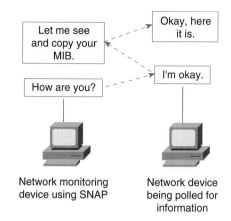

Network monitoring device using SNAP

Network device being polled for information

CMIP

CMIP was developed by the International Organization for Standardization (ISO). Currently CMIP is not implemented as much as SNMP, particularly in new installations. To obtain information about the network, CMIP uses a technique called *MIB reporting*. Using this technique, as shown in Figure 19-3, the central monitoring station waits for devices to report their current status to it.

FIGURE 19-3
If concern about the amount of traffic is an issue on your network, CMIP may be a useful network management tool for you.

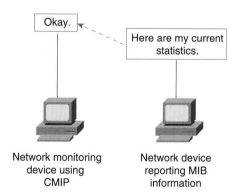

Network monitoring device using CMIP

Network device reporting MIB information

Networking Monitoring

By monitoring the day-to-day operating of the network, you will be able to establish what is "normal" for your network. For instance, by tracking the information over a period of time, you will come to learn how busy, on average, the network is. You will also discover when the peak traffic times are for the network as measured by the time of day, the time of week, and the time of month. You will learn what the network's most and least popular applications are and how they are being used. In some instances, you will even be able to identify which network users are most prone to experience difficulties when working on the network. Logs should be kept of all this information. Later, when you notice something that might be a problem, you can compare it against this baseline information showing what normal network operation should be.

Efficiency Audits

An *efficiency audit* allows you to determine that the network is performing to its potential. Like the operational audit, this audit is best performed after the network has begun to provide services to its clients.

For your network's wiring system, a set of baseline measurements meeting Institute of Electrical and Electronic Engineers (IEEE) and/or Electrical Industries Association/Telecommunications Industry Association (EIA/TIA) standards should have been provided by the installer. To ensure that your network's cabling continues to operate efficiently, you should periodically measure its performance for comparison against this baseline.

Other factors that should be included in your network's efficiency audit include a cost analysis of the network, an analysis of the ease with which the network is able to retrieve information, and an analysis of the ability of the network to ensure integrity of its data. Also included should be an evaluation of the workforce in place to support the network. Finally, the efficiency audit should include an assessment of the network's clients and their capabilities in terms of using the network's hardware and software.

Security Audits

A *security audit* reviews the security requirements of the network and what kind of software and hardware security system best meets them. Only observation and experience in how the network and its clients use and access data will provide you with the information needed to complete this audit.

Types of information that should be contained in this type of audit include a list of which segments require limited authorized access or encryption of data; which devices, files, and directories require locks or password protection; which files should be provided with archived backup; how frequently backup procedures should be performed; the type of virus protection being utilized by the network; and, most importantly, information regarding what emergency and disaster procedures will be employed by the network.

If you are uncertain about the types of information that your audits should contain, check with other network administrators to learn how they conduct audits of their networks and what types of network management tools they find most helpful in performing these tasks. Or, you can check with the manufacturers of your network's operating system. They will be able to recommend appropriate network auditing software that can guide you in securing adequate and comprehensive monitoring and analysis of your network.

Network Analyzers

You may want to investigate adding a *network analyzer* to your network. Also called a *protocol analyzer*, this device keeps track of statistical information much like a network monitor does. However, it offers a more sophisticated level of service than does a network monitor. In fact, these devices are so sophisticated and intelligent that they not only detect and identify problems, such as bottlenecks, but they fix them as well.

Troubleshooting Problems on the Network

The key to successfully troubleshooting problems on a network is information. As a general rule, the more information you have, the easier it should be to solve the problem. Information obtained during the audits you conducted will provide a baseline set of measurements with which to compare current data detailing the problem. Additional information must be gathered after the problem has arisen. Just as you did with the information you obtained during the audits, you must record and document this information as well as any solution provided. Such a log or journal is important because it provides a record of your contributions to the system. Later it can be used to justify requests for additional equipment, personnel, and training. The problems and solutions documented in the log can be useful tools to train additional troubleshooters for your network. The journal also allows you to track trends that help anticipate problems and propose solutions, either with situations or individuals.

Documenting Network Problems

Some network problems will be detected by the network administrator using the network management software and hardware tools. The network support staff will learn of other problems when the network's clients report them. All client requests for help should be documented in a trouble report. The information recorded in each report should be divided into five general categories.

The first category should be an ID number that has been assigned to the call. This will be useful in filing the information or entering it into a database.

The second category should consist of preliminary information. It should include the name of the individual who reported the problem; the time the problem was reported; the method by which the problem was reported; whether the problem was related to previous calls reporting trouble and the ID numbers of those reports; the location of where the problem occurred; whether the problem can be replicated for network support staff; the time when the problem first appeared; whether anything was done differently or changed just before the problem occurred; and whether the problem was periodic or constant in nature.

The third category should consist of information that network support staff gather at the site where the problem occurred. It should include comments by support staff regarding the PC environment, such as power, temperature, humidity, and any others; support staff observations about the problem or difficulty; and a list of what actions were taken to remedy the problem.

The fourth category should provide information that indicates whether the PC had to be taken to a repair area for further servicing, a list of any actions taken, and the result of those actions.

The final category that should appear on the trouble report should be the summary. The summary should list whether the problem was a hardware, software, or user problem: If the problem was a software problem, what software was involved; if the problem was a hardware problem, what hardware was involved.

Analyzing and Solving Network Problems

Once you have collected all the information available about a problem, start listing possible causes. Based on the performance history you have at your disposal, you should be able to prioritize these causes from most likely to least likely. It will help if you keep in mind how data flows on your network while you do this. Using this list of possibilities, use your network's management tools to further identify the cause of the problem.

Even if you are limited in the types of network management tools at your disposal, you can still successfully troubleshoot problems on your network.

Instead of relying heavily on such network management tools as monitors and analyzers, though, you will need to use the *replacement method*.

To understand how the replacement method works, when a problem occurs, assume you have one healthy entity and one nonfunctioning one. For example, if the information you gather leads you to believe that the problem lies in a particular workstation, get another one that you know works.

Start at the most basic level: the cabling. Switch the patch cords on the PCs. If the malfunctioning machine begins to work properly and the healthy PC becomes sick, then you've found the problem on the first try. If nothing changes in the malfunctioning device, replace the patch cords to their original locations and move on to the next most basic level. Continue switching components until the malfunctioning device works and the healthy one quits functioning. Be prepared: Using the replacement method to troubleshoot the problem could take a while.

If you've tried everything and still cannot solve the problem, don't overlook the obvious. Lack of knowledge, experience, or proper management tools could be part of the problem. Once you've reached this conclusion, don't hesitate to call in the experts. In the long run, consultants armed with sophisticated diagnostic management tools, more knowledge, and more experience can save you and your organization time, money, and effort. In the process, they can provide you with a valuable learning experience.

The key to successfully troubleshooting problems on the network is to isolate the problem by systematically working your way through a simple hierarchy of troubleshooting procedures.

Troubleshooting Procedures

As you gain experience in working with your network and clients, you will develop a hierarchy of troubleshooting procedures that are best suited for you. In the meantime, the following guidelines may be useful.

In most networks, usually the users—not the hardware or software—are responsible for so-called network problems. Therefore, a logical first step in troubleshooting a user-identified problem is to fix the user.

If you determine that the problem did not originate due to user actions, move to the next most frequent source of network problems: the hardware. Begin by making sure you have the right tools to diagnose the problem. Next, determine whether the problem is local to the device. If necessary, take the PC to a network connection that you know is good and replace it with a portable PC. If you determine that the problem is not local, focus on the network's hardware. SNMP can help you determine whether there is a problem with a particular network segment. Look at the network's wiring system first. See if there were any recent cable changes. Use diagnostic tools such as a time domain reflecto-meter. Check all cable connections on the known faulty segment. Begin with connections at the work area first and work back to the wiring closet. If you decide that the cabling and its connections are not at fault, look at the net-work's file servers. If you have multiple servers, try to determine which is the most likely candidate for causing the problem. If you think the problem lies with a workstation, check the wiring hub, cable, connector, and workstation memory. Don't neglect to use any diagnostic utilities built into the device's net-work interface card to help diagnose and solve the problem. If you eliminate the network's hardware, follow the appropriate diagnostic procedures to check and fix any software problems.

Network Performance Evaluations

Periodic evaluations of the network are important maintenance and preven-tion tools that can help ensure that it continues to operate at an acceptable level. The first evaluation should occur after the network has been in operation for a reasonable period of time. It should be based on information provided by the system's network management tools. Once they have been compiled, the results of the evaluation should be presented in the form of an *evaluation report*. The evaluation report will allow network management to see whether the network is continuing to work as anticipated and needed by the organiza-tion. The purpose of the evaluation report is to reveal the network's strengths and weaknesses so they can be corrected if necessary.

For example, logs maintained by a network analyzer could indicate a trend toward a slower rate of traffic on certain segments of the network. An updated audit of the network's hardware and software could reveal the addition of sev-eral new network devices running multimedia applications on those segments. When both sets of data are taken together and presented in an evaluation report, this information can be used by network management as the basis for formulating changes in the system and how it operates.

Procedures for Making Changes to a Network

Network administrators must keep in mind that all organizations change and grow. Consequently, a network that was implemented even a year ago may no longer meet the needs and requirements of that organization. As the organiza-tion changes and evolves, so must the network.

When a network administrator believes that changes need to be implemented in a network, particularly those that will alter the way users interface with the network, the services that will be provided by that network, access to informa-tion housed in applications that run on the network, or those that will involve additional time, expense, and labor, he or she should draft a *request for change*. This document should be circulated for review.

The individuals who review the request for change vary from organization to organization. Ideally, the list of reviewers should include individuals in the organization who not only possess a degree of technical knowledge, but are familiar with the types of services, applications, and work the organization must handle.

In some instances, the request for change may trigger responses from reviewers. Usually, such responses range from a brief analysis to extensive investigation and analysis. Occasionally, such investigations may result in a return to an earlier point in the network's life cycle. At others, they could require a complete redesign of the network. If problems identified in the evaluation report are severe and far reaching enough, it could even mean a return to the study phase. In short, a request for change could result in a greatly modified network.

Summary

- The first step in managing a network is to document it.
- To document a network, the following audits must be performed:
  - An inventory audit and a facility audit can be used to help troubleshoot problems on the network.
  - An operational audit allows you to view the day-to-day operations of the network through the use of specialized hardware and software management tools.
  - A security audit reviews the security requirements of the network and what kind of software and hardware security system best meets them.
  - An efficiency audit allows you to determine that the network is performing to its potential.
- Audits are needed to establish a baseline of performance against which a network's continuing performance can be measured.
- Procedures and questions can be helpful in troubleshooting problems, particularly those identified by clients.
- Periodic evaluations of the network are important maintenance and prevention tools that can help ensure that the network continues to operate at an acceptable level.
- Information gathered during a network evaluation is used to prepare an evaluation report that can become the basis for a request for change.

Review Questions

1. What is the purpose of an inventory audit?

   A. To identify the location of every network component

   B. To monitor and analyze the network's performance

   C. To collect vendor specification documents for every network component

   D. To take stock of all hardware and software on the network

2. What is the purpose of a facility audit?

   A. To identify the types of hardware and devices on the network

   B. To identify the location of every network component

   C. To monitor and analyze the network's performance

   D. To transfer the information on a building's blueprints to cut sheets

3. How does a network map aid in locating problems with a network's physical components?

   A. It provides the name of the user of the problem device.

   B. It provides the settings on the problem device.

   C. It provides operating requirements for applications used on the problem device.

   D. It provides addresses for the problem device.

4. Which of the following correctly describes SNMP?

   A. SNMP is rarely used in new installations.

   B. SNMP is a TCP/IP standard.

   C. SNMP uses a concept known as MIB.

   D. SNMP is the best choice for networks with a large amount of traffic.

5. Which of the following correctly describes how CMIP functions?

   A. It uses MIB polling.

   B. It has the central monitoring station wait for devices to report the current status.

C. It copies each device's local MIB.

D. The way it obtains information from devices contributes significantly to network traffic.

6. What is the purpose of an efficiency audit?

A. To monitor and analyze the network's performance

B. To determine whether the network is performing to its potential

C. To identify the types of hardware and devices on the network

D. To provide information regarding emergency and disaster recovery

7. What is the purpose of a security audit?

A. To match security requirements with building and privacy codes

B. To assess the capabilities of clients to use the network hardware and software

C. To identify the network's ability to ensure integrity of data

D. To identify the hardware and software system required for network security

8. After collecting performance data, what are the steps you would use to analyze and solve a network problem?

A. Determine whether the problem is periodic or constant; list possible causes; prioritize causes

B. Prioritize causes; identify cause using network management tools or the replacement method; track trends to anticipate future problems

C. List possible causes; prioritize causes; identify cause using network management tools or the replacement method

D. Determine whether the problem can be replicated; prioritize possible causes; identify cause using network management tools or the replacement method

9. Which of the following is likely to be included in an evaluation report?

A. Identification of network hardware and software that does not conform to industry standards

B. Logs indicating a trend toward a slower rate of traffic on certain sements of the network

    C. A description of instances and the location of unauthorized access to files

    D. A description of the types of users prone to experience difficulties using the network

10. What should a written request for change to improve network performance and security include?

    A. The rationale behind each change requested

    B. The type, number, and location of each device on the network

    C. A comparison of present performance and anticipated optimal performance

    D. A breakdown of costs for equipment and labor

QuickTime Movie Reference

The following table is a list of the movies you'll find on this book's CD-ROM.

Movie Name	Title and Description	Chapter
Movie 1.1	**What Is Internetworking?** A collection of networks	1
Movie 1.2	**The Evolution of Internetworking** The growth of the computer industry.	1
Movie 1.3	**The Evolution of Internetworking** Standalone computers with printers attached.	1
Movie 1.4	**The Evolution of Internetworking** Replacing old printers on a LAN with high-speed network printers.	1
Movie 1.5	**The Evolution of Internetworking** New offices—each has a LAN, software, hardware, and network administrator.	1
Movie 1.6	**The Evolution of Internetworking** Three problems—duplication of equipment and resources, inability to communicate efficiently, and lack of LAN network management.	1
Movie 1.7	**The OSI Model** The ISO researched networks, including DECnet, SNA, and TCP/IP.	1
Movie 1.8	**The OSI Model** The OSI model enhances interoperability and comprehension.	1
Movie 1.9	**The OSI Model Conceptual Framework** Protocols allow communication to occur.	1
Movie 1.10	**The Internet** Technology and networking.	1

Movie Name	Title and Description	Chapter
Movie 1.11	**The OSI Model Conceptual Framework** Protocols allow communication to occur.	1
Movie 2.1	**Network Interface Cards** The MAC address is hard coded onto the NIC.	2
Movie 3.1	**Internetworking Devices Connect Networks** Repeaters, bridges, LAN extenders, routers, and WANs are introduced.	3
Movie 3.2	**Internetworking Devices** Connect greater numbers of nodes, localize traffic, merge existing networks.	3
Movie 3.3	**Repeaters Providing Solutions** Repeaters provide the solution to two problems: too many nodes and not enough cable.	3
Movie 3.4	**Repeaters Amplifying Signals** A repeater cleans, amplifies, and resends a signal that is weakened by long cable length.	3
Movie 3.5	**Repeater Disadvantages** Repeaters can't filter traffic.	3
Movie 3.6	**Collisions** Two stations transmit simultaneously and both are damaged. Backoff algorithms determine when to retransmit.	3
Movie 3.7	**Bridges** Bridges divide a network into segments and filter traffic.	3
Movie 3.8	**Bridge Problems** Bridges always propagate frame.	3
Movie 3.8	**Routers** Problem of excessive broadcast traffic can be solved by a router.	3
Movie 3.9	**Router/Bridge Difference** Bridging occurs at Layer 2 and routing occurs at Layer 3.	3

Movie Name	Title and Description	Chapter
Movie 3.10	**Router Operation** Many different types of media use routers and encapsulation.	3
Movie 4.1	**Ethernet and 802.3 LANs** Ethernet and 802.3 LANs are broadcast networks.	4
Movie 4.2	**CSMA LANs** CSMA LANs use Ethernet and 802.3.	4
Movie 5.1	**IP Addressing Format** An IP address has a network number and a host number, and uses dotted-decimal notation.	5
Movie 5.2	**Where to Get an IP Address** You can get IP addresses from an ISP and InterNIC.	5
Movie 5.3	**IP Class Addresses** Class B addresses explained.	5
Movie 5.4	**IP Class Addresses** Class C addresses explained.	5
Movie 5.5	**IP Address Classes** Five classes of addresses explained.	5
Movie 5.6	**IP Reserved Addresses** Extensions explained.	5
Movie 5.7	**Addressing Without Subnets** An explanation of addressing without subnets.	5
Movie 5.8	**Addressing With Subnets** An explanation of addressing with subnets.	5
Movie 5.9	**Subnet Addresses** A subnet address includes the network number, subnet number, and host number.	5
Movie 5.10	**Creating Subnet Addresses** Bits explained.	5
Movie 6.1	**Address Resolution** MAC addresses and ARP explained.	6
Movie 10.1	**Broadcast Transmission** Source node to network transmission.	10

Movie Name	Title and Description	Chapter
Movie 10.2	**Reachability** The TCP/IP host sends an ICMP echo request.	10
Movie 10.3	**ICMP Time Exceeded Message** Time to Live field.	10
Movie 10.4	**TCP Sliding Window** Flow control explained.	10
Movie 10.5	**Router Can't Deliver** ICMP destination unreachable message.	10
Movie 11.1	**Distance-Vector Algorithms** Routing updates explained.	11
Movie 11.2	**Simple Split Horizon** Split horizon explained.	11
Movie 11.3	**Hold-Down Timer** When a router goes down and updates.	11
Movie 11.4	**OSPF Routers** Link-state advertisements explained.	11
Movie 11.5	**Link-State Algorithms** Link-state algorithms explained.	11
Movie 11.6	**Routers and Network Administrators** The responsibilities of the network administrator.	11
Movie 18.1	**Router Operation** Determination, transportation, and switching.	18
Movie 18.2	**Routed Versus Router Protocols** Routed and router protocols explained.	18
Movie 18.3	**Dynamic Routing Protocols** Dynamic protocols, such as RIP, explained.	18
Movie 18.4	**RIP** RIP explained.	18
Movie 18.5	**RIP Problems** Hop-count limit is a problem in RIP.	18
Movie 18.6	**IGRP** Multipath routing explained.	18

Movie Name	Title and Description	Chapter
Movie 18.7	**IGRP** Metrics explained.	18
Movie 18.8	**RIP/IGRP** Metric differences explained.	18
Movie 18.9	**Routing Table** Static routes and dynamic routes explained.	18
Movie 18.10	**Static Routes** Static routes explained.	18
Movie 18.11	**Dynamic Routes** Dynamic routes explained.	18

Command Summary

This appendix contains a summary of the commands used in this book and is intended to provide a quick reference. Each command is listed separately with a short description. In addition, the table contains cross-references to the chapter in which the command is introduced and explained. This appendix should add to your understanding of the commands used to configure Cisco routers.

Command	Description	Chapter
access-enable	Enables the router to create a temporary access list entry in a dynamic access list.	12
access-template	Manually places a temporary access list entry on a router to which you are connected.	12
appn	Sends a command to the APPN subsystem.	12
atmsig	Executes ATM signaling commands.	12
b	Boots the operating system manually.	16
bandwidth	Sets a bandwidth value for an interface.	15
banner motd	Specifies a message-of-the-day banner.	15
bfe	Sets manual emergency modes.	12
boot system	Specifies the system image that the router loads at startup.	16
calendar	Manages the hardware calendar.	12
cd	Changes the current device.	12
cdp enable	Enables Cisco Discovery Protocol on an interface.	13
clear	Resets functions.	12
clear counters	Clears the interface counters.	13

Command	Description	Chapter
`clockrate`	Configures the clock rate for the hardware connections on serial interfaces, such as network interface modules and interface processors to an acceptable bit rate	15
`cmt`	Starts or stops FDDI connection management functions.	12
`config-register`	Changes the configuration register settings.	16
`configure`	Allows you to enter changes to an existing configuration and maintain and store configuration information at a central site.	12, 15, 18
`configure memory`	Loads configuration information from nonvolatile random-access memory.	15
`configure terminal`	Configures the terminal manually from the console terminal.	15, 16
`connect`	Opens a terminal connection.	12
`copy`	Copies configuration or image data.	12
`copy flash tftp`	Copies the system image from Flash memory to a TFTP server.	16
`copy running-config startup-config`	Stores the current configuration in RAM into NVRAM.	15, 16
`copy running-config tftp`	Stores the current configuration in RAM on a network TFTP server.	15
`copy tftp flash`	Downloads a new image from the TFTP server to Flash memory.	16
`copy tftp running-config`	Loads configuration information from a network TFTP server.	15
`debug`	Uses debugging functions.	12
`debug ip rip`	Displays RIP routing updates as they are sent and received.	18
`delete`	Deletes a file.	12
`dir`	Lists the files on a given device.	12

Command	Description	Chapter
`disable`	Turns off privileged commands.	12
`disconnect`	Disconnects an existing network connection.	12
`enable`	Turns on privileged commands.	12
`enable password`	Sets a local password to control access to various privilege levels.	15
`enable secret`	Specifies an additional layer of security over the `enable password` command.	15
`erase`	Erases Flash or configuration memory.	12
`erase startup-config`	Erases the contents of NVRAM.	14, 15
`exit`	Exits any configuration mode, or closes an active terminal session and terminates the EXEC.	12, 15
`format`	Formats a device.	12
`help`	Gets a description of the interactive help system.	12
`history`	Enables the command history function.	12
`interface`	Configures an interface type and enters interface configuration mode.	15
`ip address`	Assigns an address and a subnet mask and starts IP processing on an interface.	17
`ip default-network`	Establishes a default route.	18
`ip domain-lookup`	Enables name-to-address translation in the router.	17
`ip host`	Makes a static name-to-address entry in the router's configuration file.	17
`ip name-server`	Specifies the addresses for up to six name servers to use for name and address resolution.	17
`ip route`	Establishes static routes.	18
`lat`	Opens a LAT connection.	12

Command	Description	Chapter
`line`	Identifies a specific line for configuration and starts the line configuration command collection mode.	15
`lock`	Locks the terminal.	12
`login`	Logs in as a particular user. Enables password checking at login.	12, 15
`logout`	Exits from EXEC mode.	12
`media-type`	Specifies the physical connection.	15
`mbranch`	Traces down a branch of a multicast tree for a specific group.	12
`mrbranch`	Traces up a branch of a multicast tree for a specific group.	12
`mrinfo`	Requests neighbor and version information from a multicast router.	12
`mstat`	Shows statistics after multiple multicast traceroutes.	12
`mtrace`	Traces the path from a source to a destination branch for a multicast distribution tree.	12
`name-connection`	Names an existing network connection.	12
`ncia`	Starts/stops the NCIA server.	12
`network`	Assigns a Network Information Center–based address to which the router is directly connected.	18
`no shutdown`	Restarts a disabled interface.	15
`pad`	Opens an X.29 PAD connection.	12
`ping`	Sends an echo request; diagnoses basic network connectivity.	10, 12, 17
`ppp`	Starts the IETF Point-to-Point Protocol.	12
`pwd`	Displays current device.	12

Command	Description	Chapter
`reload`	Halts and performs a cold return; reloads the operating system.	12, 14, 16
`rlogin`	Opens an rlogin connection.	12
`router`	Starts a routing process by first defining an IP routing protocol. For example, `router rip` selects RIP as the routing protocol.	15, 18
`rsh`	Executes a remote command.	12
`sdlc`	Sends SDLC test frames.	12
`send`	Sends a message over tty lines.	12
`service password-encryption`	Enables the password encryption function.	15
`setup`	Enters the `setup` command facility.	12, 14, 18
`show`	Shows running system information.	2
`show buffers`	Provides statistics for the buffer pools on the network server.	13
`show cdp entry`	Displays information about a neighbor device listed in the CDP table.	13
`show cdp interface`	Displays information about the interfaces on which CDP is enabled.	13
`show cdp neighbors`	Displays the results of the CDP discovery process.	13
`show flash`	Displays the layout and contents of Flash memory.	13, 16
`show hosts`	Displays a cached list of host names and addresses.	17
`show interfaces`	Displays statistics for all interfaces configured on the router.	13
`show ip interface`	Displays the status and global parameters associated with an interface.	18
`show ip protocols`	Displays the parameters and current state of the active routing protocol process.	18

Command	Description	Chapter
`show ip route`	Displays the contents of the IP routing table.	13, 18
`show memory`	Shows statistics about the router's memory, including memory-free pool statistics.	13
`show processes`	Displays information about the active processes.	13
`show protocols`	Displays the configured protocols. This command shows the status of any configured Layer 3 protocol.	13
`show running-config`	Displays the current configuration in RAM.	13, 14, 15, 16
`show stacks`	Monitors the stack use of processes and interrupt routines and displays the reason for the last system reboot.	13
`show startup-config`	Displays the saved configuration, which is the contents of NVRAM.	14, 15, 16
`show version`	Displays the configuration of the system hardware, the software version, the names and sources of configuration files, and the boot images.	13, 16
`shutdown`	Disables an interface.	15
`telnet`	Logs in to a host that supports Telnet.	13, 17
`term ip`	Specifies the format of network masks for the current session.	17
`trace`	Determines a path that packets will take when traveling to their destination.	13, 17
`verify`	Verifies the checksum of a Flash file.	12
`xremote`	Enters XRemote mode.	12
`where`	Lists active connections.	12
`which-route`	Does OSI route table lookup and displays results.	12

Command	Description	Chapter
`write`	Writes the running configuration to memory, a network, or a terminal.	12
`write erase`	The `erase startup-config` command replaces this command.	15
`write memory`	The `copy running-config startup-config` command replaces this command.	15
`x3`	Sets X.3 parameters on PAD.	12
`xremote`	Enters XRemote mode.	12

Answers to Review Questions

This appendix contains the answers to the review questions at the end of each chapter.

Chapter 1

1. A
2. B
3. B
4. A
5. D
6. A
7. A
8. B
9. C
10. D

Chapter 2

1. C
2. D
3. B
4. B
5. B
6. D
7. A

8. C

9. B

10. A

Chapter 3

1. A

2. D

3. D

4. A

5. B

6. B

7. A

8. B

9. A

10. B

Chapter 4

1. A

2. A

3. C

4. A

5. A

6. A

7. B

8. D

9. C

10. A

Chapter 5

1. D
2. A
3. B
4. D
5. C
6. C
7. A
8. D
9. C
10. A

Chapter 6

1. C
2. D
3. D
4. A
5. A
6. B
7. A
8. A
9. C
10. C

Chapter 7

1. B

2. C

3. A

4. D

5. B

6. C

7. A

8. D

9. B

10. C

Chapter 8

1. D

2. C

3. A

4. D

5. B

6. D

7. C

8. A

9. A

10. B

Chapter 9

1. A
2. A
3. C
4. C
5. C
6. B
7. B
8. D
9. A
10. C

Chapter 10

1. A
2. B
3. B
4. A
5. A
6. C
7. B
8. A
9. C
10. B

Chapter 11

1. C
2. B
3. A
4. A
5. A
6. A
7. D
8. A
9. A
10. A

Chapter 12

1. A
2. B
3. C
4. A
5. D
6. A
7. D
8. B
9. C
10. D

Chapter 13

1. A

2. C

3. C

4. B

5. C

6. B

7. A

8. C

9. A

10. A

Chapter 14

1. B

2. C

3. A

4. D

5. A

6. C

7. D

8. B

9. C

10. B

Chapter 15

1. B
2. A
3. C
4. D
5. D
6. B
7. A
8. C
9. C
10. A

Chapter 16

1. C
2. D
3. A
4. B
5. A
6. B
7. A
8. D
9. A
10. B

Chapter 17

1. C
2. D
3. A
4. A
5. D
6. C
7. A
8. B
9. D
10. A

Chapter 18

1. A
2. B
3. A
4. C
5. D
6. B
7. B
8. C
9. B
10. D

Chapter 19

1. D
2. B
3. D
4. C
5. B
6. B
7. D
8. C
9. B
10. A

Computer Basics

Introduction

This appendix looks at the components of a computer and at the role of computers in a network. This text takes a ground-up approach to networking, starting with the most basic component of a network, the computer. The more you know about computers, the easier it is to understand how networks are built.

To get an idea of the role of computers, it helps to think of the Internet. You can compare the Internet to a living organism: the computers play the role of the cells within that organism. Computers are sources of information and receivers of information, both giving to and taking from the Internet. Although cells often can live independently of the organism of which they are a part, the organism itself cannot live entirely without the cells that comprise it. Computers and the Internet depend on each other to some extent for survival. Computers can exist without the Internet, but as time goes on computers are becoming more and more dependent on the Internet.

The computer also plays a vital role in the work world. Companies use computers and computer software in different ways, but some uses are common to most companies. Servers are used to store important data and to manage employee accounts. Spreadsheet software is used to organize financial information. Word processor software is used to generate memos and text documents. Database software is used to maintain detailed records of customer. Web browsers are used to access company Web sites. Today, of course, computers are absolutely essential to the success of a company.

This appendix introduces you to the inner workings of a computer and gives you the foundation you need to begin the study of networking.

Computer Components

Because computers are important building blocks in a network, it is important to be able to recognize and name the major components of a personal computer (PC). Many networking devices are themselves special-purpose computers with many of the same parts as "normal" PCs. To use your computer as a reliable means of obtaining information, such as accessing Web-based curriculum, your computer must be in good working order, which means you might occasionally need to troubleshoot simple problems in your computer's hardware and software. You should be able to recognize, name, and state the purpose of the following PC components.

Small, Discrete Components

- Transistor—A device that amplifies (enlarges) a signal or opens and closes a circuit.
- Integrated circuit—An electronic device made out of semiconductor material (material that can control the amount of electricity it conducts).
- Resistor—A device that offers resistance to the flow of an electric current.
- Capacitor—An electronic component that stores energy in the form of an electrostatic field (an electric field that is not changing); it consists of two conducting metal plates separated by an insulating material.

FIGURE D-1
Capacitors.

■ Connector—The part of a cable that plugs into a port or an interface.

FIGURE D-2
Connectors.

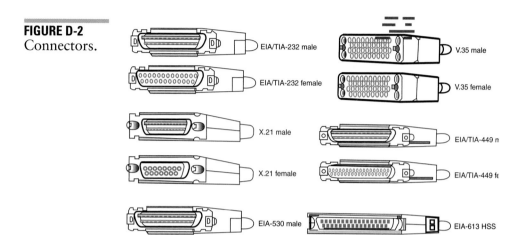

- EIA/TIA-232 male
- EIA/TIA-232 female
- X.21 male
- X.21 female
- EIA-530 male
- V.35 male
- V.35 female
- EIA/TIA-449 m
- EIA/TIA-449 fe
- EIA-613 HSS

■ Light emitting diode (LED)—A device that lights up when electricity passes through it.

■ Solder—An easily melted alloy (mixture of metals) used for joining metals.

Personal Computer Subsystems

■ Printed circuit board (PCB)—A thin plate on which chips and other electronic components are placed.

■ CD-ROM drive—A compact disc read *only memory* drive, which is a device that can read information from a CD-ROM.

FIGURE D-3
CD-ROM
drive.

■ Central Processing Unit (CPU)—The central processing unit (CPU) is the brains of the computer where most calculations take place.

FIGURE D-4
Central processing units (CPUs).

■ *Floppy disk drive*—A disk drive that can read and write to floppy disks.

FIGURE D-5
Floppy disk drive.

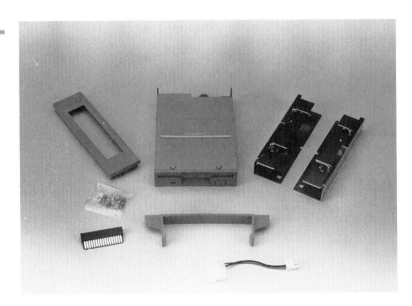

■ *Hard disk drive*—The device that reads and writes data on a hard disk.

■ *Microprocessor*—A silicon chip that contains a CPU. In the world of PCs, the terms *microprocessor* and *CPU* are interchangeable.

■ *Motherboard*—The main circuit board of a personal computer.

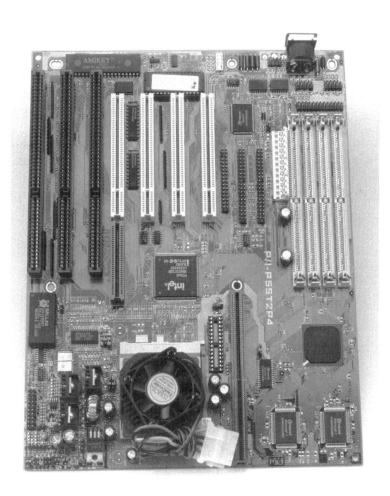

■ *Bus*—A collection of wires through which data is transmitted from one part of a computer to another. It connects all the internal computer components to the CPU.

FIGURE D-8
The dark gray lines are part of the bus.

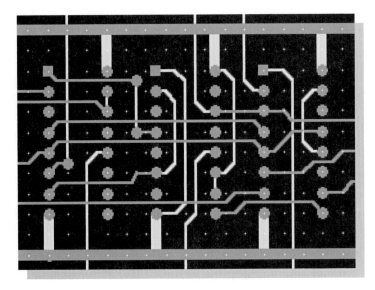

■ *Random access memory (RAM)*—A type of computer memory where any byte of memory can be accessed without touching the preceding bytes.

FIGURE D-9
Random access memory (RAM).

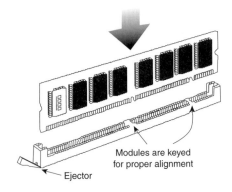

Modules are keyed for proper alignment

Ejector

■ *Read-only memory (ROM)*—Computer memory on which data has been prerecorded; after data has been written onto a ROM chip, it cannot be removed and can only be read.

■ *System unit*—The main part of a PC; the system unit includes the chassis, microprocessor, main memory, bus, and ports, but does not include the keyboard, monitor, or any external devices connected to the computer.

■ *Expansion slot*—An opening in a computer where a circuit board can be inserted to add new capabilities to the computer.

■ *Power supply*—The component that supplies power to a computer.

FIGURE D-12
Power sup-
ply.

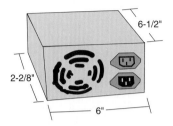

Backplane Components

Expansion card—A printed circuit board you can insert into a computer to give it added capabilities.

FIGURE D-13
Expansion
card.

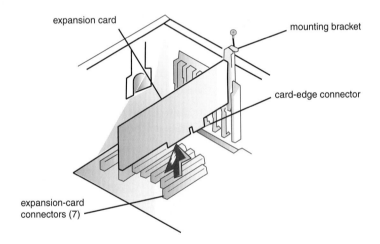

■ *Backplane*—The large circuit board that contains sockets for expansion cards. A backplane is distinguished from a motherboard by the fact that it might contain almost no logical circuitry for performing computing functions.

■ *Network card*—An expansion board inserted into a computer so the computer can be connected to a network.

■ *Modem*—The modem (modulator/demodulator) is a device that enables a computer to transmit data over telephone lines; there are internal (installed as expansion cards) and external (connected to ports) modems.

- *Video card*—A board that plugs into a PC to give it display capabilities.

FIGURE D-14
Video card.

- *Sound card*—An expansion board that enables a computer to manipulate and output sounds.
- *Interface*—A piece of hardware, such as an electrical connector, that allows two devices to be connected together.

FIGURE D-15
Interfaces on a Cisco 1601 router.

- *Port*—An interface on a computer to which you can connect an electronic device.

FIGURE D-16
An ISDN port on a Cisco 1603 router.

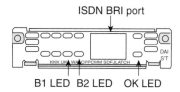

■ *Parallel port*—An interface capable of transferring more than one bit simultaneously. It is used to connect external devices such as printers.

FIGURE D-17
Parallel port
expansion
card.

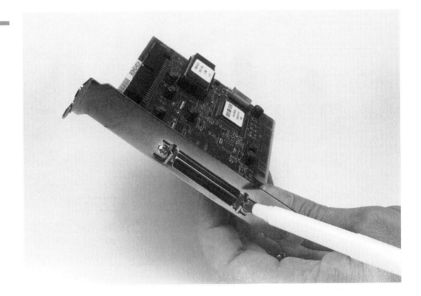

■ *Serial port*—An interface that can be used for serial communication (data communication in which only 1 bit is transmitted at a time).

FIGURE D-18
Serial port
expansion
card.

■ *Mouse port*—A port designed for connecting a mouse to a PC.

- *Power cord*—A cord used to connect an electrical device to an electrical outlet to provide power to the device.

Figure D-19 shows the basic components of an idealized computer. You can think of the internal components of a PC as a network of devices, all attached to the system bus. In a sense, a PC is a small computer network.

FIGURE D-19
The main components of a computer are the CPU, the memory, and the interfaces.

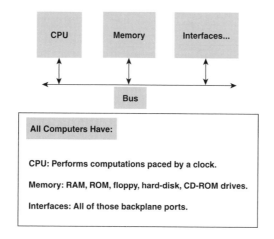

Information and electric power are constantly flowing in a PC. It helps to understand networking—designing, building, and maintaining networks—by thinking of the computer as a miniature network, with all the various devices within the system unit attached to, and communicating with, each other. The following are some of the important information flows (almost all of which occur via the bus):

- *Boot instructions*—Stored in ROM until they are sent out.
- *Software applications*—Stored in RAM after they have been loaded.
- *RAM and ROM*—Constantly talk to the CPU via the bus.
- *Application information*—Stored in RAM while applications are being used.
- *Saved information*—Flows from RAM to some form of storage device.
- *Exported information*—Flows from RAM and the CPU, via the bus and expansion slots, to the serial port, parallel port (usually for printers), video card, sound card, or network card.

Network Interface Cards

A network interface card (NIC) is a printed circuit board that provides network communication capabilities to and from a personal computer. Also called a *LAN adapter*, it plugs into a motherboard and provides a port for connecting to the network.

A *network card* communicates with the network through a serial connection (one bit transmitted at a time), and with the computer through a parallel connection (more than one bit transmitted at a time). Each card requires an IRQ, an I/O address, and an upper memory address for DOS and for Windows 95/98. IRQ, or interrupt request line, is a hardware line over which devices can send interrupts to the microprocessor. An interrupt is a signal informing a program that an event has occurred, such as running out of memory. An I/O address is a location in memory used to enter data or to retrieve data from a computer. In DOS-based systems, upper memory refers to the memory area between the first 640 kilobytes (KBs) and 1 megabyte (MB).

FIGURE D-20
A PCI bus is pictured on the right and an ISA bus on the left.

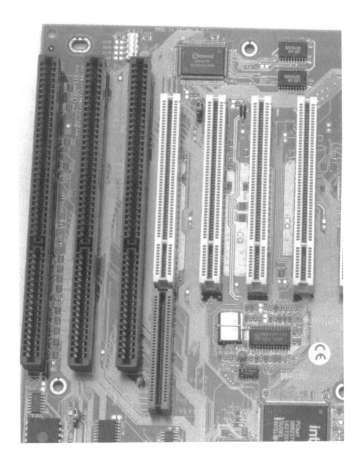

When you select a network card, consider the following three factors:

- Type of network (for example, Ethernet, Token Ring, or FDDI)
- Type of cable (for example, twisted-pair, coaxial, or fiber-optic)
- Type of system bus (for example, PCI or ISA)

The NIC allows networks to function and is, therefore, considered a key component. From time to time, you might need to install a NIC. Some possible situations that might require you to do so include the following:

- Adding a NIC to a PC that does not already have one.
- Replacing a bad or damaged NIC.
- Upgrading from a 10-Mbps (megabits, or millions of bits, per second) NIC to a 10/100-Mbps NIC.
- Altering settings on a NIC jumper. A *jumper* is a metal bridge that closes an electrical circuit; typically, a jumper consists of a plastic plug that fits over a pair of pins. The jumper is moved in order to change settings, such as the IRQ (especially on older NICs).

To perform the installation, you should have the following resources:

- Knowledge of how the network card is configured, including jumpers, plug-and-play software, and *erasable programmable read-only memory* (EPROM is a type of memory that retains its contents until it is exposed to ultraviolet light).
- Use of network card diagnostics, including the vendor-supplied diagnostics and a loopback test. (A test signal sent to a network destination that is returned as received to the originator; in the case of a network card, the test signal travels between the PC and network card, whether or not there is an external cable attached.)
- Capability to resolve hardware resource conflicts—these resources might include IRQ, I/O Base Address, or *direct memory address* (DMA is used to transfer data from RAM to a device without going through the CPU).

Laptop Components

Laptop computers and notebook computers are becoming increasingly popular, as are palm top computers, personal digital assistants, and other small computing devices. The information described in the previous sections also pertains to laptops. The main difference is that components in a laptop are smaller. The expansion slots become Personal Computer Memory Card International Association (PCMCIA) slots, where network cards, modems, hard drives, and other useful devices, usually the size of a thick credit card, can be inserted into various places along the perimeter.

Software

Now that you have a good idea of what's involved with computer hardware, you need the second ingredient: computer software. The purpose of software is to allow you to interact with the computer or networking device, to get it to do what you want it to do.

So, after the PC hardware is set up, the software must be configured. For example, the following tasks need to be completed prior to viewing Web-based curriculum:

STEP 1. Select the NIC.

STEP 2. Input the correct TCP/IP settings, including network address settings (TCP/IP is introduced in Chapter 10).

STEP 3. Adjust the monitor (if necessary).

STEP 4. Install and set up the browser.

STEP 5. Perform a few other tasks (if necessary).

Browsers

A Web server is a software application used to locate and display Web pages. A Web browser interfaces with a user by sequentially contacting a Web server, requesting information, receiving information, and then displaying the results onscreen. A browser is software that interprets hypertext markup language (HTML), the language used to create Web page content. HTML can display graphics and play sound, movies, and other multimedia files. Hyperlinks, elements in an electronic document that link to another place in the same document or to an entirely different document, allow the user to connect to other Web pages and to files that can be downloaded.

The two most popular browsers are Netscape Communicator and Internet Explorer (IE). Here are some of the similarities and differences between these two browsers:

Netscape

- First popular browser
- Takes less disk space
- Considered by many to be simple
- Displays HTML files
- Does e-mail, file transfers, and other functions

Internet Explorer (IE)

- Powerfully connected to other Microsoft products
- Takes more disk space
- Considered more difficult to use
- Displays HTML files
- Does e-mail, file transfers, and other functions

Plug-ins

There are also many proprietary (privately owned and controlled) file types that standard Web browsers are not able to display. To view these files, you must configure your browser to use plug-in applications. These applications work in conjunction with the browser to launch the program required to view the special files.

- Shockwave—Plays multimedia (integrated text, graphics, video, animation, and/or sound) files; created by Macromedia Authorware, Director, and Flash programs.
- QuickTime—Plays movies and sounds that have been saved in the Apple QuickTime file format.
- RealAudio—Plays audio files that have been saved in RealAudio format.
- RealPlayer G2—Plays movie files with high resolution that have been saved in RealPlayer format.

Office Applications

Beyond configuring your computer to view Web-based curriculum, you use your computer to perform many other useful tasks. In business, employees regularly use a set of applications that come in the form of an office suite, such as Microsoft Office. The office applications typically include spreadsheet software, word processing software, database management software, presentation software, and a personal information manager that includes an e-mail program. Spreadsheet software contains tables consisting of columns and rows and is often used with formulas to process and analyze data. Word processing software is an application used to create and edit text documents; modern word processor programs allow the user to create sophisticated documents that include graphics and richly formatted text. Database software is used to store, maintain, organize, sort, and filter records (a record is a collection of information identified by a common theme, such as a customer's name).

Presentation software is used to design and develop presentations to deliver at meetings, classes, or sales presentations. Personal information managers include such things as e-mail, contact lists, a calendar, and a to do list. Office applications are now as much a part of everyday work as typewriters were before the advent of the PC.

Networks

A network is an intricately connected system of objects or people. Networks are all around you, even inside you. Your own nervous system and cardiovascular system are networks. The cluster diagram, shown in Figure D-21, shows several types of networks; you might think of others. Notice the groupings:

FIGURE D-21
The term network is used in many different ways, but the meaning is similar in each case to that of a computer network.

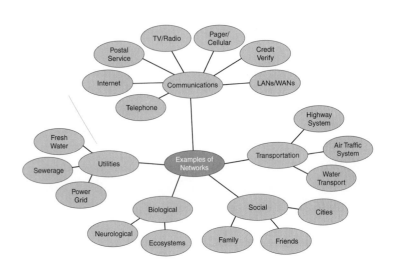

- Communications
- Transportation
- Social
- Biological
- Utilities

Data communication networks are designed to make it possible for two computers that are located anywhere in the world to be able to communicate with each other. They also make it possible for different types of computers to communicate, regardless of whether they are Macintosh, PC, or mainframe computers. The only major concern is that all computers and devices understand the other languages, or protocols.

Protocol means a formal description of a set of rules that govern how devices on a network exchange information. Most data networks are classified as local-area networks (LANs), metropolitan-area networks (MANs), or wide-area networks (WANs). LANs usually are located in single buildings or campuses, and handle interoffice communications. MANs are data networks designed for a town or city. WANs cover a large geographical area, and interconnect cities and countries. Internetworking is the practice of connecting LANs, MANs, and WANs together.

Early computers were standalone devices. Each one operated on its own, independent from any other computer. As time progressed, it became apparent that this was not an efficient or cost effective manner in which to operate businesses. What was needed was a solution that would successfully address the following two questions:

1. How to avoid duplication of equipment and resources (such as requiring a separate printer for every pair of PCs)?

2. How to share and exchange information efficiently?

One early solution to these problems was the creation of local-area networks (LANs). Because they could connect all of the workstations, peripherals (external devices attached to a computer), terminals, and other devices in a single building, LANs made it possible for businesses using computer technology to efficiently share such things as files and printers.

As computer use in businesses grew, it soon became apparent that even LANs were not sufficient. In a LAN system, each department or business was a kind of electronic island.

What was needed was a way for information to move efficiently and quickly from one business to another. The solution, then, was the creation of metropolitan-area networks (MANs) and wide-area networks (WANs). Because WANs could connect user networks over a large geographic area, they made it possible for businesses to communicate with each other across great distances.

Early development of LANs, MANs, and WANs was chaotic in many ways. The early 1980s saw a tremendous growth in networking. Companies recognized how much money they could save and how much productivity they could gain by using networking technology. For example, memos could be distributed instantaneously over the network to all employees without requiring someone to print out the document, make sufficient copies, and physically distribute them to all the employees. Companies began to add networks and to expand existing networks almost as rapidly as new network technologies and products were introduced.

By the mid-1980s, growing pains were felt. Many of the network technologies that had emerged had been built by using hardware and software implementations from a number of different manufacturers and developers. Consequently, many of the new network technologies were incompatible. It became increasingly difficult for networks using different specifications, such as Ethernet and Token Ring, to communicate with each other. Not surprisingly, much of the work since the mid-1980s has involved creating and implementing networking technologies and standards that allow different vendors' networking devices or technologies to work together on the same network. For example, there are now *bridges* (devices that connect two LANs or two segments of the same LAN) that allow for Ethernet and Token Ring networks to communicate.

As with all other technological implementations, there is a need to somehow measure the capabilities of LANs and WANs to determine their usefulness to companies and end users. The primary way this is done is by using the measure of *bandwidth* to describe the capabilities of the networks. This term can be difficult to understand, but it is an essential concept in networking. This is the topic of the next section.

Bandwidth

Bandwidth is the measure of how much information can flow from one place to another in a given amount of time. There are two common uses of the word bandwidth: one deals with analog signals, and the other with digital signals (these signals are explored in Appendix F, "Signaling and Data Transmission"). You will work with digital bandwidth, simply called bandwidth, for the remainder of the text.

You have already learned that the most basic unit used to describe the flow of digital information, from one place to another, is the bit. The next term you need to know is the one used to describe the basic unit of time. It is the second. Now you see where term bits per second (bps) comes from.

Bits per second is a unit of bandwidth. Of course, if communication happened at this rate, 1 bit per 1 second, it would be very slow. The American Standard Code for Information Interchange (ASCII, pronounced ask-ee) is a code for representing English characters as numbers, with each letter assigned a number from 0 to 127. Now, imagine trying to send the ASCII code for your name and address at 1 bit per second—it would take minutes! Fortunately, much faster communication is now possible. Table D-1 summarizes the various units of bandwidth.

TABLE D-1   Units of Bandwidth

Unit of Bandwidth	Abbreviation	Equivalence
Bits per second	Bps	1 bps = fundamental unit of bandwidth
Kilobits per second	Kbps	1 kbps = 1000 = 10^3 bps
Megabits per second	Mbps	1 Mbps = 1,000,000 bps + 10^6 bps
Gigabits per second	Gbps	1 Gbps = 1,000,000,000 bps = 10^9 bps

Bandwidth is a very important element of networking, yet it can be rather abstract and difficult to understand. The following are three analogies that might help you picture what bandwidth is:

1. Bandwidth is like the width of a pipe (see Figure D-22). Think of the network of pipes that brings water to your home and carries sewage away from it. Those pipes have different widths: the city's main water pipe might be 2 meters wide, whereas the kitchen faucet might be 2 centimeters wide. The width of the pipe measures the water-carrying capacity of the pipe. In this analogy, the water is like information and the width of the pipe is like bandwidth. In fact, many networking experts will talk in terms of "putting in bigger pipes," meaning more bandwidth; that is, more information-carrying capacity.

FIGURE D-22
The wider the pipe, the greater the rate of fluid that can flow through it.

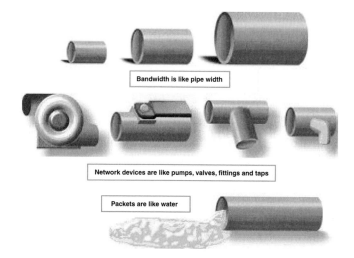

Bandwidth is like pipe width

Network devices are like pumps, valves, fittings and taps

Packets are like water

2. Bandwidth is like the number of lanes on a highway (see Figure D-23). Think about a network of roads that serves your city or town. There might be eight-lane highways, with exits onto two- and three-lane roads, which might then lead to two-lane undivided streets, and eventually to your driveway. In this analogy, the number of lanes is like bandwidth, and the number of cars is like the amount of information that can be carried.

FIGURE D-23
The more lanes in a highway, the greater the capacity for traffic flow..

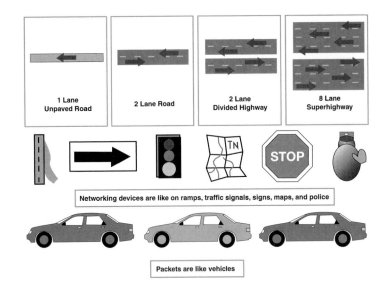

3. Bandwidth is like the quality of sound in an audio system. The sound is the information, and the quality of the sound you hear is the bandwidth; that is, the sound is the data and the measure of the frequency of the sound is the bandwidth. If you were to rank your preferences on how you would rather hear your favorite song—over the telephone, on an AM radio, on an FM radio, or on a CD-ROM—you would probably make the CD your first preference, then FM radio, then AM radio, and finally the telephone. The actual analog bandwidths for these are, respectively, 20 kHz, 15 kHz, 5 kHz, and 3 kHz.

Keep in mind that the true, actual meaning of bandwidth, in this context, is the maximum number of bits that can, in theory, pass through a given area of space in a specified amount of time under the given conditions. The analogies used here are to make it easier to understand the concept of bandwidth.

Bandwidth is a very useful concept. It does, however, have its limitations. No matter how you send your messages, no matter what kind of cable you use, bandwidth is limited. This is due both to the laws of physics and to the current technological advances.

Table D-2 illustrates the maximum digital bandwidth possible, including length limitations, for some common types of cable. Always remember that limits are both physical and technological (technology drives the quality of the manufacturing of the cable, which in turn determines bandwidth limitations).

TABLE D-2   Maximum Bandwidths and Length Limitations.

Typical Media	Maximum Theoretical Bandwidth	Maximum Physical Distance
50-Ohm Coaxial Cable (Ethernet 10Base2, ThinNet)	10-1000 Mbps	200 m
75-Ohm Coaxial Cable (Ethernet 10Base 5, Thicknet)	10-100 Mbps	500 m
Category 5 Unshielded Twisted Pair (UTP) (Ethernet 100Base-TX) (Fast Ethernet)	100 Mbps	100 m
Multimode (62.5/125um) Optical Fiber 100Base-FX	100 Mbps	200 m
Singlemode (10um core) Optical Fiber 1000Base-LX	1000 Mbps (1.000 Gbps)	3000 m
Other technologies being researched	2400 Mbps (2.400 Gbps)	40 km = 40,000 m
Wireless	2.0 Mbps	100 m

Bandwidth is also limited by the capacity of the specific technology, such as ISDN (integrated services digital network), subscribed from the service provider.

Table D-3 summarizes different WAN services and the bandwidth associated with each service. Which service do you use at home? At school?

TABLE D-3   WAN Services and Bandwidths.

Type of WAN Service	Typical User	Bandwidth
Modern	Individuals	33 kbps = 0.033 Mbps
Frame Relay	Small institutions (schools); reliable WANs	56 kbps = 0.056 Mbps

continues

TABLE D-3   WAN Services and Bandwidths. (Continued)

Type of WAN Service	Typical User	Bandwidth
ISDN	Telecommuters, small businesses	128 kbps = 0.128 Mbps
T1	Larger entities	1.544 Mbps
T3	Larger entities	44.736 Mbps
STS-1 (OC-1)	Phone companies; DataComm company backbones	51.840 Mbps
STS-3 (OC-3)	Phone companies; DataComm company backbones	155.251 Mbps
STS-48 (OC-48)	Phone companies; DataComm company backbones	2.488320 Gbps

Imagine that you are lucky enough to have a brand new cable modem (a modem designed to operate over cable TV lines), or your local store just installed an ISDN (integrated services digital network) line, or your school just received a 10-MB Ethernet LAN. Imagine the movie you want to view, or the Web page or software you want to download takes forever to receive. You probably believed you were getting all the bandwidth that was advertised. There is another important concept you should have considered; it's called throughput.

Throughput refers to actual, measured bandwidth, at a specific time of day, using specific Internet routes (paths that data will follow on the Internet), while downloading a specific file. Unfortunately, for many reasons, the throughput is often far less then the maximum possible digital bandwidth of the medium that is being used. Some of the factors that determine throughput and bandwidth include the following:

- Internetworking devices (such as routers and switches)
- Type of data being transferred
- Topology (the shape of a network, such as *ring* or *star*)
- Number of users
- User's computer
- Server computer

■ Power and weather-induced outages

When you design a network, it is important to consider the theoretical bandwidth (recall that this is the maximum number of bits that can, in theory, pass through a given area of space in a specified amount of time). Your network will be no faster than your media will allow. When you actually work on networks, you will want to measure throughput and decide if the throughput is adequate for the user (see Figure D-24).

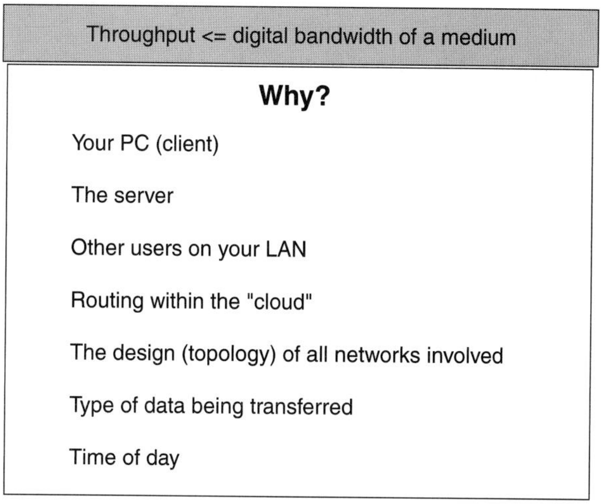

FIGURE D-24
Throughput is the actual amount of data passing through a given area of space in a specific amount of time.

Throughput <= digital bandwidth of a medium
Why?
Your PC (client)
The server
Other users on your LAN
Routing within the "cloud"
The design (topology) of all networks involved
Type of data being transferred
Time of day

An important part of networking involves making decisions about which medium to use. This often leads to questions regarding the bandwidth required by the user's applications. The graphic summarizes a simple formula that will help you with such decisions. The formula is Estimated Time = Size of File / Bandwidth (see Figure D-25). The resulting answer represents the fastest that data could be transferred. It does not take into account any of the previously discussed issues that affect bandwidth, but does give you a rough estimate of the time it will take to send information using that specific medium/application.

FIGURE D-25
Here's a formula for computing the time it takes to download a file.

BW = Maximum theoretical bandwidth of the "slowest" link between the source host and the destination host.

P = Actual throughput at the moment of transfer.

T = Time for file transfer to occur.

S = File size in bits.

$$\text{Best Download} \quad T = \frac{S}{BW}$$

$$\text{Typical Download} \quad T = \frac{S}{P}$$

Now that you are familiar with the units for digital bandwidth, try the following sample problem:

Problem:
GB stands for gigabyte and one gigabyte is one billion bytes. Similarly, 1 Gbps is one billion bits per second. SONET stands for *synchronous optical network* and is a standard for connecting fiber-optic transmission systems. OC-48 stands for a 2.488 Gbps *optical carrier* network conforming to the SONET standard. With these definitions out of the way, which would be faster: sending a floppy disk full of data over an ISDN line, or sending a 10 GB hard drive full of data over an OC-48 line?

Why Is Bandwidth Important?

1. First, bandwidth is finite (not infinite). Regardless of the media, the laws of physics limit bandwidth. For example, the bandwidth limitation (due to the physical properties of the twisted-pair phone wires that come into many homes) is what limits the throughput of standard phone modems to about 56 Kbps (1 Kbps is 1 kilobit per second or 1000 bits per second). The bandwidth of the electromagnetic spectrum (the full range of wavelengths for electromagnetic waves) is finite. There are only so many frequencies in the radio wave, microwave, and infrared spectrum. Consequently, the FCC (Federal Communications Commission) has a whole division to control bandwidth and who uses it. Fiber-optic cable permits such a large capacity for bandwidth that, in practice, it can

appear to be limitless. However, the technology used to make extremely high bandwidth networks, which fully utilize the potential of optical fiber, are just now being developed and implemented.

2. Knowing how bandwidth works, and that it is finite, can save you a lot of money. For example, the cost of various connection options from Internet service providers depends in part on how much bandwidth, on average and at peak usage (maximum attainable), you require.

3. As a networking professional, you will be expected to know about bandwidth and throughput. They are major factors in analyzing network performance. In addition, as a network designer of new networks, bandwidth will always be a major design issue.

4. It is not uncommon that once a person or an institution starts using a network, they eventually want more and more bandwidth. New multimedia software programs require much more bandwidth than those used in the mid-1990s. Creative programmers and users are busily designing networks that are capable of performing more complex tasks, thus requiring greater bandwidth.

Summary

- Computers are vital components of every network. The more you know about computers, the easier it is to understand networks.

- It is important to be familiar with the components of a computer and to be able to install a NIC. Also, troubleshooting PCs is a necessary skill for someone who works on networks.

- Software is the piece of the puzzle that allows the user to interface (connect with and make use of) the hardware. In networking, Web browsers and e-mail are commonly used software programs. In general, office applications, browsers, and e-mail programs are used to conduct business.

- The two main types of networks are LANs and WANs. WANs connect LANs together. LANs and WANs use protocols as languages to allow for computers and networking devices to communicate with each other.

- Bandwidth and throughput are measures of the speed or capacity of a network.

Electronics and Signals

Introduction

The function of the physical layer is to transmit data by defining the electrical specifications between the source and the destination. After it reaches a building, electricity is carried to workstations, servers, and network devices via wires concealed in walls, floors, and ceilings. Data, which can consist of such things as text, pictures, audio, or video, travels through the wires and is represented by the presence of either electrical pulses on copper conducting wires or light pulses in optical fibers.

In this appendix, you will learn about the basic theory of electricity, which provides a foundation for understanding networking at the physical layer of the OSI model. The concepts you learn here will help you understand how data is transmitted through physical media, such as cables and connectors, and the factors that affect data transmission (discussed in Chapter 2, " The Physical and Data Link Layers").

Basics of Electricity

All matter is composed of atoms. *The Periodic Table of Elements* (see Figure E-1) lists all known types of atoms and their properties.

FIGURE E-1
The Periodic Table of Elements

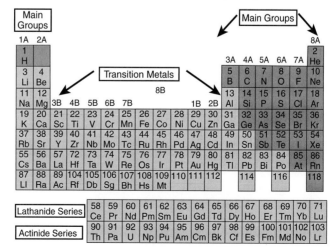

Periodic Table of Elements

The names of the parts of the atom are

- *Nucleus*—The center part of the atom, formed by protons and neutrons.
- *Protons*—Particles with a positive charge that, along with neutrons, form the nucleus.
- *Neutrons*—Particles with no charge (neutral) that, along with protons, form the nucleus.
- *Electrons*—Particles with a negative charge that orbit the nucleus.

To help you understand the electrical properties of elements/materials, locate helium on the periodic chart. It has an *atomic number* of 2, which means that it has two protons and two electrons. It has an *atomic weight* of 4. By subtracting the atomic number (2) from the atomic weight (4), you learn that helium also has two neutrons.

Example:
Atomic number of helium = 2

```
  2 protons
+ 2 electrons
  4 atomic weight
- 2 atomic number
  2 neutrons
```

The Danish physicist, Niels Bohr, developed a simplified model to illustrate atoms. Figure E-2 shows the model for a helium atom. Notice the scale of the parts. If the protons and neutrons of this atom were the size of a soccer ball in the middle of a soccer field, then the electrons would be the size of cherries and would be orbiting near the outermost seats of the stadium. The space inside the atom would be the size of the soccer field.

This model provides a setting useful for discussing the concepts of force within an atom. Coulomb's (Electric Force) Law states that *opposite charges* react to each other with a force that causes them to be attracted to each other, and *like charges* react to each other with a force that causes them to repel each other. A force is a pushing or pulling motion—in the case of opposite and like charges, the force increases as the charges move closer to each other.

FIGURE E-2
The helium atom has two protons, two electrons, and two neutrons.

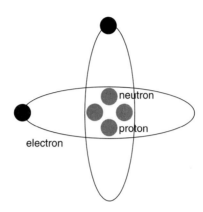

Refer to Bohr's model of the helium atom in Figure E-2. If Coulomb's Law is true, and if Bohr's model describes helium atoms as stable, then there must be other laws of nature at work. How can these two concepts be consistent?

Question 1: Why don't the electrons fly in towards the protons?

1. Coulomb's Law—Like charges repel.

2. Bohr's model—Protons are positive charges. There is more than one proton in the nucleus.

Question 2: Why don't the protons fly away from each other?

The answer to these questions is that there are other laws of nature that must be considered. Following are the answers to each of the preceding questions.

Answer 1: The electrons stay in orbit, even though they are attracted by the protons, because they have just enough velocity to keep orbiting and to not let themselves be pulled into the nucleus.

Answer 2: The protons do not fly apart from each other because of a nuclear force that is associated with neutrons. The nuclear force is an incredibly strong force that acts as a kind of glue to hold the protons together.

The protons and neutrons are bound together by a very powerful force; however, the force that binds electrons to their orbit around the nucleus is weaker. Figure E-3 illustrates these forces. It is as a result of this "weaker" force that electrons in certain types of atoms can be pulled free from their atoms and made to *flow*. This is electricity—a free flow of electrons.

FIGURE E-3
Forces within
an atom.

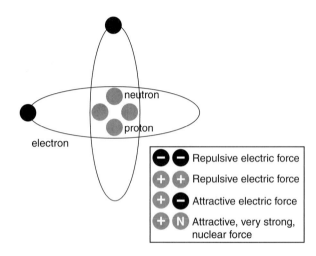

Types of Electrical Materials

Groups of atoms form *molecules*. In turn, *materials* are composed of molecules. Materials are classified as belonging to one of three groups, depending on how easily electricity (free electrons) flows through them. The three types are *electrical insulators*, *electrical conductors*, and *electrical semiconductors*.

Electrical Insulators

Electrical insulators, or *insulators*, are materials that allow electrons to flow through them with great difficulty, or not at all. Electrical insulators are not the same kind of thermal insulators, or insulation, that keep your house warm in winter. Examples of electrical insulators include plastic, glass, air, dry wood, paper, rubber, and certain atoms such as helium. These materials have very stable chemical structures, with orbiting electrons tightly bound within the atoms.

A good example of an electrical insulator is glass. Fiber-optic cable is made of glass, and it serves as a medium for carrying light pulses. Because it does not carry electrical signals, it is immune to induced electrical signals and impulses. And because glass is an electrical insulator, using fiber-optic links within a network avoids the problem of network ground loops.

Electrical Conductors

Electrical conductors, or *conductors,* are materials that allow electrons to flow through them with great ease. They flow easily because the outermost electrons are bound very loosely to the nucleus, and are easily freed. At room temperature, these materials have a large number of free electrons that can provide conduction. The introduction of voltage, (discussed in detail in the following "Voltage" section), causes the free electrons to move and a current to flow.

The periodic table categorizes some groups of atoms by listing them in columns. The atoms in each column belong to particular chemical families. Although they might have different numbers of protons, neutrons, and electrons, their outermost electrons have similar orbits and behave similarly when interacting with other atoms and molecules. The best conductors are metals, such as copper (Cu), silver (Ag), and gold (Au). All of these metals are located in one column of the periodic chart, and have electrons that are easily freed, making them excellent materials for carrying a *current.*

Other conductors include solder (a mixture of lead (Pb) and tin (Sn)) and water. Water is a conductor because of the presence of *ions.* An ion is an atom that has more electrons, or fewer electrons, than a neutral atom. The human body is made of approximately 70% (ionic) water, which means that our bodies are also conductors.

Of course, conductors are pervasive in the world of networking. Conductors allow electrical signals to transmit through a computer and over a network.

Electrical Semiconductors

Semiconductors are materials that can control the amount of electricity they conduct. These materials are listed together in one column of the periodic chart. Examples include carbon (C), germanium (Ge), and the alloy gallium arsenide (GaAs). The most important semiconductor, however, and the one that makes the best microscopic-sized electronic circuits, is silicon (Si).

Silicon is very common and can be found in sand, glass, and many types of rocks. The region around San Jose, California is known as Silicon Valley because the computer industry, which depends on silicon microchips, started in that area. The *switches, or gates,* inside a microprocessor are made up of semiconductors.

TABLE E-1   A Summary of the Three Main Types of Electrical Materials

Insulators	Electrons flow poorly	Plastic Paper Rubber Dry Wood Air Glass
Conductors	Electrons flow well	Copper (Cu) Silver (Ag) Gold (Au) Solder Water with Ions Humans
Semiconductors	Electron flow can be precisely controlled	Carbon (C) Germontum (Ge) Gallium Arsenide (GaAs) Silicon (Si)

Whether materials are classified as insulators, conductors, or semiconductors, it is the knowledge of how each one controls the flow of electrons, and how they work together in various combinations, that is the basis for all electronic devices.

Measuring Electricity

As with any other physical process or concept, we need to be able to measure electricity in order to make use of it. There are numerous ways of measuring electricity—we'll focus on *voltage, current, resistance,* and *impedance.*

Voltage

Voltage, sometimes referred to as *electromotive force (EMF),* is an electrical force, or pressure, that occurs when electrons and protons are separated. The force that is created pushes toward the opposite charge and away from the like charge. This process occurs in a battery, where chemical action causes electrons to be freed from the battery's negative terminal, and to travel to the opposite, or positive, terminal. The separation of charges results in voltage. Voltage also can be created by friction (static electricity), by magnetism (electric generator), or by light (solar cell).

Voltage is represented by the letter "V," and sometimes by the letter "E," for electromotive force. The unit of measurement for voltage is volt (V), and is defined as the amount of work per unit charge needed to separate the charges.

Current

Electrical current, or *current*, is the flow of charges that is created when electrons move. In electrical circuits, current is caused by a flow of free electrons. When voltage is applied, and there is a path for the current, electrons move from the negative terminal (which repels them) along the path to the positive terminal (which attracts them).

Current is represented by the letter "I." The unit of measurement for current is ampere (amp), and is defined as the number of charges per second that pass by a point along a path.

There are two ways in which electrical current flows: *alternating current* and *direct current*.

Alternating Current

Alternating current (AC) varies with time by changing *polarity,* or direction, about 60 times per second. AC flows in one direction, and then reverses its direction and repeats the process. AC voltage is positive at one terminal and negative at the other; then it reverses its polarity, so that the positive terminal becomes negative and the negative terminal becomes positive. This process repeats itself continuously.

Alternating current is the type of electricity that we use most often in daily life. Electricity is brought to your home, school, and office by power lines and these power lines carry electricity in the form of alternating current. AC power is suitable for many types of devices, but is totally unsuitable for use within low-voltage devices, such as computers.

Direct Current

Direct current (DC) always flows in the same direction, and DC voltages always have the same polarity. One terminal is always positive, and the other is always negative. They do not change or reverse.

Direct current can be found in flashlight batteries, car batteries, and as power for the microchips on the motherboard of a computer. The power supply in your system converts AC line power into DC, which is what the computer requires for operation. Many external peripherals (such as printers, external modems, and external storage drives) come with an *AC adapter* that looks like a little, heavy black box that plugs into the wall. That little black box is also a power converter, changing the AC power from the wall into DC power that the computer uses. Usually, the input and output electrical specifications are printed right on it.

It is important to understand the difference between DC and AC and when each is applied.

We can quantify a material's capability to allow current to flow. This is made possible by the concepts of *resistance* and *impedance.*

Resistance

Materials through which current flows offer varying amounts of opposition, or *resistance,* to the movement of electrons. Materials that offer very little or no resistance are called *conductors.* Those that do not allow the current to flow, or severely restrict its flow, are called *insulators.* The amount of resistance depends on the chemical composition of the materials.

Resistance is represented by the letter "R." The unit of measurement for resistance is the ohm (Ω). This symbol is pronounced "omega" and is a capital letter in the Greek alphabet. Greek letters are used extensively in math and physics.

For AC and DC electrical systems, the flow of electrons is always from a negatively charged source to a positively charged source. However, for the controlled flow of electrons to occur, a complete circuit is required. Generally speaking, electrical current follows the path of least resistance. Because metals such as copper provide little resistance, they are frequently used as conductors for electrical current. Conversely, materials such as glass, rubber, and plastic provide more resistance. Therefore, they do not make good electrical conductors. Instead, these materials are frequently used as insulators. They are used on conductors to prevent shock, fires, and short circuits.

Impedance

Impedance is the total opposition to current flow (due to AC and DC voltages). The term *resistance* is generally used when referring to DC voltages. Impedance is the general term, and is the measure of how the flow of electrons is resisted, or impeded.

Impedance is represented by the letter "Z." Its unit of measurement, like that for resistance, is the ohm (Ω). You often hear engineers or technicians speak of *matching* impedances; this just means that you have to use the right equipment with each type of medium utilized in a network. For example, UTP cable has a characteristic impedance of 100 ohms and STP has a characteristic impedance of 150 ohms, so the NIC's must accommodate these respective impedances to prevent reflection (resulting in corrupted signals).

The concepts of voltage, current, and resistance are related. Currents only flow in closed loops, called *circuits*. These circuits must be composed of conducting materials, and must have sources of voltage. Voltage causes current to flow, while resistance and impedance oppose it.

The formulas $P=I^2R$ and $V=IR$ relate power (P), resistance (R), and voltage (V). For example, with a fixed resistance, as in unshielded twisted-pair cable, increasing the voltage by a factor of 5 results in decreasing power by a factor of 25 (the square of the factor 5)!

Water flow (see Figure E-4) helps to explain the concepts of voltage, current, and resistance. The higher the water (and the greater the pressure), the more the water flows. The water current depends on how open the tap is. Similarly, the higher the voltage (the greater the electrical pressure), the more current produced. The electric current then encounters resistance that, like the water tap, reduces flow. If it is on an AC circuit, the amount of current depends on how much impedance is present. The pump is like a battery: it provides pressure to keep the flow moving.

FIGURE E-4
Useful parallels can be made between water flow and electricity.

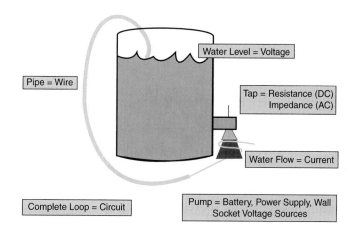

The following list summarizes the electrical concepts encountered thus far. These concepts are the basis upon which signaling and data transmissions are described in Appendix F, "Signaling and Data Transmission." Understanding these electrical concepts makes it relatively easy to understand the processes occurring at the physical layer of the OSI model.

- Electrons flow in closed loops call circuits
- Definitions
  - *Voltage*—Electrical pressure due to the separation of electrical charge (+ and -)
  - *Current (I)*—Flow of charged particles, usually electrons
  - *Resistance*—Property of a material that opposes and can control electrical flow
  - *Impedance*—Equivalent to resistance but for AC and pulsed circuits
  - *Short Circuit*—Conducting path
  - *Open Circuit*—Discontinuity in conducting path
- Voltage causes currents; resistance and impedance limit currents

Electrical Grounds

Another electrical concept that comes up frequently in networking is that of an electrical *ground*. Understanding the term *ground* can be difficult because people use the term for many different purposes:

- Ground can refer to the place on the earth that touches your house (probably by way of the buried water pipes), eventually making an indirect connection to your electric outlets. When you use an electric appliance that has a plug with three prongs, the third prong is the ground. It gives the electrons an extra conducting path to flow to the earth, rather than through your body.

- Ground can also mean the reference point, or the 0 volts level, when making electrical measurements. Voltage is created by the separation of charges, which means that voltage measurements must be made between two points. A *multimeter* (which measures voltage, current, and resistance) has two wires for that reason. The black wire is referred to as the ground, or reference ground. A negative terminal on a battery is also referred to as 0 volts, or the reference ground.

Figure E-5 shows a familiar object: electricity as supplied through wall outlets. The top two connectors supply power. The round connector on the bottom protects people and equipment from shocks and short circuits. This connector is called the safety ground connection. In electrical equipment where a safety ground is used, the safety ground wire is connected to any exposed metal part of the equipment. The motherboards and computing circuits in computing equipment are electrically connected to the chassis of the computer. This also connects them to the safety grounding wire, which is used to dissipate static electricity.

FIGURE E-5
The familiar neutral, hot, and safety ground wires in a wall outlet.

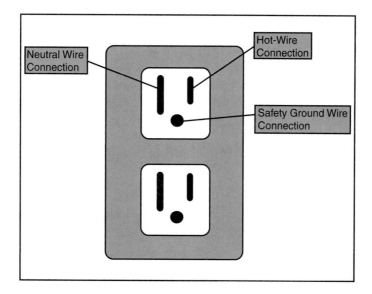

Neutral Wire Connection

Hot-Wire Connection

Safety Ground Wire Connection

The purpose of connecting the safety ground to exposed metal parts of the computing equipment is to prevent such metal parts from becoming energized with a hazardous voltage resulting from a wiring fault inside the device.

An accidental connection between the hot wire and the chassis is an example of a wiring fault that could occur in a network device. If such a fault were to occur, the safety ground wire connected to the device would serve as a low resistance path to the earth ground. The safety ground connection provides a lower resistance path than your body.

When properly installed, the low resistance path, provided by the safety ground wire offers sufficiently low resistance and current carrying capacity to prevent the build up of hazardously high voltages. The circuit links directly to the hot connection to the earth.

Whenever an electrical current is passed via this path into the ground, it causes protective devices such as circuit breakers and Ground Fault Circuit Interrupters (GFCIs) to activate. By interrupting the circuit, circuit breakers and GFCIs stop the flow of electrons and reduce the hazard of electrical shock. The circuit breakers protect you and your house wiring, but further protection, often in the form of surge suppressors and Uninterrupted Power Supplies (UPSs), is required to protect computing and networking equipment.

The power that is consumed by computers and networking equipment is supplied from a pole-mounted transformer (see Figure E-6). The transformer, which is also connected to the earth ground, reduces the high voltages originating from a power plant to the 120 or 240 volts used by typical consumer electrical appliances.

FIGURE E-6
Surge suppressors, uninterruptible power supplies, and wall outlets all connect to a transformer and to the earth ground.

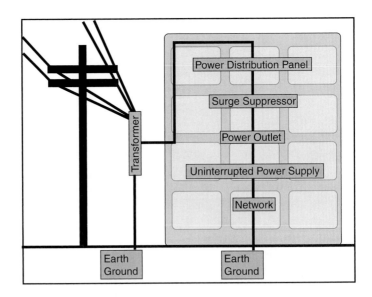

Now we see how electricity makes it to our homes, our schools, and our work places from the power plant. All the electrical considerations we've seen thus far play a role in the fundamental building block of electronic devices—the *circuits* that compose the ever present electronic equipment we use.

A Simple Circuit

Electrons flow only in circuits that are closed, or complete, loops. The diagram in Figure E-7 shows a simple circuit, typical of a lantern-style flashlight. The chemical processes in the battery cause charges to be separated, which provides a voltage, or electrical pressure, enabling electrons to flow through various devices. The lines represent a conductor, usually copper wire.

You can think of a switch as two ends of a single wire that can be opened (or broken) and then closed (also known as fixed or shorted) to prevent or to allow electrons to flow. The bulb provides resistance to the flow of electrons, causing the electrons to release energy in the form of light. The circuits involved in networking use the same concepts as in this very simple circuit, but are much more complex.

Circuits are the bottom line in networking equipment, including computers. All electronic devices are ultimately composed of circuits and switches. The simple example in Figure E-7 is replicated millions of times in the electronic devices we use. Typically, a microchip contains three to five million of these switches within one quarter-inch square.

FIGURE E-7
A simple circuit used in a 6-volt flashlight.

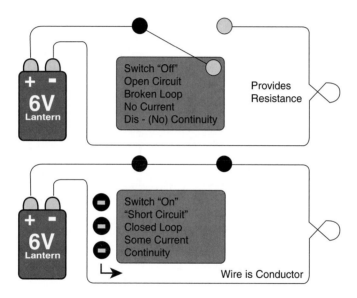

Summary

- Electricity is based on the capability of electrons of certain types of atoms to separate, or flow, from the confines of these atoms.

- Opposite charges attract and like charges repel. Electricity flows from negative to positive within electrical circuits.

- Materials can be classified as either insulators, conductors, or semiconductors, depending on their capability to allow electrons to flow.

- The concepts of voltage, current, resistance, and impedance provide a means of measuring electricity, which is required to be able to design and manufacture electronic devices.

- Alternating current and direct current are the two types of current. AC is used to provide power to our homes, schools, and work places. DC is used with electrical devices that depend on a battery to function.

- Electrical grounds provide a baseline from which to measure voltage. They also are used as a safety mechanism to prevent hazardous shocks.

- All electronic equipment is composed of electrical circuits that regulate the flow of electricity via switches.

Signaling and Data Transmission

Introduction

Appendix E, "Electronics and Signals," establishes the underlying physical principles governing computer networking. The physical layer of the OSI model is the setting in which the requisite physical phenomena is harnessed for the purposes of signaling. *Signaling* is the means by which data transmission is made possible. *Data transmission* is the means by which networking devices can operate within the remaining layers of the OSI model.

It is interesting to see the bottom-up approach that makes the world of networking possible. All of what we learn and do in computer networking is ultimately dependent on the underlying physics of electricity. Just as it is easier to learn about IP addressing and subnetting if we have a solid understanding of binary numbers and associated base conversions, it is much easier to understand networking at the physical and data link layers if we have a solid understanding of the physics of electricity.

In this appendix, you will study in detail the various concepts related to signaling and data transmission. This appendix culminates in a discussion of the formation of frames from bits at the physical layer, which completes your study of the physical layer.

Signals and Noise in Communication Systems

The term *signal* refers to a desired electrical voltage, light pattern, or modulated electromagnetic wave. Each of these entities can carry networking data. The two main types of signaling are *analog* and *digital*. Let's take a look at the specific attributes of each of these types of signals.

Comparing Analog and Digital Signals

One type of signal is analog. An analog signal has the following characteristics:

- It is wavy.
- It has a continuously varying voltage-versus-time graph.
- It is typical of things in nature.
- It has been widely used in telecommunications for more than 100 years.

Figure F-1 shows a *sine wave*. The two important characteristics of a sine wave are its *amplitude (A)*, its height and depth, and its *period (T)*, the length of one complete cycle (in our case, this is a time measurement). You can calculate the *frequency (f)* of the wave, measured in cycles per second, with the formula f = 1/T.

FIGURE F-1

Here is an example of an analog signal. This particular signal is in the form of a sine wave.

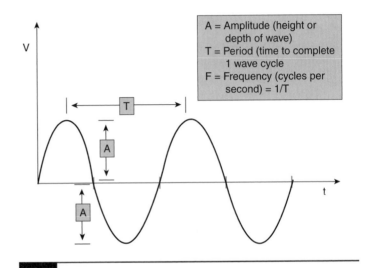

A = Amplitude (height or depth of wave)
T = Period (time to complete 1 wave cycle
F = Frequency (cycles per second) = 1/T

• Continuous voltage
• Can have any voltage
• "Wavy" voltage as time progresses
• Many encodings possible

Another type of signal is digital. A digital signal has the following characteristics:

- It has discrete, or jumpy, voltage-versus-time graphs.
- It is typical of technology (man-made), rather than nature.

Figure F-2 shows a digital networking signal. A digital signal has a fixed amplitude, but its amplitude, period, and frequency can be altered. Digital signals can be approximated by square waves (see Figure F-3), which have instantaneous transitions from low to high voltage states. Although this is an approximation, it is a reasonable one, and is used frequently herein.

FIGURE F-2
Here is an example of a digital signal.

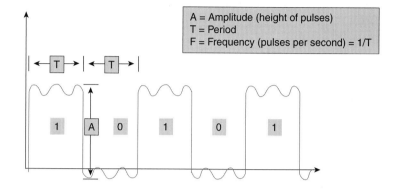

A = Amplitude (height of pulses)
T = Period
F = Frequency (pulses per second) = 1/T

- Not continuous (discreet) pulses
- Can only have one of two voltage levels
- Voltage jumps between levels
- Made up of many particular sine waves

FIGURE F-3
Here's a square wave. These waves can be approximated by a series of sine waves.

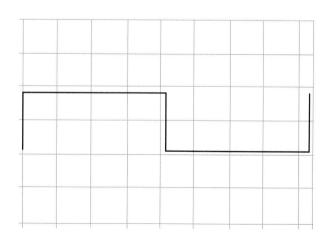

Using Digital Signals To Build Analog Signals

Jean Baptiste Fourier (1768-1830), a French mathematician, is responsible for proving mathematically that a special sum of sine waves with harmonically related frequencies, all multiples of some basic frequency, can be added together to create any wave pattern. The fundamental principle here is that complex waves can be built out of simple waves. This is how voice recognition devices and heart pacemakers work.

A square wave, or a square pulse, can be built by using the right combination of sine waves. Figure F-4 shows how the square wave (digital signal) can be built with sine waves (analog signals). This is important to remember as you examine what happens to a digital pulse as it travels along networking media. The infinite sum of sine waves that "adds up to" a square wave is called a *Fourier series* (this topic is studied in advanced engineering mathematics).

FIGURE F-4
Here's a square wave being approximated by a series of sine waves.

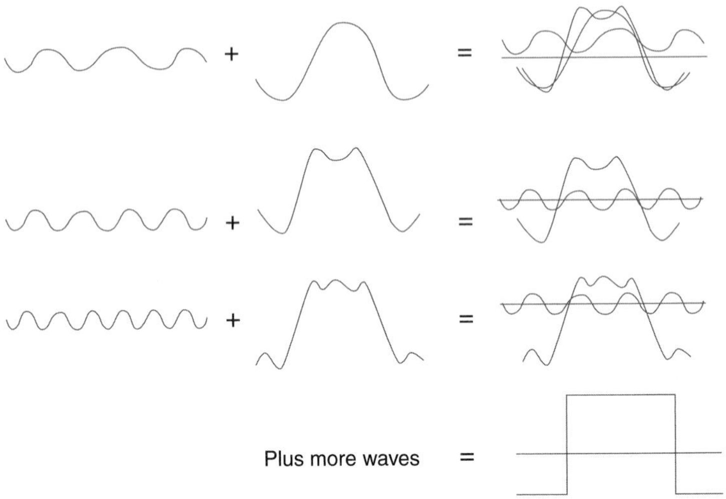

Now you know that digital waves can be approximated by sums of sine waves. Therefore, digital signals can be constructed from analog signals. Next, you'll see how electrical signals represent a bit.

Representing One Bit on a Physical Medium

Data networks have become increasingly dependent on digital (binary, two-state) systems. The basic building block of information is a binary digit, known as a bit or pulse. One bit, on an electrical medium, is the electrical signal corresponding to binary 0 or binary 1. This can be as simple as 0 volts for binary 0 and +5 volts for binary 1, or a more complex encoding. The signal reference ground is an important concept relating to all networking media that uses voltages to carry messages.

To function correctly, a signal reference ground must be physically close to a computer's digital circuits. Engineers have accomplished this by designing circuit boards to contain ground planes. The computer cabinets are used as the common point of connection for the circuit board ground planes to establish the signal reference ground. Signal reference ground establishes the 0 volts line in diagrams, such as Figure F-5.

With optical signals, binary 0 would be encoded as low light, or no light, intensity (darkness). Binary 1 would be encoded as a higher-light intensity (brightness), or other more complex patterns.

With wireless signals, binary 0 might be a short burst of waves; binary 1 might be a longer burst of waves, or another more complex pattern. The 0 bit is commonly represented by a horizontal line appearing on the t-axis (it's black in Figure F-5). It's also common to use +5 volts to indicate the 1 bit (the upper horizontal black line in the voltage versus time graph on the left).

FIGURE F-5
The signal reference ground is used to set a baseline.

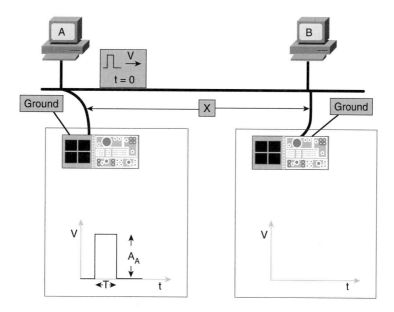

The following six things can affect a single bit:

- Propagation
- Attenuation

- Reflection
- Noise
- Timing problems
- Collisions

Propagation

Propagation means to travel through a medium. When a NIC puts out a voltage or light pulse onto a physical medium, that square pulse made up of waves travels along the medium (propagates). Propagation means that a lump of energy, representing 1 bit, travels from one place to another. The speed at which it propagates depends on the actual material used in the medium, the geometry (structure) of the medium, and the frequency of the pulses. The time it takes the bit to travel from one end of the medium and back is referred to as the *round trip time* (*RTT*). Assuming no other delays, the time it takes the bit to travel down the medium to the far end is RTT/2 (see Figure F-6).

The fact that the bit travels does not cause a problem for the network. The signaling occurs so quickly that to humans it sometimes appears to be instantaneous. In any case, it is important to account for the various timings involved with signaling in a network.

There are two extreme situations to consider. Either the bit takes "0" time to travel, meaning it travels instantaneously, or it takes forever to travel. The first case is wrong according to Albert Einstein, whose Theory of Relativity says no information can travel faster than the speed of light in a vacuum. This means that the bit takes at least a small amount of time to travel. The second case is also wrong, because with the right equipment, you can actually time the pulse. Lack of knowledge of propagation time is a problem, because you might assume the bit arrives at some destination either too soon or too late.

This problem can be resolved. Again, propagation time (see Figure F-6) is not inherently a problem; it's simply a fact that you should be aware of. If the propagation time is too long, you should reevaluate how the rest of the network deals with this delay. If the propagation delay is too short, you might have to slow down the bits, or save them temporarily (known as *buffering*), so the rest of the networking equipment can catch up with the bit.

Attenuation

Attenuation is the loss of signal strength as a signal traverses a physical medium, particularly in the case that the maximum recommended length for a cable is exceeded. This means that a 1-bit voltage signal loses amplitude as energy passes from the intrinsic signal to the cable (see Figure F-7). Although choosing materials carefully (such as using copper instead of carbon) and taking geometry (the shape and positioning of the wires) into account can reduce electrical attenuation, some loss is unavoidable due to electrical resistance. Attenuation also occurs with optical signals; the optical fiber absorbs and scatters some of the light energy as the light pulse, 1 bit, travels down the fiber. This can be minimized by the wavelength, or color, of the light that you choose. This can also be minimized by whether or not you use single mode or multimode fiber, and by the actual glass that is used for the fiber. Even with these choices, some signal loss is unavoidable.

FIGURE F-6
The familiar formula Distance = Rate x Time comes in handy sometimes in networking. Here is one application of the D=RT formula: computing the propagation delay (half the round-trip time) for a bit traveling from host A to host B.

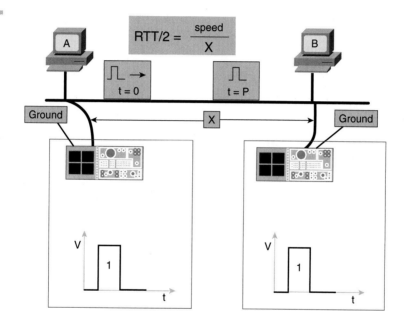

Attenuation also takes place with radio waves and microwaves, as they are absorbed and scattered by molecules in the atmosphere.

Attenuation can affect a network because it limits the length of network cabling over which you can send a message. If the cable is too long, 1 bit sent from the source can look like a 0 bit by the time it gets to the destination.

You can resolve this problem by choosing the appropriate networking media for a given design scenario. Another way to fix the problem is to use a repeater after a certain distance limitation is met. There are repeaters for electrical, optical, and wireless bits.

Reflection

To understand reflection, imagine having a slinky or a jump rope stretched out with a friend holding the other end. Now, imagine sending your friend a pulse or a 1-bit message. If you watch carefully, you can see that a small wave (pulse) returns (reflects) to you..

FIGURE F-7
Attenuation is the loss of signal energy as the distance traveled by a bit on the cable increases. You can see this indicated by the reduced height and protracted base of the square wave pictured on the right relative to its original condition on the left.

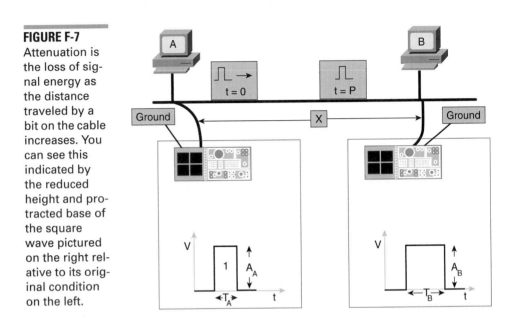

Reflection occurs in electrical signals. When voltage pulses, or bits, encounter a discontinuity, some energy can be reflected. This can occur wherever there is a change in a material's connection to another, or even the same, material. If not carefully controlled, this energy can confuse other bits. Remember, although you are focused on only 1 bit at a time right now, in real networks you send millions or billions of bits every second, thus requiring you to keep track of this reflected pulse energy. Depending on the cabling and connections that the network uses, reflections might or might not be a problem. A complex electrical characteristic involving resistance (the opposition to the flow of electrons) and reactance (the opposition to changes in voltage and current) is known as impedance.

Reflection also occurs with optical signals. Optical signals reflect whenever they encounter a discontinuity in the glass fiber, such as when a connector is plugged into a device. You can see this effect at night if you look out a window. You can see your reflection in the window even though the window is not a mirror. Some of the light that is reflected off your body reflects in the window. This also happens with radio waves and microwaves as they encounter different layers in the atmosphere.

This can cause problems on your network (see Figure F-8). For optimal network performance, it is important that the network media have a specific impedance in order to match the electrical components in the NICs. Unless the network media have the correct impedance, the signal suffers some reflection and interference is created. Then, multiple reflecting pulses can occur. Whether the system is electrical, optical, or wireless, impedance mismatches cause reflections. If enough energy is reflected, the binary, two-state system can become confused by all the extra energy bouncing around. You can resolve this by ensuring that all networking components are carefully impedance matched. You can avoid discontinuities in impedance through a variety of technologies.

FIGURE F-8
Reflection is caused by discontinuities in the medium. This could be a result of kinks in a cable or poorly terminated cables.

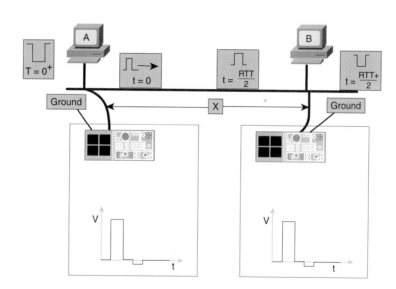

Noise

Noise in data communications is the unwanted addition of electrical signals to voltage, optical, or electromagnetic signals. In other words, each bit gets additional unwanted signals from various sources. Too much noise can corrupt a binary 1, changing it to a binary 0, and thus destroying the 1-bit message. Or, a 0-bit message can be mistaken for a 1 bit due to noise. No electrical signal is without noise; however, you must keep the signal-to-noise (S/N) ratio as high as possible. Figure F-9 shows five sources of noise that can affect a bit on a wire.

FIGURE F-9
Five sources of noise on a cable.

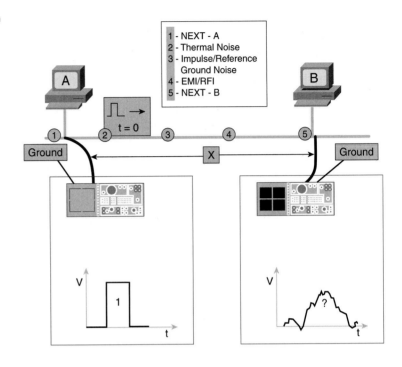

1 - NEXT - A
2 - Thermal Noise
3 - Impulse/Reference Ground Noise
4 - EMI/RFI
5 - NEXT - B

NEXT

When electrical noise on the cable originates from signals on other wires in the cable, this is known as *crosstalk*. NEXT stands for *near-end crosstalk*. When two wires are near each other and untwisted, energy from one wire can wind up in an adjacent wire and vice versa. This can cause noise at both ends of a terminated cable. Actually, many forms of crosstalk exist that must be considered when building networks.

NEXT can be addressed by termination technology, strict adherence to standard termination procedures, and use of quality twisted-pair cables.

Thermal Noise

Thermal noise is the random motion of electrons caused by temperature fluctuations of the media, and usually has a relatively small impact on signals. Nothing can be done about thermal noise other than to give the signals large enough amplitudes so the thermal noise influence is inconsequential.

AC Power/Reference Ground Noise

AC power and reference ground noises are serious problems in networking. AC line noise creates problems in homes, schools, and offices. Electricity is carried to appliances and machines by wires concealed in walls, floors, and ceilings. Consequently, inside these buildings, AC power line noise is all around. If not properly dealt with, power line noise can cause problems for a network.

Ideally, the signal reference ground should be completely isolated from the electrical ground. Isolation keeps AC power leakage and voltage spikes off the signal reference ground. The problem is that the chassis (case) of a computing device serves as the signal reference ground and as the AC power line ground. Because there is a link between the signal reference ground and the power ground, problems with the power ground can lead to interference with the data system. Such interference can be difficult to detect and trace. Usually, the problem occurs because electrical contractors and installers are not concerned about the length of the neutral and ground wires that lead to each electrical outlet. Unfortunately, when these wires are long, they can act as antennas for electrical noise. This noise interferes with the digital signals (bits) that computers must be able to recognize and process.

AC line noise coming from a nearby video monitor or hard disk drive can be enough to create errors in a computer system. It does this by interfering (changing the shape and voltage level) with the desired signals, preventing a computer from detecting the leading and trailing edges of the square waves. This problem can be compounded further when a computer has a poor ground connection.

To avoid the problem of AC/reference ground noise as described above, it is important to work closely with the electrical contractor and the power company. This enables you to get the best and shortest electrical ground. One way to do this is to investigate the cost of getting a single power transformer dedicated to your LAN installation area. If you can afford this option, you can control the attachment of other devices to your power circuit. Restricting how and where devices, such as motors or high-current electrical heaters, attach can eliminate much of the electrical noise generated by them.

When working with your electrical contractor, you should ask that separate power distribution panels, known as breaker boxes, be installed for each office area. Because the neutral wires and ground wires from each outlet come together in the breaker box, taking this step increases your chances of shortening the length of the signal ground. Although installing individual power distribution panels for every cluster of computers increases the up-front cost of power wiring, it reduces the length of the ground wires and limits several kinds of signal-burying electrical noise.

EMI/RFI

External sources of electrical impulses that can attack the quality of electrical signals on the cable include lighting, electrical motors, and radio systems. These types of interference are referred to as *electromagnetic interference (EMI)* and *radio frequency interference (RFI)*. Each wire in a cable can act like an antenna. When this happens, the wire actually absorbs electrical signals from other wires in the cable and from electrical sources outside the cable. If the resulting electrical noise reaches a high enough level, it can become difficult for NICs to discriminate the noise from the data signal. This is particularly a problem because most LANs use frequencies in the 1 to 100 megahertz (MHz) range, which happens to be where FM radio signals, TV signals, and many appliances have their operating frequencies as well.

To understand how electrical noise, regardless of the source, impacts digital signals, imagine that you want to send data, represented by the binary number 1011001001101, over the network. Your computer converts the binary number to a digital signal. Figure F-10 shows what the digital signal for 1011001001101 looks like. The digital signal travels through the networking media to the destination. The destination happens to be near an electrical outlet that is fed by both long neutral and long ground wires. These wires act as possible antennas for electrical noise. Figure F-10 shows what electrical noise looks like. Because the destination computer's chassis is used for both the earth ground and the signal reference ground, the noise generated interferes with the digital signal that the computer receives. Figure F-10 shows what happens to the signal when it is combined with this electrical noise. Instead of reading the signal as 1011001001101, the computer reads the signal as 1011000101101, making the data unreliable (corrupted).

There are many ways to limit EMI and RFI. One way is to increase the size of the conductors. Another way is to improve the type of insulating material used. However, such changes increase the size and cost of the cable faster than they improve its quality. Therefore, it is more typical for network designers to specify a cable of good quality and to provide specifications for the maximum recommended cable length between nodes.

Two techniques that cable designers have used successfully in dealing with EMI and RFI are *shielding* and *cancellation*. In cable that employs shielding, a metal braid or foil surrounds each wire pair or group of wire pairs. This shielding acts as a barrier to any interfering signals. However, as with increasing the size of the conductors, using braid or foil covering increases the diameter of the cable and the cost. Therefore, cancellation is the more commonly used technique to protect the wire from undesirable interference.

FIGURE F-10
The first graph is a digital signal, the second graph represents electrical noise, and the third graph shows the combined result. Note the red 0 and 1 are permuted relative to the original.

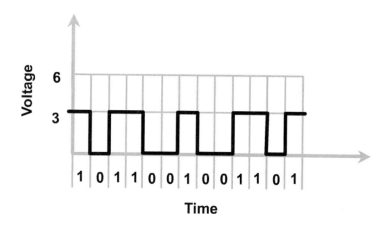

1 | 0 | 1 | 1 | 0 | 0 | 1 | 0 | 0 | 1 | 1 | 0 | 1

Time

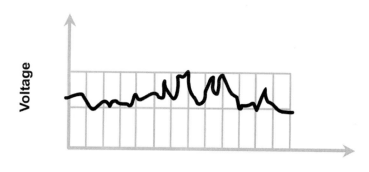

Time

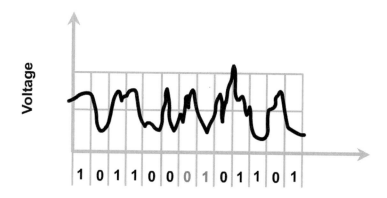

1 | 0 | 1 | 1 | 0 | 0 | 0 | 1 | 0 | 1 | 1 | 0 | 1

When electrical current flows through a wire, it creates a small, circular magnetic field around the wire (see Figure F-11). The direction of these magnetic lines of force is determined by the direction in which the current flows along the wire. If two wires are part of the same electrical circuit, electrons flow from the negative voltage source to the destination along one wire. Then, the electrons flow from the destination to the positive voltage source along the other wire. When two wires in an electrical circuit are placed close together, their magnetic fields are the exact opposite of each other. Thus, the two magnetic fields cancel each other out. Moreover, they cancel out some outside magnetic fields as well. Twisting the wires can enhance this cancellation effect. By using cancellation in combination with twisted wires, cable designers can provide an effective method of providing self-shielding for wire pairs within the network media.

FIGURE F-11
Electrical current in a wire induces a magnetic field around the wire.

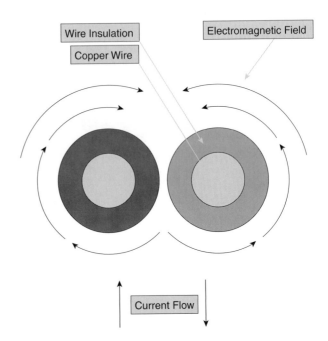

Wire Insulation

Copper Wire

Electromagnetic Field

Current Flow

Dispersion, Jitter, and Latency (Timing Problems)

Although dispersion, jitter, and latency are actually three different things that can happen to a bit, they are grouped together because they each affect the same thing: the timing of a bit. Because you are trying to understand what problems might occur as millions and billions of bits travel on a medium in one second, timing matters a lot.

Dispersion is when the signal broadens in time (see Figure F-12). The degree of dispersion depends on the type of media involved. If serious enough, one bit can start to interfere with the next bit, resulting in confusion as to which bit is which. Because you want to send millions or billions of bits per second, you must be careful not to allow the signals to spread out. You can minimize dispersion by designing cable properly, by limiting cable lengths, and by finding the proper impedance. In optical fibers, you can control dispersion by using laser light of a very specific wavelength. For wireless communications, you can minimize dispersion by the frequencies used to transmit.

FIGURE F-12
Dispersion elongates digital signals sometimes to the point where networking devices cannot distinguish where one bit ends and another begins.

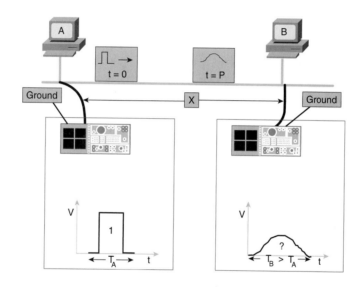

All digital systems are clocked, meaning that clock pulses govern electronic activity. Clock pulses cause a CPU to calculate, data to store in memory, and the NIC to send bits. If the clock on the source host is not synchronized with the destination, which is quite likely, you get timing *jitter*. This means that bits arrive a little earlier or later than expected. You can fix jitter by using a series of complicated clock synchronizations, including hardware, software, or protocol synchronizations.

Latency, also known as *delay*, has two main causes. First, Einstein's Theory of Relativity states that nothing can travel faster than the speed of light in a vacuum (3.0 x 10^8 m/s). Wireless networking signals travel slightly less fast than the speed of light (2.9 x 10^8 m/s). Signals on copper cables travel 2.3 x10^8 m/s, and in optical fiber they travel 2.0 x 10^8 m/s. So to travel a distance, a bit takes at least a small amount of time to get to its destination. Second, if the bit goes through any devices, the transistors and electronics introduce more latency. Some solutions to the latency issue are careful use of internetworking devices, utilizing various encoding strategies, and implementing appropriate layer protocols.

Modern networks typically work at speeds from 1 Mbps to 155 Mbps or greater. Soon, they will work at 1 Gbps or 1 billion bits per second. If bits are broadened by dispersion, then 1s can be mistaken for 0s, and 0s for 1s. If groups of bits get routed differently and there is no attention paid to timing, the jitter can cause errors as the receiving computer tries to reassemble packets into a message. If groups of bits are late, the intermediate networking devices and the destination computers might get hopelessly overwhelmed by a billion bits per second.

Collisions

A *collision* occurs when two bits from two different communicating computers simultaneously propagate on a shared medium. In the case of shared media, the voltages of the two binary signals are added and cause a third voltage level. This voltage variation is not allowed in a binary system, which only understands two voltage levels. The bits are destroyed. Figure F-13 illustrates a collision.

FIGURE F-13
Collisions are a common phenomenon on Ethernet networks.

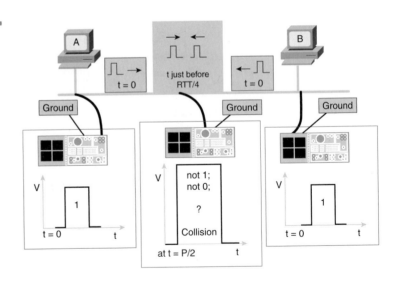

Some technologies, such as Ethernet, function by negotiating whose turn it is to transmit on the shared media when hosts are attempting to communicate. In some instances, collisions are a natural part of the functioning of a network. However, excessive collisions can slow the network down or bring it to a halt. Therefore, a lot of network design goes into minimizing and localizing collisions.

There are many ways to deal with collisions. One way is to detect them and simply have a set of rules for dealing with them when they occur, as in Ethernet. Another way is to try to prevent collisions by allowing only one computer at a time to transmit on a shared media environment. This requires that a computer have a special bit pattern, called a token, to transmit. This is the technology used with Token Ring and FDDI.

Messages in Terms of Bits

You now know that within a medium, a bit can experience attenuation, reflection, noise, dispersion, or collisions. Of course, you'll transmit far more than 1 bit. In fact, you'll transmit billions of bits in one second. All of the effects described so far can occur to one bit apply indirectly to the various protocol data units (PDUs) of the OSI model: 8 bits equals 1 byte, multiple bytes comprise one frame (see Figure F-14), frames contain packets, and packets contain segments. Segments carry the message you want to communicate. This brings us full circle, back to the layers of the OSI model serviced by the physical layer: the data link, network, transport, session, presentation, and application layers.

FIGURE F-14
Bits string together to form bytes, and bytes link together to form frames.

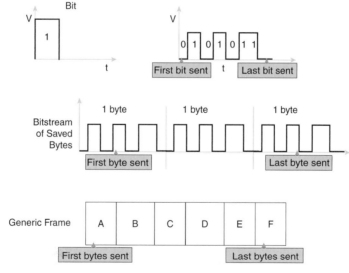

A, B, C, D, E, F multiple, often many, bytes

Encoding Networking Signals

When you want to send a message over a long distance, there are two problems you must solve: how to express the message (*encoding* or *modulation*), and which method to use to transport the message (*carrier*).

Throughout history there have been a variety of ways in which the problem of carrying a long distance communication has been solved: runners, riders, horses, optical telescopes, carrier pigeons, and smoke signals (see Figure F-15). Each method of delivery required a form of encoding. For example, smoke signals announcing that good hunting had just been found might be three short puffs of smoke, carrier pigeon messages relaying that someone had reached a destination safely might be a picture of a smiling face.

FIGURE F-15
Historical versions of transmitting signals with encoding.

☐ Smoke Signals

☐ Telegraph/Morse Code

☐ Telephone

☐ TV/Radio

☐ Pony Express

☐ Carrier Pigeon

In more modern times, the creation of Morse code revolutionized communications. Two symbols, the dot and the dash, encode the alphabet. For example, ••• --- ••• means SOS (see Figure F-16), the universal distress signal. Modern telephones, FAX, AM, FM, short wave radio, and TV all encode their signals electronically, typically using the modulation of different waves from different parts of the electromagnetic spectrum.

Encoding is the process of converting binary data into a form that can travel on a physical communications link. *Modulation* means using the binary data to manipulate a wave. Computers use three particular technologies, all of which have their counterparts in history. These technologies are: encoding messages as voltages on various forms of copper wire; encoding messages as pulses of guided light on optical fibers; and encoding messages as modulated, radiated electromagnetic waves.

FIGURE F-16
Historical versions of transmitting signals with encoding.

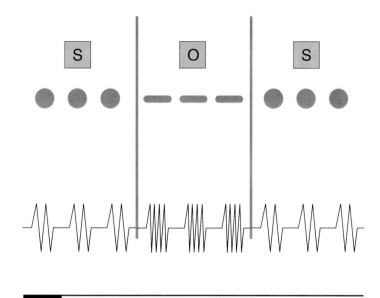

Morse code was the first widespread use of voltages to encode messages.

Encoding and Modulation

Encoding converts 1s and 0s into something real and physical, such as:

- An electrical pulse on a wire
- A light pulse on an optical fiber
- A pulse of electromagnetic waves in space

Two methods of accomplishing this are *NRZ encoding* and *Manchester encoding*. Figure F-17 illustrate these methods.

NRZ (non-return to 0) encoding is the simplest. It is characterized by a high signal and a low signal (often +5 or +3.3 V for binary 1 and 0 V for binary 0). In optical fibers, binary 1 might be a bright LED or laser light, and binary 0 might be darkness or no light. In wireless networks, binary 1 might mean a carrier wave is present, and binary 0 might mean that no carrier is present.

Manchester encoding is more complex, but is more immune to noise and is better at remaining synchronized. In Manchester encoding, the voltage on copper wire, the brightness of LED or laser light in optical fiber, or the power of an electromagnetic wave has the bits encoded as transitions. Specifically, in

Manchester encoding, upward transitions in the signal mean binary 1 and downward transitions mean binary 0.

FIGURE F-17
NRZ encoding and Manchester encoding are the primary methods of encoding.

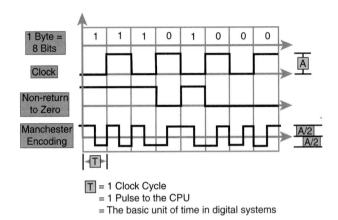

Closely related to encoding is modulation, which takes a wave and changes (modulates) it so that it carries information. To give you an idea of what modulation is, examine the following three forms of modifying, or modulating, a carrier wave to encode bits:

- *AM (amplitude modulation)*—The amplitude of a carrier sine wave is varied to carry the message.

- *FM (frequency modulation)*—The frequency of the carrier wave is varied to carry the message.

- *PM (phase modulation)*—The phase (beginning and ending points of a cycle) of the carrier wave is varied to carry the message.

Other more complex forms of modulation also exist. Figure F-18 shows three ways binary data can be encoded onto a carrier wave by the process of modulation. Binary 11 (note: read as "one one", not "eleven"!) can be communicated on a wave by either AM (wave on/wave off), FM (wave wiggles a lot for 1s, a little for 0s), or PM (one type of phase change for 0s, another for 1s).

FIGURE F-18
hree ways for
encoding
binary data
into a carrier
wave.

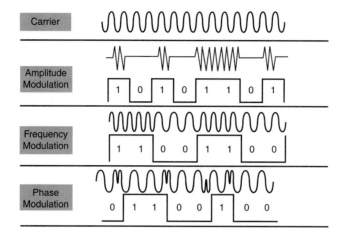

Messages can be encoded in a variety of ways:

- As voltages on copper; Manchester and NRZ encodings are popular on copper-based networks.

- As guided light; Manchester and 4B/5B encodings are popular on fiber-based networks.

- As radiated EM waves; a variety of encoding schemes (variations on AM, FM, and PM) are used on wireless networks.

Summary

- The computer converts the binary number to a digital signal.

- When a computer attached to a network receives data in the form of digital signals, it recognizes the data by measuring and comparing the voltage signals it receives to a reference point called the signal reference ground.

- Ideally, the signal reference ground should be completely isolated from the electrical ground. Isolation would keep AC power leakage and voltage spikes off the signal reference ground.

- If not properly addressed, power line noise can present serious problems for a network.

- The five types of noise are NEXT, thermal noise, AC power/reference, ground noise, and EMI/RFI.

- Timing problems include dispersion, jitter, and latency.
- Collisions occur when two bits from two different communicating computers simultaneously propagate on a shared medium.
- The two primary methods of encoding bits are NRZ encoding and Manchester encoding.
- The three main types of modulation for carrier waves are frequency modulation, amplitude modulation, and phase modulation.

Binary and Hexadecimal Conversion

Introduction

Computers are electronic devices made up of electronic switches. At the lowest levels of computation, computers depend on these electronic switches to make decisions. As such, computers react only to electrical impulses. These impulses are understood by the computer as either "on" or "off" states, or as 1s or 0s. Because the computer can't speak your language, you need to learn to speak the computer's language. That is the language of *binary arithmetic*.

The *binary number system*, or *Base 2*, is made up entirely of 0s and 1s. Computers use Base 2 in expressing IP addresses. One of the goals of this appendix is to provide a better understanding of the process of converting between binary numbers (used with IP addresses) and their equivalent decimal values.

At higher levels of computation, computers sometimes process information using the *hexadecimal number system*, or *Base 16*. Base 16 is a number system that uses 16 characters: 0, 1, 2, 3, 4, 5, 6, 7, 8, 9, A, B, C, D, E, and F. Computer scientists use Base 16 because it makes expressing bytes more manageable. This is because 16 is a power of 2: 16=2×2×2×2. Only two hexadecimal digits are needed to represent one 8-bit byte. Of course, Base 15 or Base 20 would not work as well because neither 15 nor 20 are powers of 2.

Computers don't think in the *decimal number system*, or *Base 10*, as humans do. Electronic devices are structured in such a way that binary and hexadecimal numbering is natural: computers have to *translate* in order to use decimal numbering. It's like a person who speaks two languages, one is their first language and the other is their second language: it is faster and more accurate to communicate in the first language.

In this appendix, you will learn how to think in binary and hexadecimal numbering systems so you can make the necessary translations when performing certain networking tasks, such as designing an IP addressing scheme for a network (binary) or working with memory addresses or MAC addresses on a router (hexadecimal).

As you know, it takes time and practice to learn new concepts in math. You won't master binary and hexadecimal numbers the first time you read about them. So, if you are learning about the binary and hexadecimal numbering systems for the first time, remember that it is a step-by-step process.

Preliminaries

How Do You Know What Base Someone Is Referring To?

The binary numbering system uses two characters, 0 and 1. Any decimal number you can imagine can be expressed in binary. The characters used in the decimal number system are 0, 1, 2, 3, 4, 5, 6, 7, 8, and 9. Because both number systems use the characters 0 and 1, there is a potential for confusion. For example, what does 10110 mean? Well, it depends on whether you're referring to 10110 in Base 10 or 10110 in Base 2. Because of the potential for confusion, sometimes mathematicians write 10110_{10} to mean 10110 in Base 10 and 10110_2 to mean 10110 in Base 2. However, writing down these subscripts every time you write a number quickly becomes very tedious, so what you usually do is make it clear from the context what base is being referred to without explicitly writing down the base. So, first make sure that it is clear in your mind when you look at a *string* of characters, such as 10110, that you know what base the person who wrote 10110 was thinking of when he wrote it. If you are unsure, then the person who wrote it did a poor job of making it clear or did not intend to refer to a particular base (this is what a computer scientist calls a *string*, an abstract list of characters strung together).

Some Miscellaneous Facts

There is one important *convention* (agreed upon rule) that should be made clear and that almost goes without saying. It is taken for granted after years of working with decimal numbers: The convention is to read, write, and pronounce strings, such as 10110, from left to right. For example, you read 10110 as "one, zero, one, one, zero".

If you come across a string like 10110, it usually is coming from some kind of computer output. There are specific notations that certain programs, such as protocol analyzers, use to differentiate between binary, decimal, and hexadecimal notation. For example, the % sign precedes a binary string; thus, %10110 means 10110 in Base 2. In addition, the 0x sign precedes a hexadecimal string, so 0x10110 means 10110 in Base 16.

One practical consideration to keep in mind when using different bases is that the bigger the base, the less characters used to express the number. For example, the decimal number 16 in Base 2 is 10000 and the decimal number 16 in Base 16 is 10. In addition, although we focus only on Base 2 and Base 16, there is no numerical limit to the base you can use. Although it is not practical for computer-related work, you could work in Base 23,037 or Base 1,002,395. To illustrate, the decimal number 15 is represented by the letter F in Base 16, the decimal number 20 is represented by the letter K in Base 21, and the decimal number 29 is represented by the letter T in Base 30. What character in Base 36 represents the decimal number 35 (assuming you use the English alphabet)?

Another important fact to keep in mind is that each base you work in has a fixed set of characters. For example, Base 2 has 2 characters, Base 10 has 10 characters, and Base 16 has 16 characters. Note that no character 2 exists in Base 2 (just 0 and 1—you know you can't be working in binary if there's a number with a 2 in it!). No character 3 exists in Base 3 (just 0, 1, and 2). No character 9 exists in Base 9 (just 0, 1, 2, 3, 4, 5, 6, 7, and 8). No character A exists in Base 10 (just 0, 1, 2, 3, 4, 5, 6, 7, 8, and 9). No character G exists in Base 16 (just 0, 1, 2, 3, 4, 5, 6, 7, 8, 9, A, B, C, D, E, and F). You get the idea. Also, note that the number of characters in a base is equal to the decimal value of the base. Here are a couple silly examples: 0 is the only character in Base 1 (so you can't express any number greater than 0 in Base 1!) and there are no characters in Base 0.

Whether you're working in Base 2, 10, 16, or whatever, numbers are expressed as strings of characters, such as 101011 in Base 2, 14932 in Base 10, or A2E7 in Base 16. This is actually a convenience. Did you know that writing the decimal number 124 is actually a shortcut? It is short for 1×100+2×10+4×1, which would be tedious to write out. Imagine if every time you wrote down a decimal number you had to express it this way! Each number in a string of characters represents a value that depends on its *place* in the string. For example, the character 7 in the Base 10 number 23761 represents 7×100, or 700. You also can use tables with columns to emphasize the importance of place value when converting between bases. Among other things, the tables help illustrate that when you read strings of characters from left to right, the characters represent decreasing place values. For example, in the decimal number 234, 2 represents 2 hundreds, 3 represents 3 tens, and 4 represents 4 ones. In summary, two things are essential to understand with each string of characters: the characters in the string and their place value in the string.

Base Conventions

You use the words *ten, eleven, twelve, thirteen, …, twenty, twenty-one,* and so on only when working in decimal. These *are* decimal (Base 10) numbers. When you say "thirty," it is just a short way of saying "three tens." When you talk about the string 23 in Base 5, you don't say "twenty-three in Base 5," you say "two three in Base 5." Saying "twenty-three" would mean "two tens and three"—you are talking in Base 10 when you say "twenty-three." You pronounce numbers differently when working in bases *other than ten*. As another example, 101 in Base 2 is spoken "one zero one in Base 2," or just "one zero one" if it's clear that you're referring to Base 2. You wouldn't say "one hundred one in Base 2" or "one hundred one." The reason for this is you don't want to confuse people by verbalizing a string of characters in Base 10 when the string represents a Base 2 number.

Note that the string "21" in "3A2 in Base 21" is pronounced "twenty-one" and it means exactly that, 21 in decimal. To emphasize this, sometimes people just write "3A2 in Base twenty-one." Another example: the string "16" in "Base 16" is "sixteen;" that is, it is assumed that 16 is a decimal number (as opposed to 16 in another base). As a last example, "847 in Base 20" is spoken "eight four seven in Base twenty." The convention is to think, read, write, and speak in decimal when referring to the string appearing after the word "Base."

One other thing to keep in mind is the role of the character 0. Every base uses the character 0. *Whenever the character 0 appears on the left side of a string of characters, it can be removed without changing the value of the string of characters.* For example, in Base 10, 02947 equals 2947. In Base 2, 0001001101 equals 1001101. Sometimes people include 0s on the left side of a number to emphasize places that would otherwise not be represented. Because the 8-bit byte is sometimes thought of as a unit, binary strings are often *padded out* to be eight characters long. For example, when *subnetting*, the decimal number 6 is most conveniently expressed as 00000110 in binary. It's very common when working with IP addresses to express binary numbers with 0s in the front because, with IP addresses, you work with *octets* (strings of eight characters at a time). For example, it's not unusual to express the binary number 10000 as 00010000.

Working with Exponents

Last, you need to work with *powers* of numbers, called *exponents*, when dealing with different number systems. Recall from mathematics that powers are used to represent repeated multiplication of the same number. The following example illustrates how exponents work with the number 2—the rules hold for other numbers as well. First, $2^0=1$, which is spoken "two to the zero equals one" (2 is called the *base* and 0 is called the *exponent*). This fact is not derived from previous knowledge, it is part of the definition of 2^n, where *n* is an *integer*. Second, $2^1=2$ ("two to the one equals two") according to mathematical definition. Third, $2^2=2\times2=4$: "two to the two equals two times two equals four." Continuing, $2^3=2\times2\times2=8$: "two to the three equals two times two times two equals eight." This provides a pattern that can be used for any power of 2. A common mistake is to confuse taking powers with multiplying, so be careful: $2^4\neq2\times4=8$, $2^4=2\times2\times2\times2=16$.

Exponents are very convenient when working with binary numbers. For example, the number of objects that n bits can represent is calculated by using the formula s^n. If there are 8 bits set aside for describing or naming an object, then there are $2^8=256$ possible variations for assigning a binary number to that object. This fact is very important to understand: if there are 8 bits available, that means there are eight *slots* or places for a binary number—there are 256 different binary numbers that can be expressed with 8 bits and there are 256 different strings consisting of 0s and 1s that can be formed with 8 slots or places.

You have seen many concepts up to this point regarding different bases and how to work with them. You should now have a better understanding of the fundamentals necessary to be able to work in different numbering systems.

Binary Numbers

First, you will learn how to use tables to represent numbers in a particular base. Then, you will learn about the two main concepts of interest: converting binary numbers to decimal numbers, and converting decimal numbers to binary numbers. After that, you will learn how to *count* in binary, which is useful when determining *subnetwork addresses*.

In Base 10, you work with powers of ten. For example, 23,605 in Base 10 means $2\times10,000+3\times1000+6\times100+0\times10+5\times1$. Note that $10^0=1$, $10^1=10$, $10^2=100$, $10^3=1000$, and $10^4=10,000$. In addition, even though $0\times10=0$, you don't leave out the 0 in 23,605 because, if you did, you would have $2365=2\times1000+3\times100+6\times10+5\times1$, which is not what you meant to express by 23,605: the 0 acts as a *placeholder*. On the other hand, if for some reason you wanted to focus on the one hundred thousand place and the one million place, you would express 23,605 as 0,023,605.

As the previous paragraph demonstrates, if you want to literally express the meaning of a decimal number, you can use powers of 10 (10^0, 10^1, 10^2, and so on). You use the expanded form of the powers (1, 10, 100, and so on) when you focus on the actual value of a decimal number. It helps to use tables to keep track of all this. Table G-1 has three rows: the first row lists *powers of 10*; the second row expresses the *expanded* (multiplied out) *powers of 10*; and the third row is where you place numbers to communicate how many (between 0 and 9) of that power of 10 you want.

TABLE G-1

10^7	10^6	10^5	10^4	10^3	10^2	10^1	10^0
10,000,000	1,000,000	100,000	10,000	1000	100	10	1

For example, Table G-2 shows how to express 23,605 in a Base 10 table.

TABLE G-2

10^4	10^3	10^3	10^1	10^0
10,000	1000	100	10	1
2	3	6	0	5

The pattern for expressing binary numbers is very similar to what you just read about decimal numbers. Binary numbers use the principle of place value just as decimal numbers do. The difference is that you use powers of 2 instead of powers of 10, and you use only the characters 0 and 1 (there's no 2, 3, 4, 5, 6, 7, 8, or 9). So, the binary table (comparable to Table G-1) has three rows: the first row lists *powers of 2*; the second row expresses the *expanded* (multiplied out) *powers of 2*; and the third row is where you place numbers to communicate how many (between 0 and 1) of that power of 2 you want (see Table G-3). *Notice that the second row has numbers written in Base 10!*

TABLE G-3

2^7	2^6	2^5	2^4	2^3	2^2	2^1	2^0
128	64	32	16	8	4	2	1

As an example, you can *break down* the binary number 1101 by placing the digits in a binary table (see Table G-4). After making the table, you can use it to convert the binary number to its Base 10 equivalent.

TABLE G-4

2^3	2^2	2^1	2^0
8	4	2	1
1	1	0	1

You can use Table G-4 to *convert* the binary number 1101 to Base 10:

1101=1×8+1×4+0×2+1×1=8+4+0+1=13.

As another example, you can examine the binary number 10010001 by placing the digits in a binary table (see Table G-5). After making the table, you can use it to convert the binary number to its Base 10 equivalent.

TABLE G-5

2^7	2^6	2^5	2^4	2^3	2^2	2^1	2^0
128	64	32	16	8	4	2	1
1	0	0	1	0	0	0	1

You can use Table G-5 to convert the binary number 10010001 to Base 10:

10010001=1×128+0×64+0×32+1×16+0×8+0×4+0×2+1×1=128+16+1=145.

The binary number 11111111 occurs as often as any other in networking (see Table G-6).

TABLE G-6

2^7	2^6	2^5	2^4	2^3	2^2	2^1	2^0
128	64	32	16	8	4	2	1
1	1	1	1	1	1	1	1

You can use Table G-6 to convert the binary number 11111111 to Base 10:

11111111=1×128+1×64+1×32+1×16+1×8+1×4+1×2+1×1=255.

Most of the work you do with binary numbers in networking involves working with one byte, or one octet, at a time; that is, working with 8-bit binary numbers.

An IP address is expressed as a dotted-decimal number, W.X.Y.Z, where W, X, Y, and Z are decimal numbers whose binary representations each consist of 8 bits. The smallest decimal value that can be represented by one byte

(00000000 in binary) is 0. The largest decimal value that can be represented by one byte (11111111 in binary) is 255, as calculated in Table G-6. It follows that the range of decimal numbers that can be represented by a byte is 0 to 255, a total of 256 possible values. Therefore, in an IP address, the decimal numbers (W, X, Y, and Z) are between 0 and 255. Some examples of IP addresses are 140.57.255.0, 204.65.103.243, and 5.6.7.8.

Now you know how to convert a binary number to a decimal number. As an exercise, use a table to show that the binary number 11111001 is equal to the decimal number 249. After doing several problems like this, you can develop your own shortcuts that might not include using a table at all.

Converting a Decimal Number into a Binary Number

Converting a decimal number into a binary number is one of the most common procedures performed while working with IP addresses. As with most problems in math, there are several ways to solve the problem. This section introduces one method, but feel free to use another method if you find it easier.

To convert a decimal number to binary, you first find the largest power of 2 that fits into the decimal number. Consider the decimal number 35. If you refer to Table G-3, what's the largest power of 2 that is less than or equal to 35? Well, 64 is too large, but 32 just fits, so you know that there is be a 1 in the 2^5 column. Now, how much is left over? You find this by subtracting 32 from 35: 35–32=3. Next, you look at each remaining powers of 2, one column at a time. Because the next smaller power of 2 is 2^4, you determine if 2^4, or 16, is less than or equal to 3. Because it is not, you put a 0 in the 2^4 column. The next power is 2^3, so you decide if 2^3, or 8, is less than or equal to 3; it is not, so you put a 0 in the 2^3 column as well. Next, is 2^2, or 4, less than or equal to 3? It is not, so place a 0 in the 2^2 column. Next, is 2^1, or 2, less than or equal to 3? It is, so place a 1 in the 2^1 column. Now, how much is left over? Subtract: 3–2=1. Finally, you ask if 2^0, or 1, is less than or equal to the remainder 1? Because it is, you put a 1 in the 2^0 column. Therefore, the decimal number 35 is equal to the binary number 00100011 or 100011. That's it. Table G-7 summarizes this process.

TABLE G-7

2^7	2^6	2^5	2^4	2^3	2^2	2^1	2^0
128	64	32	16	8	4	2	1
0	0	1	0	0	0	1	1

As a second example of converting a decimal number to binary, consider the decimal number 239. Notice that we're taking the byte-oriented approach here; that is, we're working with numbers between 0 and 255, which are the decimal numbers that can be expressed with one byte. If you refer to Table G-3, what's the largest power of 2 that is less than or equal to 239? You can see that 128 meets the criteria, so you put a 1 in the 2^7 column. Now, how much is left over? You find this by subtracting 128 from 239: 239–128=111. Because the next smaller power of 2 is 2^6, you determine if 2^6, or 64, is less than or equal to 111. Because it is, you put a 1 in the 2^6 column. How much is left over? You find this by subtracting 64 from 111: 111–64=47. The next power is 2^5, so you decide if 2^5, or 32, is less than or equal to the remainder 47; it is, so you put a 1 in the 2^5 column as well. How much is left over? Find this by subtracting 32 from 47: 47–32=15. Next, is 2^4, or 16, less than or equal to 15? It is not, so place a 0 in the 2^4 column. Next, is 2^3, or 8, less than or equal to 15? It is, so place a 1 in the 2^3 column. How much is left over? Subtract: 15–8=7. Next, is 2^2, or 4, less than or equal to the remainder 7? It is, so place a 1 in the 2^2 column. How much is left over? Subtract: 7–4=3. Next, is 2^1, or 2, less than or equal to 3? It is, so you put a 1 in the 2^1 column. How much is left over? Subtract: 3–2=1. Finally, you ask if 2^0, or 1, is less than or equal to the remainder 1? Because it is, you put a 1 in the 2^0 column. Therefore, the decimal number 239 is equal to the binary number 11101111. Table G-8 summarizes the result.

TABLE G-8

2^7	2^6	2^5	2^4	2^3	2^2	2^1	2^0
128	64	32	16	8	4	2	1
1	1	1	0	1	1	1	1

This procedure works for any decimal number. Consider the decimal number 1,000,000 (one million). What's the largest power of 2 less than or equal to 1,000,000? With a little patience, you can find that 2^{19}=524,288 and 2^{20}=1,048,576, so 2^{19} is the largest power of 2 that fits into 1,000,000. If you continue with the procedure previously described, you determine that the decimal number one million is equal to the binary number 11110100001001000000.

You see that binary numbers take up a lot more space than decimal numbers. This is partly why humans don't think in binary. Probably the main reason humans use Base 10, though, is because we have 10 fingers. If we had 12 fingers, we would probably think in Base 12.

Counting in Binary

You can divide a network into *subnetworks* (*subnets* for short) by "borrowing bits" from the leftmost portion of the host field of the network IP address. The borrowed bits allow you to differentiate the subnets by the binary strings that define them. For example, if you borrow 2 bits from the fourth octet of the Class C network 200.10.20.0, you form four subnets. The four possible combinations obtainable from 2 bits are the binary strings 00, 01, 10, and 11. You normally discard the first and the last subnets (associated with all 0s and all 1s). Note that 00, 01, 10, and 11 is how you count from 0 to 3 in binary.

So, when determining the subnet addresses for a given IP network, it is useful to be able to count in binary. Counting in binary allows you to explicitly list the binary representations of the subnet IP addresses obtained by borrowing bits.

With 4 bits, you can express $2^{14}=16$ possible combinations of 0s and 1s. For your reference, here's a list of the first 16 binary numbers in order (counting from 0 to 15 in binary):

`0, 1, 10, 11, 100, 101, 110, 111, 1000, 1001, 1010, 1011, 1100, 1101, 1110, 1111.`

Even and Odd

Sometimes it's useful to recognize how the concepts of *even* and *odd* translate into binary numbers. An even decimal number is one that is a multiple of 2 (such as 0, 2, 4, 6, 8, 10, 12, and so on). Notice in the second row of Table G-9 that all the numbers are multiples of 2 except the one on the right: 1.

TABLE G-9

2^7	2^6	2^5	2^4	2^3	2^2	2^1	2^0
128	64	32	16	8	4	2	1

If you think about it, this means that *a binary number is a multiple of 2 if and only if the rightmost digit is a 0*. Therefore, **a binary number is even if and only if the rightmost digit is 0.** An odd number is one that is not even (such as the decimal numbers 1, 3, 5, 7, 9, 11, and so on). Hence, **a binary number is odd if and only if the rightmost digit is 1.**

Here are some examples: the binary number 10011 is odd (19 in decimal) and the binary number 1010100010 is even (674 in decimal).

Hexadecimal Numbers

In Base 16, or *hexadecimal*, you work with powers of sixteen. You use hexadecimal notation with data link layer addressing (such as MAC addresses) and when referring to memory addresses in electronic devices. The 16 hexadecimal characters are 0, 1, 2, 3, 4, 5, 6, 7, 8, 9, A, B, C, D, E, and F. The A corresponds to the decimal number 10; B to 11; C to 12; D to 13; E to 14; and F to 15. Some examples of hexadecimal numbers are 2A384C5D9E7F, A001, and 237. Again, you have to be careful that it is clear from the context as to what base you're referring; otherwise, the previous example of 237 might be mistaken for a decimal number.

There are two special notations used with hexadecimal numbers. Sometimes, you see notation like 0x1A3B or 1A3Bh. These mean the same thing: 1A3B in hexadecimal. To reiterate, if you see a string preceded by "0x" or followed by "h", you know to interpret the string as a hexadecimal number. In particular, you see these notations when you work with memory registers.

Another fact that is important to understand is that one hexadecimal character can represent any decimal number between 0 and 15. In binary, 15 is 1111 and A is 1010. It follows that *4 bits are required to represent a single hexadecimal character in binary*. A MAC address is 48 bits long (6 bytes), which translates to 48÷4=12 hexadecimal characters required to express a MAC address. You can check this by typing **winipcfg** in Windows 95/98 or **ipconfig /all** in Windows NT4/2000 at the command prompt.

Table G-10 is a hexadecimal table (comparable to Table G-1) that has three rows. The first row lists *powers of 16*; the second row expresses the *expanded* (multiplied out) *powers of 16*; and the third row is where you place numbers to communicate how many (between 0 and F) of that power of 16 you want. *Notice that the second row has numbers written in Base 10!* This table uses only four columns because the powers of 16 become very large as the exponent increases; also, it is common to express hexadecimal characters in groups of two or four.

TABLE G-10

16^3	16^2	16^1	16^0
4096	256	16	1

Consider the hexadecimal number 3A. You can determine the value of 3A in decimal by using a hexadecimal table (see Table G-11).

TABLE G-11

16^1	16^0
16	1
3	A

You can use Table G-11 to convert the hexadecimal number 3A to Base 10:

3A=3×16+A×1=3×16+10×1=48+10=58.

Now, consider the hexadecimal number 23CF. Table G-12 helps put it in perspective.

TABLE G-12

16^3	16^2	16^1	16^0
4096	256	16	1
2	3	C	F

You can use Table G-12 to convert the hexadecimal number 23CF to Base 10:

23CF=2×4096+3×256+C×16+F×1=2×4096+3×256+12×16+15×1
.=8192+768+192+15=9167.

The smallest decimal value that can be represented by four hexadecimal characters, 0000, is 0. The largest decimal value that can be represented by four hexadecimal characters, FFFF, is 65,535. It follows that the range of decimal numbers that can be represented by four hexadecimal characters is 0 to 65,535, a total of 65,536 or 2^{16} possible values.

Now you know how to convert a hexadecimal number to a decimal number. As an exercise, use a table to show that the hexadecimal number 8D2B3 converts to the decimal number 578,227. As with binary to decimal conversion, after repeating this procedure several times, you'll probably develop your own shortcuts that might include not using a table at all.

Converting a Decimal Number into a Hexadecimal Number

Again, there's more than one way to proceed, so stick with your favorite method. The following process demonstrates one way to go about this conversion. If you are already comfortable with a particular method, you might want to skip the rest of this section.

To convert a decimal number into a hexadecimal number, the idea is to first find the largest power of 16 that is less than or equal to the decimal number, and then to determine how many times it fits into the decimal number. Now that you've been through a similar process with decimal to binary conversion, you can just get right to it. One difference to note is that the highest power of 16 to fit into a decimal number sometimes fits multiple times.

Consider the decimal number 15,211. Looking at Table G-10, what's the largest power of 16 that is less than or equal to 15,211? Well, 4096 meets the criteria. How many times does it fit in 15,211? Checking, you see that 4096 fits three times and no more (4096×3=12,288), so you know there will be a 3 in the 4096 (or 16^3) column. Now, how much is left over? You find this by subtraction: 15,211–12,288=2923. Next, you see that 256 fits 11 times (and no more) into 2923 (256×11=2816), so you know there is a B (not 11!) in the 256 (or 16^2) place. Subtracting, you get 2923–2816=107. Because 16 fits six times (and no more) into 107 (16×6=96), you know there is a 6 in the 16 (or 16^1) column. Subtracting, you get 107-96=11, so the last digit is a B. The hexadecimal value for the decimal number 15,211 is 3B6B. Table G-13 summarizes this process.

TABLE G-13

16^3	16^2	16^1	16^0
4096	256	16	1
3	B	6	B

Converting a Hexadecimal Number into a Binary Number

It's relatively easy to convert a hexadecimal number into a binary number. You can do it one hexadecimal character at a time. Note that this method does not work in general for converting between various bases; the method only works here because 16 is a power of 2: $16=2^4$.

As an example, the hexadecimal number A3 is equal to the binary number 10100011 because A converts to 1010 and 3 converts to 0011. *Be especially careful to include four binary digits for each hexadecimal character for this method to work.* (If you forgot to do this in the last example, your result would be 101011, which you can check is incorrect.) The hexadecimal number F0F0 converts to 1111000011110000 because F converts to 1111 in binary and 0 converts to 0000 in binary. Last, the broadcast MAC address FF-FF-FF-FF-FF-FF converts to the binary equivalent of 11111111-11111111-11111111-11111111-11111111-11111111. You see that hexadecimal representations take up much less space than their binary counterparts.

This concludes the discussion of binary and hexadecimal numbers. Remember that these concepts take some time to get used to, but you can do it. Stick with it and, after getting a lot of practice over time, you'll be explaining it to others!

Exercises

1. Convert the binary number 1010 to Base 10.
2. Convert the Base 2 number 11110000 to decimal notation.
3. Convert the binary number 10101111 to a decimal number.
4. Convert the decimal number 1111 to binary notation.
5. Convert the decimal number 249 to Base 2.
6. Convert the decimal number 128 to Base 2.
7. Convert the decimal number 65 to a binary number.
8. Convert the Base 10 number 63 to binary notation.
9. Convert the Base 10 number 31 to a binary number.
10. Convert the decimal number 198 to binary notation.
11. Is the binary number 11100011 even or odd?
12. Convert 0xAB to Base 10.
13. Convert ABCDh to Base 10.
14. Convert 0xFF to decimal notation.
15. Convert the decimal number 249 to Base 16.
16. Convert the decimal number 65,000 to hexadecimal notation.
17. Convert 0x2B to Base 2.
18. Convert 0x10F8 to Base 2.
19. Change the MAC address 00-A0-CC-3C-4A-39 to binary notation.
20. Change both the IP address 166.122.23.130 and the subnet mask 255.255.255.128 to dotted-hexadecimal form.

Network Troubleshooting

Introduction

By performing router labs, you become more familiar with the troubleshooting process. In this appendix, you explore troubleshooting in more detail. To some extent, troubleshooting is an individualized process. However, some principles are common to any troubleshooting methodology. In the following pages, we use the language of the OSI model to put troubleshooting in perspective as it relates to Semester 2 router labs. Then, we present a general problem-solving approach for networking.

Troubleshooting Semester 2 Labs

You gained quite a bit of skill in troubleshooting during the time you spent configuring routers in Semester 2 (see Figure H-1). You learned to work upward from layer 1 of the OSI model, progressing from the physical layer to the data link layer to the network layer and beyond. A review of some of the common layer 1, layer 2, and layer 3 issues you learned to resolve follows.

Layer 1 errors can include

- Broken cables
- Disconnected cables
- Cables connected to the wrong ports
- Intermittent cable connections
- Cables incorrectly terminated
- Wrong cables used for the tasks at hand (must use cross-connects, rollovers, and straight-through cables correctly)
- Transceiver problems
- DCE cable problems
- DTE cable problems
- Devices powered off

FIGURE H-1
Here is the
Semester 2 lab
configuration
with all the
usual settings.

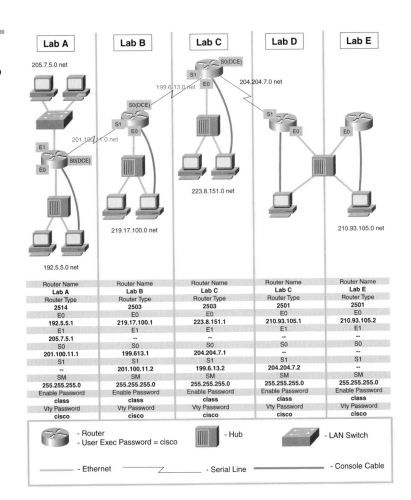

Router Name **Lab A**	Router Name **Lab B**	Router Name **Lab C**	Router Name **Lab C**	Router Name **Lab E**
Router Type **2514**	Router Type **2503**	Router Type **2503**	Router Type **2501**	Router Type **2501**
E0	E0	E0	E0	E0
192.5.5.1	219.17.100.1	223.8.151.1	210.93.105.1	210.93.105.2
E1	E1	E1	E1	E1
205.7.5.1	--	--	--	--
S0	S0	S0	S0	S0
201.100.11.1	199.613.1	204.204.7.1	--	--
S1	S1	S1	S1	S1
--	201.100.11.2	199.6.13.2	204.204.7.2	--
SM	SM	SM	SM	SM
255.255.255.0	255.255.255.0	255.255.255.0	255.255.255.0	255.255.255.0
Enable Password **class**	Enable Password **class**	Enable Password **class**	Enable Password **class**	Enable Password **class**
Vty Password **cisco**	Vty Password **cisco**	Vty Password **cisco**	Vty Password **cisco**	Vty Password **cisco**

- Router
- User Exec Password = cisco

- Hub

- LAN Switch

——— - Ethernet   ——/—— - Serial Line   ━━━━ - Console Cable

FIGURE H-2
Always start
troubleshoot-
ing by
analyzing
layer 1 issues.

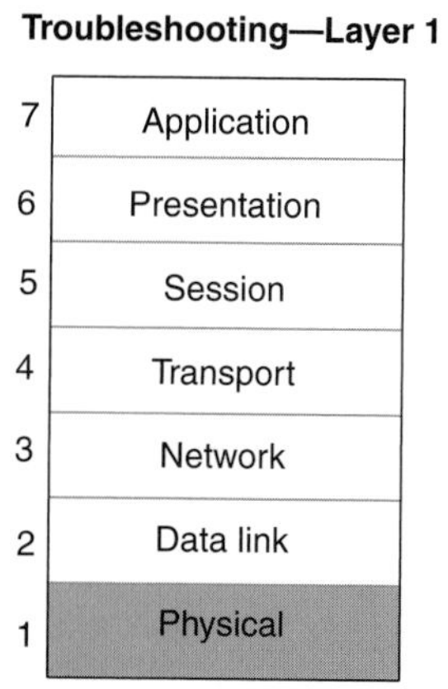

Troubleshooting—Layer 1

FIGURE H-3
The second OSI
layer you
should trouble-
shoot is layer 2.

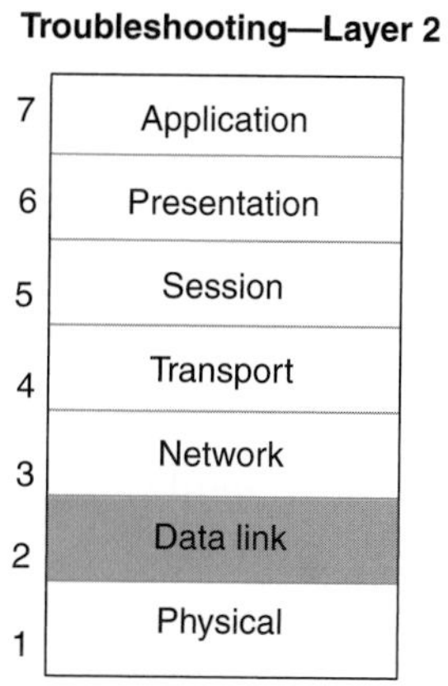

Troubleshooting—Layer 2

Layer 2 errors can include

- Improperly configured serial interfaces
- Improperly configured Ethernet interfaces
- Incorrect clock rate settings on serial interfaces
- Improper encapsulation set on serial interfaces (HDLC is default)
- Faulty NIC

FIGURE H-4

Normally, you complete your troubleshooting with layer 3 of the OSI model.

Troubleshooting—Layer 3

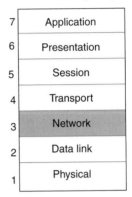

7	Application
6	Presentation
5	Session
4	Transport
3	Network
2	Data link
1	Physical

Layer 3 errors can include

- Routing protocol not enabled
- Wrong routing protocol enabled
- Incorrect network/IP addresses
- Incorrect subnet masks
- Incorrect interface addresses
- Incorrect DNS to IP bindings (host table entries)
- Wrong autonomous system number for IGRP

It's important to be familiar with troubleshooting the layer 1, layer 2, and layer 3 errors previously listed. That's not the end of the story, however, because you also need to know where to look for help if you can't immediately determine why a network is not working as desired. Figure H-5 lists some of these resources. One resource that networking professionals use frequently is the documentation website at CCO (Cisco Connection Online: www.cisco.com)

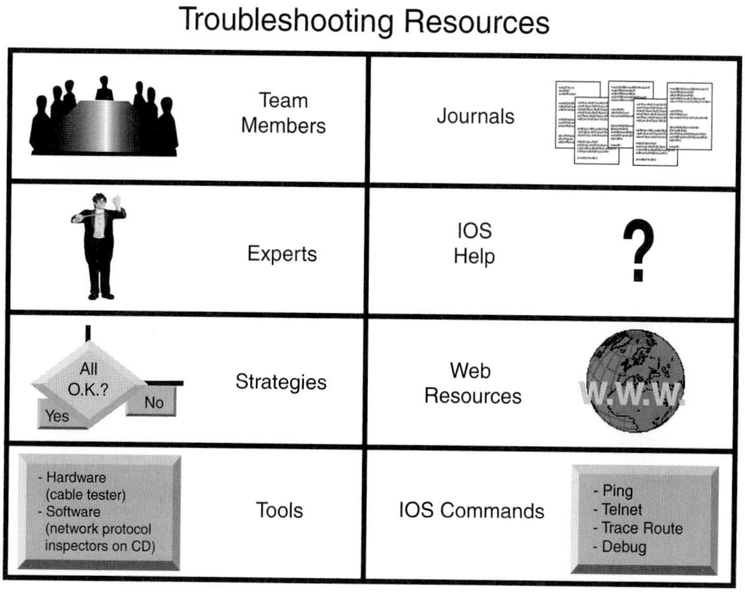

FIGURE H-5
Here is a list of troubleshooting resources, in case the usual troubleshooting techniques don't work

Troubleshooting Resources

A General Model for Troubleshooting

It's useful to have a general method to refer to when troubleshooting computer networks. This section outlines one such method, which is used by many networking professionals.

The steps are as follows:

STEP 1. *Define the problem.* What are the symptoms and the potential causes?

STEP 2. *Gather the facts.* Isolate the possible causes.

STEP 3. *Consider the possibilities.* Based on the facts gathered, narrow the focus to those areas relevant to the specific problem. This is the step where you set the boundaries for the problem.

STEP 4. *Create an action plan.* Devise a plan in which you manipulate only *one* variable at a time.

STEP 5. *Implement the action plan.* Perform each step carefully while testing to see if the symptom disappears.

STEP 6. *Observe the results.* Determine whether you resolved the problem. If so, the process is complete.

STEP 7. *Repeat the process.* If you did not resolve the problem, move to the next, most likely cause on your list. Return to step 4, and repeat the process until you solve the problem.

Applying the Model for Troubleshooting

Here is an example of how you can apply the troubleshooting model in a router lab.

FIGURE H-6
The familiar Semester 2 router lab diagram

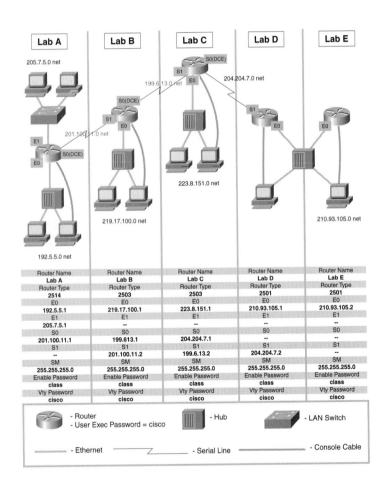

Router Name	Router Name	Router Name	Router Name	Router Name
Lab A	**Lab B**	**Lab C**	**Lab D**	**Lab E**
Router Type	Router Type	Router Type	Router Type	Router Type
2514	2503	2503	2501	2501
E0	E0	E0	E0	E0
192.5.5.1	219.17.100.1	223.8.151.1	210.93.105.1	210.93.105.2
E1	E1	E1	E1	E1
205.7.5.1	--	--	--	--
S0	S0	S0	S0	S0
201.100.11.1	199.613.1	204.204.7.1	--	--
S1	S1	S1	S1	S1
--	201.100.11.2	199.6.13.2	204.204.7.2	--
SM	SM	SM	SM	SM
255.255.255.0	255.255.255.0	255.255.255.0	255.255.255.0	255.255.255.0
Enable Password	Enable Password	Enable Password	Enable Password	Enable Password
class	**class**	**class**	**class**	**class**
Vty Password	Vty Password	Vty Password	Vty Password	Vty Password
cisco	**cisco**	**cisco**	**cisco**	**cisco**

- Router
- User Exec Password = cisco

- Hub

- LAN Switch

——— - Ethernet   ———⁄——— - Serial Line   ——— - Console Cable

When trying to ping Lab-E from Lab-A, you receive a series of time out messages.

```
lab-a#ping lab-e

Type escape sequence to abort.
Sending 5, 100-byte ICMP Echos to 210.93.105.2, timeout is 2 seconds:
.....
Success rate is 0 percent (0/5)
```

You now begin step 1 of the troubleshooting model:

STEP 1. *Define the problem.* What are the symptoms and the potential causes?

Begin by listing the symptoms:

— Unable to ping Lab-E from Lab-A.

Then, list the potential causes by layer:

a. Layer 1

— Bad cable
— Cable not connected
— Power loss on hub

b. Layer 2

— Interface shut down
— Improper encapsulation set (HDLC is the default on serial interfaces)
— Incorrect clock rate settings on serial interfaces

c. Layer 3

— Wrong interface address
— Wrong subnet mask
— Wrong routing information

STEP 2. *Gather the facts.* Isolate the possible causes.

You can do this by using the router's show commands to isolate the problem. Begin by testing the whole network. Because this network is under the control of one management, the routing table of each router contains all the networks in the WAN.

Type **show ip route** at the privileged EXEC prompt on
Lab-A. This shows the routing table for Lab-A. All eight
networks should be displayed. In the following, only seven
of the eight networks appear in the routing table:

```
lab-a#show ip route
Codes: C - connected, S -  static, I - IGRP, R - RIP, M - mobile, B - BGP
    D - EIGRP, EX - EIGRP external, O - OSPF, IA - OSPF inter area
    N1 - OSPF NSSA external type 1, N2 - OSPF NSSA external type 2
    E1 - OSPF external type 1, E2 - OSPF external type 2, E - EGP
    i - IS-IS, L1 - IS-IS level-1, L2 - IS-IS level-2, * - candidate default
    U - per-user static route, o - ODR

Gateway of last resort is not set

C  205.7.5.0/24 is directly connected, Ethernet1
R  219.17.100.0/24 [120/1] via 201.100.11.2, 00:00:24, Serial0
R  199.6.13.0/24 [120/1] via 201.100.11.2, 00:00:24, Serial0
R  204.204.7.0/24 [120/2] via 201.100.11.2, 00:00:24, Serial0
C  192.5.5.0/24 is directly connected, Ethernet0
R  223.8.151.0/24 [120/2] via 201.100.11.2, 00:00:24, Serial0
C  201.100.11.0/24 is directly connected, Serial0
```

STEP 3. *Consider the possibilities.* Based on the facts gathered, narrow the
focus to those areas relevant to the specific problem. Set the boundaries of the problem. To do this, you must simplify the search area;
move from the big picture to a more focused and detailed look of
where the problem could be.

The information from the routing table shows that network
204.204.7.0 is two hops away, which is displayed as [120/2]
in the line R 204.204.7.0/24 [120/2] via 201.100.11.2,
00:00:24, Serial0. Two hops from Lab-A is Lab-C, which is
the last router that shared its RIP information. You should
begin troubleshooting at the last router from which you
received information. Now, gather information on a smaller
scale. Focus on a single router. Telnet to the router Lab-C.
At Lab-C, type **show run** to see the router's running
configuration. Be sure to log the configuration file (write the
configuration in your journal or copy and paste the
configuration into a Notepad file).

```
lab-a#lab-c
Trying lab-c (199.6.13.2)... Open


User Access Verification

Password:
lab-c>ena
Password:
lab-c#show run
```

```
interface Ethernet0
  ip address 223.8.151.1 255.255.255.0
!
interface Serial0
  ip address 204.204.7.1 255.255.255.0
  no ip mroute-cache
  clockrate 56000
!
interface Serial1
  ip address 199.6.13.2.255.255.255.0
```

```
Building configuration...                          !
                                                   interface BRI0
                                                    no ip address
                                                    shutdown
Current configuration:                             !
!                                                  router rip
version 11.3                                         network 199.6.13.0
service timestamps debug uptime                     network 204.204.7.0
service timestamps log uptime                       network 223.8.151.0
no service password-encryption                     !
!                                                  ip host lab-a 192.5.5.1 205.7.5.1
hostname lab-c                                      ip host lab-b 201.100.11.2.219.17.100.1
!                                                  <more>
enable password class
<more>
```

Gather information on the interface connected to the last
displayed network from the **show ip route** command. At the
prompt, type **show int s0**; this displays all the current
information about the interface. Log this information.

```
lab-c#sho int s0
Serial0 is up, line protocol is up
 Hardware is HD64570
 Internet address is 204.204.7.1/24
 MTU 1500 bytes, BW 1544 Kbit, DLY 20000 usec,,
  reliability 255/255, txload 1/255, rxload 1/255
 Encapsulation HDLC, loopback not set, keepalive set (10 sec)
 Last input 00:00:01, output 00:00:00, output hang never
 Last clearing of "show interface" counters never
 Input queue: 0/75/0 (size/max/drops); Total output drops: 0
 Queueing strategy: weighted fair
 Output queue: 0/1000/64/0 (size/max total/threshold/drops)
  Conversations 0/1/256 (active/max active/max total)
  Reserved Conversations 0/0 (allocated/max allocated)
5 minute input rate 0 bits/sec, 0 packets/sec
5 minute output rate 0 bits/sec, 0 packets/sec
 185 packets input, 12570 bytes, 0 no buffer
 Received 185 broadcasts, 0 runts, 0 giants, 0 throttles
 0 input errors, 0 CRC, 0 frame, 0 overrun, 0 ignored, 0 abort
 241 packets output, 20487 bytes, 0 underruns
 0 output errors, 0 collisions, 21 interface resets
 0 output buffer failures, 0 output buffers swapped out
 10 carrier transitions
 DCD=up DSR=up DTR=up RTS=up CTS=up
```

STEP 4. *Create an action plan.* Devise a plan in which you manipulate only
one variable at a time.

From the information about Lab-C's running configuration,
you see that everything is correctly configured. Looking then
at the information from the **show int s0** report, you see that
the interface is up and the line protocol is up. This tells you
that the cable is connected to a device on the other end and
that the data link layer is functional. If the cable is not
connected properly, the line protocol will be down. From

these two show commands, you know that this router is correctly configured and functioning. The problem must be at the next router, Lab-D. This is an example of the process of elimination, or of simplifying the problem. A good action plan would start by attempting to telnet to router Lab-D, and then moving to Lab-D's terminal to check the running configuration for errors. If you do not find errors in the configuration, you might need to examine the S1 interface.

STEP 5. *Implement the action plan.* Perform each step carefully while testing to see if the symptom disappears.

You tried to telnet to router Lab-D and failed. You must now go to the terminal connected to Lab-D. Enter privileged EXEC mode and type **show run**. From this report, you notice that the routing protocol on Lab-D is IGRP instead of RIP (which router Lab-C uses). To correct this error, you need to enter global configuration mode, type **no router igrp 111**, and enter the command **router rip**. Now enter the network commands **network 210.93.105.0** and **network 204.204.7.0** (these are the networks directly connected to Lab-D). Then, type **Ctrl-Z** and issue the **copy run start** command.

STEP 6. *Observe the results.* Determine whether you resolved the problem. If so, the process is complete.

Now, test connectivity by pinging Lab-A and Lab-E.

```
lab-d#ping lab-a

Type escape sequence to abort.
Sending 5, 100-byte ICMP Echos to 192.5.5.1, timeout is 2 seconds:
!!!!
Success rates is 100 percent (5/5), round-trip min/avg/max = 96/100/108 ms

lab-d#ping lab-e

Type escape sequence to abort.
Sending 5, 100-byte ICMP Echos to 210.93.105.2, timeout is 2 seconds:
!!!!
Success rate is 100 percent (5/5), round-trip min/avg/max =  1/3/4 ms
```

STEP 7. Repeat the process. If you did not resolve the problem, move to the next, most likely cause on your list. Return to step 4, and repeat the process until you solve the problem.

Although you found an error in the configuration file of the router and corrected it, this might not successfully restore connectivity. Some problems have compound, or multiple, causes. If this fails to fix the problem, return to step 4 and develop a new action plan. Just as most network problems are caused by user error, your action plan might also contain errors. Most errors in an action plan are omissions, simply overlooked causes. The process of troubleshooting can be frustrating. Remember, don't panic. If you reach a point at which you need help, don't be afraid to ask.

To put all this in perspective, Figure H-7 shows a flowchart for the troubleshooting model.

FIGURE H-7
Each person develops his own trouble-shooting methods. It helps to have a general method to refer to should all else fail.

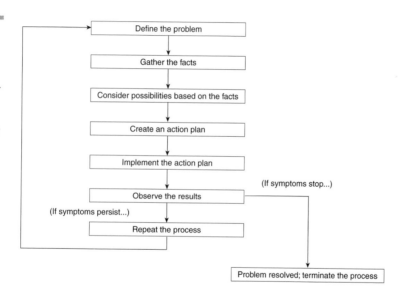

With this guide, you can resolve most network failures that confront you. As a networking professional, troubleshooting plays a vital role in day-to-day work, so it is critical that you get a lot of hands-on experience to improve your troubleshooting skills. For many, troubleshooting is the most enjoyable and rewarding part of networking. With a little time and patience, the process of troubleshooting will become second nature.

This glossary attempts to gather and define the terms and abbreviations related to networking. As with any growing technical field, some terms evolve into several meanings. Where necessary, multiple definitions and abbreviation expansions are presented. Multiword terms are alphabetized as if there were no spaces; hyphenated terms, as if there were no hyphens.

Terms in this glossary are typically defined under their abbreviations. Each abbreviation expansion is listed separately, with a cross-reference to the abbreviation entry. In addition, many definitions contain cross-references to related terms.

We hope that this glossary adds to your understanding of internetworking technologies.

Numerics

4B/5B local fiber   4-byte/5-byte local fiber. Fibre Channel physical medium used for FDDI and ATM. Supports speeds of up to 100 Mbps over multimode fiber.

8B/10B local fiber   8-byte/10-byte local fiber. Fiber Channel physical medium that supports speeds up to 149.76 Mbps over multimode fiber.

10Base2   A 10-Mbps baseband Ethernet specification using 50-ohm thin coaxial cable. 10Base2, which is part of the IEEE 802.3 specification, has a distance limit of 185 meters per segment. *See also* Ethernet and IEEE 802.3.

10Base5   A 10-Mbps baseband Ethernet specification using standard (thick) 50-ohm baseband coaxial cable. 10Base5, which is part of the IEEE 802.3 baseband physical-layer specification, has a distance limit of 500 meters per segment. *See also* Ethernet and IEEE 802.3.

10BaseF   A 10-Mbps baseband Ethernet specification that refers to the 10BaseFB, 10BaseFL, and 10BaseFP standards for Ethernet over fiber-optic cabling. *See also* 10BaseFB, 10BaseFL, 10BaseFP, and Ethernet.

10BaseFB   A 10-Mbps baseband Ethernet specification using fiber-optic cabling. 10BaseFB is part of the IEEE 10BaseF specification. It is not used to connect user stations, but provides a synchronous signaling backbone that allows additional segments and repeaters to be connected to the network. 10BaseFB segments can be up to 2,000 meters long. *See also* 10BaseF and Ethernet.

10BaseFL A 10-Mbps baseband Ethernet specification using fiber-optic cabling. 10BaseFL is part of the IEEE 10BaseF specification and, although able to interoperate with FOIRL, is designed to replace the FOIRL specification. 10BaseFL segments can be up to 1,000 meters long if used with FOIRL, and up to 2,000 meters if 10BaseFL is used exclusively. *See also* 10BaseF and Ethernet.

10BaseFP A 10-Mbps fiber-passive baseband Ethernet specification using fiber-optic cabling. 10BaseFP is part of the IEEE 10BaseF specification. It organizes a number of computers into a star topology without the use of repeaters. 10BaseFP segments can be up to 500 meters long. *See also* 10BaseF and Ethernet.

10BaseT A 10-Mbps baseband Ethernet specification using two pairs of twisted-pair cabling (Category 3, 4, or 5): one pair for transmitting data and the other for receiving data. 10BaseT, which is part of the IEEE 802.3 specification, has a distance limit of approximately 100 meters per segment. *See also* Ethernet and IEEE 802.3.

10Broad36 A 10-Mbps broadband Ethernet specification using broadband coaxial cable. 10Broad36, which is part of the IEEE 802.3 specification, has a distance limit of 3,600 meters per segment. *See also* Ethernet and IEEE 802.3.

100BaseFX A 100-Mbps baseband Fast Ethernet specification using two strands of multimode fiber-optic cable per link. To guarantee proper signal timing, a 100BaseFX link cannot exceed 400 meters in length. Based on the IEEE 802.3 standard. *See also* 100BaseX, Fast Ethernet, and IEEE 802.3.

100BaseT A 100-Mbps baseband Fast Ethernet specification using UTP wiring. Like the 10BaseT technology on which it is based, 100BaseT sends link pulses over the network segment when no traffic is present. However, these link pulses contain more information than do those used in 10BaseT. Based on the IEEE 802.3 standard. *See also* 10BaseT, Fast Ethernet, and IEEE 802.3.

100BaseT4 A 100-Mbps baseband Fast Ethernet specification using four pairs of Category 3, 4, or 5 UTP wiring. To guarantee proper signal timing, a 100BaseT4 segment cannot exceed 100 meters in length. Based on the IEEE 802.3 standard. *See also* Fast Ethernet and IEEE 802.3.

100BaseTX A 100-Mbps baseband Fast Ethernet specification using two pairs of either UTP or STP wiring. The first pair of wires is used to receive data; the second is used to transmit. To guarantee proper signal timing, a 100BaseTX segment cannot exceed 100 meters in length. Based on the IEEE 802.3 standard. *See also* 100BaseX, Fast Ethernet, and IEEE 802.3.

100BaseX A 100-Mbps baseband Fast Ethernet specification that refers to the 100BaseFX and 100BaseTX standards for Fast Ethernet over fiber-optic cabling. Based on the IEEE 802.3 standard. *See also* 100BaseFX, 100BaseTX, Fast Ethernet, and IEEE 802.3.

100VG-AnyLAN A 100-Mbps Fast Ethernet and Token Ring media technology using four pairs of Category 3, 4, or 5 UTP cabling. This high-speed transport technology, developed by Hewlett-Packard, can be made to operate on existing 10BaseT Ethernet networks. Based on the IEEE 802.12 standard.

A

A&B bit signaling A procedure used in T1 transmission facilities in which each of the 24 T1 subchannels devotes 1 bit of every sixth frame to the carrying of supervisory signaling information.

ABM Asynchronous Balanced Mode. An HDLC (and derivative protocol) communication mode supporting peer-oriented, point-to-point communications between two stations, where either station can initiate transmission.

access list A list kept by routers to control access through or to the router for a number of services (for example, to prevent packets with a certain IP address from leaving a particular interface on the router).

access method 1. Generally, the way in which network devices access the network medium. 2. Software within an SNA processor that controls the flow of information through a network.

ACK *See* acknowledgment.

acknowledgment Notification sent from one network device to another to acknowledge that some event (for example, receipt of a message) occurred. Sometimes abbreviated ACK. *Compare with* NAK.

active monitor A device responsible for performing maintenance functions on a Token Ring network. A network node is selected to be the active monitor if it has the highest MAC address on the ring. The active monitor is responsible for such ring maintenance tasks as ensuring that tokens are not lost and that frames do not circulate indefinitely.

adapter *See* NIC.

address A data structure or logical convention used to identify a unique entity, such as a particular process or network device.

address mapping   A technique that allows different protocols to interoperate by translating addresses from one format to another. For example, when routing IP over X.25, the IP addresses must be mapped to the X.25 addresses so that the IP packets can be transmitted by the X.25 network.

address mask   A bit combination used to describe which portion of an address refers to the network or subnet and which part refers to the host. Sometimes referred to simply as *mask*.

address resolution   Generally, a method for resolving differences between computer addressing schemes. Address resolution usually specifies a method for mapping network layer (Layer 3) addresses to data link layer (Layer 2) addresses.

Address Resolution Protocol   *See* ARP.

adjacency   A relationship formed between selected neighboring routers and end nodes for the purpose of exchanging routing information. Adjacency is based on the use of a common media segment.

Advanced Research Projects Agency   *See* ARPA.

advertising   A router process in which routing or service updates are sent so that other routers on the network can maintain lists of usable routes.

AEP   AppleTalk Echo Protocol. A protocol used to test connectivity between two AppleTalk nodes. One node sends a packet to another node and receives a duplicate, or echo, of that packet.

AFP   AppleTalk Filing Protocol. A presentation-layer protocol that allows users to share data files and application programs that reside on a file server. AFP supports AppleShare and Mac OS file sharing.

agent   1. Generally, software that processes queries and returns replies on behalf of an application. 2. In NMSs, a process that resides in all managed devices and reports the values of specified variables to management stations.

algorithm   A well-defined rule or process for arriving at a solution to a problem. In networking, algorithms are commonly used to determine the best route for traffic from a particular source to a particular destination.

ANSI   American National Standards Institute. A voluntary organization composed of corporate, government, and other members that coordinates standards-related activities, approves U.S. national standards, and develops positions for the United States in international standards organizations. ANSI helps develop international and U.S. standards relating to, among other things, communications and networking. ANSI is a member of the IEC and the International Organization for Standardization.

API   application programming interface. A specification of function-call conventions that defines an interface to a service.

AppleTalk   A series of communications protocols designed by Apple Computer consisting of two phases. Phase 1, the earlier version, supports a single physical network that can have only one network number and be in one zone. Phase 2 supports multiple logical networks on a single physical network and allows networks to be in more than one zone. *See also* zone.

application   A program that performs a function directly for a user. FTP and Telnet clients are examples of network applications.

application layer   Layer 7 of the OSI reference model. This layer provides services to application processes (such as e-mail, file transfer, and terminal emulation) that are outside the OSI reference model. The application layer identifies and establishes the availability of intended communication partners (and the resources required to connect with them), synchronizes cooperating applications, and establishes agreement on procedures for error recovery and control of data integrity. Corresponds roughly with the transaction services layer in the SNA model. *See also* data link layer, network layer, physical layer, presentation layer, session layer, and transport layer.

APPN   Advanced Peer-to-Peer Networking. An enhancement to the original IBM SNA architecture. APPN handles session establishment between peer nodes, dynamic transparent route calculation, and traffic prioritization for APPC traffic.

ARA   AppleTalk Remote Access. A protocol that provides Macintosh users direct access to information and resources at a remote AppleTalk site.

area   A logical set of network segments (CLNS, DECnet, or OSPF based) and their attached devices. Areas are usually connected to other areas via routers, making up a single autonomous system.

ARIN   An organization that serves the Internet community by supplying user assistance, documentation, training, registration service for Internet domain names, network addresses, and other services. Formerly called *InterNIC*.

ARP   Address Resolution Protocol. An Internet protocol used to map an IP address to a MAC address. Defined in RFC 826. *Compare with* RARP.

ARPA   Advanced Research Projects Agency. A research and development organization that is part of the U.S. Department of Defense. ARPA is responsible for numerous technological advances in communications and networking. ARPA evolved into DARPA, and then back into ARPA again in 1994.

ARPANET   Advanced Research Projects Agency Network. A landmark packet-switching network established in 1969. ARPANET was developed in the 1970s by BBN and funded by ARPA (and later DARPA). It eventually evolved into the Internet. The term *ARPANET* was officially retired in 1990.

ASBR   Autonomous System Boundary Router. An ABR located between an OSPF autonomous system and a non-OSPF network. ASBRs run both OSPF and another routing protocol, such as RIP. ASBRs must reside in a nonstub OSPF area.

ASCII   American Standard Code for Information Interchange. An 8-bit code (7 bits plus parity) for character representation.

Asynchronous Balanced Mode   *See* ABM.

Asynchronous Transfer Mode   *See* ATM.

asynchronous transmission   Digital signals that are transmitted without precise clocking. Such signals generally have different frequencies and phase relationships. Asynchronous transmissions usually encapsulate individual characters in control bits (called start and stop bits) that designate the beginning and end of each character. *Compare with* synchronous transmission.

ATM   Asynchronous Transfer Mode. An international standard for cell relay in which multiple service types (such as voice, video, or data) are conveyed in fixed-length (53-byte) cells. Fixed-length cells allow cell processing to occur in hardware, thereby reducing transit delays. ATM is designed to take advantage of high-speed transmission media such as E3, SONET, and T3.

ATM Forum   An international organization jointly founded in 1991 by Cisco Systems, NET/ADAPTIVE, Northern Telecom, and Sprint that develops and promotes standards-based implementation agreements for ATM technology. The ATM Forum expands on official standards developed by ANSI and ITU-T, and develops implementation agreements in advance of official standards.

ATP   AppleTalk Transaction Protocol. A transport-level protocol that provides a loss-free transaction service between sockets. The service allows exchanges between two socket clients in which one client requests the other to perform a particular task and to report the results. ATP binds the request and response together to ensure the reliable exchange of request/response pairs.

attenuation   Loss of communication signal energy.

AURP   AppleTalk Update-Based Routing Protocol. A method of encapsulating AppleTalk traffic in the header of a foreign protocol, allowing the connection of two or more discontiguous AppleTalk internetworks through a foreign network (such as TCP/IP) to form an AppleTalk WAN. This connection is called an *AURP tunnel*. In addition to its encapsulation function, AURP maintains routing tables for the entire AppleTalk WAN by exchanging routing information between exterior routers.

authentication   In security, the verification of the identity of a person or process.

B

backbone   Part of a network that acts as the primary path for traffic that is most often sourced from, and destined for, other networks.

backbone cabling   Cabling that provides interconnections between wiring closets and the POP, and between buildings that are part of the same LAN.

backoff   The retransmission delay enforced when a collision occurs.

bandwidth   The difference between the highest and lowest frequencies available for network signals. Also used to describe the rated throughput capacity of a given network medium or protocol.

bandwidth reservation   The process of assigning bandwidth to users and applications served by a network. It involves assigning priority to different flows of traffic based on how critical and delay sensitive they are. This makes the best use of available bandwidth, and if the network becomes congested, lower-priority traffic can be dropped. Sometimes called *bandwidth allocation*.

Banyan VINES   *See* VINES.

Basic Rate Interface   *See* BRI.

B channel   bearer channel. In ISDN, a full-duplex, 64-kbps channel used to send user data. *Compare with* D channel, E channel, and H channel.

binary   A numbering system characterized by ones and zeros (1 = on; 0 = off).

BOOTP   Bootstrap Protocol. A protocol used by a network node to determine the IP address of its Ethernet interfaces to affect network booting.

bootstrap   A simple, preset operation to load instructions that in turn cause other instructions to be loaded into memory, or cause entry into other configuration modes.

Bootstrap Protocol   *See* BOOTP.

BPDU   bridge protocol data unit. A Spanning-Tree Protocol hello packet that is sent out at configurable intervals to exchange information among bridges in the network.

BRI   Basic Rate Interface. An ISDN interface composed of two B channels and one D channel for circuit-switched communication of voice, video, and data. *Compare with* PRI.

bridge   A device that connects and passes packets between two network segments that use the same communications protocol. Bridges operate at the data link layer (Layer 2) of the OSI reference model. In general, a bridge filters, forwards, or floods an incoming frame based on the MAC address of that frame.

broadcast   A data packet that is sent to all nodes on a network. Broadcasts are identified by a broadcast address. *Compare with* multicast and unicast. *See also* broadcast address.

broadcast address   A special address reserved for sending a message to all stations. Generally, a broadcast address is a MAC destination address of all ones. *Compare with* multicast address and unicast address. *See also* broadcast.

broadcast domain   A set of all devices that will receive broadcast frames originating from any device within the set. Broadcast domains are typically bounded by routers (or in a switched network, by VLANs) because routers do not forward broadcast frames.

bus topology   A linear LAN architecture in which transmissions from network stations propagate the length of the medium and are received by all other stations. *Compare with* ring topology, star topology, and tree topology.

C

cable range   A range of network numbers that is valid for use by nodes on an extended AppleTalk network. The cable range value can be a single network number or a contiguous sequence of several network numbers. Node addresses are assigned based on the cable range value.

caching   A form of replication in which information learned during a previous transaction is used to process later transactions.

call setup time   The time required to establish a switched call between DTE devices.

carrier   An electromagnetic wave or alternating current of a single frequency, suitable for modulation by another, data-bearing signal.

Category 1 cabling   One of five grades of UTP cabling described in the EIA/ TIA 568B standard. Category 1 cabling is used for telephone communications and is not suitable for transmitting data. *Compare with* Category 2 cabling, Category 3 cabling, Category 4 cabling, and Category 5 cabling. *See also* UTP.

Category 2 cabling   One of five grades of UTP cabling described in the EIA/ TIA 568B standard. Category 2 cabling is capable of transmitting data at speeds up to 4 Mbps. *Compare with* Category 1 cabling, Category 3 cabling, Category 4 cabling, and Category 5 cabling. *See also* UTP.

Category 3 cabling   One of five grades of UTP cabling described in the EIA/ TIA 568B standard. Category 3 cabling is used in 10BaseT networks and can transmit data at speeds up to 10 Mbps. *Compare with* Category 1 cabling, Category 2 cabling, Category 4 cabling, and Category 5 cabling. *See also* UTP.

Category 4 cabling   One of five grades of UTP cabling described in the EIA/ TIA 568B standard. Category 4 cabling is used in Token Ring networks and can transmit data at speeds up to 16 Mbps. *Compare with* Category 1 cabling, Category 2 cabling, Category 3 cabling, and Category 5 cabling. *See also* UTP.

Category 5 cabling   One of five grades of UTP cabling described in the EIA/ TIA 568B standard. Category 5 cabling is used for running CDDI and can transmit data at speeds up to 100 Mbps. *Compare with* Category 1 cabling, Category 2 cabling, Category 3 cabling, and Category 4 cabling. *See also* UTP.

CCITT   Consultative Committee for International Telegraph and Telephone. An international organization responsible for the development of communications standards. Now called the ITU-T. *See* ITU-T.

CDDI   Copper Distributed Data Interface. An implementation of FDDI protocols over STP and UTP cabling. CDDI transmits over relatively short distances (about 100 meters), providing data rates of 100 Mbps using a dual-ring architecture to provide redundancy. Based on the ANSI Twisted-Pair Physical Medium Dependent (TPPMD) standard. *Compare with* FDDI.

Challenge Handshake Authentication Protocol   *See* CHAP.

CHAP   Challenge Handshake Authentication Protocol. A security feature supported on lines using PPP encapsulation that prevents unauthorized access. CHAP does not itself prevent unauthorized access; it merely identifies the remote end. The router or access server then determines whether that user is allowed access. *Compare with* PAP.

CIDR   classless interdomain routing. A technique supported by BGP and based on route aggregation. CIDR allows routers to group routes together in order to cut down on the quantity of routing information carried by the core routers. With CIDR, several IP networks appear to networks outside the group as a single, larger entity.

circuit   A communications path between two or more points.

circuit group   A grouping of associated serial lines that link two bridges. If one of the serial links in a circuit group is in the spanning tree for a network, any of the serial links in the circuit group can be used for load balancing. This load-balancing strategy avoids data ordering problems by assigning each destination address to a particular serial link.

Cisco IOS software   Cisco Internetwork Operating System software. Cisco system software that provides common functionality, scalability, and security for all products under the CiscoFusion architecture. The Cisco IOS software allows centralized, integrated, and automated installation and management of internetworks, while ensuring support for a wide variety of protocols, media, services, and platforms.

client   A node or software program (front-end device) that requests services from a server.

client/server computing   Distributed computing (processing) network systems in which transaction responsibilities are divided into two parts: client (front end) and server (back end). Both terms (*client* and *server*) can be applied to software programs or actual computing devices. Also called *distributed computing (processing)*. *Compare with* peer-to-peer computing.

client/server model   A common way to describe network services and the model user processes (programs) of those services. Examples include the nameserver/nameresolver paradigm of the DNS and fileserver/file-client relationships such as NFS and diskless hosts.

CMIP   Common Management Information Protocol. An OSI network management protocol created and standardized by ISO for the monitoring and control of heterogeneous networks. *See also* CMIS.

CMIS   Common Management Information Services. An OSI network management service interface created and standardized by ISO for the monitoring and control of heterogeneous networks. *See also* CMIP.

CO   central office. A local telephone company office to which all local loops in a given area connect and in which circuit switching of subscriber lines occurs.

coaxial cable   Cable consisting of a hollow outer cylindrical conductor that surrounds a single inner wire conductor. Two types of coaxial cable are currently used in LANs: 50-ohm cable, which is used for digital signaling, and 75-ohm cable, which is used for analog signal and high-speed digital signaling.

coding   Electrical techniques used to convey binary signals.

collision   In Ethernet, the result of two nodes transmitting simultaneously. The frames from each device impact and are damaged when they meet on the physical media. *See also* collision domain.

collision domain   In Ethernet, the network area within which frames that have collided are propagated. Repeaters and hubs propagate collisions; LAN switches, bridges, and routers do not. *See also* collision.

common carrier   A licensed, private utility company that supplies communication services to the public at regulated prices.

concentrator   *See* hub.

congestion   Traffic in excess of network capacity.

congestion avoidance   A mechanism by which an ATM network controls traffic entering the network to minimize delays. To use resources most efficiently, lower-priority traffic is discarded at the edge of the network if conditions indicate that it cannot be delivered.

connectionless   Data transfer without the existence of a virtual circuit. *Compare with* connection-oriented. *See also* virtual circuit.

CLNS   Connectionless Network Service. OSI network layer service that does not require a circuit to be established before data is transmitted. CLNS routes messages to their destinations independently of any other messages.

connection-oriented   Data transfer that requires the establishment of a virtual circuit. *See also* connectionless and virtual circuit.

console   A DTE through which commands are entered into a host.

contention   An access method in which network devices compete for permission to access the physical medium. *Compare with* token passing.

convergence   The speed and ability of a group of internetworking devices running a specific routing protocol to agree on the topology of an internetwork after a change in that topology.

count to infinity   A problem that can occur in routing algorithms that are slow to converge, in which routers continuously increment the hop count to particular networks. Typically, some arbitrary hop-count limit is imposed to prevent this problem.

CPE customer premises equipment. Terminating equipment, such as terminals, telephones, and modems, supplied by the telephone company, installed at customer sites, and connected to the telephone company network.

CSMA/CD carrier sense multiple access with collision detect. A media-access mechanism wherein devices ready to transmit data first check the channel for a carrier. If no carrier is sensed for a specific period of time, a device can transmit. If two devices transmit at once, a collision occurs and is detected by all colliding devices. This collision subsequently delays retransmissions from those devices for some random length of time. CSMA/CD access is used by Ethernet and IEEE 802.3.

CSU channel service unit. A digital interface device that connects end user equipment to the local digital telephone loop. Often referred to together with DSU as CSU/DSU.

cut sheet A rough diagram indicating where cable runs are located and the numbers of rooms they lead to.

D

DARPA Defense Advanced Research Projects Agency. The U.S. government agency that funded research for and experimentation with the Internet. Evolved from ARPA, and then, in 1994, back to ARPA. *See also* ARPA.

DAS 1. dual attachment station. A device attached to both the primary and the secondary FDDI rings. Dual attachment provides redundancy for the FDDI ring: If the primary ring fails, the station can wrap the primary ring to the secondary ring, isolating the failure and retaining ring integrity. Also called a Class A station. *Compare with* SAS. 2. dynamically assigned socket. A socket that is dynamically assigned by DDP upon request by a client. In an AppleTalk network, the sockets numbered 128 to 254 are allocated as DASs.

data Upper-layer protocol data.

data flow control layer Layer 5 of the SNA architectural model. This layer determines and manages interactions between session partners, particularly data flow. Corresponds to the session layer of the OSI reference model. *See also* data link control layer, path control layer, physical control layer, presentation services layer, transaction services layer, and transmission control layer.

datagram A logical grouping of information sent as a network layer unit over a transmission medium without prior establishment of a virtual circuit. IP datagrams are the primary information units in the Internet. The terms *cell,* *frame*, *message*, *packet*, and *segment* are also used to describe logical information groupings at various layers of the OSI reference model and in various technology circles.

data link control layer   Layer 2 in the SNA architectural model. Responsible for the transmission of data over a particular physical link. Corresponds roughly to the data link layer of the OSI reference model. *See also* data flow control layer, path control layer, physical control layer, presentation services layer, transaction services layer, and transmission control layer.

data link layer   Layer 2 of the OSI reference model. Provides transit of data across a physical link. The data link layer is concerned with physical addressing, network topology, line discipline, error notification, ordered delivery of frames, and flow control. The IEEE divided this layer into two sublayers: the MAC sublayer and the LLC sublayer. Sometimes simply called *link layer*. Roughly corresponds to the data link control layer of the SNA model.

DCE   data communications equipment (EIA expansion) or data circuit-terminating equipment (ITU-T expansion). Devices and connections of a communications network that comprise the network end of the user-to-network interface. The DCE provides a physical connection to the network, forwards traffic, and provides a clocking signal used to synchronize data transmission between DCE and DTE devices. Modems and interface cards are examples of DCEs. *Compare with* DTE.

D channel   delta channel. 1. Full-duplex, 16-kbps (BRI) or 64-kbps (PRI) ISDN channel. *Compare with* B channel, E channel, and H channel. 2. In SNA, a device that connects a processor and main storage with peripherals.

DDN   Defense Data Network. A U.S. military network composed of an unclassified network (MILNET) and various secret and top-secret networks. DDN is operated and maintained by DISA.

DDP   Datagram Delivery Protocol. An AppleTalk network-layer protocol responsible for the socket-to-socket delivery of datagrams over an AppleTalk internetwork.

DDR   dial-on-demand routing. A technique whereby a router can automatically initiate and close a circuit-switched session as transmitting stations demand. The router spoofs keepalives so that end stations treat the session as active. DDR permits routing over ISDN or telephone lines sometimes using an external ISDN terminal adapter or modem.

DECnet   A group of communications products (including a protocol suite) developed and supported by Digital Equipment Corporation. DECnet/OSI (also called *DECnet Phase V*) is the most recent iteration and supports both

OSI protocols and proprietary Digital protocols. Phase IV Prime supports inherent MAC addresses that allow DECnet nodes to coexist with systems running other protocols that have MAC address restrictions.

DECnet Routing Protocol   *See* DRP.

default route   A routing table entry that is used to direct frames for which a next hop is not explicitly listed in the routing table.

demarc   A demarcation point between carrier equipment and CPE.

demultiplexing   The separating of multiple input streams that have been multiplexed into a common physical signal back into multiple output streams. *See also* multiplexing.

designated router   An OSPF router that generates LSAs for a multiaccess network and has other special responsibilities in running OSPF. Each multiaccess OSPF network that has at least two attached routers has a designated router that is elected by the OSPF Hello protocol. The designated router enables a reduction in the number of adjacencies required on a multiaccess network, which in turn reduces the amount of routing protocol traffic and the size of the topological database.

destination address   An address of a network device that is receiving data. *See also* source address.

destination service access point   *See* DSAP.

DHCP   Dynamic Host Configuration Protocol. A protocol that provides a mechanism for allocating IP addresses dynamically so that addresses automatically can be reused when hosts no longer need them.

dial-on-demand routing   *See* DDR.

dialup line   A communications circuit that is established by a switched-circuit connection using the telephone company network.

distance-vector routing algorithm   A class of routing algorithms that iterate on the number of hops in a route to find a shortest-path spanning tree. Distance-vector routing algorithms call for each router to send its entire routing table in each update, but only to its neighbors. Distance-vector routing algorithms can be prone to routing loops, but are computationally simpler than link state routing algorithms. Also called Bellman-Ford routing algorithm.

DNS   Domain Name System. The system used in the Internet for translating names of network nodes into addresses.

DoD Department of Defense. The U.S. government organization that is responsible for national defense. The DoD has frequently funded communication protocol development.

dotted-decimal notation The common notation for IP addresses in the form *a.b.c.d*, where each number represents, in decimal, 1 byte of the 4-byte IP address. Also called dotted notation or four-part dotted notation.

DRP DECnet Routing Protocol. A proprietary routing scheme introduced by Digital Equipment Corporation in DECnet Phase III. In DECnet Phase V, DECnet completed its transition to OSI routing protocols (ES-IS and IS-IS).

DSAP destination service access point. The SAP of the network node designated in the Destination field of a packet. *Compare with* SSAP. *See also* SAP (service access point).

DSU digital service unit. A device used in digital transmission that adapts the physical interface on a DTE device to a transmission facility such as T1 or E1. The DSU is also responsible for such functions as signal timing. Often referred to together with CSU, as CSU/DSU. *See also* CSU.

DTE data terminal equipment. A device at the user end of a user-network interface that serves as a data source, destination, or both. DTE connects to a data network through a DCE device (for example, a modem) and typically uses clocking signals generated by the DCE. DTE includes such devices as computers, routers, and multiplexers. *Compare with* DCE.

dual attachment station *See* DAS.

dual counter-rotating rings A network topology in which two signal paths, whose directions are opposite each other, exist in a token-passing network. FDDI and CDDI are based on this concept.

dual-homed station A device attached to multiple FDDI concentrators to provide redundancy.

dual homing A network topology in which a device is connected to the network by way of two independent access points (points of attachment). One access point is the primary connection, and the other is a standby connection that is activated in the event of a failure of the primary connection.

dynamic routing Routing that adjusts automatically to network topology or traffic changes. Also called *adaptive routing*. Requires that a routing protocol be run between routers.

E

E1   A wide-area digital transmission scheme used predominantly in Europe that carries data at a rate of 2.048 Mbps. E1 lines can be leased for private use from common carriers. *Compare with* T1.

E3   A wide-area digital transmission scheme used predominantly in Europe that carries data at a rate of 34.368 Mbps. E3 lines can be leased for private use from common carriers. *Compare with* T3.

E channel   echo channel. A 64-kbps ISDN circuit-switching control channel. The E channel was defined in the 1984 ITU-T ISDN specification, but was dropped in the 1988 specification. *Compare with* B channel, D channel, and H channel.

echo channel   See E channel.

EEPROM   electrically erasable programmable read-only memory. EPROM can be erased using electrical signals applied to specific pins.

EIA   Electronic Industries Association. A group that specifies electrical transmission standards. The EIA and TIA have developed numerous well-known communications standards, including EIA/TIA-232 and EIA/TIA-449.

encapsulation   Wrapping of data in a particular protocol header. For example, upper-layer data is wrapped in a specific Ethernet header before network transit. Also, when bridging dissimilar networks, the entire frame from one network can simply be placed in the header used by the data link layer protocol of the other network. *See also* tunneling.

encoding   The process by which bits are represented by voltages.

Enhanced IGRP   Enhanced Interior Gateway Routing Protocol. An advanced version of IGRP developed by Cisco. Provides superior convergence properties and operating efficiency, and combines the advantages of link state protocols with those of distance vector protocols. *Compare with* IGRP. *See also* IGP, OSPF, and RIP.

EPROM   erasable programmable read-only memory. Nonvolatile memory chips that are programmed after they are manufactured and, if necessary, can be erased by some means and reprogrammed. *Compare with* EEPROM and PROM.

ES-IS   End System-to-Intermediate System. An OSI protocol that defines how end systems (hosts) announce themselves to intermediate systems (routers). *See also* IS-IS.

Ethernet   A baseband LAN specification invented by Xerox Corporation and developed jointly by Xerox, Intel, and Digital Equipment Corporation. Ethernet networks use CSMA/CD and run over a variety of cable types at 10, 100, and 1,000 Mbps. Ethernet is similar to the IEEE 802.3 series of standards.

excess rate   Traffic in excess of the insured rate for a given connection. Specifically, the excess rate equals the maximum rate minus the insured rate. Excess traffic is delivered only if network resources are available and can be discarded during periods of congestion. *Compare with* insured rate and maximum rate.

F

Fast Ethernet   Any of a number of 100-Mbps Ethernet specifications. Fast Ethernet offers a speed increase ten times that of the 10BaseT Ethernet specification, while preserving such qualities as frame format, MAC mechanisms, and MTU. Such similarities allow the use of existing 10BaseT applications and network management tools on Fast Ethernet networks. Based on an extension to the IEEE 802.3 specification. Compare with Ethernet. *See also* 100BaseFX, 100BaseT, 100BaseT4, 100BaseTX, 100BaseX, and IEEE 802.3.

fault management   Four categories of network management— accounting management, configuration management, performance management, and security management—defined by ISO for management of OSI networks. Fault management attempts to ensure that network faults are detected and controlled.

FDDI   Fiber Distributed Data Interface. A LAN standard, defined by ANSI X3T9.5, specifying a 100-Mbps token-passing network using fiber-optic cable, with transmission distances of up to 2 km. FDDI uses a dual-ring architecture to provide redundancy. *Compare with* CDDI and FDDI II.

FDDI II   An ANSI standard that enhances FDDI. FDDI II provides isochronous transmission for connectionless data circuits and connection-oriented voice and video circuits. *Compare with* FDDI.

Fiber Distributed Data Interface   *See* FDDI.

fiber-optic cable   A physical medium capable of conducting modulated light transmission. Compared with other transmission media, fiber-optic cable is more expensive but is not susceptible to electromagnetic interference. Sometimes called *optical fiber.*

File Transfer Protocol   *See* FTP.

filter   Generally, a process or device that screens network traffic for certain characteristics, such as source address, destination address, or protocol, and determines whether to forward or discard that traffic based on the established criteria.

firewall   A device that controls who may access a private network and is itself immune to penetration.

firmware   Software instructions set permanently or semipermanently in ROM.

Flash memory   Nonvolatile storage that can be electrically erased and reprogrammed so that software images can be stored, booted, and rewritten as necessary. Flash memory was developed by Intel and is licensed to other semiconductor companies.

flash update   A routing update sent asynchronously in response to a change in the network topology. *Compare with* routing update.

flat addressing   A scheme of addressing that does not use a logical hierarchy to determine location.

flow   A stream of data traveling between two endpoints across a network (for example, from one LAN station to another). Multiple flows can be transmitted on a single circuit.

flow control   A technique for ensuring that a transmitting entity does not overwhelm a receiving entity with data. When the buffers on the receiving device are full, a message is sent to the sending device to suspend the transmission until the data in the buffers has been processed. In IBM networks, this technique is called *pacing*.

forwarding   A process of sending a frame toward its ultimate destination by way of an internetworking device.

fragment   A piece of a larger packet that has been broken down into smaller units. In Ethernet networks, also sometimes referred to as a frame less than the legal limit of 64 bytes.

fragmentation   The process of breaking a packet into smaller units when transmitting over a network medium that cannot support the original size of the packet.

frame   A logical grouping of information sent as a data link-layer unit over a transmission medium. Often refers to the header and trailer, used for synchronization and error control, that surround the user data contained in the unit. The terms *cell, datagram, message, packet,* and *segment* are also used to describe logical information groupings at various layers of the OSI reference model and in various technology circles.

frame forwarding A mechanism by which frame-based traffic, such as HDLC and SDLC, traverses an ATM network.

Frame Relay An industry-standard, switched data link-layer protocol that handles multiple virtual circuits by using a form of HDLC encapsulation between connected devices. Frame Relay is more efficient than X.25, the protocol for which it is generally considered a replacement. *See also* X.25.

FTP File Transfer Protocol. An application protocol, part of the TCP/IP protocol stack, used for transferring files between network nodes. FTP is defined in RFC 959.

full duplex The capability for simultaneous data transmission between a sending station and a receiving station. *Compare with* half duplex and simplex.

full mesh A network in which devices are organized in a mesh topology, with each network node having either a physical circuit or a virtual circuit connecting it to every other network node. A full mesh provides a great deal of redundancy, but because it can be prohibitively expensive to implement, it is usually reserved for network backbones. *See also* mesh and partial mesh.

G

gateway In the IP community, an older term referring to a routing device. Today, the term *router* is used to describe nodes that perform this function, and *gateway* refers to a special-purpose device that performs an application-layer conversion of information from one protocol stack to another. *Compare with* router.

Gb gigabit. Approximately 1,000,000,000 bits.

Gbps gigabytes per second.

Get Nearest Server *See* GNS.

gigabit Abbreviated Gb.

GNS Get Nearest Server. A request packet sent by a client on an IPX network to locate the nearest active server of a particular type. An IPX network client issues a GNS request to solicit either a direct response from a connected server or a response from a router that tells it where on the internetwork the service can be located. GNS is part of the IPX SAP. *See also* IPX and SAP (Service Advertising Protocol).

GUI   graphical user interface. A user environment that uses pictorial as well as textual representations of the input and output of applications and the hierarchical or other data structure in which information is stored. Conventions such as buttons, icons, and windows are typical, and many actions are performed using a pointing device (such as a mouse). Microsoft Windows and the Apple Macintosh are prominent examples of platforms utilizing GUIs.

H

half duplex   A capability for data transmission in only one direction at a time between a sending station and a receiving station. *Compare with* full duplex and simplex.

handshake   A sequence of messages exchanged between two or more network devices to ensure transmission synchronization before sending user data.

hardware address   *See* MAC address.

H channel   high-speed channel. A full-duplex ISDN primary rate channel operating at 384 kbps. *Compare with* B channel, D channel, and E channel.

HDLC   High-Level Data Link Control. A bit-oriented synchronous data link-layer protocol developed by ISO. HDLC specifies a data encapsulation method on synchronous serial links by using frame characters and checksums.

header   Control information placed before data when encapsulating that data for network transmission. *Compare with* trailer.

hello packet   A multicast packet that is used by routers using certain routing protocols for neighbor discovery and recovery. Hello packets also indicate that a client is still operating and network ready.

holddown   A state into which a route is placed so that routers will neither advertise the route nor accept advertisements about the route for a specific length of time (the hold-down period). Holddown is used to flush bad information about a route from all routers in the network. A route is typically placed in holddown when a link in that route fails.

hop   The passage of a data packet from one network node, typically a router, to another. *See also* hop count.

hop count   A routing metric used to measure the distance between a source and a destination. RIP uses hop count as its sole metric. *See also* hop and RIP.

horizontal cross-connect   A wiring closet in which the horizontal cabling connects to a path panel that is connected by backbone cabling to the main distribution facility.

host   A computer system on a network. Similar to *node*, except that host usually implies a computer system, whereas *node* generally applies to any networked system, including access servers and routers. *See also* node.

host address   *See* host number.

host number   The part of an IP address that designates which node on the subnetwork is being addressed. Also called a *host address*.

HTML   Hypertext Markup Language. A simple hypertext document formatting language that uses tags to indicate how a given part of a document should be interpreted by a viewing application, such as a Web browser.

HTTP   Hypertext Transfer Protocol. The protocol used by Web browsers and Web servers to transfer files, such as text and graphics files.

hub   1. Generally, a device that serves as the center of a star-topology network and connects end stations. Operates at Layer 1 of the OSI reference model. 2. In Ethernet and IEEE 802.3, an Ethernet multiport repeater, sometimes called a *concentrator*.

hybrid network   An internetwork made up of more than one type of network technology, including LANs and WANs.

Hypertext Markup Language   *See* HTML.

Hypertext Transfer Protocol   *See* HTTP.

I

IAB   Internet Architecture Board. A board of internetwork researchers who discuss issues pertinent to Internet architecture. Responsible for appointing a variety of Internet-related groups such as the IANA, IESG, and IRSG. The IAB is appointed by the trustees of the ISOC. *See also* IANA and ISOC.

IANA   Internet Assigned Numbers Authority. An organization operated under the auspices of the ISOC as a part of the IAB. IANA delegates authority for IP address-space allocation and domain-name assignment to the InterNIC and other organizations. IANA also maintains a database of assigned protocol identifiers used in the TCP/IP stack, including autonomous system numbers.

ICMP   Internet Control Message Protocol. A network-layer Internet protocol that reports errors and provides other information relevant to IP packet processing. Documented in RFC 792.

IDF   intermediate distribution facility. A secondary communications room for a building using a star networking topology. The IDF is dependent on the MDF. *See also* MDF.

IEC   International Electrotechnical Commission. An industry group that writes and distributes standards for electrical products and components.

IEEE   Institute of Electrical and Electronic Engineers. A professional organization whose activities include the development of communications and network standards. IEEE LAN standards are the predominant LAN standards today.

IEEE 802.2   An IEEE LAN protocol that specifies an implementation of the LLC sublayer of the data link layer. IEEE 802.2 handles errors, framing, flow control, and the network layer (Layer 3) service interface. Used in IEEE 802.3 and IEEE 802.5 LANs. *See also* IEEE 802.3 and IEEE 802.5.

IEEE 802.3   An IEEE LAN protocol that specifies an implementation of the physical layer and the MAC sublayer of the data link layer. IEEE 802.3 uses CSMA/CD access at a variety of speeds over a variety of physical media. Extensions to the IEEE 802.3 standard specify implementations for Fast Ethernet. Physical variations of the original IEEE 802.3 specification include 10Base2, 10Base5, 10BaseF, 10BaseT, and 10Broad36. Physical variations for Fast Ethernet include 100BaseTX and 100BaseFX.

IEEE 802.5   An IEEE LAN protocol that specifies an implementation of the physical layer and MAC sublayer of the data link layer. IEEE 802.5 uses token passing access at 4 or 16 Mbps over STP or UTP cabling and is functionally and operationally equivalent to IBM Token Ring. *See also* Token Ring.

IETF   Internet Engineering Task Force. A task force consisting of more than 80 working groups responsible for developing Internet standards. The IETF operates under the auspices of ISOC.

IGP   Interior Gateway Protocol. An Internet protocol used to exchange routing information within an autonomous system. Examples of common Internet IGPs are IGRP, OSPF, and RIP.

IGRP   Interior Gateway Routing Protocol. An IGP developed by Cisco to address the problems associated with routing in large, heterogeneous networks. *Compare with* Enhanced IGRP. *See also* IGP, OSPF, and RIP.

Institute of Electrical and Electronic Engineers   *See* IEEE.

insured rate   The long-term data throughput, in bits or cells per second, that an ATM network commits to support under normal network conditions. The insured rate is 100 percent allocated; the entire amount is deducted from the total trunk bandwidth along the path of the circuit. *Compare with* excess rate and maximum rate.

Integrated Services Digital Network   *See ISDN.*

interface   1. A connection between two systems or devices. 2. In routing terminology, a network connection on the router. 3. In telephony, a shared boundary defined by common physical interconnection characteristics, signal characteristics, and meanings of interchanged signals. 4. A boundary between adjacent layers of the OSI reference model.

International Organization for Standardization   *See* ISO.

Internet   The largest global internetwork, connecting tens of thousands of networks worldwide and having a culture that focuses on research and standardization based on real-life use. Many leading-edge network technologies come from the Internet community. The Internet evolved in part from ARPANET. At one time called the DARPA Internet, not to be confused with the general term *internet.*

internet   Short for internetwork. Not to be confused with the Internet. *See* internetwork.

Internet protocol   Any protocol that is part of the TCP/IP protocol stack. *See* IP. *See also* TCP/IP.

internetwork   A collection of networks interconnected by routers and other devices that functions (generally) as a single network.

internetworking   The industry devoted to connecting networks together. The term can refer to products, procedures, and technologies.

Internetwork Packet Exchange   *See* IPX.

interoperability   The capability of computing equipment manufactured by different vendors to communicate with one another successfully over a network.

IOS   Internetwork Operating System. *See* Cisco IOS software.

IP   Internet Protocol. A network-layer protocol in the TCP/IP stack offering a connectionless internetwork service. IP provides features for addressing, type-of-service specification, fragmentation and reassembly, and security. Defined in RFC 791. IPv4 (Internet Protocol version 4) is a connectionless, best-effort packet switching protocol. *See also* IPv6.

IP address   A 32-bit address assigned to hosts using TCP/IP. An IP address belongs to one of five classes (A, B, C, D, or E) and is written as four octets separated by periods (that is, dotted-decimal format). Each address consists of a network number, an optional subnetwork number, and a host number. The network and subnetwork numbers together are used for routing, and the host number is used to address an individual host within the network or subnetwork. A subnet mask is used to extract network and subnetwork information from the IP address. CIDR provides a new way of representing IP addresses and subnet masks. Also called an *Internet address*.

IP datagram   A fundamental unit of information passed across the Internet. Contains source and destination addresses along with data and a number of fields that define such things as the length of the datagram, the header checksum, and flags to indicate whether the datagram can be (or was) fragmented.

IPv6   IP version 6. A replacement for the current version of IP (version 4). IPv6 includes support for flow ID in the packet header, which can be used to identify flows. Formerly called IPng (IP next generation).

IPX   Internetwork Packet Exchange. A NetWare network-layer protocol used for transferring data from servers to workstations. IPX is similar to IP and XNS.

IPXWAN   IPX wide-area network. A protocol that negotiates end-to-end options for new links. When a link comes up, the first IPX packets sent across are IPXWAN packets that negotiate the options for the link. When the IPXWAN options are successfully determined, normal IPX transmission begins. Defined by RFC 1362.

ISDN   Integrated Services Digital Network. A communication protocol, offered by telephone companies, that permits telephone networks to carry data, voice, and other source traffic.

IS-IS   Intermediate System-to-Intermediate System. An OSI link-state hierarchical routing protocol based on DECnet Phase V routing whereby ISs (routers) exchange routing information based on a single metric to determine network topology. *See also* ES-IS and OSPF.

ISO   International Organization for Standardization. An international organization that is responsible for a wide range of standards, including those relevant to networking. ISO developed the OSI reference model, a popular networking reference model.

ISOC   Internet Society. An international nonprofit organization, founded in 1992, that coordinates the evolution and use of the Internet. In addition, ISOC delegates authority to other groups related to the Internet, such as the IAB. ISOC is headquartered in Reston, Virginia, U.S.A. *See also* IAB.

ITU-T   International Telecommunication Union Telecommunication Standardization Sector (formerly the Committee for International Telegraph and Telephone [CCITT]). An international organization that develops communication standards. *See also* CCITT.

K

kb   kilobit. Approximately 1,000 bits.

kB   kilobyte. Approximately 1,000 bytes.

kbps   kilobits per second.

kBps   kilobytes per second.

keepalive interval   The period of time between each keepalive message sent by a network device.

kilobit   Abbreviated kb.

kilobits per second   Abbreviated kbps.

kilobyte   Abbreviated kB.

kilobytes per second   Abbreviated kBps.

L

LAN   local-area network. A high-speed, low-error data network covering a relatively small geographic area (up to a few thousand meters). LANs connect workstations, peripherals, terminals, and other devices in a single building or other geographically limited area. LAN standards specify cabling and signaling at the physical and data link layers of the OSI reference model. Ethernet, FDDI, and Token Ring are widely used LAN technologies. *Compare with* MAN and WAN.

LAPB   Link Access Procedure, Balanced. A data link-layer protocol in the X.25 protocol stack. LAPB is a bit-oriented protocol derived from HDLC. *See also* HDLC and X.25.

LAPD   Link Access Procedure on the D channel. An ISDN data link-layer protocol for the D channel. LAPD was derived from the LAPB protocol and is designed primarily to satisfy the signaling requirements of ISDN basic access. Defined by ITU-T Recommendations Q.920 and Q.921.

LAT   local-area transport. A network virtual terminal protocol developed by Digital Equipment Corporation.

leased line   A transmission line reserved by a communications carrier for the private use of a customer. A leased line is a type of dedicated line.

link   A network communications channel consisting of a circuit or transmission path and all related equipment between a sender and a receiver. Most often used to refer to a WAN connection. Sometimes referred to as a line or a transmission link.

Link Access Procedure, Balanced   *See* LAPB.

Link Access Procedure on the D channel   *See* LAPD.

link layer   *See* data link layer.

link-layer address   *See* MAC address.

link-state routing algorithm   A routing algorithm in which each router broadcasts or multicasts information regarding the cost of reaching each of its neighbors to all nodes in the internetwork. Link-state algorithms create a consistent view of the network and are therefore not prone to routing loops, but they achieve this at the cost of relatively greater computational difficulty and more widespread traffic than do distance-vector routing algorithms. *Compare with* distance-vector routing algorithm.

LLC   logical link control. The higher of the two data link-layer sublayers defined by the IEEE. The LLC sublayer handles error control, flow control, framing, and MAC-sublayer addressing. The most prevalent LLC protocol is IEEE 802.2, which includes both connectionless and connection-oriented variants.

load balancing   In routing, the capability of a router to distribute traffic over all its network ports that are the same distance from the destination address. Good load-balancing algorithms use both line speed and reliability information. Load balancing increases the use of network segments, thus increasing effective network bandwidth.

local-area network   *See* LAN.

local loop   A line from the premises of a telephone subscriber to the telephone company CO.

local traffic filtering   A process by which a bridge filters out (drops) frames whose source and destination MAC addresses are located on the same interface on the bridge, thus preventing unnecessary traffic from being forwarded across the bridge. Defined in the IEEE 802.1 standard.

loop A route where packets never reach their destination but simply cycle repeatedly through a constant series of network nodes.

loopback test A test in which signals are sent and then directed back toward their source from some point along the communications path. Loopback tests are often used to test network interface usability.

LSA link-state advertisement. A broadcast packet used by link-state protocols that contains information about neighbors and path costs. LSAs are used by the receiving routers to maintain their routing tables. Sometimes called a link-state packet (LSP).

M

MAC Media Access Control. The lower of the two sublayers of the data link layer defined by the IEEE. The MAC sublayer handles access to shared media, such as whether token passing or contention will be used. *See also* data link layer and LLC.

MAC address A standardized data link layer address that is required for every device that connects to a LAN. Other devices in the network use these addresses to locate specific devices in the network and to create and update routing tables and data structures. MAC addresses are six bytes long and are controlled by the IEEE. Also known as a *hardware address*, *MAC-layer address*, or *physical address*. *Compare with* network address.

MAC address learning A service that characterizes a learning switch in which the source MAC address of each received packet is stored so that future packets destined for that address can be forwarded only to the switch interface on which that address is located. Packets destined for unrecognized broadcast or multicast addresses are forwarded out every switch interface except the originating one. This scheme helps minimize traffic on the attached LANs. MAC address learning is defined in the IEEE 802.1 standard.

MAC-layer address *See* MAC address.

MAN metropolitan-area network. A network that spans a metropolitan area. Generally, a MAN spans a larger geographic area than a LAN, but a smaller geographic area than a WAN. *Compare with* LAN and WAN.

Management Information Base *See* MIB.

mask *See* address mask and subnet mask.

MAU media attachment unit. A device used in Ethernet and IEEE 802.3 networks that provides the interface between the AUI port of a station and the common media of the Ethernet. The MAU, which can be built into a station or can be a separate device, performs physical-layer functions including the conversion of digital data from the Ethernet interface, collision detection, and injection of bits onto the network. Sometimes referred to as a *media access unit*, also abbreviated MAU, or as a *transceiver*. In Token Ring, a MAU is known as a *multistation access unit* and is usually abbreviated *MSAU* to avoid confusion.

maximum rate The maximum total data throughput allowed on a given virtual circuit, equal to the sum of the insured and uninsured traffic from the traffic source. The uninsured data might be dropped if the network becomes congested. The maximum rate, which cannot exceed the media rate, represents the highest data throughput the virtual circuit will ever deliver, measured in bits or cells per second. *Compare with* excess rate and insured rate.

Mb megabit. Approximately 1,000,000 bits.

MB megabyte. Approximately 1,000,000 bytes.

Mbps megabits per second.

MDF main distribution facility. The primary communications room for a building. The central point of a star networking topology where patch panels, hub, and router are located.

media Plural of medium. Various physical environments through which transmission signals pass. Common network media include twisted-pair, coaxial, and fiber-optic cable, and the atmosphere (through which microwave, laser, and infrared transmission occurs). Sometimes called *physical media*.

Media Access Control *See* MAC.

media access unit *See* MAU.

megabit Abbreviated Mb. Approximately 1,000,000 bits.

megabits per second Abbreviated Mbps.

megabyte Abbreviated MB. Approximately 1,000,000 bytes.

mesh A network topology in which devices are organized in a manageable, segmented manner with many, often redundant, interconnections strategically placed between network nodes. *See also* full mesh and partial mesh.

message An application-layer logical grouping of information, often composed of a number of lower-layer logical groupings such as packets. The terms *datagram*, *frame*, *packet*, and *segment* are also used to describe logical information groupings at various layers of the OSI reference model and in various technology circles.

metric *See* routing metric.

MIB Management Information Base. A database of network management information that is used and maintained by a network management protocol such as SNMP. The value of a MIB object can be changed or retrieved by using SNMP commands, usually through a GUI network management system. MIB objects are organized in a tree structure that includes public (standard) and private (proprietary) branches.

modem modulator-demodulator. A device that converts digital and analog signals. At the source, a modem converts digital signals to a form suitable for transmission over analog communication facilities. At the destination, the analog signals are returned to their digital form. Modems allow data to be transmitted over voice-grade telephone lines.

MSAU multistation access unit. A wiring concentrator to which all end stations in a Token Ring network connect. The MSAU provides an interface between these devices and the Token Ring interface of a router. Sometimes abbreviated MAU.

MTU maximum transmission unit. The maximum packet size, in bytes, that a particular interface can handle.

multicast Single packets copied by the network and sent to a specific subset of network addresses. These addresses are specified in the Destination Address field. *Compare with* broadcast and unicast.

multicast address A single address that refers to multiple network devices. Synonymous with group address. *Compare with* broadcast address and unicast address. *See also* multicast.

multimode fiber Optical fiber supporting propagation of multiple frequencies of light.

multiplexing A scheme that allows multiple logical signals to be transmitted simultaneously across a single physical channel. *Compare with* demultiplexing.

multistation access unit *See* MSAU.

multivendor network A network using equipment from more than one vendor. Multivendor networks pose many more compatibility problems than single-vendor networks. *Compare with* single-vendor network.

N

NAK   negative acknowledgment. A response sent from a receiving device to a sending device indicating that the information received contained errors. *Compare with* acknowledgment.

name resolution   Generally, the process of associating a name with a network address.

name server   A server connected to a network that resolves network names into network addresses.

NAT   network address translation. A mechanism for reducing the need for globally unique IP addresses. NAT allows an organization with addresses that are not globally unique to connect to the Internet by translating those addresses into globally routable address space. Also known as *network address translator.*

NAUN   nearest active upstream neighbor. In Token Ring or IEEE 802.5 networks, the closest upstream network device from any given device that is still active.

NCP   Network Control Program. In SNA, a program that routes and controls the flow of data between a communications controller (in which it resides) and other network resources.

neighboring routers   In OSPF, two routers that have interfaces to a common network. On multiaccess networks, neighbors are dynamically discovered by the OSPF Hello protocol.

NetBEUI   NetBIOS Extended User Interface. An enhanced version of the NetBIOS protocol used by network operating systems, such as LAN Manager, LAN Server, Windows for Workgroups, and Windows NT. NetBEUI formalizes the transport frame and adds additional functions. NetBEUI implements the OSI LLC2 protocol.

NetBIOS   Network Basic Input/Output System. An application programming interface used by applications on an IBM LAN to request services from lower-level network processes. These services might include session establishment and termination, and information transfer.

NetWare   A popular distributed NOS developed by Novell. Provides transparent remote file access and numerous other distributed network services.

NetWare Link Services Protocol   *See* NLSP.

NetWare Loadable Module   *See* NLM.

network   A collection of computers, printers, routers, switches, and other devices that are able to communicate with each other over some transmission medium.

network address   A network-layer address referring to a logical, rather than a physical, network device. Also called a *protocol address. Compare with* MAC address.

network address translation   *See* NAT.

network administrator   A person responsible for the operation, maintenance, and management of a network.

network analyzer   A hardware or software device offering various network troubleshooting features, including protocol-specific packet decodes, specific preprogrammed troubleshooting tests, packet filtering, and packet transmission.

Network Basic Input/Output System   *See* NetBIOS.

network byte order   An Internet-standard ordering of the bytes corresponding to numeric values.

Network File System   *See* NFS.

network interface   The boundary between a carrier network and a privately owned installation.

network interface card   *See* NIC.

network layer   Layer 3 of the OSI reference model. This layer provides connectivity and path selection between two end systems. The network layer is the layer at which routing occurs. Corresponds roughly with the path control layer of the SNA model. *See also* application layer, data link layer, physical layer, presentation layer, session layer, and transport layer.

network management   Using systems or actions to maintain, characterize, or troubleshoot a network.

network management system   *See* NMS.

network number   The part of an IP address that specifies the network to which the host belongs.

network operating system   *See* NOS.

networking   The interconnection of workstations, peripherals such as printers, hard drives, scanners, CD-ROMs, and other devices.

NFS   Network File System. As commonly used, a distributed file system protocol suite developed by Sun Microsystems that allows remote file access across a network. In actuality, NFS is simply one protocol in the suite. NFS protocols include RPC and XDR. These protocols are part of a larger architecture that Sun refers to as ONC.

NIC   1. network interface card. A board that provides network communication capabilities to and from a computer system. Also called an *adapter*. 2. Network Information Center. An organization whose functions have been assumed by ARIN. *See* ARIN.

NLM   NetWare Loadable Module. An individual program that can be loaded into memory and function as part of the NetWare NOS.

NLSP   NetWare Link Services Protocol. A link-state routing protocol based on IS-IS.

NMS   network management system. A system responsible for managing at least part of a network. An NMS is generally a reasonably powerful and well-equipped computer such as an engineering workstation. NMSs communicate with agents to help keep track of network statistics and resources.

node   1. An endpoint of a network connection or a junction common to two or more lines in a network. Nodes can be processors, controllers, or workstations. Nodes, which vary in routing and other functional capabilities, can be interconnected by links and serve as control points in the network. *Node* is sometimes used generically to refer to any entity that can access a network and is frequently used interchangeably with *device*. 2. In SNA, the basic component of a network and the point at which one or more functional units connect channels or data circuits.

nonextended network   An AppleTalk Phase 2 network that supports addressing of up to 253 nodes and only 1 zone.

nonseed router   In AppleTalk, a router that must first obtain, and then verify, its configuration with a seed router before it can begin operation. *See also* seed router.

non-stub area   A resource-intensive OSPF area that carries a default route, static routes, intra-area routes, interarea routes, and external routes. Non-stub areas are the only OSPF areas that can have virtual links configured across them, and are the only areas that can contain an ASBR. *Compare with* stub area.

NOS   network operating system. Distributed file systems. Examples of NOSs include LAN Manager, NetWare, NFS, VINES, and Windows NT.

Novell IPX *See* IPX.

NTP Network Time Protocol. A protocol built on top of TCP that assures accurate local time-keeping with reference to radio and atomic clocks located on the Internet. This protocol is capable of synchronizing distributed clocks within milliseconds over long time periods.

NVRAM nonvolatile RAM. RAM that retains its contents when a unit is powered off.

O

octet 8 bits. In networking, the term *octet* is often used (rather than *byte*) because some machine architectures employ bytes that are not 8 bits long.

ODI Open Data-Link Interface. A Novell specification providing a standardized interface for network interface cards (NICs) that allows multiple protocols to use a single NIC.

Open Shortest Path First *See* OSPF.

Open System Interconnection *See* OSI.

Open System Interconnection reference model *See* OSI reference model.

OSI Open System Interconnection. An international standardization program created by ISO and ITU-T to develop standards for data networking that facilitate multivendor equipment interoperability.

OSI presentation address An address used to locate an OSI application entity. It consists of an OSI network address and up to three selectors, one each for use by the transport, session, and presentation entities.

OSI reference model Open System Interconnection reference model. A network architectural model developed by ISO and ITU-T. The model consists of seven layers, each of which specifies particular network functions such as addressing, flow control, error control, encapsulation, and reliable message transfer. The lowest layer (the physical layer) is closest to the media technology. The lower two layers are implemented in hardware and software, and the upper five layers are implemented only in software. The highest layer (the application layer) is closest to the user. The OSI reference model is used universally as a method for teaching and understanding network functionality. Similar in some respects to SNA. *See* application layer, data link layer, network layer, physical layer, presentation layer, session layer, and transport layer.

OSPF   Open Shortest Path First. A link-state, hierarchical IGP routing algorithm proposed as a successor to RIP in the Internet community. OSPF features include least-cost routing, multipath routing, and load balancing. OSPF was derived from an early version of the IS-IS protocol.

OUI   organizational unique identifier. Three octets assigned by the IEEE in a block of 48-bit LAN addresses.

P

packet   A logical grouping of information that includes a header containing control information and (usually) user data. Packets are most often used to refer to network-layer units of data. The terms *datagram, frame, message,* and *segment* are also used to describe logical information groupings at various layers of the OSI reference model and in various technology circles.

packet internet groper   *See* `ping`.

PAP   Password Authentication Protocol. An authentication protocol that allows PPP peers to authenticate one another. The remote router attempting to connect to the local router is required to send an authentication request. Unlike CHAP, PAP passes the password and host name or username in the clear (unencrypted). PAP does not itself prevent unauthorized access, but merely identifies the remote end. The router or access server then determines whether that user is allowed access. PAP is supported only on PPP lines. *Compare with* CHAP.

parallel transmission   A method of data transmission in which the bits of a data character are transmitted simultaneously over a number of channels. *Compare with* serial transmission.

partial mesh   A network in which devices are organized in a mesh topology, with some network nodes organized in a full mesh, but with others that are only connected to one or two other nodes in the network. A partial mesh does not provide the level of redundancy of a full-mesh topology but is less expensive to implement. Partial-mesh topologies are generally used in the peripheral networks that connect to a fully meshed backbone.

Password Authentication Protocol   *See* PAP.

patch panel   An assembly of pin locations and ports that can be mounted on a rack or wall bracket in the wiring closet. Patch panels act like switchboards that connect workstations' cables to each other and to the outside.

path control layer   Layer 3 in the SNA architectural model. This layer performs sequencing services related to proper data reassembly. The path control layer is also responsible for routing. Corresponds roughly with the network layer of the OSI reference model. *See also* data flow control layer, data link control layer, physical control layer, presentation services layer, transaction services layer, and transmission control layer.

payload   A portion of a cell, frame, or packet that contains upper-layer information (data).

PDN   public data network. A network operated either by a government (as in Europe) or by a private concern to provide computer communications to the public, usually for a fee. PDNs enable small organizations to create a WAN without all the equipment costs of long-distance circuits.

PDU   protocol data unit. The OSI term for a packet.

peer-to-peer computing   Peer-to-peer computing calls for each network device to run both client and server portions of an application. Also describes communication between implementations of the same OSI reference model layer in two different network devices. *Compare with* client/server computing.

permanent virtual circuit   *See* PVC.

PHY   1. physical sublayer. One of two sublayers of the FDDI physical layer. 2. physical layer. In ATM, the physical layer provides for the transmission of cells over a physical medium that connects two ATM devices. The PHY is composed of two sublayers: PMD and TC.

physical address   *See* MAC address.

physical control layer   Layer 1 in the SNA architectural model. This layer is responsible for the physical specifications for the physical links between end systems. Corresponds to the physical layer of the OSI reference model. *See also* data flow control layer, data link control layer, path control layer, presentation services layer, transaction services layer, and transmission control layer.

physical layer   Layer 1 of the OSI reference model. The physical layer defines the electrical, mechanical, procedural, and functional specifications for activating, maintaining, and deactivating the physical link between end systems. Corresponds with the physical control layer in the SNA model. *See also* application layer, data link layer, network layer, presentation layer, session layer, and transport layer.

ping   packet internet groper. An ICMP echo message and its reply. Often used in IP networks to test the reachability of a network device.

PLP packet level protocol. A network-layer protocol in the X.25 protocol stack. Sometimes called *X.25 Level 3* and *X.25 Protocol*. *See also* X.25.

point-to-multipoint connection One of two fundamental connection types. In ATM, a point-to-multipoint connection is a unidirectional connection in which a single source end system (known as a root node) connects to multiple destination end systems (known as leaves). *Compare* with point-to-point connection.

point-to-point connection One of two fundamental connection types. In ATM, a point-to-point connection can be a unidirectional or bidirectional connection between two ATM end systems. *Compare with* point-to-multipoint connection.

Point-to-Point Protocol *See* PPP.

poison reverse update A routing update that explicitly indicates that a network or subnet is unreachable, rather than implying that a network is unreachable by not including it in updates. Poison reverse updates are sent to defeat large routing loops.

port 1. An interface on an internetworking device (such as a router). 2. In IP terminology, an upper-layer process that receives information from lower layers. Ports are numbered, and many are associated with a specific process. For example, SMTP is associated with port 25. A port number of this type is called a *well-known address*. 3. To rewrite software or microcode so that it will run on a different hardware platform or in a different software environment than that for which it was originally designed.

POST power-on self-test. A set of hardware diagnostics that runs on a hardware device when that device is powered up.

PPP Point-to-Point Protocol. A successor to SLIP that provides router-to-router and host-to-network connections over synchronous and asynchronous circuits. Whereas SLIP was designed to work with IP, PPP was designed to work with several network-layer protocols, such as IP, IPX, and ARA. PPP also has built-in security mechanisms, such as CHAP and PAP. PPP relies on two protocols: LCP and NCP.

presentation layer Layer 6 of the OSI reference model. This layer ensures that information sent by the application layer of one system will be readable by the application layer of another. The presentation layer is also concerned with the data structures used by programs and therefore negotiates data transfer syntax for the application layer. Corresponds roughly with the presentation services layer of the SNA model. *See also* application layer, data link layer, network layer, physical layer, session layer, and transport layer.

presentation services layer   Layer 6 of the SNA architectural model. This layer provides network resource management, session presentation services, and some application management. Corresponds roughly with the presentation layer of the OSI reference model.

PRI   Primary Rate Interface. An ISDN interface to primary rate access. Primary rate access consists of a single 64-kbps D channel plus 23 (T1) or 30 (E1) B channels for voice or data. *Compare with* BRI.

priority queuing   A routing feature in which frames in an interface output queue are prioritized based on various characteristics such as protocol, packet size, and interface type.

PROM   programmable read-only memory. ROM that can be programmed using special equipment. PROMs can be programmed only once. *Compare with* EPROM.

protocol   A formal description of a set of rules and conventions that govern how devices on a network exchange information.

protocol address   *See* network address.

protocol analyzer   *See* network analyzer.

protocol stack   A set of related communications protocols that operate together and, as a group, address communication at some or all of the seven layers of the OSI reference model. Not every protocol stack covers each layer of the model, and often a single protocol in the stack will address a number of layers at once. TCP/IP is a typical protocol stack.

proxy   An entity that, in the interest of efficiency, essentially stands in for another entity.

proxy Address Resolution Protocol   *See* proxy ARP.

proxy ARP   proxy Address Resolution Protocol. A variation of the ARP protocol in which an intermediate device (for example, a router) sends an ARP response on behalf of an end node to the requesting host. Proxy ARP can lessen bandwidth use on slow-speed WAN links.

punch tool   A spring-loaded tool used for cutting and connecting wire in a jack or on a patch panel.

PVC   permanent virtual circuit. A virtual circuit that is permanently established. PVCs save bandwidth associated with circuit establishment and tear down in situations where certain virtual circuits must exist all the time. In ATM terminology, called a *permanent virtual connection. Compare with* SVC.

Q

QoS   quality of service. A measure of performance for a transmission system that reflects its transmission quality and service availability.

queue   1. Generally, an ordered list of elements waiting to be processed. 2. In routing, a backlog of packets waiting to be forwarded over a router interface.

queuing delay   The amount of time that data must wait before it can be transmitted onto a statistically multiplexed physical circuit.

R

RAM   random-access memory. Volatile memory that can be read and written by a microprocessor.

random-access memory   *See* RAM.

RARP   Reverse Address Resolution Protocol. A protocol in the TCP/IP stack that provides a method for finding IP addresses based on MAC addresses. *Compare with* ARP.

reassembly   The putting back together of an IP datagram at the destination after it has been fragmented either at the source or at an intermediate node.

redirect   Part of the ICMP and ES-IS protocols that allows a router to tell a host that using another router would be more effective.

redundancy   1. In internetworking, the duplication of devices, services, or connections so that, in the event of a failure, the redundant devices, services, or connections can perform the work of those that failed. 2. In telephony, the portion of the total information contained in a message that can be eliminated without loss of essential information or meaning.

repeater   A device that regenerates and propagates electrical signals between two network segments.

Request for Comments   *See* RFC.

RFC   Request for Comments. A document series used as the primary means for communicating information about the Internet. Some RFCs are designated by the IAB as Internet standards. Most RFCs document protocol specifications such as Telnet and FTP, but some are humorous or historical. RFCs are available online from numerous sources.

ring   A connection of two or more stations in a logically circular topology. Information is passed sequentially between active stations. Token Ring, FDDI, and CDDI are based on this topology.

ring topology   A network topology that consists of a series of repeaters connected to one another by unidirectional transmission links to form a single closed loop. Each station on the network connects to the network at a repeater. Although logically rings, ring topologies are most often organized in a closed-loop star. *Compare with* bus topology, star topology, and tree topology.

RIP   Routing Information Protocol. An IGP supplied with UNIX BSD systems. The most common IGP in the Internet. RIP uses hop count as a routing metric.

RMON   remote monitoring. A MIB agent specification described in RFC 1271 that defines functions for the remote monitoring of networked devices. The RMON specification provides numerous monitoring, problem detection, and reporting capabilities.

ROM   read-only memory. Nonvolatile memory that can be read, but not written, by the microprocessor.

route map   A method of controlling the redistribution of routes between routing domains.

route summarization   The consolidation of advertised network numbers in OSPF and IS-IS. In OSPF, this causes a single summary route to be advertised to other areas by an area border router.

routed protocol   A protocol that can be routed by a router. A router must be able to interpret the logical internetwork as specified by that routed protocol. Examples of routed protocols are AppleTalk, DECnet, and IP.

router   A network-layer device that uses one or more metrics to determine the optimal path along which network traffic should be forwarded. Routers forward packets from one network to another based on network-layer information contained in routing updates. Occasionally called a *gateway* (although this definition of *gateway* is becoming increasingly outdated).

routing   The process of finding a path to a destination host. Routing is very complex in large networks because of the many potential intermediate destinations a packet might traverse before reaching its destination host.

routing metric   A method by which a routing algorithm determines that one route is better than another. This information is stored in routing tables and sent in routing updates. Metrics include bandwidth, communication cost, delay, hop count, load, MTU, path cost, and reliability. Sometimes referred to simply as a *metric*.

routing protocol   A protocol that accomplishes routing through the implementation of a specific routing algorithm. Examples of routing protocols are IGRP, OSPF, and RIP.

routing table   A table stored in a router or some other internetworking device that keeps track of routes to particular network destinations and, in some cases, metrics associated with those routes.

Routing Table Maintenance Protocol   *See* RTMP.

routing update   A message sent from a router to indicate network reachability and associated cost information. Routing updates are typically sent at regular intervals and after a change in network topology. *Compare with* flash update.

RPC   remote-procedure call. The technological foundation of client/server computing. RPCs are procedure calls that are built or specified by clients and executed on servers, with the results returned over the network to the clients.

RPF   Reverse Path Forwarding. A multicasting technique in which a multicast datagram is forwarded out of all but the receiving interface if the receiving interface is the one used to forward unicast datagrams to the source of the multicast datagram.

RSVP   Resource Reservation Protocol. A protocol that supports the reservation of resources across an IP network. Applications running on IP end systems can use RSVP to indicate to other nodes the nature (bandwidth, jitter, maximum burst, and so forth) of the packet streams they want to receive. RSVP depends on IPv6. Also known as *Resource Reservation Setup Protocol.*

RTMP   Routing Table Maintenance Protocol. Apple Computer's proprietary routing protocol. RTMP establishes and maintains the routing information that is required to route datagrams from any source socket to any destination socket in an AppleTalk network. Using RTMP, routers dynamically maintain routing tables to reflect changes in topology. RTMP was derived from RIP.

RTP   1. Routing Table Protocol. A VINES routing protocol based on RIP. Distributes network topology information and aids VINES servers in finding neighboring clients, servers, and routers. Uses delay as a routing metric. 2. Rapid Transport Protocol. A protocol that provides pacing and error recovery for APPN data as it crosses the APPN network. With RTP, error recovery and flow control are done end-to-end rather than at every node. RTP prevents congestion rather than reacts to it. 3. Real-Time Transport Protocol. One of the IPv6 protocols. RTP is designed to provide end-to-end network transport functions for applications transmitting real-time data, such as audio, video, or simulation data, over multicast or unicast network services. RTP provides services such as payload type identification, sequence numbering, timestamping, and delivery monitoring to real-time applications.

S

SAP 1. service access point. A field defined by the IEEE 802.2 specification that identifies the upper-layer process and is part of an address specification. Thus, the destination plus the DSAP define the recipient of a packet. The same applies to the SSAP. 2. Service Advertising Protocol. An IPX protocol that provides a means of informing network clients, via routers and servers, of available network resources and services.

SAS single attachment station. A device attached only to the primary ring of an FDDI ring. Also known as a Class B station. *Compare with* DAS. *See also* FDDI.

SDLC Synchronous Data Link Control. An SNA data link layer communications protocol. SDLC is a bit-oriented, full-duplex serial protocol that has spawned numerous similar protocols, including HDLC and LAPB.

secondary station In bit-synchronous data link-layer protocols such as HDLC, a station that responds to commands from a primary station. Sometimes referred to simply as a *secondary*.

seed router A router in an AppleTalk network that has the network number or cable range built in to its port descriptor. The seed router defines the network number or cable range for other routers in that network segment and responds to configuration queries from nonseed routers on its connected AppleTalk network, allowing those routers to confirm or modify their configurations accordingly. Each AppleTalk network must have at least one seed router.

segment 1. A section of a network that is bounded by bridges, routers, or switches. 2. In a LAN using a bus topology, a continuous electrical circuit that is often connected to other such segments with repeaters. 3. In the TCP specification, a single transport-layer unit of information. The terms *datagram*, *frame*, *message*, and *packet* are also used to describe logical information groupings at various layers of the OSI reference model and in various technology circles.

Sequenced Packet Exchange *See* SPX.

serial transmission   A method of data transmission in which the bits of a data character are transmitted sequentially over a single channel. *Compare with* parallel transmission.

server   A node or software program that provides services to clients.

service access point   *See* SAP.

Service Advertising Protocol   *See* SAP.

session   1. A related set of connection-oriented communications transactions between two or more network devices. 2. In SNA, a logical connection enabling two network addressable units to communicate.

session layer   Layer 5 of the OSI reference model. This layer establishes, manages, and terminates sessions between applications and manages data exchange between presentation layer entities. Corresponds to the data flow control layer of the SNA model.

shortest-path routing   Routing that minimizes distance or path cost through application of an algorithm.

signal reference ground   A reference point used by computing devices to measure and compare incoming digital signals to. The reference point used by computing devices to measure and compare incoming digital signals.

signaling   The process of sending a transmission signal over a physical medium for purposes of communication.

simplex   The capability for transmission in only one direction between a sending station and a receiving station. Broadcast television is an example of a simplex technology. *Compare with* full duplex and half duplex.

single-vendor network   A network using equipment from only one vendor. Single-vendor networks rarely suffer compatibility problems. *See also* multi-vendor network.

sliding window flow control   A method of flow control in which a receiver gives a transmitter permission to transmit data until a window is full. When the window is full, the transmitter must stop transmitting until the receiver advertises a larger window. TCP, other transport protocols, and several data link-layer protocols use this method of flow control.

SLIP   Serial Line Internet Protocol. A standard protocol for point-to-point serial connections using a variation of TCP/IP. The predecessor of PPP.

SMI   Structure of Management Information. A document (RFC 1155) specifying rules used to define managed objects in the MIB.

SNA   Systems Network Architecture. A large, complex, feature-rich network architecture developed in the 1970s by IBM. Similar in some respects to the OSI reference model, but with a number of differences. SNA is essentially composed of seven layers. *See* data flow control layer, data-link control layer, path control layer, physical control layer, presentation services layer, transaction services layer, and transmission control layer.

SNMP   Simple Network Management Protocol. A network management protocol used almost exclusively in TCP/IP networks. SNMP provides a means to monitor and control network devices, and to manage configurations, statistics collection, performance, and security.

socket   1. A software structure operating as a communications endpoint within a network device (similar to a port). 2. An addressable entity within a node connected to an AppleTalk network; sockets are owned by software processes known as *socket clients*. AppleTalk sockets are divided into two groups: SASs, which are reserved for clients such as AppleTalk core protocols, and DASs, which are assigned dynamically by DDP upon request from clients in the node. An AppleTalk socket is similar in concept to a TCP/IP port.

socket number   An 8-bit number that identifies a socket. A maximum of 254 socket numbers can be assigned in an AppleTalk node.

source address   An address of a network device that is sending data.

spanning tree   A loop-free subset of a Layer 2 (switched) network topology.

spanning-tree algorithm   An algorithm used by the Spanning-Tree Protocol to create a spanning tree. Sometimes abbreviated as STA.

Spanning-Tree Protocol   A bridge protocol that uses the spanning-tree algorithm, enabling a learning switch to dynamically work around loops in a switched network topology by creating a spanning tree. Switches exchange BPDU messages with other bridges to detect loops, and then remove the loops by shutting down selected switch interfaces. If the primary link fails, a standby link is activated. Refers to both the IEEE 802.1 Spanning-Tree Protocol standard and the earlier Digital Equipment Corporation Spanning-Tree Protocol on which it is based. The IEEE version supports switch domains and allows the switch to construct a loop-free topology across an extended LAN. The IEEE version is generally preferred over the Digital version.

SPF   shortest path first. A routing algorithm that iterates on length of path to determine a shortest-path spanning tree. Commonly used in link-state routing algorithms. Sometimes called *Dijkstra's algorithm*.

split-horizon updates   A routing technique in which information about routes is prevented from exiting the router interface through which that information was received. Split-horizon updates are useful in preventing routing loops.

spoofing   1. A scheme used by routers to cause a host to treat an interface as if it were up and supporting a session. The router spoofs replies to keepalive messages from the host in order to convince that host that the session still exists. Spoofing is useful in routing environments such as DDR, in which a circuit-switched link is taken down when there is no traffic to be sent across it in order to save toll charges. 2. The act of a packet illegally claiming to be from an address from which it was not actually sent. Spoofing is designed to foil network security mechanisms such as filters and access lists.

SPP   Sequenced Packet Protocol. A protocol that provides reliable, connection-based, flow-controlled packet transmission on behalf of client processes. Part of the XNS protocol suite.

SPX   Sequenced Packet Exchange. A reliable, connection-oriented protocol that supplements the datagram service provided by network-layer protocols. Novell derived this commonly used NetWare transport protocol from the SPP of the XNS protocol suite.

SQE   signal quality error. In Ethernet, a transmission sent by a transceiver back to the controller to let the controller know whether the collision circuitry is functional. Also called *heartbeat*.

SSAP   source service access point. The SAP of the network node designated in the Source field of a packet. *Compare with* DSAP. *See also* SAP.

standard   A set of rules or procedures that are either widely used or officially specified.

star topology   A LAN topology in which endpoints on a network are connected to a common central switch by point-to-point links. A ring topology that is organized as a star implements a unidirectional closed-loop star, instead of point-to-point links. *Compare with* bus topology, ring topology, and tree topology.

static route   A route that is explicitly configured and entered into the routing table, by default. Static routes take precedence over routes chosen by dynamic routing protocols.

STP   shielded twisted-pair. A two-pair wiring medium used in a variety of network implementations. STP cabling has a layer of shielded insulation to reduce EMI. Compare with UTP.

stub area   An OSPF area that carries a default route, intra-area routes, and interarea routes, but does not carry external routes. Virtual links cannot be configured across a stub area, and they cannot contain an ASBR. *Compare with* non-stub area.

stub network   A network that has only a single connection to a router.

subnet   *See* subnetwork.

subnet address   A portion of an IP address that is specified as the subnetwork by the subnet mask.

subnet mask   A 32-bit address mask used in IP to indicate the bits of an IP address that are being used for the subnet address. Sometimes referred to simply as *mask*.

subnetwork   1. In IP networks, a network sharing a particular subnet address. Subnetworks are networks arbitrarily segmented by a network administrator in order to provide a multilevel, hierarchical routing structure while shielding the subnetwork from the addressing complexity of attached networks. Sometimes called a *subnet*. 2. In OSI networks, a collection of ESs and ISs under the control of a single administrative domain and using a single network access protocol.

SNAP   Subnetwork Access Protocol. Internet protocol that operates between a network entity in the subnetwork and a network entity in the end system. SNAP specifies a standard method of encapsulating IP datagame and ARP messages on IEEE networks. The SNAP entity in the end system makes use of the services of the subnetwork and performs three key functions: data transfer, connection management, and QoS selection.

surge   Any voltage increase above 110% of the normal voltage carried by a power line.

SVC   switched virtual circuit. A virtual circuit that is dynamically established on demand and is torn down when transmission is complete. SVCs are used in situations where data transmission is sporadic. Called a *switched virtual connection* in ATM terminology. *Compare with* PVC.

synchronous transmission   Digital signals that are transmitted with precise clocking. Such signals have the same frequency, with individual characters encapsulated in control bits (called *start bits* and *stop bits*) that designate the beginning and end of each character. *Compare with* asynchronous transmission.

T

T1   A digital WAN carrier facility that transmits DS-1-formatted data at 1.544 Mbps through the telephone-switching network, using AMI or B8ZS coding. *Compare with* E1.

T3   A digital WAN carrier facility that transmits DS-3-formatted data at 44.736 Mbps through the telephone switching network. *Compare with* E3.

TACACS   Terminal Access Controller Access Control System. An authentication protocol, developed by the DDN community, that provides remote access authentication and related services, such as event logging. User passwords are administered in a central database rather than in individual routers, providing an easily scalable network security solution.

TCP   Transmission Control Protocol. A connection-oriented transport-layer protocol that provides reliable full-duplex data transmission. TCP is part of the TCP/IP protocol stack.

TCP/IP   Transmission Control Protocol/Internet Protocol. A common name for the suite of protocols developed by the U.S. DoD in the 1970s to support the construction of worldwide internetworks. TCP and IP are the two best-known protocols in the suite.

Telnet   A standard terminal emulation protocol in the TCP/IP protocol stack. Telnet is used for remote terminal connection, enabling users to log in to remote systems and use resources as if they were connected to a local system. Telnet is defined in RFC 854.

TFTP   Trivial File Transfer Protocol. A simplified version of FTP that allows files to be transferred from one computer to another over a network.

throughput   The rate of information arriving at, and possibly passing through, a particular point in a network system.

timeout   An event that occurs when one network device expects to hear from another network device within a specified period of time but does not. The resulting timeout usually results in a retransmission of information or the dissolving of the session between the two devices.

Time To Live   *See* TTL.

token   A frame that contains control information. Possession of the token allows a network device to transmit data onto the network.

token bus   A LAN architecture using token passing access over a bus topology. This LAN architecture is the basis for the IEEE 802.4 LAN specification.

token passing   An access method by which network devices access the physical medium in an orderly fashion based on possession of a small frame called a token. *Compare with* circuit switching and contention.

Token Ring   A token-passing LAN developed and supported by IBM. Token Ring runs at 4 or 16 Mbps over a ring topology. Similar to IEEE 802.5.

TokenTalk   Apple Computer's data-link product that allows an AppleTalk network to be connected by Token Ring cables.

topology   A physical arrangement of network nodes and media within an enterprise networking structure.

traceroute   A program available on many systems that traces the path a packet takes to a destination. It is mostly used to debug routing problems between hosts. There is also a traceroute protocol defined in RFC 1393.

traffic management   Techniques for avoiding congestion and shaping and policing traffic. Allows links to operate at high levels of utilization by scaling back lower-priority, delay-tolerant traffic at the edge of the network when congestion begins to occur.

trailer   Control information appended to data when encapsulating the data for network transmission. *Compare with* header.

transaction services layer   Layer 7 in the SNA architectural model. Represents user application functions, such as spreadsheets, word processing, or electronic mail, by which users interact with the network. Corresponds roughly with the application layer of the OSI reference model. *See also* data flow control layer, data link control layer, path control layer, physical control layer, presentation services layer, and transmission control layer.

transmission control layer   Layer 4 in the SNA architectural model. This layer is responsible for establishing, maintaining, and terminating SNA sessions, sequencing data messages, and controlling session level flow. Corresponds to the transport layer of the OSI reference model. *See also* data flow control layer, data link control layer, path control layer, physical control layer, presentation services layer, and transaction services layer.

Transmission Control Protocol   *See* TCP.

transport layer   Layer 4 of the OSI reference model. This layer is responsible for reliable network communication between end nodes. The transport layer provides mechanisms for the establishment, maintenance, and termination of virtual circuits, transport fault detection and recovery, and information flow control. Corresponds to the transmission control layer of the SNA model. *See also* application layer, data link layer, network layer, physical layer, presentation layer, and session layer.

trap   A message sent by an SNMP agent to an NMS, a console, or a terminal to indicate the occurrence of a significant event, such as a specifically defined condition or a threshold that was reached.

tree topology   A LAN topology similar to a bus topology, except that tree networks can contain branches with multiple nodes. Transmissions from a station propagate the length of the medium and are received by all other stations. *Compare with* bus topology, ring topology, and star topology.

TTL   Time To Live. A field in an IP header that indicates how long a packet is considered valid.

tunneling   An architecture that is designed to provide the services necessary to implement any standard point-to-point encapsulation scheme.

U

UDP   User Datagram Protocol. A connectionless transport-layer protocol in the TCP/IP protocol stack. UDP is a simple protocol that exchanges datagrams without acknowledgments or guaranteed delivery, requiring that error processing and retransmission be handled by other protocols. UDP is defined in RFC 768.

unicast   A message sent to a single network destination. *Compare with* broadcast and multicast.

unicast address   An address specifying a single network device. *Compare with* broadcast address and multicast address.

universal resource locator   *See* URL.

UPS   uninterruptable power supply. A backup device designed to provide an uninterrupted power source in the event of a power failure. UPSs are commonly installed on file servers and wiring hubs.

URL   universal resource locator. A standardized addressing scheme for accessing hypertext documents and other services using a browser.

User Datagram Protocol   *See* UDP.

UTP   unshielded twisted-pair. A four-pair wire medium used in a variety of networks. UTP does not require the fixed spacing between connections that is necessary with coaxial-type connections. *Compare with* STP.

V

VINES   Virtual Integrated Network Service. A NOS developed and marketed by Banyan Systems.

virtual circuit   A logical circuit created to ensure reliable communication between two network devices. A virtual circuit is defined by a VPI/VCI pair and can be either permanent (PVC) or switched (SVC). Virtual circuits are used in Frame Relay and X.25. In ATM, a virtual circuit is called a virtual channel. Sometimes abbreviated *VC*.

VLAN   virtual LAN. A group of devices on a LAN that are configured (using management software) so that they can communicate as if they were attached to the same wire, when in fact they are located on a number of different LAN segments. Because VLANs are based on logical instead of physical connections, they are extremely flexible.

W

WAN   wide-area network. A data communications network that serves users across a broad geographic area and often uses transmission devices provided by common carriers. Frame Relay, SMDS, and X.25 are examples of WANs. *Compare with* LAN and MAN.

watchdog packet   A method used to ensure that a client is still connected to a NetWare server. If the server has not received a packet from a client for a certain period of time, it sends that client a series of watchdog packets. If the station fails to respond to a predefined number of watchdog packets, the server concludes that the station is no longer connected and clears the connection for that station.

watchdog spoofing   A subset of spoofing that refers specifically to a router acting especially for a NetWare client by sending watchdog packets to a NetWare server to keep the session between client and server active. Useful when the client and server are separated by a DDR WAN link.

watchdog timer   1. A hardware or software mechanism that is used to trigger an event or an escape from a process unless the timer is periodically reset. 2. In NetWare, a timer that indicates the maximum period of time that a server will wait for a client to respond to a watchdog packet. If the timer expires, the server sends another watchdog packet (up to a set maximum).

window size   The number of messages that can be transmitted while awaiting an acknowledgment.

X–Y

X.25 An ITU-T standard that defines how connections between DTE and DCE are maintained for remote terminal access and computer communications in PDNs. X.25 specifies LAPB, a data link layer protocol, and PLP, a network-layer protocol. Frame Relay has to some degree superseded X.25.

XNS Xerox Network Systems. A protocol suite originally designed by PARC. Many PC networking companies, such as 3Com, Banyan, Novell, and UB Networks used or currently use a variation of XNS as their primary transport protocol.

Z

ZIP Zone Information Protocol. An AppleTalk session-layer protocol that maps network numbers to zone names. ZIP is used by NBP to determine which networks contain nodes that belong to a zone.

zone In AppleTalk, a logical group of network devices.

zone multicast address A data-link-dependent multicast address at which a node receives the NBP broadcasts directed to its zone.